JOHN WARDEN and the RENAISSANCE of
AMERICAN AIR POWER

JOHN WARDEN and the RENAISSANCE of
AMERICAN AIR POWER

John Andreas Olsen

POTOMAC BOOKS, INC.
WASHINGTON, D.C.

Library of Congress Cataloging-in-Publication Data
Olsen, John Andreas, 1968–
  John Warden and the renaissance of American air power / John Andreas Olsen.— 1st ed.
    p. cm.
  Includes bibliographical references and index.
  ISBN-13: 978-1-59797-084-6 (alk. paper)
  1. Warden, John A., 1943– 2. United States. Air Force—Officers—Biography. 3. Air power—United States. 4. Persian Gulf War, 1991—Aerial operations, American. I. Title.
  UG626.2.W3685O47 2007
  956.7044'248092—dc22
  [B]
                        2006028002

Printed in the United States of America on acid-free paper that meets the American National Standards Institute Z39-48 Standard.

Potomac Books, Inc.
22841 Quicksilver Drive
Dulles, Virginia 20166

First Edition

10 9 8 7 6 5 4 3 2 1

To my parents,
Karin Anne and Nikolai Bøe Olsen

CONTENTS

FOREWORD

The atomic bombs that ended the Second World War had a profound effect on military thinking worldwide, and nowhere more than in the United States. The air force initially had a monopoly on the means of delivery of the new weapon, but the army and navy immediately began working towards acquiring one for themselves. At the same time, military doctrine began changing to accommodate a nuclear environment. Not even a limited war in Korea could shake the belief among the services that a major nuclear war against the Warsaw Pact in Central Europe should be the planning focus.

Only after the second "aberration," the war in Vietnam, would emphasis finally shift away from nuclear war. For the air force, this signaled a wholesale change in force structure, doctrine, and leadership. The "bomber mafia" of Strategic Air Command (SAC), who for three decades had held sway, receded into the background. It was fighter pilots who had borne the brunt of the war in Southeast Asia, flying the most sorties and suffering the heaviest casualties. As a result, the fighter pilots gradually took over the key leadership positions within the air force.

There was a downside to that change. During the decades when SAC had been in the ascendant, most tactical airmen had given little thought to issues of air strategy. Instead, they focused on tactics and the battle for air superiority. As a result, the air force found itself in a position where its leaders had devoted a great deal of thought and doctrinal ink to the extreme poles of the conflict spectrum—nuclear war and the tactical air battle. The area between these extremes—conventional air war at the operational and strategic levels—had been ignored.

Enter John A. Warden III.

As John Andreas Olsen points out in this masterful biography, Warden had delved deeply into the subject of strategy ever since his cadet days in Colorado Springs. An autodidact, he taught himself the principles of grand strategy.

His formal graduate education at Texas Tech merely reinforced this personal predilection. While a student at the National War College in 1986, Warden turned his focus to airpower. The resulting thesis, which was published by National Defense University (NDU) Press and later Brassey's as *The Air Campaign: Planning for Combat*, outlined his ideas on the importance of strategic conventional air operations. The book was controversial. Although today one is struck by how mild in tone and nonprovocative the book's theme, at the time (1987), its discussion of the importance of air superiority, air interdiction, and the heretical belief that ground forces could at times support the operational air campaign, met with resistance even within the air force. The commander of Tactical Air Command (TAC) had said that his mission was to support the army; how could a mere colonel advocate something grander? It is a measure of how profoundly war has changed over the past two decades that Warden's basic themes are now accepted as a starting point for joint doctrine.

Let me digress here slightly with a lesson in leadership. In 1970 a young air force officer had completed his PhD dissertation, which was soon published. The officer, Perry McCoy Smith, had written a book critical of the air force's means of achieving independence after the Second World War. *The Air Force Plans for Peace* caught the attention of some generals in the Pentagon who were displeased with Smith's blunt conclusions, and an officer on the Air Staff was instructed to devise a suitable punishment for the outspoken writer. The officer, Russell Dougherty, who would later become a full general, read the book and decided Smith had made an honest if unpopular argument. He urged against punitive action. Smith's career was spared. Fifteen years later Smith was himself a general and commandant of the National War College at NDU when Warden was a student there. Smith read Warden's manuscript on the air campaign and was tremendously impressed and pushed to have it published. When Warden later became controversial because of his activities during the first Persian Gulf War (discussion to follow in this foreword), his book was reprinted and began to raise eyebrows among some in the air force. Smith, by then retired and a major television commentator, supported Warden by recommending his book on national TV as a "must read" to understand the war then unfolding. It was a dramatic gesture. The lesson: visionary leaders must protect and promote original thinkers who challenge conventional thinking. The determination and wisdom of Generals Dougherty and Smith paid great dividends to the nation.

After an operational tour as a wing commander that could not be labeled a success, in 1988 John Warden took over the directorate of Warfighting Concepts Development on the Air Staff. There he began inculcating his views on air warfare into his subordinates (and, one should note, his superiors as well).

When Saddam Hussein moved south in August 1990, the theater commander, Gen. Norman Schwarzkopf, knew that he had insufficient ground forces to defend Saudi Arabia, much less liberate Kuwait. As an alternative, Schwarzkopf asked the air force for an air plan, and Warden was designated to produce one. Olsen's description of this planning effort is exciting, informed, and accurate. Warden titled his plan "Instant Thunder"—to distinguish it from the failed gradual escalation air effort of Vietnam called "Rolling Thunder." In contrast to Vietnam's air campaign, Instant Thunder called for a sharp, hard, and massive air assault against Iraq's centers of gravity, especially against its leadership. Warden, like most airmen of his generation, had flown combat over Vietnam and been scarred by the experience. Those ghosts needed to be expunged.

As Olsen notes, Warden's plan was flawed. It promised results that were too extravagant, and it ignored the possibility that it would not be able to coerce Saddam into pulling his forces out of Kuwait. However, and this cannot be over-emphasized, Warden's plan, vigorously pushed to the country's top decision makers, shaped the entire debate on the subsequent air campaign. TAC, which was still mired in a tactical focus and advocating air support to a massive ground assault—certain to be extremely bloody—was especially irritated at the upstart colonel from the Pentagon. Fortunately for the nation and the coalition, Warden's views were accepted as the baseline for theatre planning efforts. The air campaign devastated Iraqi forces over the month preceding the ground assault, saving thousands of coalition lives and proving to be a decisive factor in the war's outcome.

Yet, Warden's trenchant and aggressive advocacy had won him enemies. Instead of being hailed as a hero and promoted—or at least given a medal—Warden was ignored. After leaving the Pentagon and serving a year in the White House as an adviser to the vice president, Warden was posted to Maxwell AFB to take over the Air Command and Staff College. This seemed an enlightened decision—take a leading air theorist and put him charge of educating future air leaders. But Warden still had detractors, and although the commandant was usually a general officer's slot, Warden remained a colonel throughout his three-year tenure.

Olsen covers this period extremely well. Determined to reform what he saw as an outdated curriculum, Warden moved quickly, decisively, and radically. As he was fond of saying, "I'm not an evolutionary kind of guy." Focusing on the need to graduate officers who understood and could articulate airpower in a broad sense, while also understanding the dynamics of actually writing an air campaign plan, Warden redirected the faculty's efforts. There were dissenters, but Warden simply bypassed or preempted them as he had at other times in his career. It is the nature of academic institutions that few changes are long lasting—there are too many forces resisting change. Nonetheless, Warden's curriculum and its emphasis on air campaign planning set a new tone that has, in part, survived. Indeed, some of Warden's key concepts—parallel warfare, inside-out operations, and his Five Rings targeting scheme—have become common currency within the air force.

Olsen portrays John Warden as a fascinating individual. At times charming while at others seemingly distracted and preoccupied, he inspired both devoted advocates and bitter enemies throughout his career. As Olsen perceptively notes, Warden's signature characteristic was that his greatest strengths were at once his greatest weaknesses. That is to say, the qualities that made him so successful—his aggressiveness, bureaucratic fearlessness, creativity, and a disregard for rank that moved him to bypass recalcitrant superiors—were precisely the same traits that often landed him in hot water.

In retrospect, John Warden had a major impact on the air force and the way it approached modern war. His contributions while on the Air Staff helped give rise to several important ideas that would later bear fruit: the Global Reach–Global Power white paper, the genesis of the Expeditionary Air Force organizational structure, and the emerging ideas on parallel warfare and effects-based operations. His Instant Thunder air campaign plan, although only a blueprint that was heavily modified for use in war, was still a seminal document that shaped U.S. thinking on "Desert Storm" and, indeed, airpower doctrine ever since. His efforts at the Air Command and Staff College were, in a sense, an attempt to institutionalize his ideas on air warfare for a new generation—in some ways his most difficult and important challenge of all.

John Warden is a genuine original. Now retired and running his own future-oriented consulting company in Montgomery, Alabama, he continues to raise eyebrows with his original and iconoclastic ideas. His theories on airpower and war continue to evolve, and he remains a respected and visionary spokesman regarding such topics on television, the radio, and in the print media. John Andreas Olsen has done an important service in bringing the story of this great airman to light.

COL. PHILLIP S. MEILINGER (USAF, RETIRED)

PREFACE

In researching this book I have relied on four major sources. First were the written accounts listed in the bibliography, including the extensive *Gulf War Air Power Survey* (*GWAPS*) and the excellent analyses by the U.S. Air Force historians at Bolling Air Force Base. In the latter group Diane T. Putney's *Airpower Advantage* is the best single volume on the planning of the 1991 air campaign, and my work benefited greatly from her research. Second, I have drawn on primary documentation from Operation Desert Storm and on papers, memoranda, and notes directly related to Col. John A. Warden—from his early days in uniform until his retirement. Third, many of my findings derived from the *Desert Story Collection*, which includes lengthy interviews with those officers who participated in the planning and execution of the air campaign. The research team—Air Force Cols. Suzanne B. Gehri, Edward C. Mann, and Richard T. Reynolds—worked independently from the *GWAPS* and the USAF historians, and the comprehensive record they compiled contributed significantly to this book. Since most of the interviews took place in the months immediately after the war they complement my fourth major source: personal interviews with more than two hundred officers who worked with Warden at different stages of his career. These interviews were conducted primarily by telephone, frequently by written correspondence, but often also through personal meetings. I will not list all these people here, and many preferred not to be named, but I hope they realize that their insight was highly appreciated and that I have kept the notes from every single interview and piece of correspondence.

I would, however, like to acknowledge a few of the officers who took the time to read and comment on large portions of the manuscript. Gens. Charles A. Horner, David A. Deptula, William J. Breckner, Peter D. Robinson, and Perry M. Smith, in addition to Cols. Richard T. Reynolds and Larry Weaver, added constructive criticism and perspective. I am also grateful to Gen. H. Norman

Schwarzkopf, who spent more than an hour with me; former Secretary of the Air Force Donald B. Rice, with whom I spent several hours; and seven former air force chiefs of staff who took the time to talk with me about Warden and his impact on their beloved service.

I am, of course, especially grateful to Warden himself. He cooperated fully during the research and writing of this book, in particular by submitting to numerous extensive interviews and commenting on manuscript drafts. Most notably, his cooperation was unreserved: Warden neither sought, nor did he seem to desire, to direct, limit, or otherwise influence me in terms of what I could or could not write about him. As a result this book is not hagiographical; rather, it reflects an attempt to remain balanced in both its portrayal of Warden and in its analysis of his ideas and accomplishments. That Warden never tried to influence the content is thus especially admirable, since it cannot be pleasant to have one's career, and personality, scrutinized by an outsider. I am also grateful to Warden's family: Margie, Betsy, and John IV all took the time from their busy schedules to help me with information and reflection.

In my attempt to be fair to the subject, the reader, and history I benefited from the analytical insight of Richard P. Hallion, Edward N. Luttwak, Phillip S. Meilinger, David R. Mets, Daniel R. Mortensen, Richard R. Muller, and Alan Stephens, all of whom spent considerable time reviewing the evolving manuscript. I also benefited from the insight of Air Force Col. Robyn S. Read, Lt. Col. Kerry Evans, and Majs. Peter A. Engelmann and William E. Young.

Most of the writing was done at the German Staff College in Hamburg and I would like to thank all my fellow students for their interest in my project, and especially Wing Cmdr. Adam Sansom and my tutor, Lt. Col. Thomas Andrejews, for commenting on various drafts. I am indebted to Steven Weingartner for his absolute support, Ned Willmott for his analysis and thought-provoking comments, and Margaret S. MacDonald for her magnificent editorial skills. I am also grateful to Potomac Books: Katie Freeman, Don Jacobs, Julie Kimmel, Don McKeon, Claire Nobel, and the rest of the team did a fantastic job in turning the manuscript into a book.

At home I am blessed with a caring family. I would particularly like to thank my brother, Claus Ivar Olsen, and his wife, Gøril Pharm, for their friendship; and my parents, Karin Anne and Nikolai Bøe Olsen—to whom I dedicate this book—for their lifelong encouragement and inspiration. Finally, my deepest appreciation goes to my wife, Tine, whose love is unselfish and unconditional. She is, truly, an angel.

ABBREVIATIONS

AAA	antiaircraft artillery
ABF	Air Battle Force
ACMI	Air Combat Maneuvering Instrumentation
ACSC	Air Command and Staff College
ACTS	Air Corps Tactical School
AFB	Air Force Base
AFIA	Air Force Intelligence Agency
AFM	Air Force Manual
AFMC	Air Force Mobility Command
ATO	Air Tasking Order
AWC	Air War College
BDA	bomb damage assessment
BEN	basic encyclopedia number
C^2	command and control
C^3	command, control, and communications
CADRE	Center for Airpower Development, Research, and Education
CAS	close air support
CASF	Composite Air Strike Force
CENTAF	Central Command Air Forces
CENTCOM	Central Command
CENTO	Central Treaty Organization
CEP	circular error probable
CIA	Central Intelligence Agency
CINC	commander in chief
CONOPS	concept of operations
DG	Distinguished Graduate
DIA	Defense Intelligence Agency
DPG	Defense Planning Guidance

FAC	forward air controller
FM	Field Manual
GWAPS	*Gulf War Air Power Survey*
HARM	high-speed antiradiation missile
INTJ	Introvert, Intuitive, Thinking, and Judging
KTO	Kuwait theater of operations
MAAP	Master Air Attack Plan
MAP	Master Attack Plan
MBTI	Myers-Briggs Type Indicator
MEI	Management Effectiveness Inspection
MIT	Massachusetts Institute of Technology
MORS	Military Operations Research Society
MWR	morale, welfare, and recreation
NATO	North Atlantic Treaty Organization
NBC	nuclear, biological, and chemical
NCA	National Command Authority
NCO	non-commissioned officer
NDU	National Defense University
NSA	National Security Agency
NSC	National Security Council
NWC	National War College
OPLAN	Operations Plan
OPORD	operational order
ORI	Operational Readiness Inspection
OSD	Office of the Secretary of Defense
PGM	precision-guided munition
PME	professional military education
POL	petroleum, oil, and lubricants
PSYOPS	psychological operations
QDR	Quadrennial Defense Review
ROTC	Reserve Officer Training Corps
SAAS	School of Advanced Airpower Studies
SAC	Strategic Air Command
SAM	surface-to-air-missile
SEAD	suppression of enemy air defenses
SIOP	Single Integrated Operational Plan
SPEAR	Strike Projection Evaluation and Anti-Air Research
TAC	Tactical Air Command
TACEVAL	Tactical Evaluation (NATO)
TALD	Tactical Air-Launched Decoy
Texas A&M	Agricultural and Mechanical College of Texas

Texas Tech	Texas Technical University
TFS	Tactical Fighter Squadron
TFW	Tactical Fighter Wing
TRADOC	Training and Doctrine Command
USAF	United States Air Force
USAFE	U.S. Air Forces in Europe
USSBS	U.S. Strategic Bombing Survey
WSO	weapon system operator
XO	Plans and Operations
XOO	Directorate of Operations (XO)
XOX	Directorate of Plans (XO)
XOXW	Deputy Directorate for Warfighting Concepts (XOX)
XOXWC	Concepts Division (XOXW)
XOXWD	Doctrine Division (XOXW)
XOXWF	Force Assessment Division (XOXW)
XOXWP	Long-Range Planning Division (XOXW)
XOXWR	Requirements Division (XOXW)
XOXWS	Strategy Division (XOXW)

Introduction:

THE POWER OF IDEAS

To borrow a saying that has come down through the centuries, there are moments "when the world turns." In Operation Desert Storm the world saw a military campaign that blended novel elements to produce an unprecedented result. Forty-eight hours after the air attacks against Iraq began in the early hours of January 17, 1991, U.S. aircraft armed with precision-guided bombs, operating in tandem with preprogrammed cruise missiles, had rendered Iraq's civilian and military leadership all but deaf, dumb, and blind. With few exceptions, President Saddam Hussein and his top commanders in Baghdad were unable to communicate with their security forces, commanders in the field, and the population at large. The Iraqi air defense system was similarly affected: while many individual control centers with their radars, missile launchers, and antiaircraft guns still functioned, the centralized command and control system required to coordinate their efforts had ceased to exist and what remained was unable to mount an effective defense.

In the days that followed, the situation steadily worsened for the Iraqi state, society, and military as the air offensive broadened to include attacks on supply, infrastructure, and lines of communication. Coalition aircraft ranging deep into Iraq struck at critical rail and road bridges, oil production and storage facilities, and water distribution centers. The devastation visited upon these installations quickly achieved its intended purpose of degrading the position of the Iraqi military in Kuwait. Essential commodities such as fuel, ammunition, food, and water failed to reach deployed troops in quantities sufficient to maintain their combat capability. Direct attacks against the formations and units further reduced their combat effectiveness and caused morale to plummet. By the time coalition ground forces launched their offensive on February 24, the Iraqi army could scarcely defend itself, much less take meaningful offensive action against its enemy. In a ground campaign that saw fighting end four days after it began, coalition forces drove the Iraqis out of Kuwait and advanced into Iraq itself, shattering the Iraqi army in the process.

Coalition ground forces deserve much credit for their impressive performance on the battlefield, but in assessing the speed and scale of the victory it is important to grasp the simple fact that their accomplishments were, in very large measure, made possible by the comprehensive air offensive. The fighting unfolded without the ebb and flow of alternate fortunes that normally mark major military campaigns, because the air offensive had decided the issue of victory and defeat well before the ground offensive began. The primary function of the land campaign was to complete the victory that had already been won.

The most original aspect of the air effort—the strategic air campaign—had wider implications for the U.S. Air Force, signifying a renaissance in American air power theory after a period of decline. Ideas pioneered in the 1930s focused on bombing key economic and societal nodes to achieve decisive results, and spurred the establishment of an independent U.S. Air Force following the Second World War. But the advent of the nuclear age, combined with the prevalent belief that only ground forces could win military victories, resulted in the air force's focusing either on deterrence and the delivery of nuclear weapons or on air-to-air tactics and ground-support missions. Only in the late 1980s did a new movement seek to revive the concept of independent strategic air attacks with conventional weapons.

Military success has a thousand fathers, and many claimed paternity of the 1991 victory. Yet the origins of the air campaign, and the philosophy behind it, can be traced to a small coterie of dedicated and determined airmen whose efforts were guided by one man in particular: Col. John A. Warden III. When Iraq invaded Kuwait on August 2, 1990, Warden was the deputy director of Warfighting Concepts, a branch of the Air Staff, and had already been working extensively on air power strategy, theory, and doctrine. As an outspoken advocate of using air power as the dominant element in a military campaign, rather than merely as support to the ground commander's scheme of maneuver, he had acquired a reputation as a radical theorist. Warden insisted that the air force should move away from its brute force-oriented warfighting approach to one that focused on strategic paralysis and systemic effects. He suggested that destroying ground forces might have little to do with winning wars and even less to do with winning the peace for which wars were fought.

In the days immediately following the Iraqi occupation of Kuwait, Gen. H. Norman Schwarzkopf, commander in chief of Central Command, asked the Air Staff to put together a plan for a retaliatory air response—a job that fell within Warden's purview. Schwarzkopf thus presented Warden with a unique opportunity, the kind that men of ideas seek but so seldom find: a chance to put his theories to the test. Brimming with energy and self-assurance, Warden was not slow to act upon it: he led an effort that presented Schwarzkopf with a plan for a full-blown strategic air campaign in less than forty-eight hours. Warden's proposed plan advocated precision attacks on the Iraqi leadership; on its command, control, and communication apparatus; and on a selection of electrical facilities, supply dumps, and infrastructure. He maintained that air power would bring about victory in six to nine days and he believed it would be unnecessary to target a single tank in Kuwait. Schwarzkopf was delighted.

Gen. Colin Powell, chairman of the Joint Chiefs of Staff, was also impressed, but he insisted that the United States should also cripple Iraqi forces in Kuwait and southern Iraq. He wanted "to leave smoking tanks as kilometer posts all the way to Baghdad." Warden modified his plan to encompass both the strategic air campaign and an operational air campaign that would complete Iraq's defeat by winning air superiority over Kuwait and paralyzing the Iraqi ground forces. He insisted, however, that air power could attack ground forces directly, achieve operational paralysis, and thereby avoid a large ground campaign.

Instant Thunder, as Warden called his plan, became the conceptual underpinning for the air campaign planning effort. Through it Warden introduced a concept for an air offensive that ensured both a strategic and an operational dimension missing from the contingency plans and from air force practice at the time. After the war Powell acknowledged the significance of Warden's intellectual contribution, stating, "his original concept remained at the heart of the Desert Storm air war."[1] Schwarzkopf also praised Warden, declaring, "together we mapped out the strategic concept that ultimately led to our country's great victory in Desert Storm."[2] David Halberstam, author of *War in a Time of Peace*, asserted, "If one of the newsmagazines had wanted to run on its cover the photograph of the man who had played the most critical role in achieving victory, it might well have chosen Warden instead of Powell or Schwarzkopf."[3] Several distinguished military historians, officers, and other experts have concluded that Warden defined the very terms of reference for the 1991 military strategy and thereby introduced a new approach to the conduct of war.[4]

Warden's view of the enemy as a "system" and of the primary importance of the enemy's command, control, and communication apparatus within that system, combined with his belief in bombing for functional disruption, strategic paralysis, and systemic effect, has played an important role in changing the U.S. view of warfighting at the strategic and operational levels. Warden's major imperative—the need to understand that strategic war may have little to do with the destruction of the enemy's military forces—has earned increasing acceptance throughout the military services as they move away from the brute force premise of attrition and annihilation models. Having developed a coherent theory for the employment of air forces in support of national objectives during times of war, and explained that theory succinctly to officers, policy makers, and the public,

Warden is probably the most influential American air power theorist since the Second World War. At the very least he has become the symbol of the renaissance in aerospace thinking that took place in the 1990s and continues to this day.

These achievements might suggest that the air force honors Warden for his role in what was perhaps the most successful air campaign in history and for his influence on air power theory. Yet nothing could be further from the truth. Throughout his thirty-year air force career, Warden provoked dissension, with some praising him as a visionary, others condemning him as a fanatic with no respect for authority and rank. Even as they responded to Schwarzkopf's initial call for a strategic air option, Warden and his team encountered fierce opposition from senior officers in the air force, who disagreed with his concept, resented his involvement in the planning, and viewed him as a strictly academic thinker divorced from the realities of military operations.

The hostility toward Warden reflects in part the difficulty of introducing new concepts into a vast military organization and in part honest disagreement with his theories, but it was his personality and working methods that provoked the strongest opposition. The character traits that made him successful as a theorist and strategist were the same qualities that made him a controversial leader, colleague, and subordinate. While some admired his moral courage and his readiness to act on his beliefs, his self-confidence and dedication to his personal vision angered many senior leaders, who believed that he lacked both common sense and the common touch. In a strongly hierarchical organization he refused to accept bureaucratic boundaries, and did not hesitate to bypass the established chain of command to advance his agenda through the system. Drawing chiefly on his own intuition and convictions, he constantly devised unusual solutions to problems, ignoring existing alternatives.

Although a fighter pilot by trade, Warden did not conform to the fighter community image: he lacked the deep sense of camaraderie and love of flying that fighter pilots valued, and he never fully appreciated that subordinates and superiors were often more concerned with solid personal relationships and daily matters than with grand ideas. While some welcomed his analytical skills, his drive to implement changes, and the courage that he showed in thinking and acting in ways that challenged the mainstream, others thought that he was simply not a "people person." Many fighter pilots felt alienated from Warden, who was unfailingly polite, soft-spoken, and private: he seldom told jokes, rarely laughed whole-heartedly, never swore, and showed little interest in small talk. As one four-star general expressed it, "Warden was not your typical sloppy pilot type who would hang around in the bar and talk about air maneuvers." Even his sense of humor reflected a twist of British understatement and irony that his peers did not always appreciate. His somewhat formal behavior made him a solitary figure in a profession that laid great stress on socialization and companionship. He was, quintessentially, "an intellectual maverick who did not fit in." Perhaps not surprisingly, despite his achievements as a planner and thinker, Warden was denied promotion to the rank of brigadier general and retired from the service as a colonel. The very mention of his name still elicits both warm affection and cold contempt inside and outside the U.S. Air Force.

This book endeavors to come to grips with the character of this warrior-scholar whom officers of all ranks swore by or swore about. It draws on both written accounts and extensive interviews and discussions with Warden himself and more than two hundred senior officers—admirers and antagonists alike—who worked for him, or for whom he worked, at different stages of his career. Taking a chronological approach, the narrative examines the development of Warden's influential and controversial ideas concerning the application of air power. It discusses and analyzes his published and unpublished works and describes and explains his role in planning Operation Desert Storm. The book assesses the origins, evolution, and legacy of his strategic thought, and by exploring substance as well as process it paints a picture of the man as perceived by his contemporaries. It shows how a combative colonel played a significant part in conceiving a new form of warfare, developed a nearly messianic drive to proselytize airmen mired in conventional thinking even when it was obvious that his effort might cost him his career, and succeeded in restoring air campaign planning and theory to the forefront of the air force agenda.

At first glance it may seem as though the book is exclusively about a single personality, but in essence it seeks to tell the story of a human lightning rod who overcame an entrenched bureaucracy to effect changes in the way modern military operations are planned and executed. His influence, not as an individual, but as a leading intellectual warrior, has extended far beyond anything his supporters and detractors dreamed possible. The true theme of this book is the power of ideas, and how the right ideas and the strength of character needed to implement them have strongly influenced the foundation of U.S. warfighting in the twenty-first century.

The John Warden story, then, is really about the willingness to follow what Robert Frost coined "The Road Not Taken":

> *Two roads diverged in a yellow wood,*
> *And sorry I could not travel both*
> *And be one traveler, long I stood*
> *And looked down one as far as I could*
> *To where it bent in the undergrowth;*
>
> *Then took the other, as just as fair,*
> *And having perhaps the better claim,*

Because it was grassy and wanted wear;
Though as for that the passing there
Had worn them really about the same,

And both that morning equally lay
In leaves no step had trodden black.
Oh, I kept the first for another day!
Yet knowing how way leads on to way,
I doubted if I should ever come back.

I shall be telling this with a sigh
Somewhere ages and ages hence:
Two roads diverged in a wood, and I—
I took the one less traveled by,
And that has made all the difference.[5]

1

ORIGINS: THE EARLY YEARS

We are all products of our environment, and genetic factors vie with education and society in shaping the individual. To understand John Ashley Warden III we must first understand the historical, social, and intellectual characteristics of the society in which he grew up and the personalities of the family members who exerted the greatest influence on his profession, values, and ideas.

Brig. Gen. John A. Warden

John Ashley Warden III, born December 21, 1943, was the fourth in his family to pursue a military career. His great-grandfather, after fighting for the Confederacy in the Civil War, had moved west and settled as a farmer in McKinney, Texas. His son, the first John Ashley Warden, joined the army in 1908 after earning a bachelor of science degree in engineering and completing the Army Reserve Officer Training Corps (ROTC) program at the Agricultural and Mechanical College of Texas (Texas A&M). In 1914 he deployed to the Philippines, serving with the Eighth and Ninth Cavalry at Fort McKinley,[1] and stayed in the Pacific until the United States entered the First World War in April 1917. He was then sent to France with his regiment, but to his disappointment the war ended before the unit ever saw battle. With the end of hostilities, Major Warden accepted the attractive position of assistant military attaché to the American Embassy in Paris, an assignment that introduced him to the world of policy and diplomacy, and through reading, studying, and writing reports on national security, he developed an interest in political-military affairs. He was also fortunate enough to have his entire family with him: his wife, née Jane Robinson Abernathy, and their three children—John Jr., Henry Edward, and Nancy Jane.[2]

The family returned to the United States in 1923, moving to Fort D. A. Russell, Cheyenne, Wyoming, where Warden found himself relegated to conducting low-intensity policing activities on horseback. After his experience with international relations in Paris he considered the new assignment less than satisfying, but he endured it because he had been selected for the army's Command and General Staff School at Fort Leavenworth, Kansas, which trained and qualified officers for higher command. Warden had by then developed into a ranked polo player, which probably played a role in the army's decision to send him to New York City to work with the Horse Cavalry Reserve Unit after he graduated. The assignment involved the not very onerous challenge of working on military contingency deployment plans, but gave him the opportunity to enjoy a social life that revolved around the professional polo players in the city during the latter part of the 1920s.

However, by the end of the decade, Warden had come to realize that the horse cavalry had no future, and he transferred to the Quartermaster Corps. In 1933–1934 he led an unprecedented mobilization of men, material, and transportation when President Franklin D. Roosevelt established the Civilian Conservation Corps. Thereafter he attended the Army Industrial College in Washington, DC, and the Naval War College in Newport, Rhode Island. He was then assigned to the Atlanta General Depot at Fort McPherson, with quartermaster responsibilities for an area that stretched from North Carolina to Florida.

Compared to his contemporaries, Warden had acquired a great deal of formal education, and his added operational experience led to his promotion to colonel in 1937. He served briefly as the first commandant of Fort Lee, Virginia, and was then promoted to brigadier general in May 1941 and assigned to Fort Francis E. Warren, Wyoming.[3] After the United States entered the Second World War in December 1941, the fort witnessed an immense mobilization in terms of activity and manpower: at one point Warden was in charge of training nearly twenty thousand quartermasters.

Once again Warden received orders to prepare for war. He was sent to India, and as Base Sector One commander in Karachi he organized the reception, storage, and distribution of supplies for the China-Burma-India theater of operations. Again, however, he never saw actual combat, which, according to his younger son, was a cause of professional and personal disappointment. When the war ended he became the commanding officer of the Quartermaster Depot at Charlotte, North Carolina, and it was from this post that he retired from the army in January 1947. Having served his country as a military officer for thirty-nine years, Warden returned to McKinney and decided to enter politics. He joined the Democratic Party—the only realistic option in Texas at that time—and served as a state legislator in Collin County for two terms (1951–1954). He stayed in McKinney until his death in 1973.

Col. Pete Warden and the B-52

His younger son and John A. Warden III's uncle, Henry Edward "Pete" Warden, had not planned on a military career, but when Germany invaded Poland in September 1939 he abandoned his postgraduate studies at the Massachusetts

Institute of Technology (MIT) and joined the Army Air Corps. He subsequently earned his wings in June 1940 and shortly thereafter deployed with the Twentieth Pursuit Squadron to Nichols Field in central Luzon in the Philippines. He was primarily a P-40 pilot, but after a few months he also became the depot inspector. When the Japanese attacked on December 8, 1941, leaving Nichols Field untenable, he was forced to move with parts of the depot team to the outskirts of Manila in an attempt to prolong resistance. After the main Japanese landings in Lingayen Gulf two weeks later, Gen. Douglas A. MacArthur, the commander in the Philippines, ordered national and local forces to withdraw to the Bataan Peninsula, declaring Manila an open city. However, Warden chose to stay behind enemy lines in order to salvage aircraft that would otherwise be lost during the immediate retreat. His team managed to save eight; Warden himself flew the last aircraft out of Manila only hours after the Japanese entered the capital.

Brig. Gen. Harold H. George, the air commander responsible for the region, then instructed Warden to take a few enlisted men to the island of Mindanao to find, assemble, and save more aircraft. Warden soon discovered three aircraft in packing crates, and while test-flying one he shot down what appears to have been a Japanese "Betty" bomber. With the end of the resistance in the Philippines in May 1942, Warden left for Australia, where he assembled, modified, and overhauled aircraft at the Fifth Air Service Command. He soon proved himself an innovative officer who achieved results, although not necessarily by following the technical manuals and procedures.

When he returned to the United States after almost four years in the Pacific, he was assigned to Wright Field, Dayton, Ohio—"the engineering center of the Air Force." At that time the air force was engaged in fierce debates over whether it should focus on a bomber with straight wings and propeller-driven engines or one with swept wings and turbojet engines. The latter would be able to fly at higher altitudes and at high speed, which would make it more effective within the zone of engagement. However, aircraft with turbojets consumed far more fuel, and their shorter range would require a large tanker fleet for air-to-air refueling. The preliminary design program for the XB-52 indicated that costs would be high. Air force leaders also disagreed about the size of the aircraft and confronted considerable uncertainty about the quality of jet engines. Moreover, while the B-36 propeller plane could be delivered immediately, the B-52 would take years to develop.

In May 1945 Col. Donald L. Putt, chief of the Bombardment Branch, appointed Warden as the chief of the branch's engineering division, with responsibility for running the Northrop XB-35 and the Convair XB-36 programs. Warden strongly identified with the three-bomber concept, which involved light, medium, and heavy bombers, stating, "the most important of the three airplanes is the heavy [bomber], whose mission will be the delivery of the special bomb load to the strategic target system."[4]

When Boeing was awarded a contract to build an experimental long-range heavy bomber Warden became the designated project officer and the leading spokesman for a new generation of bombers based on turbojet propulsion. His unrelenting support for both the B-47 and the B-52 gained him friends and enemies alike, and earned him the reputation as "one of the founding fathers of the B-52." According to Walter J. Boyne, the author of *Beyond the Wild Blue*, Warden exercised far more authority than he actually had when he told Boeing, on October 21, 1948, to design the B-52 with jet engines:

> Pete Warden undoubtedly knew that he had more information on air-craft and engine projects than any other individual, and that to ad-vance the USAF's need for a long-range bomber, he was responsible for making value judgments, causing programs to happen, and then seeing to their approval. In the case of the long-range bomber, Boeing had not been able to get the required range from the B-47-size jet bomber projects they were investigating. Intuitively, they felt that a larger, turbo prop bomber would have the required range. Unfortu-nately, the Wright T-35 turboprop engines, although they had been increased in power, still did not provide the necessary range, and worse, would not be ready for production until four years later in 1952. War-den apparently considered all this, urged Pratt & Whitney to pursue what became the J57 engine, and once he had their commitment, in-structed Boeing to design a very large aircraft based on the J57. The B-52 was the result.[5]

Lori S. Tagg, author of *Development of the B-52*, dedicated her book to Pete Warden, and insisted that the United States owes a considerable gratitude to this "progressive and persuasive jet-nut." Boeing may have completed the design drawings and engineering, but Warden and his small staff played an important role in keeping the B-52 project alive at crucial times despite heavy criticism.[6]

As the new bombers went into production and test flights, Gen. George C. Kenney, the commandant of Air University, requested that Warden join a research program at the Air War College. In late 1953, after Warden had been promoted to the rank of colonel at the age of thirty-eight, his technological in-sight and operational grasp caught the attention of Brig. Gen. Bernard A. Schriever, who personally ensured that he was put in charge of long-range planning at the Air Warfare Systems Division in the Pentagon. Maj. Gen. Donald N. Yates, com-mander of the Air Force Missile Test Center at Patrick AFB, also seems to have been impressed with Warden, arranging for him to become the deputy com-mander for tests in 1957. Three years later, Schriever, as the three-star commander of the Air Force Research and Development Command at Andrews AFB, made certain that Warden was given a central role in reorganizing what would become the Air Force Systems Command.

In this position, Warden became eligible for promotion to general rank. However, Warden was not one to play the political games required: he operated on the philosophy that it was easier to ask for forgiveness than to ask for permission, and when the Air Staff wanted him to do something he considered a waste of effort he silently ignored it. His involvement with the B-52 also defined him as a controversial figure, one who could not be fully controlled. Given Warden's maverick tendencies, the Promotion Board voted against him, and Warden retired from the air force in 1964, at the age of forty-nine. Shortly thereafter he became the corporate director of plans for North American Aviation; he stayed with the company for six years before he and his wife, Joanna, decided to devote their full time to managing their 550 acres of farmland near Columbus, Mississippi.

John A. Warden, Jr., and Kathleen Day

Pete Warden's elder brother, John A. Warden, Jr., planned for a career as a military officer, but it was not to be. He attended the ROTC program at Texas A&M, graduating with a bachelor of science degree in electrical engineering in 1935. As a second lieutenant he enjoyed his service as an active reserve officer, but after two years he was incorrectly diagnosed with tuberculosis and dismissed from the army. He accepted an engineering position with the Otis Elevator Company, but in 1943, with his father deployed to India, his brother stationed in Australia, and his country seeking men to win the war, he felt obligated to serve. He departed for the Pacific theater of operations in the spring of 1943; his wife, née Kathleen Marie Day, stayed with his mother in McKinney, where she gave birth to their only child, John A. Warden III.

John Warden, Jr., spent the war years first in Australia and then building docks, airfields, bridges, and roads in New Guinea. When the war ended, his corps moved into the westernmost point of the three main islands of Japan to take part in the occupation and reconstruction.[7] He returned to the United States in 1946 and rejoined his old firm, where he continually gained responsibility, finally supervising the southwest region, with an office in New Orleans, Louisiana. The Otis archive reveals that he received "excellent ratings" and that colleagues found him "brilliant, dependable and cooperative." He was known for having "excellent product knowledge, sound judgment and a wonderful attitude." Although quiet and soft-spoken, he "inspired confidence."[8]

Kathleen Day was the single most important reason why her son gained a lifelong appreciation for books. She had excelled in her schoolwork, but for economic reasons had never attended college. Although she regretted this all her life, she acquired a sound education by reading and studying on her own. The boy's interest was reinforced by his paternal grandmother, who knew long passages of Shakespeare by heart and urged her grandson to read different types of literature. Thus, from an early age the boy was encouraged to read, think, and express his views. Both of his parents were well read in history, politics, and current affairs, and introduced their son at an early age to the world of newspapers, magazines, and books, which in turn provided the material for wide-ranging discussions at the dinner table.

John Warden III had a happy, secure, and loving childhood. He grew up in an atmosphere of traditional family values: his parents adhered to basic Christian beliefs, although they were not active in any particular church community. Both his mother and father had a positive and encouraging attitude toward life, convinced that people determine their own future and that most limitations to growth are self-imposed. They fostered their son's perseverance and self-reliance. At the same time, his upbringing retained a certain formality in behavior, dress, and conversation. His father, like his father before him, was a gentleman of the old school who used reason and logic rather than emotion to support his positions, and seldom, if ever, raised his voice. His mother instilled in her son her own dedication to integrity and respect for others, but also taught him to question conventional wisdom. Although he learned to submit to authority when necessary, the boy also developed a stubborn streak that sometimes led him to persist in views that were not popular with those around him.

This family background obviously predisposed John Warden III toward a military career. His grandfather convinced his grandson of the nobility of the officer's calling, and his father, a man of deep convictions, always remained entirely positive about military life. Although Warden spent many summers with his grandfather in McKinney, enjoying his grandfather's political campaigning and entertaining stories about his personal experiences in two world wars and travels throughout the continent and abroad, it was his father who most influenced and supported his decision to pursue a military career. His uncle's example, in turn, made the air force seem the most natural choice: Pete Warden had more than four thousand flying hours, of which some two hundred were combat missions. The responsibilities he held during his career, together with the attention he had received from the higher echelons of the USAF, played their part in convincing his nephew that the USAF was a more dynamic, future-oriented, and free-thinking institution than the other services.

Young Warden did well in high school, and in 1959 he asked his congressman in Pennsylvania to nominate him for the USAF Academy. After a long bureaucratic admission process involving interviews, physical tests, and academic assessments, the academy offered him a position. He had been accepted at MIT and at Indiana University, but the prospect of continuing the family's military tradition while also earning an engineering degree proved the most appealing option, and he enrolled as a cadet in 1961.

2

LEARNING TO FLY: FROM THE AIR FORCE ACADEMY TO SPAIN

Warden stood outside the mainstream even in the earliest portions of his military career. As a cadet he was troubled by the lack of importance that the Air Force Academy apparently accorded to the role of air power in warfare. His first operational assignments—in Korea, Vietnam, and Spain—revealed a disturbing lack of plans for effective use of air force assets, and stimulated his lifelong interest in improving the planning process. His frustrations with the rules of engagement that shackled pilots in Vietnam also prompted him to question the underpinnings of national strategy, and would later play a decisive role when he developed the concept for the strategic air campaign against Iraq. In an essay written in 1972 he already suggested that the air force should realign its priorities and recognize air superiority, rather than close air support, as its real primary mission.

Signing Up for the USAF

In the 1960s the Air Force Academy in Colorado Springs still enrolled only men; the students were divided into four groups of six squadrons, each squadron containing a mix of cadets from all four class levels. The seventeen-year-old Warden was appointed to the Nineteenth ("Playboy") Squadron of the Fourth Group. He quickly settled in and came to enjoy life on campus, enrolling in a range of courses and benefiting from the school's many athletic activities. He appreciated the academy's positive and dynamic atmosphere, which allowed him both to play and work hard.

Warden decided early on to make the most out of his academic opportunities and selected a heavy load of extra coursework. He soon realized that he preferred small classes, where he could state his opinion and engage in discussions, to large lecture courses. He also discovered that his real interests lay in the humanities rather than science; he consequently chose as many courses as possible in the fields of history and international studies rather than detailed courses on mechanics and engineering. The academy's two-semester military history course covered not only battles and campaigns, but also theory, doctrine, logistics, train-ing, industrial mobilization, and other perspectives.[1]

Although history became his favorite subject, Warden encountered dis-concerting problems. The curriculum introduced the cadets to the ideas of lead-ers such as Gen. Henry H. Arnold and Gen. Carl A. Spaatz, and of the Air Corps Tactical School, but the revisionist approach that prevailed at the academy led to an emphasis on management of the air effort rather than on the conduct and consequences of war making and war fighting. The history department faculty seemed to have little appreciation of air power's achievements against Germany and Japan during the Second World War. Warden had not given much thought to air power as a subject and his instructors did not provide much inspiration for further exploration. The students learned that the true American heroes were army generals such as Douglas A. MacArthur and George S. Patton, and that the real action had taken place on the battlefield. Even humanities and social science courses tended to focus on facts and statistics rather than on ideas. In addition, Warden believed that most courses were too broadly focused and did not allow the cadets sufficient time for in-depth analysis. For these reasons he was left un-satisfied: his major subject, engineering, did not inspire him and the courses in his favorite subject, military history, left a great deal to be desired.[2]

When Warden was well into his second year, these elements of dissatisfac-tion came together and led to serious doubts about dedicating his life to the air force. If the decisive battles took place on the ground—fought, led, and won by army officers—and conventional air power played merely secondary and sup-porting roles, perhaps he should transfer to the army and enroll at West Point. During the following summer vacation he shared his concerns with his uncle, at that time with Systems Command, and a civilian air force historian, Joseph Engels. Both men assured the young cadet that high technology would change the con-duct of war considerably. With aircraft becoming leaner and meaner, Pete War-den was convinced that air power would play an increasingly important role in warfare. He insisted that if his nephew still wanted to pursue a military career, he should remain in the air force.

His doubts allayed by his uncle's certainty and by the prospect of starting pilot training after graduation, Cadet Warden decided to stay on for the time being. Most important, an instructor, Maj. Roger P. Fox, took a keen interest in the young cadet's enthusiasm for military history and strategy. He introduced Warden to a book that would become a source of immense inspiration and influ-ence: Maj. Gen. J. F. C. Fuller's *The Generalship of Alexander the Great*. At the academy, Fuller became Warden's "intellectual mentor," and Alexander the Great his "favorite commander."

While he enjoyed legends, Warden was most fascinated by the Macedonian conqueror's battles and sieges, particularly by his preference for avoiding tradi-tional force-on-force confrontation. Warden stayed up into the early hours, carefully studying the battles of Granicus, Issus, and Hydaspes, and covering maps with arrows and notes. He further distilled from Alexander's campaigns the concept of concentrating the effort on the core of the opposing forces—the enemy leadership—rather than on troops in the field or vessels at sea: an approach illustrated by the Battle of Arbela, in which Alexander defeated Darius III by directly attacking the leader despite the associated risks. Alexander not only focused on the enemy's critical vulnerabilities in the conduct of military operations, but also followed his conquests by imposing governing systems that to some extent respected the religion and customs of the people. Fox spent considerable time with Warden, discussing how Alexander conducted his military operations to achieve political aims, and how he encouraged his opponents to surrender and convert rather than imposing his will by slaughter and slavery. This, to Warden, demonstrated not simply military leadership, but true statesmanship.

Fuller, with his intellectual intensity, wide-ranging interests, literary scope, and articulate writing style, served as an early inspiration that would last throughout Warden's lifetime. Fuller's thinking indicated an intellectual inclination toward the radical rather than the conservative and nostalgic, and Warden found these qualities appealing. Compulsory engineering classes provided Warden with a method for analyzing the essence of strategy and history in a deductive, scientific, and systematic fashion, which made Fuller's ability to reduce the strategy and principles of war to their essence especially appealing. He was encouraged by Fuller's belief that a systematic study of history and strategy could prepare officers for battle, and accepted Fuller's dictum that there were striking resemblances between the conditions that prevailed in the fifth century before Christ and those that governed the present age. Like Fuller, Warden believed that studying great military campaigns could inform and educate military officers on the art and science of war.[3] During his active military career, Fuller had developed into a spokesman for a rational and methodical approach to warfare, insisting that the physical and social sciences were governed by identical forces and could be dealt with in the same way. Thus, the principles of war represented "the tip of the iceberg . . . an iceberg labeled Science of War."[4]

In presenting a holistic theory of war, Fuller, very confident of his own intellect, insisted that he was "trying to do for war what Copernicus did for astronomy, Newton for physics, and Darwin for natural history."[5] Warden recognized Fuller's controversial sides—Fuller had been a Nazi sympathizer who was blacklisted in Britain during the Second World War and who became involved with a number of marginal activities—but he still believed that the self-educated British pioneer understood the alchemy of war better than anyone else and that his focused attention to the factors that made battles decisive provided valuable guidance.

Although fascinated by history and eager to read and discuss what he learned, Warden was also action-oriented throughout his four years at the academy. For example, unhappy with some of the exercises in which the students had to participate, he took the lead in developing a volunteer commando-raid exercise for the squadron during the last school year, insisting that it should be as realistic as possible. He succeeded in persuading a few dozen enlisted rangers from nearby Fort Carson to come to the academy and operate as the Red Team, the simulated enemy, defending an area that the Playboy Squadron was to infiltrate. The rangers also set up a prisoner-of-war camp. The exercise proved a huge success, with only one cadet caught. The structure of the exercise that Warden had developed, with attack and deception tactics and extensive use of walkie-talkies, expanded the following year and became the foundation of an annual training program.

Socially, however, Warden was only partly in tune with the other cadets. Classmates such as Michael C. Short, Howard M. Estes III, and Michael E. Ryan, all of whom would later achieve general rank, recalled that although Warden took part in the main social events, several characteristics singled him out from the crowd.[6] He obviously read more than the other students and the range of his interests was also unusual. He earned respect for being intellectually agile, thoughtful, and an articulate debater, but he was never fully accepted as "one of the guys"—and he did not seem to care. For example, his preference for wearing a coat and tie rather than t-shirts and jeans outside of class set him apart from the rest. He gave the impression of being serious, formal, and determined for his age. He did not even join his classmates in chasing women, because he was already spoken for.

During his last year at the academy he had worked up the courage to propose to his high-school sweetheart, Marjorie "Margie" Ann Clarke. He had been "the new kid in town" when he joined her class for their senior year at Conestoga High School in Berwyn, Pennsylvania. He first attracted her attention when the class began to discuss the forthcoming election for class president. He told them that he had been president of his tenth grade class in Harrisburg, but had lost the election the following year because he had not taken the full electorate into account. Although he was not running for office, he wanted them to make sure that they had identified all the students who were eligible to vote. Margie found him both "handsome and intelligent" and the two started dating. They were not quite a couple when he started at the academy and she went off to college in New Hampshire, but they stayed in touch and over the four years they met ever more often when school breaks allowed. During the spring break of 1965 he proposed and she accepted.[7]

Warden graduated on June 9, 1965, with a bachelor's degree in science and a major in national security affairs. Academically he ranked in the middle of the class: he did well in history and social science, but his grades in engineering—the courses that counted the most—were mediocre. His entry in the class yearbook stated:

John came to the Academy directly out of high school at Berwyn, Pennsylvania. He became a tolerable skier as a member of the Ski Club, and a good rider in the Saddle Club. He also belonged to the Mountaineering Club and the Forensic Society. John was manager of the Tennis Team for one year and coached the Squadron intramural Field Hockey team his first class year. He was on the Dean's List for five semesters. After graduation, John plans on going to flying school and then making a long, profitable career out of the Air Force. He has an ardent desire to go to Viet Nam.[8]

This description was not unusual in that most cadets took an interest in sports, most wanted to become pilots, and Vietnam was clearly on the agenda. As a cadet Warden already considered it his duty to fight for his country, and he wanted to get to Southeast Asia as soon as possible. Even though some of his educational experience was unsatisfactory, Warden's years at the academy further deepened the patriotism that he inherited from his family. People and events at the academy convinced him that the air force represented a worthy ethos of integrity and dedication to the country and he intended to be part of it.

Deployment to South Korea: Flying the F-4 Phantom II

After receiving his undergraduate degree, Second Lieutenant Warden embarked on a one-year pilot training program at Laredo AFB, Texas. He found the year interesting and progressively more challenging as he learned to fly the three training aircraft: the T-41, the military version of the four-seat Cessna 172; the T-37, the twin-engine jet used to teach fundamental aircraft handling, including instruments, night flying, and formations; and the T-38, the twin-engine, high-altitude, supersonic jet trainer.

Warden was ranked in the middle of his class, and upon receiving his pilot wings in July 1966 he was selected for the F-4 *Phantom II.* The year also proved rewarding on a personal level: Margie and he had used the Christmas break to get married, on his twenty-second birthday, December 21, 1965; and on December 5, 1966, they became the parents of twins—Elizabeth Kathleen and John IV.

The USAF pilots selected for the F-4 program began their platform-specific training with a radar-intercept course and simulation training for the back seat position at Davis-Monthan AFB in Tucson, Arizona. They were next sent to MacDill AFB in Tampa, Florida, to become "combat capable." At MacDill Warden learned the basic skills needed to fly the jet: takeoffs, landings, basic aerobatics, and basic instrument flight. He appreciated the aircraft and, like most of his colleagues, found it incredibly powerful. When Warden began to fly the F-4C it had been in the USAF inventory for only three years, but it had already demonstrated both strengths and weaknesses: it could carry twice the bomb load of the B-17 *Flying Fortress,* which gave it a notable conventional air-to-ground capacity, but its bombing accuracy was poor. A 500-pound bomb had to hit within twenty-five feet to destroy a truck, yet one study revealed that the circular error probable (CEP) for all bombs dropped in Vietnam was over three hundred feet.[9]

In April 1967 Warden reported to the 334th Tactical Fighter Squadron (TFS) at the Fourth Tactical Fighter Wing (TFW), Seymour-Johnson AFB, Goldsboro, North Carolina. The wing's mission was to constitute forces that could be deployed to Europe as part of its commitment to the North Atlantic Treaty Organization (NATO), but it also supplied personnel for rotational tours in Southeast Asia. Warden was determined to do well and became "combat ready" in August 1967 along with his front seater, Capt. Larry Van Sickle. A few months later his squadron deployed to South Korea in response to the *Pueblo* incident. The USS *Pueblo* had been collecting signals intelligence in the Sea of Japan, using the cover of conducting hydrographical research, when it was attacked by North Korean torpedo boats on January 23, 1968. *Pueblo* was the first U.S. Navy ship to be seized on the high seas for more than 150 years, and the United States responded by sending fighter squadrons to the region, including seventy-two F-4s from the Fourth TFW. The total deployment was one of the largest and fastest movements since the 1958 Lebanon crisis.

The dispatched formations were proud that they were able to deploy on such short notice, reaching the theater ready for combat within forty-eight hours. On arrival, however, Warden and his colleagues discovered that the air force had no plan for using them, and this became his squadron's first concern. With the aircraft parked wing-tip to wing-tip on the runway at Kunsan, Warden wondered if the United States had forgotten the lessons of Pearl Harbor and the Arab-Israeli war of the previous year. When the squadron finally received operational contingency orders for attacking possible targets in Wonsan it was instructed to fly at 20,000 feet, "straight and level," and without electronic countermeasures: it was an open invitation to be shot down. With the guidance of those who had recent experience in Vietnam, the squadron subsequently took matters into its own hands and made changes as best it could.

Realizing that Kunsan was too crowded for effective operations, the air force ordered the entire wing to disperse, and Warden's squadron moved to Kwang-ju. The base was used primarily for training new South Korean recruits, but the squadron was given decentralized authority to prepare itself for possible engagements. As it happened, it was never called beyond cockpit alert, but the short operational experience gave Warden a glimpse of a sobering reality: the air force was ready to deploy at short notice, but it lacked operational plans for employing its forces in any coherent fashion.

Although being deployed to South Korea held the potential for action, Warden concluded early on that he would probably not witness combat unless he went to Vietnam. He recalled his uncle's assertion that it was preferable to deploy as part of a unit rather than as an individual, but that option was not available. Warden was impatient: he wanted to serve his country in the ongoing war, he wanted to be where the action was, and he wanted to go sooner rather than later. He faced a predicament, however. He did not want to be tied to the back seat of the F-4, "a place nobody wanted to be,"[10] and he was not willing to wait for the opportunity to complete the standard program to upgrade to the front seat position. Since the USAF was short of forward air controllers (FACs), he volunteered for this role, although he would certainly have preferred to go to Vietnam as a fighter pilot. Ironically, by the time the air force had completed the paperwork and approved Warden's transition, he had almost finished the F-4 upgrade program, but he could not reverse the assignment.

Warden started OV-10 *Bronco* training at Hurlburt AFB, Fort Walton Beach, Florida. The *Bronco* was a twin-turboprop short takeoff and landing aircraft designed for observation, helicopter escort, gunfire spotting, limited ground attack, armed reconnaissance, and forward air control missions. Newly promoted to captain, he would now fly the *Bronco* to find and identify enemy positions, which in turn would guide the fighter-bombers conducting the attacks. Warden liked the aircraft: he found it highly maneuverable and even enjoyable to fly. After the *Bronco* transition course, he left the United States for survival training in the Philippine jungles.

Deployment to South Vietnam: Flying the OV-10 *Bronco*

When Captain Warden reached Southeast Asia on January 29, 1969, Operation Rolling Thunder had just ended. The operation, which consisted of direct, independent application of air power, had been designed to force North Vietnam to abandon its war in the south and admit defeat at the negotiating table. The codename described an intentionally gradualist strategy, implemented in the form of a targeting process that prohibited systematic attacks against Hanoi and Haiphong, airfields, and supply lines along the Chinese border. The airmen were subject to strict rules of engagement and these restrictions precluded an effective campaign against the enemy's infrastructure.[11] When President Lyndon B. Johnson declared a halt to all bombing of North Vietnam north of the 20th parallel, Rolling Thunder had achieved little, despite almost a million sorties flown and several hundred aircraft lost to enemy fire.

The entire U.S. strategy in Vietnam suffered from a fundamental problem: President Johnson and his advisors underestimated the enemy's determination and compounded their mistake by misreading the nature of the conflict. A psychological dimension added to the actual difficulties on the battlefield. The infamous Tet Offensive, a series of attacks launched against some forty cities and towns throughout South Vietnam in early 1968, had severely undermined public support for the war. For all practical purposes the American forces and their allies had succeeded in destroying the Viet Cong as an effective fighting force and thereby prevented the North Vietnamese from achieving any real military success, yet this tactical victory proved almost irrelevant. The U.S. media portrayed, and the American public perceived, the offensive as a North Vietnamese victory because the Viet Cong's ability to launch such an offensive belied the U.S. government's repeated assertions that the communists were incapable of resisting U.S. military power. The disturbing images emerging from the Tet Offensive—of body bags and the shooting of prisoners—further contributed to a credibility gap that the administration was unable to close. Thus, in essence, U.S. forces found themselves fighting a war of attrition against a fiercely determined enemy without a coherent strategy for winning or the backing of public opinion at home.

The year 1968 had also proved the bloodiest of the Vietnam conflict, with the highest rate at which American ground forces were killed. In response, President Johnson initiated the next phase of the conflict, "Vietnamization," designed to turn the war over to the South Vietnamese. The effort intensified under the newly elected president, Richard M. Nixon, and on January 25, 1969, Nixon proposed "mutual withdrawal" of troops and canceled all bombing of North Vietnam.

Captain Warden first participated in compulsory "in-country" FAC training and was then assigned to Tay Ninh, some sixty miles northwest of Saigon. For the first time Warden engaged in joint operations with army forces: his squadron's primary mission was to assist the First Brigade of the First Air Cavalry Division by performing reconnaissance and close air support. Warden soon observed that air power could secure lines of communication in ways that land power could not. However, while aerial firepower on occasion could provide salvation for a beleaguered American ground force, half of the ground battles lasted less than twenty minutes—too short a time for ground forces to call upon air power for assistance.[12] Warden considered close air support a rather ineffective application of air power, but he enjoyed the flying, the team spirit, and the fact that he was fighting for his country. He took pride in military honor and duty, and believed that U.S. forces were at least holding the North Vietnamese in check.

After six months at Tay Ninh Warden was transferred to the air force's Twenty-third Tactical Air Support Squadron at Nakhon Phanom Royal Thai Air Base, an operational base located close to the Mekong River, some four hundred miles northeast of Bangkok. Reconnaissance remained his most important mission, but interdiction replaced ground support operations. Warden felt as though he had participated in two different kinds of wars: the first applied air power against ground forces, where the threat was basically small-arms fire, while the latter used air power against infrastructure and supplies to affect the enemy at the operational level of war. He considered the latter type of operation more useful than close air support, although he was not dogmatic in his belief. From a flying standpoint interdiction was also clearly more dangerous: he now faced the full range of antiaircraft artillery and if shot down over Laos he was more likely to be captured than if shot down over South Vietnam.

The interdiction campaign became synonymous with attacks on the Ho Chi Minh Trail: an elaborate system of mountain and jungle trails linking not only Hanoi to Saigon, but also Cambodia and Laos to North and South Vietnam. The initially small trail had developed into an intricate track system including paths for troops and vehicles, with a total length of nearly 12,500 miles along the Truong Son Mountains. Air operations focused on four elements: the road and travel routes, the supply dumps, the vehicles on the trail itself, and the guns defending the trail. Although such elements made for attractive targets, the rules of engagement restricted efficiency. For example, the North Vietnamese would line up their trucks during the day in preparation for crossing the border under the cover of darkness, but as long as they were on home territory they were "off limits."[13] Warden and his colleagues thus experienced the frustration of having to engage their targets only after the enemy had the chance to disperse. The attacks prevented the North Vietnamese from establishing a complete supply base in South Vietnam, but Warden and his colleagues believed that U.S. fighter-bombers could achieve far more if allowed to attack the enemy at the source.

Unable to interdict the enemy flow where it began in the North, Warden and his fellow airmen were relegated to guiding tactical air strikes in constrained areas. Although the nearly unarmed FAC was vulnerable in its long searches at low altitude, the North Vietnamese quickly learned that to fire at a FAC would draw the attention of fighter-bombers and thereby reduce their chance of survival. Nevertheless, navigator Maj. Gary B. Mcintire recalls that one day Warden's aircraft was severely damaged by antiaircraft artillery fire as he flew back from the Ho Chi Minh Trail. The following day Warden sought to retaliate, flying lower than he should to increase his chances of success, only to have his aircraft further damaged by the same enemy firing unit. When he returned to the base, his squadron commander grounded him for a few days to signal to the other pilots that such risks were not worth taking.[14] Returning safely to the base became the airmen's daily measure of merit, and winning was defined as coming home in one piece at the end of a year's tour.

Warden had conducted 266 combat missions by the time his tour ended. Colleagues remember him as an ardent patriot who believed strongly in the larger cause of the war. Overall, they viewed him as aggressive, motivated, and competent, as well as mission-oriented. They also considered him friendly, outspoken, and private—all at the same time; they often observed him sitting by himself, reading and thinking, and when he engaged in conversations he held strong opinions.

Warden first gave voice to a personal strategic outlook during his farewell dinner at Nakhon Phanom. In his obligatory speech Warden stated that he would never again accept being part of a sham: he was happy to fight the North Vietnamese or other communists, but he viewed the war's rules of engagement as a cardinal sin.[15] He argued that the American effort was coming unraveled because the strategy applied force incorrectly. Warden concluded that the limits *of* air power stemmed from the limits put *upon* air power: air power was being misused by politicians who picked targets in the White House during the infamous Tuesday luncheons, and by a gradualist approach that sought to send signals rather than win the war. Even the measures of merit were misleading: body counts for the ground war and sortie rates for the air war.

Warden expressed his frustration, but affirmed that he was still proud of his country and his service. He then took it upon himself to be the lead singer of the Air Force Song. The words of the song had very real meaning for Warden, but some of those present found his behavior and speech strange.[16] Still, they sang along and enjoyed doing so: after all, Warden had served well with them and this was his going-away party. Moreover, while certain members of his audience may have thought Warden presumptuous for believing he understood matters of national interest better than the president and his advisors, many fighter pilots, necessarily focused on the tactics of air operations, agreed that the restrictions imposed on them made no sense, and Warden had stated their objections in clear terms.

Warden recalls that an officer from the U.S. Special Forces, who had not heard the whole speech, thought Warden had argued that the war itself was immoral. The officer took offense and after dinner suggested that the two should settle the issue with a fistfight outside the officers' club. Warden assured him that there was a misunderstanding, and when he had explained his position the Special Forces officer agreed fully.

Vietnam taught Warden an important lesson: good tactics could not compensate for a flawed strategy. Allowed to operate only in support of ground forces or in interdiction missions in an inhospitable environment, Warden and his colleagues questioned not only the operational procedures and the limits put upon air power, but also the lack of any coherent political and strategic plan. Warden made a resolution: if he ever found himself in another war he would do everything he could to make sure that the United States would win.[17] The experience of witnessing a losing campaign from the inside exerted a profound influence on his way of thinking: twenty years later, when Iraq invaded Kuwait, he viewed it as an opportunity and obligation to "get it right."

Deployment to Spain: Back to the F-4

As his Vietnam tour came to an end, the personnel center in Texas suggested that Warden become a T-28 instructor pilot at Keesler AFB in Biloxi, Mississippi, training the South Vietnamese as part of the Vietnamization program. Warden considered such an assignment unchallenging and insisted that he would rather return to flying fighter aircraft, even if this meant starting from scratch on the front seat checkout that he had left unfinished when he went to war. The authorities relented, and when he returned from Vietnam in January 1970, he was assigned as an F-4 pilot to the 613th TFS of the 401st TFW at Torrejon Air Base outside Madrid. The original F-4 had been upgraded twice since its inception and Warden became a member of the F-4 cadre that would witness the conversion of the wing to the E-model. His tour with the USAF in Europe (USAFE) provided for steady career progress: he completed the upgrade to front seat and was appointed assistant flight commander within the first two years.

The primary mission of Warden's squadron, nicknamed "the Squids," was to remain on nuclear alert; they were to deploy to Incirlik Air Base, outside Adana, Turkey, in the event of war. Warden therefore had to study the Single Integrated Operational Plan (SIOP) series—the concepts for employing nuclear weapons. He developed a general knowledge of the overall concept and an intimate knowledge of the aspects related to his own mission, but grew increasingly dissatisfied with large portions of the tactics that related to the local plan because he simply did not find the nuclear threat credible. Warden openly stated the belief that conventional air battles with the Soviet Union were much more likely than nuclear action, and therefore the air superiority mission needed to be practiced and improved. Capt. Kenneth F. Keller, who served with Warden at Torrejon, remembered that Warden was a "good pilot" who was "exceptionally serious about the business of war." He recalled Warden's eagerness to discuss what had gone wrong in Vietnam and his determination to help the air force improve itself at the tactical level.[18]

Halfway through his tour in Spain Warden became the assistant director of wing operations and training and began to commit some of his thoughts to paper. By the summer of 1972 his ideas coalesced in the first of his theoretical writings: an essay, "Employment of Tactical Air in Europe," which he submitted to his USAFE superiors in the form of a memorandum.[19] Warden's basic hypothesis was that both the Warsaw Pact and NATO were obsessed with close air support as the primary air power mission, at the expense of the more important objective—gaining and maintaining air superiority. The paper suggested that the Soviet orientation toward the concept left the United States with five basic options for employing air power in a large-scale conventional war in Europe: (1) complete dedication of forces to attacks on Soviet rear bases and their lines of communications; (2) complete dedication of forces to block Soviet armored thrusts at their heads; (3) complete dedication of forces to counter-air operations by attacking the enemy in the air or on the ground; (4) complete dedication of forces to the defense of allied installations; and (5) division of forces to address a combination of any or all of the previous four options.

Warden argued that the first option would "result in a deadly attrition of our forces without producing substantial results," and that the second would play directly into Soviet hands. He characterized the number of sorties required against Soviet armor as absolutely staggering even in a permissive environment. Warden argued that the U.S.S.R. would impose heavy casualties on U.S. forces that attacked its main forces; moreover, the vast antiaircraft artillery and surface-to-air missile (SAM) facilities in Eastern Europe and the U.S.S.R. would make fighting the Warsaw Pact over its territory exceedingly difficult and dangerous.

Warden favored the third option: the USAFE should focus on defensive counter-air operations to achieve air superiority over NATO territory. In seeking air superiority, he emphasized, the USAFE had to concentrate its forces "at a given time and place," but he left the tactics open for further discussion: "perhaps forces should be employed in a squadron or wing size. Perhaps repeated two or four ship flights are the answer." He further noted, "if Soviet air can be destroyed over the land battle with acceptable friendly loss rates, the Soviet ground thrusts are deprived of a necessary adjunct of their operations. We suggest with near certainty that the Soviets *must* concentrate a large proportion of their Air Forces over the ground battle area."

The fourth option would make sense if NATO were certain that the Soviets would attack particular targets, but allowing the enemy to come so far without initial opposition entailed a variety of risks. The fifth option would be feasible if the air commander had a "unified objective" and avoided spreading his forces too thinly. Warden concluded:

> We submit that our case for the attainment of Air Superiority is substantiated for we have noted that one, the Soviets depend on CAS [close air support] for offensive ground operations; two that we cannot provide effective close air support of our own ground forces in the face of enemy air opposition; and three, we can destroy Soviet Air in our environment. Thus, our goal must be to do this in the most expeditious manner. . . . The greatest number of counter air targets will be in our own backyard, our own airspace, in the air. By attacking the enemy there, we eliminate the need for costly penetration of his territory with concomitant loss of aircrews who there abandon their disabled aircraft. And, by attacking Soviet Aircraft over our territory without fear of extensive SAM and AAA [antiaircraft artillery] threats, we realize several advantages. . . . The mission of USAFE is Air Superiority to be gained in the air.[20]

The essay showed Captain Warden's serious interest in planning air operations at the tactical level, and his skepticism regarding then-current planning. Although the viewpoint reflected in this early thought piece—especially his warning against attacking the enemy in the rear—was far more defensive than that in his later writings, the essay was a precursor to *The Air Campaign* in a double sense. It revealed Warden's systematic thinking about the need to concentrate forces in time and place, his interest in big-wing tactics, and his sense that the air force needed to identify a mission other than the nuclear scenario or support to the army. Perhaps more important, as early as the summer of 1972, Captain Warden suggested in written form that the air force and the army had an unhealthy obsession with close air support: gaining air superiority would be the real determinant of success in modern war and the fight for air superiority should therefore receive first priority. The essay also exemplified Warden's characteristically deductive and methodical approach to analysis: after identifying the problems he suggested concrete solutions without apologizing for not adhering to conventional wisdom—all features that would become his trademark.

From Warden's perspective, the most interesting part of the assignment to Spain was serving as the wing's first representative to the Shahbaz exercise: the annual combined air defense exercise that covered Turkey and Iran. The exercise was part of an effort designed to support the Central Treaty Organization (CENTO), formed in 1959 by Turkey, Pakistan, Iran, Britain, and the United States to check Soviet ambitions in the Middle East. The Americans had assumed a supervisory role since CENTO's inception but had never previously participated in direct military exercises with its treaty partners. Now, as part of the attempt to consolidate relations with Iran, the 401st TFW was tasked with taking the exercise a step further: for the first time, USAFE sent a fighter contingent to Tehran to participate in the forthcoming exercise. This assignment gave Warden the opportunity to visit Beirut, Ankara, Istanbul, Tel Aviv, and Tehran. As part of the exercise he flew over the Caspian Sea and along the Soviet border, took part in negotiations at the senior military level, and dealt with issues such as host nation support and pre-positioning of assets, discovering that he could make important decisions.

His participation in the Shahbaz exercise confirmed his opinion that the air force had no credible concept for how to gain and sustain air superiority, and he took it upon himself to investigate how air power could make a meaningful contribution "with just a handful of airplanes."[21] Among the ideas he explored at the time was achieving air superiority through large and independent sweeps rather than the traditional four-ship packages with close escort.[22]

His job as assistant director meant less flying, but he was pleased that he could devote more time to his growing interest in realistic training and planning. His responsibilities enabled Warden to deal with planning and operations for one of the world's political hot spots, the Persian Gulf, and gave him the opportunity to consider ways to improve performance at the tactical level. Torrejon was in many ways a rather liberal establishment: since it was not the USAFE's first priority, the 401st Wing was free to explore many different approaches to its mission, testing various options and then deciding how to proceed. U.S. forces in Spain were not on the front line, at least compared to formations in Germany, and the wing was not subjected to direct command and control from NATO headquarters. Such a remote assignment also created stronger bonds among the Americans assigned to the base: as a captain, Warden had far better access to the wing's leadership than he would have had at a fighter wing in the United States.

Fortunately, Warden had tolerant and encouraging superior officers. Warden's efforts to improve planning caught the attention of Col. Charles L. Donnelly Jr., who had been appointed wing commander in November 1973. Donnelly enjoyed hosting dignitaries, representing his country, and discussing matters of policy and bilateral relations between the United States and Spain, and he showed a genuine interest in both his officers and enlisted men at the 401st TFW. Warden considered him an excellent leader: mission-oriented, imperturbable, demanding, polite, and—perhaps most important—collegial and open-minded about new ideas. Warden also found that Donnelly encouraged a free exchange of opinions without losing his own authority in the decision-making process.[23] Donnelly, in turn, thought highly of Warden: they spent many hours together discussing ways to improve the employment of air power at a tactical level, and at meetings Donnelly seemed to pay attention to the captain's contributions.[24] Moreover, Donnelly and Warden shared an interest in history, often exchanging books and debating their relevance.

Both Donnelly and Warden were intrigued by the idea of securing air superiority as a result of concentrated and aggressive operations. They agreed that the air force needed to think more deeply and broadly about conventional air power as well as the existing nuclear capability. Warden impressed Donnelly and the colonel apparently worried that Warden's qualities could easily be overlooked in the bureaucratic maze. Air force officers may have both mentors and sponsors: the former advise, guide, and ensure that an officer develops various skills, while the latter take an active role in advancing the younger officer's career. In Warden's case Donnelly, who eventually became a four-star general, served both functions, which proved of no small importance to Warden's career. Lt. Col. Michael P. C. Carns, the commander of 613th TFS, also developed ties to Captain Warden. He, too, seems to have been impressed by the young dynamic officer who had so many ideas: many years and promotions later he would remain one of Warden's strongest supporters.

Hardworking and dedicated, Warden received extremely high evaluations and had the prospect of becoming a fighter instructor pilot, which in turn had the potential to lead to a flight commander position. Thus, when the air force suggested that he should enroll in a two-year master's degree program in residence, he hesitated. He did not want to spend too much time away from the operational environment, and the degree that he was offered belonged to the intelligence branch—a prospect he found not at all attractive. But Donnelly convinced him to accept, arguing that it would be good for his career if he earned a master's degree sooner rather than later and that the anticipated follow-on intelligence assignment could be avoided. In the summer of 1974, after almost six years abroad, Warden returned to American soil and again concentrated on the academic component of his chosen profession.

3

THE MAKING OF
A STRATEGIC THINKER

W arden's interest in generalship, strategy, and the art of war intensified in 1974–1975, the year that he spent earning his master's degree at Texas Technical University (Texas Tech). He used the opportunity to read widely and ponder anew aspects of the Second World War, and his thesis focused exclusively on decision making at the grand strategic level. In style and methodology the thesis foreshadowed his later writings: it combined a comprehensible, broad approach with a commendable grasp of strategy, but was based on radical premises that led to both sound and debatable conclusions. In subsequent assignments to the Pentagon as a staff officer, first in the Middle East and Africa Division and then as assistant executive officer to the air force chief of staff, he attracted considerable attention from the highest level of command. His years in the Pentagon stimulated Warden to think more clearly about the strategic and operational levels of war and convinced him that the Air Staff held exceptional opportunities for networking and pushing new ideas.

Master's Studies
From a list of options for a postgraduate degree program, Warden had selected political science at Texas Tech, located on the high plains near Lubbock. Highly motivated to advance his career, Warden quickly realized that he could compress the normal two-year program into a single year. Again, however, he found his classes disappointing and some of the same doubts that he had entertained about air force education more than ten years earlier returned.

He was nevertheless determined to make good use of the opportunity to dedicate a full year to academia. Fortunately, one man came to his rescue: Frederick H. Hartmann, the author of *Germany Between East and West* and *The Relations of Nations*. Warden later reflected that, had it not been for Hartmann, the year would have been a complete waste of time.[1] Hartmann, who was spending his sabbatical year from the Naval War College at Texas Tech, had just finished the manuscript for *The Game of Strategy*. The two men found common ground through their shared interest in strategy, which Hartmann defined as "the art and science of predicting and producing outcomes."[2] Warden changed classes so that he could attend all those that Hartmann taught. In turn, Hartmann readily agreed to supervise Warden's thesis, "The Grand Alliance: Strategy and Decision."

Rather than concentrate on the tactics and technicalities of flying aircraft, Captain Warden chose to focus on the highest level of decision making: on how countries go to war and how they win and lose wars. He cited three reasons for his choice of subject. First, he wanted to learn more about the decisions that had resulted in the polarized cold war world. Second, he wanted to improve his knowledge and understanding of strategy, and for the modern era, the Second World War provided the obvious frame of reference. Third, his service in Europe had led him to question the effectiveness of NATO decision making, which encouraged him to study coalition warfare, again with the Second World War as the natural subject.

As he prepared his thesis, Warden discovered that he enjoyed writing. He developed a systematic method for his research: he read through source materials relatively fast and noted a few citations, hypotheses, and key arguments. Using index cards and an archive system, he later reviewed his notes and decided which sources and sets of ideas he should explore further. He found that this approach— starting with a broad overview and then proceeding to specific instances—worked well, and he used it in preparing his subsequent publications.

The main hypothesis underlying Warden's thesis was that the Anglo-American Alliance had failed "to integrate military and political affairs into a grand strategy." As a result, military victories "brought new problems even as they solved old ones,"[3] and thus the outcome of the Second World War was unnecessarily flawed. Warden argued that the three individuals whom he identified as the most influential American decision makers—President Franklin D. Roosevelt, Gen. George C. Marshall, and Gen. Dwight D. Eisenhower—were all products of an environment that tended to dissociate war from politics. As military campaigns developed their own momentum, the desired military end-state, "the utter destruction of the Axis," had replaced any political post-war vision, with the consequence that "there was nobody in charge of the most important part of war—its political purpose."[4] In this Warden agreed with Fuller, who had stated, "in war victory is no more than a means to an end; peace is the end, and should victory lead to a disastrous peace, then politically, the war will have been lost."[5]

Warden further asserted that while the Allies had agreed on the desired military outcome, "destruction of the fighting ability of their opponents," and on the decision to deal with the European theater first, including an attack on the German homeland, the Americans and the British had differed fundamentally on crucial questions of strategy. The United States had favored paralyzing enemy forces by massive, immediate, and direct attacks on Germany through France, whereas the British, already committed to operations in the Mediterranean theater, sought to bring that campaign to a successful end before completing Germany's defeat in northwest Europe. These divergent strategies led to unwarranted compromises and flawed decisions: to invade North Africa instead of concentrating on France from the outset; to invade Sicily; to invade Italy before moving into the heartland of Germany; to engage in a broad front across France, rather than the British-preferred option of swift attacks across the northern plains of Germany; and to halt Allied forces at the river Elbe, which had "repercussions which are still very much with us today." His thesis stated the U.S. decision makers had failed to appreciate the importance of "shaking hands with the Russians as far to the east as possible" at a time when the potential Russian threat should have been obvious, and had thus virtually given away Berlin and Prague.[6] Warden reasoned that by the spring of 1945 it was clear that the Germans preferred to surrender to Allied troops and thus fled toward the Western Front: he concluded that capturing Berlin ahead of Russian troops would not have produced the anticipated bloodbath and would have enabled the Allies to secure all of Germany behind Anglo-American lines.

Warden identified yet another factor that had overshadowed the political focus: the moral dimension. In his understated fashion he noted: "Hitler was not a nice man, but dislike of an individual is a shaky ground for national security decisions."[7] Fuller, again, influenced his interpretation of events, as shown clearly toward the end of the thesis:

> The two countries of the Grand Alliance, with "inveterate antipathy" and mesmerized by the evil of Hitler, went blindly to war dressed in shining armor and mounted on magnificent white chargers. They were predominantly unable to see across Germany to the equal peril that lay to the East. Rather than attain a satisfactory postwar balance of power, the Allies set their sights on military victory.[8]

The thesis was unusual in that Warden tried to strike a balance between the British and the American perspectives, an uncommon approach in the mid-1970s. In the final chapter, titled "The Fruits of Victory," Warden evaluated the different military options available at the time, stating the opinion that the U.S. approach of direct attack could have succeeded, although the British indirect approach would have been preferable, but that "short-term considerations" drove "long-term considerations" to the extent that the Western allies settled on the least effective of strategic compromises.[9] He concluded that both countries showed little imagination in terms of strategy and had failed to consider the postwar situation adequately. The last three paragraphs of the thesis summarized his position on "lessons learned":

> Coalition warfare is a trying experience. That it was so for the Americans and the British, despite shared values, culture, and language, only serves to emphasize the point. Imagine the problems which would beset two allied nations of more divergent background or with different languages. Recognition of the difficulty of this problem is half the battle in avoiding failing to solve it. The solution must depend on the circumstances.
>
> When, in the summer of 1944, the United States became preponderant in men and equipment, it became for all practical purposes the senior partner and that fact had its effects. Although differences of opinion did not end, long debates over strategy did. The Americans decided. Thereafter, the military strategy, for good or for ill, was at least coherent, which it certainly was not before the summer of 1944. If, in comparable future situations, one partner can be acknowledged as the *primus inter pares*, it may prevent the confusion and vacillation prevalent in the Grand Alliance of World War II. The results, though, will depend upon the senior partner's grasp of grand strategy.
>
> The over-riding requirement for an agreed and sound grand strategy is the most important lesson to be derived from a study of the experiences of Great Britain and the United States in World War II. Had there been a sound Alliance Grand Strategy, the world would certainly be different today. The Alliance would have been able to have looked calmly and rationally beyond the immediate danger then posed by Germany. Had it done so, it would have recognized that, "A Russian state from the Urals to the Northern Sea can be no great improvement over a German state from the North Sea to the Urals." The lessons and the rules of grand strategy, known to the discerning since the days of Alexander the Great, might have been applied more effectively in order to steer the Ship of State safely down the eddying currents of the tumultuous history of our times.[10]

The thesis offered valuable insight, but its arguments were not unassailable. Warden's outlook was inordinately influenced by Fuller, who considered the communist conquest of Eastern Europe the worst possible outcome of the Second World War, and he sometimes took his arguments to extreme conclusions. That the communist threat was comparable to the Nazi threat is at least open to discussion: from the European standpoint, communism was a matter of rivalry and enmity, but Nazism was a matter of cult and annihilation. Admittedly,

Warden's assertion stemmed from concerns with the balance of power rather than ideology: he believed that by destroying Germany the Allies had also destroyed a bulwark against the East that European regimes since the Roman Empire had striven to maintain. While one threat undoubtedly replaced another after the war, communism was well established and the ideological differences between the East and the West would no doubt have manifested themselves whether Eisenhower had stopped at the Elbe or advanced further to the east.

Warden's conclusions reflect the realities of the cold war and his personal experiences in Korea, Vietnam, and Spain. His interpretations also derive from the literature of the 1950s and 1960s on which he based his findings. Warden's strong objections to communism may explain why his thesis barely acknowledged Soviet contributions to the allied victory or the suffering the Russians experienced on the Eastern Front, where they lost an average of more than nineteen thousand men per day between June 22, 1941, and May 12, 1945.[11] Warden warned against judging events in hindsight, but he failed to appreciate that the Grand Alliance had to fight where it was, rather than where it wanted to be, and that a nation entering a war belatedly cannot determine its terms of reference.[12] Although Warden stated upfront that the thesis would only focus on the Anglo-American relationship, the third partner in the alliance should at least have been identified.

The thesis was a case study, and many of the factors analyzed were specific to the historical situation, but Warden drew a valid universal conclusion: a grand strategy depends on the integration of political and military dimensions. In his own words, "methods of war change, but the principles of war, the strategy of war—and peace—have not changed since Miltiades repulsed the Great King on the Plains of Marathon."[13] This belief—that universal rules and principles determine success in warfare—became the bedrock of Warden's strategic thinking, but he had not yet tied his knowledge and experience of tactical air power from Vietnam and his various deployments into the grand strategic dimension. Warden's thesis was unconventional, well structured, well written, and focused despite its broad sweep, and it deserved the high marks it received.

His studies at Texas Tech introduced Warden to planning at the national level and the ways in which individuals and bureaucracies could influence the flow and outcome of wars. He devoted considerable time to thinking about strategy and developed a genuine interest in military and political theory. The insights he gained would serve as the basis for his later actions and writings: indeed, many of the concepts underlying the strategic air campaign in Operation Desert Storm were already starting to crystallize in Warden's mind in 1975. Paramount among them were the need for leaders to define the desired political end-state clearly and to coordinate those objectives with military strategies in order to have a coherent grand strategy; the danger of settling for compromises in the absence of an overall vision; and the importance of imaginative and thorough military planning that included a postwar picture. He concluded that in the Second World War "there was no consideration of what the defeat of the Axis was supposed to accomplish beyond the defeat of the Axis."[14]

Gradually Warden started to develop his own ideas about how states should wage war, and how the military should fight, to ensure success. Perhaps most important, he developed a profound aversion to the frontal "man-to-man" approach that Marshall and Eisenhower endorsed, and a strong preference for the British indirect approach.[15] Warden generally agreed with Basil Liddell Hart, who had stated, "the most decisive victory is of no value if a nation be bled white while gaining it."[16] Liddell Hart also noted that the aim of grand strategy should be to discover and pierce the Achilles' heel of the opposing government's power to wage war. A strategist, Liddell Hart believed, should think in terms of paralyzing, not of killing, and should not consider the army as the only focus to achieve victory. Warden also began to share some of Liddell Hart's skepticism about Carl von Clausewitz, whom the British captain had dubbed "the Mahdi of Mass" and castigated as the prophet whose clarion call had misled generations into the belief that the best way to wage war was to form the greatest possible concentration of men and weapons and launch it straight ahead against the enemy. While Warden agreed it was better to neutralize enemy forces than to annihilate them, he shared Clausewitz's and Liddell Hart's conviction that the ultimate purpose of war was political.

First Pentagon Tour

Warden was now prepared to serve in the nation's capital, but finding a desirable position required considerable effort, and for the only time in his career he actively "worked his own assignment." The prospective job in the Air Staff's Intelligence Directorate had never appealed to him; by contrast, during his posting to Spain, Col. Donnelly and others had spoken very positively about the work environment in the Air Staff's Directorate of Plans and the challenges that such an assignment entailed. Through his association with Hartmann, Warden had become fascinated with the process by which planning efforts were transformed into contingency and war plans, and while he knew relatively little about the planning directorate he intuitively realized that he wanted to work there. His studies further strengthened his conviction that the important decisions were made in planning environments: as he saw it, "Plans" opened all doors for the future, while "Intelligence" did not.

Halfway through the academic year he wrote to the Air Staff, requesting that he be posted to the Directorate of Plans. The responses to his letters were discouraging, indicating a change would be difficult because Intelligence had paid for his education. Warden took a week off from the university and went to the Pentagon to seek help from an academy classmate, a distant relative, and Major Keller, with whom he had worked in Spain. Keller, now assigned to the Europe/NATO Division, did his best to obtain Warden's release from the Intelligence assignment.[17] After considerable arguing Warden succeeded in obtaining a position in the Planning Directorate, although he had to settle for the Middle East and Africa Division—far smaller and less prestigious than the Europe/NATO Division, where he had hoped to work, or the Pacific Division. Still, Warden's eagerness to work in the Pentagon set him apart from his fellow fighter pilots, most of whom viewed an assignment in the Air Staff as a necessary evil to be endured before they could return to flying.

MIDDLE EAST AND AFRICA DIVISION
In August 1975, when Warden arrived at the Pentagon, repercussions of the Yom Kippur War dominated his division's concerns. On October 6, 1973, Egyptian forces had crossed the Suez Canal while Syrian forces pushed across the Golan Heights. The Arabs won a series of victories at the outset, which created a lasting impression of triumph that Israeli success in the latter stages of this war could not dispel. Although the Israelis managed to recover and ultimately defeat their enemies, they had lost twenty-five hundred men and almost a quarter of their aircraft. Syrian and Egyptian losses were even higher, but Israel had lost face and Arab forces perceived this as a political victory.

At the military level, the war had produced immediate lessons about the importance of the fluidity, tempo, and intensity of modern warfare, which suggested that strategies based on holding a line and imposing attrition on the enemy were outdated. The Yom Kippur War also led to profound changes in the U.S. policy toward the Middle East. Israel's vulnerability in the opening days of the war, which surprised both the Soviet Union and the United States, called into question the U.S. strategy of maintaining stability through "imbalance." The Nixon and later the Ford administration adopted a policy favoring regional balance of power: rather than support Israel unconditionally, the United States sought to assist both the Jewish state and its Arab neighbors. This marked the beginning of the process that would lead to the Camp David Accords and Egypt's becoming a major recipient of U.S. aid.

Warden was first assigned to the Lebanon and Morocco Desk. As a junior officer he was given a great deal of routine work, and he had to familiarize himself with a range of procedures and documents. After a few months, under the supervision of Col. Lurie J. Morris and later Col. Thomas W. Sawyer, he was entrusted with leading the project to develop an American air base in Morocco. The State Department eventually approved the basic concept, but it was never implemented because Gerald Ford lost the 1976 election. However, the change of governments proved fortunate for Warden, as the new administration began to recognize the Middle East and the Persian Gulf as an important region in its own right, and this was reflected in military plans, procurements, and contingency developments. Warden became a member of the Air Force Transition Team, which was established to update incoming officials on military affairs. Although this meant extra work, the assignment enabled him to meet regularly with general officers in the Pentagon, staff workers on Capitol Hill, and members of the intelligence community throughout Washington, DC.

Warden's experiences soon convinced him that America's one-dimensional focus on Europe as the potential flashpoint of a conflict between NATO and the Warsaw Pact was misplaced. As he saw it, if the Soviets decided to go to war they would attack where they would run less risk and receive higher returns: the Middle East—more specifically, the Persian Gulf. The United States therefore needed to move away from the "one-and-a-half-war" strategy, according to which the United States might have to divert some of its forces temporarily to defend Israel—the half war—before deploying to continental Europe to fight a full-blown war against the Warsaw Pact. Warden saw three flaws in this strategy. First, the Yom Kippur War had proved that Israel could defend itself against any conceivable combination of attacks. Second, the Soviets were unlikely to attack Israel directly; they would probably attack the Persian Gulf first, most likely through Iran and Iraq, and then move westward. Third, a Soviet attack on the Persian Gulf would not necessarily be merely a precursor to a war in Europe; the oil-rich area and its ports were worth controlling in their own right. Thus, the national strategy missed the real dangers that the Soviet Union posed to the West's strategic flank. In meeting with staff members of the National Security Council, Warden argued that the United States needed to reorganize its force structure and dedicate adequate troops to meet a Soviet threat that would manifest itself outside the traditional Central European theater.

Warden faced immediate resistance from both military and civilian intelligence agencies, whose Soviet experts asserted that the Warsaw Pact had deployed only three divisions to the region, which proved that no real threat existed. Warden countered that there were twenty-three divisions with considerable offensive capability in the Caucasus region and the Turkish military district, and these forces could deploy on short notice. His opponents responded that those forces were earmarked for deployment to Europe rather than the Middle East if a crisis occurred. When Warden insisted that it was risky to rely on such an assumption, one intelligence officer admitted that he did not know whether the twenty-three divisions would be deployed to the Middle East or to Europe in the event of war, but told Warden that the U.S. armed forces needed the assessment to justify their own number of troops in Europe.

The mindset that such confrontations revealed made Warden increasingly impatient with the intelligence community. He believed that it resulted from a

rigid organizational structure: the intelligence community had two entirely separate compartments dealing with the Soviet Union. One assessed the region west
of the Urals and its threat to main Europe, while the other dealt with the eastern
side of the mountains and its threat to China and Japan.[18] As Warden saw it,
nobody took responsibility for assessing the totality of the situation. Moreover,
the intelligence officers with whom he talked seemed unable to recognize how
easily the Soviet Union could attack and control oil and warm water ports if it
decided to seize the Straits of Hormuz. Warden also realized that war planning
should not focus on territory per se, but on underlying strategic interests. He
believed the United States faced many threats other than a massive Soviet offensive through the German heartland: "[we had] to get people to start thinking on
a global scale and not think that the Fulda Gap was the center of gravity of the
world."[19] He also dared to suggest that air power could sometimes stop and even
destroy an attacking army. Characteristically, this notion met resistance even inside the air force.

Warden's third commanding officer in the Air Staff, Col. Richard W.
Masson, appreciated these ideas and recognized that certain general officers within
the Directorate of Plans and Operations also supported them. Masson, who had
taught political science at the USAF Academy when Warden was a cadet, found
the newly promoted major's views more than useful. Still, the person perhaps
most receptive to Warden's ideas was the director of plans, then Maj. Gen. Richard L. Lawson. He had previously served in the White House as a military assistant to President Nixon; thus, he knew his way around political circles and had
developed a serious interest in politico-military affairs. This served Lawson well,
since at the time the Air Staff's Directorate of Plans (XOX) functioned in essence
as the air force's "State Department," addressing air force issues on a country-to-
country basis with immense latitude. As Warden saw it, Lawson was "all over
Washington": he would have lunch with the director of political and military
affairs in the State Department one week and meet representatives of the White
House the next.

Lawson later recalled that he could not help noticing Warden from the
beginning, "for here was a major who obviously had a hard time keeping quiet
during meetings normally reserved for generals," and when he spoke he was "im-
pressively eloquent in arguing his case."[20] Lawson found that Warden had serious
ideas about "force structures, concepts and doctrine that normally did not interest pilots."[21] He gladly gave Warden even more responsibility. In Lawson's view,
he had an officer who was "one-hundred percent loyal and a great visionary,"
although he had to be "closely tracked," because if left without supervision for
too long he would "wander off into his castle, convincing himself that air power
could accomplish everything." Lawson made sure Warden was given "tasks where
his ability to think strategically and conceptually would be appreciated," and the
two met on a weekly basis.[22]

Warden, for his part, greatly admired Lawson's ability to analyze important concepts and act accordingly. Warden was also allowed a role that gave him an immense amount of flexibility. For example, he suggested to Masson that the Middle East and Africa Division create a strategy desk to analyze overarching challenges rather than assign individuals to only one country or region. While he did not succeed in creating this organizational change, he personally was allowed to take on such a freewheeling role. At the time, the air force chief of Plans and Operations (XO) represented the three-star level on the Joint Staff; thus, Warden was also involved whenever a decision or discussion paper—a so-called "green paper"—related to the Middle East was being forwarded to the three- and four-star generals.[23] The small size of the Middle East Division, at a time when the Persian Gulf was receiving increased political attention, played to Warden's advantage.

As Washington began to develop a more energetic military approach to the Persian Gulf region, U.S. officials speculated openly about the possibility of executing amphibious and airborne operations to secure critical oil-producing areas. On several occasions Warden had expressed his opinion that a region as important as the Persian Gulf should not be merely part of the responsibility of the European Command. During what would normally have been a routine review of a rudimentary contingency plan for the Persian Gulf area, Warden wrote a memorandum that questioned the desirability of European Command's having responsibility for an area so far away geographically and politically from its central concerns. This, of course, raised the issues of what organization should have that responsibility and what the accompanying force structure should be. The air force chief of staff, Gen. David C. Jones, liked the idea and ensured those views were heard. Warden then played an important role in the collective effort that developed the basis for what became the Rapid Deployment Force, which became the Rapid Deployment Joint Task Force in 1980 and eventually CENTCOM in 1983.

After studying the base structure in the region and combining his findings with his tactical air power experience in Korea, Vietnam, and Spain, Warden suggested a conceptual plan to his superiors whereby thirteen tactical fighter wings would be deployed into Saudi Arabia and southern Iran. The number reflected two main considerations: it provided for sufficient aircraft (primarily F-4s) to defend the region and it did not exceed local bed-down capabilities; moreover, it was logistically sustainable.

At about this time, Checkmate—a unit established in 1976 to study U.S. and allied conventional warfighting against the Soviet Union and to identify attendant requirements, problems, and limitations—began to expand its interests beyond the Soviets in Central Europe. Warden convinced Checkmate to examine the Persian Gulf and provided the organization with his scenario concepts and accompanying force structure recommendations. Although its models were attrition-oriented, Checkmate's work lent support to and generated interest in Warden's concepts, and its Red Team evaluated his proposal, extending it on the basis of war-gaming exercises.

Warden then divided his warfighting concept into two parts. Most senior officers who heard his briefing warmly supported the first portion of the plan: "to leap-frog those forces forward" to drive the Soviet forces back as air superiority was gained and extended.[24] The second part was far more controversial, as it suggested a direct attack on the Soviet Union. It reflected Warden's belief in offensive and aggressive use of air power, and, ultimately, his conviction that there was no such thing as a limited war. If the president was ready to commit forces to war, the United States should use every possible means to win, short of nuclear attacks: victory could never be gained by constant cycles of concessions and escalation.

> I am reminded of Wellington's idea from a long time ago that a great country cannot have a little war. There is no such thing as a limited war. It just does not make any sense; and again, you need to identify what you were after, and you had to go get it. If you were not prepared to expend the effort that was going to assure victory, then you should not play. It is far better not to play than it is to play and get beaten or wander off in some stalemate situation like Vietnam . . . We really started developing and arguing frequently this idea that you should not focus war planning on territory, that territory is a tactical thing that you use and it is no big deal, it sorts itself out after the war is over. We can defeat the Soviets in Iran with air power alone. There is no way you were going to get enough troops on the ground that are going to be of any value. You do not have any reason to do that, because you can do it with air power and you can do it with thirteen tactical fighter wings.[25]

By the late 1970s Warden had become a quintessential air power advocate. He pushed the issue of what air power could do separate from ground forces in the theater of operations further than most. The Air Staff gave him his first experience of serving on a team that strongly opposed existing war plans, and the changes that resulted from his work made the Pentagon years especially gratifying to him. He concluded that even as a major he could influence events if he were persistent enough. His experiences confirmed his intuitive belief that it was sometimes necessary to bypass bureaucratic and institutional compartmentalization to achieve results. With top-cover support an officer could cut a few corners and achieve a great deal in a short period of time. He observed and learned from the stamina that enabled his superior officers, first Major General Lawson and later Maj. Gen. James H. Ahmann, to translate political guidance into military action plans.

Overall, Warden made an excellent impression on his superiors in the Air Staff, as well as on some senior generals. Promoted to the rank of major before he had turned thirty-four, Warden was recognized as an extraordinary staff officer and a creative researcher with exceptional ability to present conclusions and suggestions for further action. According to his last division chief, Col. Richard B. Goetze, Jr.:

> It was immediately evident upon assuming leadership of the Middle East and Africa Division, that John Warden was a unique officer. He was out of the office a great deal briefing his deployment concepts for response to a hypothetical conflict in the greater Middle East. The senior leadership within the XO community supported his concepts and encouraged his travels to brief the highest levels within the defense establishment. As a Major, John was getting exposure to senior officials in the government that was normally reserved for Colonels and flag officers. When not on briefing trips, John worked well with his colleagues and was a responsive and responsible action officer. The Middle East and Africa Division was blessed with many officers whose intellect, and experience in the area were exceptional. Even within this exceptional group John's intellect, energy, and articulate briefings marked him as a very special person.[26]

EXECUTIVE ASSISTANT TO THE CHIEF OF STAFF

After almost four years in the Middle East and Africa Division, Warden was earmarked for promotion to lieutenant colonel. One who sought to take advantage of the situation was Col. William M. Constantine, who had become executive officer to the air force chief of staff, Gen. Lew Allen Jr., in July 1978. A few months after assuming his new responsibilities he attended a presentation that Warden gave to the Air Force Board—the senior generals in the Air Staff—on dangers and opportunities in the Middle East, including the concept of the thirteen fighter wings. He was very impressed by Warden's arguments and particularly by his concise manner of speaking and the confident way in which he responded to questions. In the spring of 1979, when Constantine was asked to find an assistant at the lieutenant colonel level, he thought of Warden:

> I recalled my recent experience in observing John Warden's impressive presentation: my thoughts about his confident demeanor, how well he articulated his positions and how well he handled himself and stood

his ground, under the pressure of some tough questioning. I thought that this was the kind of officer that could operate very effectively in the high-pressure environment of the office of the chief of staff.[27]

When Constantine asked Warden if he were interested in the position, Warden hesitated, noting that he had been away from operations for a long time. Constantine argued that a year or two in the office of the chief of staff could only benefit him, and Warden became assistant executive officer on May 25, 1979.

Constantine quickly made Warden a full partner, rather than considering him a subordinate, and the position gave Warden in-depth understanding of the air force organization and its leaders. It also enabled him to improve his performance as a staff officer, since he often faced extremely tight deadlines and thus needed to identify core issues and develop articulate presentations for his superiors in a short time. Although most of Warden's work was administrative, which he disliked, he learned how the paperwork machine functioned and how to work around it. He also continued to involve himself in a wide range of issues; for example, Constantine and he deserve credit for naming the F-16. The air force had already approved the name *Falcon*, which reflected the Air Force Academy mascot, but Dassault Aircraft Corporation owned the copyright of the name, which it used for one of its small executive jets, and obviously did not want the public to confuse its Falcon with a combat aircraft. Constantine and Warden, understandably dissatisfied with suggested options such as *Eaglet* or *Mustang II*, came up with *Fighting Falcon*. After the office of the USAF judge advocate general reviewed the legal aspects, General Allen informed Dassault of the new name on July 21, 1980. The same day the air force conducted the official christening ceremony for the F-16 *Fighting Falcon* at Hill AFB in Utah.

Constantine remembers that Warden was "courteous and respectful" in communicating with the senior officers whom they had to deal with on a daily basis, that he was in tune with the nature of his position as an assistant executive officer, and that he did not "try to exploit the position to his advantage." He gave Warden an outstanding report and recalls that what impressed him most was Warden's "unusual strategic vision, fiercely independent nature, questioning attitude, interest and dedication toward effecting change and devotion to duty and mission."[28]

Gen. Allen recalls that Warden was "brilliant" when it came to "vision and working capacity" and that he was "very effective, creative and extremely motivated."[29] He liked the "aggressive attitude" that Warden brought into the office and his relentless interest in improving the service. He also appreciated the many memoranda with Warden's coherent and well-argued assessments of what he believed had to be changed and improved. The chief of staff's view was essentially the same as Lawson's: he, too, found that at times Warden was "pushing the envelope" too hard: "every now and then he went a bit over the edge."[30] Still, Allen believed it was his duty to encourage such an "unusual creative talent," because Warden's "enthusiasm, dedication, and intelligence outweighed any concerns about his lack of restraint."[31] Allen also recalls that overall the Air Staff proved receptive to Warden's critical thinking, although some reacted negatively to a lieutenant colonel who always had an opinion and seemed unable to keep quiet in meetings when he disagreed with other participants—and he tended to disagree a great deal.

Col. Joseph W. Ashy, who succeeded Constantine in September 1980, made it clear from the start that Warden would no longer have the "direct line" to Allen; if he wanted to present something to the chief of staff he should inform Ashy first so that they could coordinate the effort. Ashy also pointed out that he would not share the same degree of responsibility with his assistant as Constantine had. Nevertheless, Ashy found that Warden adapted well to the new "rules of engagement" and the two established a good working relationship.[32] Warden also continued to interact frequently with senior officers in the Pentagon.

After Warden had spent eighteen months as assistant executive officer, Ashy, who believed that Warden had done "a great job" and was "a fine subordinate," told him that he had to make an important decision: did he want to stay in the Air Staff, dealing with issues of policy and strategy, or did he want to return to the cockpit and the operational field?[33] Warden, knowing full well that only the latter option would lead to command, replied that he wanted to return to the operational world. He had even told Constantine a few months earlier that his strongest wish was to be the leader of the first F-15 squadron to engage the Soviet Union in battle. When Constantine left the Air Staff he had tried to ensure that Warden would move into the F-15 environment; he believed Warden could be "the best leader the Air Force ever saw."[34] Ashy did not share his predecessor's unconditional enthusiasm for Warden, but he "made a few phone calls to ensure that Warden was given the opportunity to prove himself."[35] Having received glowing efficiency reports throughout his Air Staff tenure, and with the added advantage of having served as an assistant executive to the chief of staff, Warden was offered the chance to convert to the F-15C *Eagle*, a clear sign that the air force had great plans for him.

4

OPERATIONAL ASSIGNMENTS

Warden's unorthodox ideas found more appreciation in the Pentagon than in the operational world. In each of the three operational assignments that followed his conversion to the F-15, Warden challenged existing procedures, and some of the controversy that accompanied his actions presaged later events in his career.

Eglin AFB: Director of Wing Inspections

For a fighter pilot there was nothing grander than being offered the chance to operate the new and technologically advanced F-15 *Eagle*. The F-15 was the first purely air-to-air fighter aircraft requested by the air force since the F-86 *Saber* and the F-104 *Starfighter*. The *Eagle* had been designed as an all-weather, extremely maneuverable, tactical fighter aircraft that would allow the air force to gain and maintain air superiority. It embodied lessons learned over decades in the skies over Germany, Korea, and Vietnam: more thrust, improved maneuverability, better cockpit visibility, a powerful radar, long-range missiles, an internal gun, and cockpit switches that were easy to operate.[1] Although it carried many of the same weapons as the updated F-4, it was faster and more agile, and had vastly greater endurance and combat range. The air force believed that this blend of unmatched maneuverability, acceleration, range, weapons, and avionics made the F-15 a state-of-the-art aircraft that could penetrate all enemy defense systems and prevail over the existing and anticipated Soviet threat.

In February 1981 Warden arrived at Luke AFB, approximately twenty miles west of Phoenix, Arizona, and began the conversion from the F-4 to the F-15C. He may not have shared the typical fighter pilot's enthusiasm for flying, but he was glad to be back in the cockpit. Like most of his colleagues, he found the F-15 superior to the F-4 in every way: not only was it more capable, it was also more pleasant to fly.[2] At thirty-seven he was older than most of his fellow pilots and he outranked them; yet that he was given the opportunity to fly the

F-15 at that relatively late age clearly indicated that he was destined for senior leadership. He therefore received considerable attention from the staff during the training period. According to Maj. Gregory S. Martin, at the time an assistant operations officer and later a four-star general, Warden was "precise and decisive in his actions," "appreciative of the instructors, staff and colleagues," and not "your typical sloppy pilot type who would hang around in the bar and talk about air maneuvers."[3] He also noted that at times, because of his intensity, Warden could come across as somewhat regimented. Still, Warden's systematic preparation allowed him to perform well in his pilot training, and after he passed the qualifying tests he learned that his first assignment would be at the Thirty-third TFW at Eglin AFB, in the Florida panhandle.

Col. Stanton R. Musser, the wing commander, did not have a squadron leader position available for Warden in May 1981. Musser knew nothing about Warden prior to his arrival, but as he reviewed his new subordinate's efficiency reports and engaged him on operational matters, he was impressed by his ability to think innovatively beyond the immediate tactical and technical dimensions of the aircraft. He decided to put Warden in charge of preparing the Thirty-third TFW for inspections,[4] convinced that Warden, "with his vision, intellect and dedication," would do an excellent job.[5] Technically, Warden's title was assistant deputy for operations, but in reality he became responsible for designing wing-level exercises, with the primary mission of ensuring that the wing could pass external readiness tests. Warden would not have chosen this position, and it was certainly less rewarding than being a squadron commander, but he put all his energy into his new assignment and found the job both challenging and interesting.

At any given time all wings in the air force needed to prepare for three types of no-notice inspections. Management Effectiveness Inspections (MEIs) focused on administrative procedures, programs, and processes, such as bookkeeping, unit management, and the daily routines involved in running a wing. Operational Readiness Inspection (ORI) Phase I measured the organization's ability to mobilize and deploy its aircraft, personnel, and a range of supply items. Finally, ORI Phase II was mission oriented, focusing on sortie generation, intercepts, bombing accuracy, and weapon expertise. Wings could earn five grades: "Outstanding," "Excellent," "Satisfactory," "Marginal," and "Failure." The latter two required that a wing retake the test within a few weeks.

Warden spent considerable time during the first weeks reading about the inspection requirements and the wing's local procedures. As he tried to make the wing more efficient, he first insisted that each part of the wing develop a self-testing system that matched the inspection criteria, and he created schemes, checklists, and overall procedures for such self-assessments. The first major test during his tenure, an ORI Phase II in which an inspection team from TAC measured the wing's operability and survivability, took place on August 13–20, 1981, and the wing received the overall rating of "Excellent."

On the surface this was gratifying, but Warden was more concerned about the deployment phase than the employment phase: records showed that the wing had a significant mobilization problem. Although it was highly successful at flying combat missions, the wing struggled to get airborne within the required time frame. The fundamental problem was that the Thirty-third TFW was a tenant organization, only a small part of a base that belonged to Systems Command, and to launch air operations it depended heavily on the base's personnel and vehicles. Since the base had its own tasks and priorities, which did not always correspond to those of the wing, any mobilization of forces posed challenges in coordinating the two chains of command.

Warden discussed the problems with some of the enlisted men, especially Senior M. Sgt. Richard Miles, the senior non-commissioned officer (NCO) in his inspection office. Miles stated that the solution was obvious: it involved an alternative process for delivering supplies. The standard practice when deploying was to deliver pallets of equipment and supplies to the inspection gate one at the time: when the first pallet was cleared it was placed in a holding area before being loaded onto an available transport airplane. Only then was the next pallet inspected at the gate: thus, any delay rippled through the system and there was no way to catch up. Miles suggested that instead all pallets and equipment be delivered to the inspection point as soon as they were ready, and Warden put this new procedure into effect. Thus, rather than operate serially, the wing adopted a practice of "simultaneous processing," so that if they lacked equipment for one pallet the staff could prepare another while waiting for the problem to be rectified.

During Warden's first ORI Phase I inspection, held in October 1981, the wing was ready to deploy in less than ten hours, more than three times faster than its previous standard. The wing was confident that it would score "Outstanding," but to its disappointment the overall rating was "Satisfactory."[6] When Warden asked for an explanation TAC responded that the wing was graded on both objectives and procedures, and the wing's procedures did not follow the book. Thus, almost inconceivably, a system that improved efficiency without jeopardizing any aspect of security resulted in a mediocre assessment simply because it was innovative. However, since Warden placed far more emphasis on improving effectiveness than on earning high grades, he continued to use the new simultaneous processing in the next ORI Phase I inspection, held in June 1982, but again the wing scored "Satisfactory."

Perhaps more important, his year in the F-15 environment prompted Warden to think in depth about air-to-air operations. Rather than concentrate on the factors evaluated in official tests, he began to focus on three issues that were to consume much of his attention over the following years.

First, he had become ever more convinced that the United States should pay increasing attention to the scenario under which it would have to fight the Soviet Union in the Persian Gulf rather than in Central Europe. Since there were few forward-deployed bases in the region, Warden openly advocated long-range missions. Airmen certainly discussed such missions, which required air-to-air refueling, but the air force did not practice them extensively because they would consume extra time and fuel, and because the wing would not be required to fly long-range missions during inspections. Instead, the normal practice was for the F-15s to engage a simulated enemy in their immediate vicinity and the training philosophy favored compressing as many events as possible into a single mission: this kept fuel cost down, swift engagements were believed to strengthen the pilot's mental agility, and aircraft spent little time in transition routes. Warden sought to persuade his superiors that long-range strikes might well become the backbone for operations in the future and that in the interim the wings should at least start preparing for operations outside the European perimeter. He let it be known that he opposed the notion of limiting air-to-air engagements to defending sectors in Europe when air power could operate offensively and take the war to the enemy homeland. Arguing that forces should train as they expect to fight, he pointed out that important factors would come into play: air-to-air refueling required certain weather conditions; timing became crucial when it came to long-distance flights; and fog, friction, and uncertainty increased when a formation of aircraft had to spend several hours in the air prior to a mission. The Ninth Air Force proved somewhat receptive to these ideas. Its commander, Lt. Gen. Larry D. Welch, had already started to think along the same lines, and in fact had initiated a "Checkered Flag" program that assigned some of its wings to prepare for operations outside Europe.[7] On a local level, however, Warden seems to have pushed the issue further and harder than his colleagues and superiors at Eglin generally found acceptable, probably because many pilots had little enthusiasm for spending over 80 percent of their flying time in transition routes.

Second, Warden emphasized to the wing commander that they should practice high-altitude ingress—not an original idea, but unorthodox at the time. War plans assumed that the United States would fight the Warsaw Pact in Central Europe, where the substantial overlapping and mutually supporting SAM capabilities were thought to pose a deadly threat to aircraft flying at medium or high altitudes. Remembering lessons from Vietnam, planners believed that the fighters needed to fly under the SAM radar coverage and face only antiaircraft artillery, the lesser of two evils. The opposing school of thought, to which Warden belonged, pointed out that in Vietnam antiaircraft artillery had destroyed more aircraft than SAMs, that electronic countermeasures could reduce the effectiveness of SAMs, and that such missiles had inherent weaknesses: they were both static and predictable.[8] In addition, Warden argued, potential enemies outside Central Europe would have less capable ground-based air defense systems than the Soviets, and aircraft could either avoid the sites or destroy them. Warden insisted that the air force should practice this maneuver, because in preparing to win a war, fighter aircraft needed to operate from all angles.

Third, Warden focused on big-wing formations. Plans at the time assumed that in a war with the Soviet Union the allied air forces would deploy series of two- or four-ships (aircraft flying in formations of two and two or four and four, respectively) operating relatively independently. The air force considered four aircraft flying together the optimal tactical arrangement for exerting combat power: the coordination involved was manageable, the pilots could support each other, and the formation was highly maneuverable and agile—able to adapt to new situations. Warden contended that although Warsaw Pact forces outnumbered NATO forces, NATO and the United States could gain and maintain local air superiority by concentrating air power against their opponent at any given place and time, and he began to call for larger formations of F-15s. Again, he encountered considerable skepticism: why should the wing practice something not defined in the operational procedures? Besides, fighter pilots viewed flying in large formations purely as entertainment for air shows; in actual combat it was every man and his wingman for himself.

Meanwhile, Warden's first published article, "Planning to Win," appeared in *Air University Review* and won honorable mention in Air University's Ira Eaker essay contest. It represented his first attempt to relate strategic thinking to matters of air power: more than anything else it offered a critique of national planning. The essay developed themes from his master's thesis, emphasizing that war was not about territory per se, and that in certain circumstances a tactical retreat that included loss of territory might lay the ground for future achievements: "for wars should be fought for the peace that follows, not for the momentary triumph of arms." He echoed Fuller's and Liddell Hart's view that military victory was no more than a means to an end, but cautioned there was nothing easy about determining the true goal of war, which could range from a Carthaginian solution of total destruction to mere border adjustments. Warden then went on to argue that theater commanders had to plan on the basis of the forces they actually had at their disposition: "The commander who tries to use a strategy or war plan designed to be executed with more force than he has is courting disaster; and the planner who fails to provide a strategy or war plan built around available forces has not done his job." The commander had to be willing to "trade space for time" and to commit "air, land, or sea forces independently or as a combined team":

> The planner must remember that territory is just as much a means to
> the end as are his military forces. Space in modern warfare is three

dimensional. Air forces may attack the enemy hundreds or even thousands of miles ahead of surface forces. Theoretically, air forces can destroy enemy ground forces, but with great certainty they can slow and even stop advancement. In many ways, air forces, whether from land bases or from carriers, are the first line of attack. They are highly mobile and easy to concentrate. Air firepower can be moved much faster and with far less transport than can equivalent amounts of land firepower. Air power can control the third dimension while buying time to deploy ground forces to fight in the second dimension. This significant capability must not be ignored or denied. It may be the key to victory. The fact that an attack takes place in one theater does not mean that the current planner must respond in that theater. He must consider strategic flanks as well as tactical flanks.[9]

The essay also discussed the problems of threat analysis, which the master's thesis had touched upon. Most significantly, it showed that Warden had started to develop strongly held ideas about how air power could contribute at the operational level of war. It reflected an offensive and aggressive mindset that would manifest itself in his later writings.

Such theorizing, however, was not in his job description as the wing's inspector general, and at Eglin Warden was in no position to push his three concepts as far as he would have liked. He discussed military threat scenarios and operational preferences with his colleagues, insisting that current procedures did not fully capitalize on the potential of air power. He also emphasized that the air force needed to develop a more aggressive and offensive mindset, but his ideas had limited impact because most of his colleagues were simply too busy with their daily tasks to give serious thought to the issues he presented. Nevertheless, Warden had some success in promoting larger formations: he arranged for the New Orleans Air National Guard to fly its F-4s east along the Gulf Coast and for the Thirty-third TFW to intercept them by using F-15 formations that moved beyond the traditional four ships. His colleagues considered this an interesting exercise, but Warden was further encouraged by the results. He also secured permission to operate in a larger than normal air space, but the short duration of his tour did not allow him to take advantage of it.

Warden served under two wing commanders at Eglin, both of whom were pleased with his performance. Col. Musser reported that Warden did an "excellent job," praising his "good grasp of operations," and calling him "visionary" and "loyal," although he had to admit that sometimes his insistence on changing things could be exasperating. Musser noted that for all his strengths, Warden revealed one weakness: he did not pay sufficient attention to interpersonal relations and thus never fully connected with the younger aircrew.[10] Col. Jack Petry, who replaced Musser as the wing commander in January 1982, shared this view: though "analytical, bright, hard-working and mission oriented," Warden was not the kind of officer with whom one developed close bonds. Petry also suspected that Warden's "impressive intellect" and his early promotion to lieutenant colonel as a result of staff work rather than operational experience caused some jealousy and resentment among his peers.[11] Nevertheless, these were private concerns, and both wing commanders considered such weak spots secondary to his qualities. Both also placed high value on his ability to conceptualize the complexity of air operations and suggest improvements, calling this a vital ability that the air force desperately needed. Warden seems to have left a general impression among his fellow airmen as someone who constantly tried to "push the envelope," persistently wanted to change things, and was predominantly concerned with doctrine and policy. Again he received very good efficiency reports.

Moody AFB: Deputy Commander for Operations

Warden was on the selection list for promotion to colonel before he was offered a squadron commander position. Thus, rather than become a squadron commander at Eglin he became the assistant deputy commander for operations at the 347th TFW at Moody AFB in southern Georgia, thirty miles north of the Florida border. Being named to this position in a well-respected tactical fighter wing was a sign of recognition, but it meant that after earning the certificate required for the F-15, both as a mission commander and a four-ship flight leader, he would again work with the F-4. He welcomed the new challenge and made up his mind that as soon as he was given operational responsibilities he would pursue his ideas further, especially the concept of big-wing formations.

While the primary mission for Eglin's F-15s was air-to-air combat, the F-4s at Moody focused on air-to-ground operations, specializing in using the AGM-65 *Maverick*—a tactical missile designed for close air support, interdiction, and the suppression of enemy air defenses. In the 1970s many considered the 347th the best wing in TAC: *Time Magazine* had even depicted a formation of its F-4s on its cover.

However, when Col. Eugene L. Vosika became the wing commander in August 1981 he feared that all was not as well as it seemed.[12] Shortly after he arrived the wing did poorly on a deployment inspection, but most of the wing's officers viewed this as a momentary lapse because the wing passed when it retook the test shortly thereafter. Within the first few weeks of his new assignment, Vosika identified two elements that needed improvement. First, he believed that the wing's extraordinary reputation had imbued some of the officers and enlisted men with arrogance rather than a healthy self-confidence. Second, the pilots, although expert at flying, had difficulty in interpreting the Air Tasking Order (ATO), also known as the Fragmentary Order or simply as the frag, that provided all the data associated with an air operation. The ATO informed pilots who would fly where and when, and which ordnance should be dropped on which targets: it bristled with details and acronyms and Vosika found that his pilots often could not translate it into action in a timely manner.[13]

When Warden arrived in August 1982 Vosika quickly concluded that he was an officer who could help him remedy these shortcomings. Most important, Warden could deal with the ATO: Vosika later recalled that Warden was an "analytical, detail-oriented and effective officer who was very capable when it came to decoding the frag."[14] Warden was also eager to improve both the wing's warfighting concepts and its morale, but he told Vosika that his concerns went further: he wanted to improve the professionalism of pilot officers by making them more familiar with military history and encouraging them to think of themselves as officers first and as pilots second. Vosika appreciated Warden's initiative, but his fighter pilot colleagues did not: many of them dismissed history as "bunk" and considered themselves just as professional as Warden.

Shortly after he assumed his new duties as assistant director of operations, Warden participated in a Red Flag exercise—a combat squadron training exercise in which crewmembers flew several different missions on a highly instrumented range at Nellis AFB in southern Nevada. Most officers considered the exercise uniquely valuable in preparing pilots, logisticians, and technicians for the real world, but the experience confirmed for Warden his conviction that the air force was thinking too narrowly about future threat scenarios: it focused all of its planning on Central Europe and did not take alternative contingencies seriously into account. He was given the chance to test his high-altitude ingress and egress tactics against the Aggressors, the team that simulated the enemy, but was not allowed to go further. As a result, he could not rid himself of the belief that the exercise, and the policies behind it, did not address key issues at the operational level of war.

Warden enjoyed his first year at Moody: he planned exercises, oversaw improvements in air-to-air tactics, flew with the three squadrons, became familiar with local procedures, and dealt with the inevitable paperwork that assistant positions entail. He also established a very good working relationship with his immediate superior, Col. Douglas B. Cairns. Indeed, when Cairns's tour came to an end on October 1, 1983, he convinced his superiors that Warden should succeed him. Cairns recalls that Warden did "an excellent job," proved himself able to combine new training procedures with the established ones, and was "a very good pilot and a great mission commander with high morale and high integrity." But before he left he gave Warden some advice: "you need to be a bit more political when insisting on making changes and you need to be more adaptive—there are certain club-rules that you are better off not breaking."[15] He recalled that Warden seemed astounded by the feedback and thanked him for his frankness.

By the time Warden took on his new responsibilities as director of operations, Col. Harald G. Hermes had replaced Vosika as the wing commander and Col. Billy G. McCoy accompanied him as the new vice commander. The wing remained busy, although it generated fewer sorties than in the late 1970s. The squadrons were still in high demand, participating in one deployment after the other: one squadron commander, Lt. Col. John Golden, experienced fourteen deployments and eight Red Flag exercises over a period of eighteen months.[16] Lt. Gen. John T. Piotrowski, who had replaced Welch as the commander of the Ninth Air Force, was nevertheless concerned that despite its busy schedule the wing had "gone soft" on its primary mission.[17] Piotrowski decided to arrange for inspections to check the status quo. The MEI, held September 19–26, 1983, gave the overall rating of "Satisfactory" and the no-notice ORI Phase I, held September 26–30, produced a rating of "Excellent."[18] The ability to switch rapidly from the MEI to the ORI without any prior warning was no small feat, and Hermes and McCoy, both of whom had their private doubts about the wing when they arrived, concluded that the 347th knew its business well.

Not until the wing received the overall score of "Marginal" in an ORI Phase II, held from November 30 to December 7, did its shortcomings become apparent. During the inspection the squadrons scored high on air-to-air missions, but they could not hit their ground targets.[19] Those attending the inspection privately thought that the real score should have been "Failure," but the wing's overseas commitment meant that politics came into play and the score seems to have been upgraded in the classified report.

A marginal score on an MEI, or even an ORI Phase I, could be explained away, but failing to pass the warfighting inspection, when everyone knew it was coming and understood the criteria, left the wing humiliated and embarrassed. The officers immediately sought a scapegoat. Since the wing had received its lowest ratings in operations they directed considerable blame at the director of operations, Col. Warden. After all, they reasoned, the wing had performed well under the previous leadership. How could the great 347th Wing's performance in its primary mission have deteriorated so quickly?

The critics found the explanation they sought in the training conducted during the critical weeks prior to the ORI Phase II. Rather than focus on perfecting the basic mission of air-to-ground operations, Warden had led large parts of the wing into a huge air-to-air exercise at Tyndall AFB in northwest Florida. In their view, Warden had sacrificed the interest of the wing to his private obsession with big-wing tactics and air-to-air operations at a time when he should have concerned himself with fine-tuning air-to-ground operations.

Warden's decision had in fact resulted from his conviction that in an actual war the wing's F-4 packages might well have to undertake air-to-air operations to enable subsequent air-to-ground operations: if they failed in the first mission the second would become irrelevant. The NATO alliance had only four F-15 wings, and with two of them dedicated to Europe only a limited number would be available if a crisis erupted elsewhere. Moreover, the F-15 did not have air-to-ground capability, while the F-4 could perform multiple roles, since it was equipped with systems for long-range visual identification of both airborne and ground targets. Over the previous months, beginning when he was still assistant director of operations, Warden had pushed for exploring air-to-air formations with as many as twenty-four aircraft in the air simultaneously, and had finally succeeded in obtaining support for a major exercise. He still believed that by moving toward large packages, Western forces could outnumber the enemy at any given time and place, even if the enemy had more aircraft in its overall inventory. If the huge formations were applied against a single point, in sectors or in waves, options for employing the forces would expand greatly compared to the possibilities that resided in the traditional two- or four-ships. Thus, while Moody's three squadrons never ceased to practice air-to-ground operations, Warden gave priority to mastering the complexities of coordinating such an air-to-air armada.

The exercise at Tyndall represented the first important test of Warden's ability as an operational commander. It had not been easy to convince his colleagues that this was a worthwhile undertaking; most of them considered such huge operations too labor-intensive in terms of technicians, supply, and aircrew. However, both Hermes and the Ninth Air Force commander explicitly agreed to the unprecedented air-to-air exercise, and the results were impressive. Even skeptics agreed that the big air-to-air formations, high-level ingress, and long-range missions were feasible approaches that, when practiced, would improve the wing's warfighting capability.[20]

Warden believed that the exercise had validated his ideas and that the air force should intensify its exploration of big-wing formations. For example, it seemed that the overall command and control system depended too heavily on radio communication, and he therefore insisted that big-wing formations operate in radio silence. The concept, like that of big wings, was not spectacular per se, but few had bothered to test it because it required detailed and immensely time-consuming precoordination. The next move would be to have these formations operate at night, also without radio. The Tyndall exercise, in its small way, may have proved a catalyst in bringing such ideas into the mainstream, because in the later 1980s and throughout the 1990s, the air force practiced big-wing tactics with increasing frequency.

Despite this success in breaking new ground at the conceptual level, the timing of the exercise had resulted in a genuine problem for the 347th TFW. Warden's assistant deputy commander for operations, Lt. Col. Joe Prater, later reflected that the entire wing should share the blame for not having opposed the air-to-air exercise forcefully enough when preparing for the inspection. Still, at the heart of the matter, he believed, Warden "neglected the day-to-day business of getting bombs on target, which caused a problem because the most important job as the Deputy Commander for Operations is to get the daily business done."[21] Col. Robert A. Ator, commander for combat support, and Maj. William A. Peck, assistant operations officer, both found Warden unimpressive as a leader.[22] Some members of the inspection team also found it strange that Warden had not focused on fine-tuning the operations that would inevitably be tested.[23] Although Warden was not openly called to account, there was a tacit perception at the time that he deserved the greatest share of the blame for the inspection failure.[24]

Warden certainly bears some responsibility for the miserable inspection results, but closer scrutiny reveals that much of the bitterness directed at him was probably unjustified. He had been the director of operations for only two months and the exercise had been approved by higher command. Warden had made no attempt to subvert any element of the chain of command, and none of his superiors had suggested that the exercise at Tyndall should be canceled. The inspector general, then Brig. Gen. Michael J. Dugan, stated years later that he remembered the inspection vividly and that "the profound failure of the wing was a collective failure that could not be pinned on Warden personally in any way, shape or form."[25] Colonel Hermes, the wing commander, argued along the same lines and took full responsibility for what happened, as did Colonel McCoy, the vice commander who found himself in the middle of the debacle:[26]

> Linking the ORI failure to a brief Tyndall deployment (Warden's "folly") is like blaming McDonalds for obesity. John Warden has perhaps been unjustly tagged for what was not the central cause of our exposed shortfalls. However, the stories abound with that notion. After all these years, and rethinking my time at Moody, I am convinced that the ill timed air-to-air deployment to Tyndall was a very, very small part of our problem. Sure, we should have shifted our focus immediately to air-to-ground training, but we were "soft" in almost every area. I seriously doubt it would have made any difference. Despite all that has been chronicled about the failure, John Warden has had to bear the heaviest cross. In some ways, I think he was the scapegoat for the failure. More visible was the fact that the wing was ill prepared to conduct operations under simulated chemical conditions, we could not break a frag order to fly our required sortie rate, and, more importantly, we simply could not hit the target.[27]

Perhaps the most interesting part of the story is not the failed test, or the extent to which Warden can or cannot be blamed for it, but the collective effort that the leadership made to restore the wing's efficiency. Hermes responded to the situation in the old-fashioned way: face-to-face with the entire wing. By doing so he bonded individuals into a team and established the needed calm at a time of crisis.[28] Together with McCoy and Warden, his most powerful associates, he identified the problem, decided on the necessary course of action, and laid out his plan, which in essence involved nurturing constructive attitudes by every man and woman on the base.[29] He ordered that almost every practice session include worst-case conditions. For instance, the wing had performed poorly when operating in chemical suits and Hermes insisted that they needed to practice these tasks to perfection—an unpopular decision in hot and humid southern Georgia. Many of the nonflying personnel, who believed that they bore no responsibility for the operational shortcomings, objected, but the united leadership ensured that the wing carried out this aspect of the training.

During these months Warden proved himself: reshaping and recasting the wing became his unquestioned first priority; his big ideas had to wait. He made no attempt at self-justification and acknowledged that the inspection had been fair. Hermes recalled that Warden worked day and night, never complained, and always remained enthusiastic and focused. Warden set an example by running in full chemical gear in the middle of the day, pushing the limits as always. No obstacles discouraged him, and his dedication to finding the best solutions earned him increased respect in the fighter community and its supporting units. He talked with his men, paid attention to their concerns and proposals, and devoted considerable time to helping decode the frag. McCoy had such confidence in Warden that he decided to focus on maintenance while giving Warden a free hand in operational matters.

Believing that competition would motivate the pilots to perform their best, Warden initiated a scoreboard (often referred to as the Shield of Shame) that listed each squadron's results for operational performance, such as sortie rates and bombing accuracy. He stressed the importance of real-time feedback, making every effort to ensure a more rapid response from the intelligence branch to the pilots' performance during training exercises. He also took a personal interest in the flying missions, and particularly in the wing's bombing accuracy.

Many factors contributed to the vast improvement, and when the inspection team returned on April 23–30, 1984, the 347th Wing scored "Excellent." Indeed, some observers thought that the wing had done so well that it deserved a rating of "Outstanding," but the "Marginal" grade two months earlier caused TAC to believe that the entire inspection system would come into question if the grades differed so greatly in such a short period. Thus, the score was again, to some extent, politically motivated, this time to the wing's disadvantage.

Warden's dedication had convinced Hermes and McCoy that they could not have had a better man to help them restore the 347th Wing to its earlier excellence, and both insisted that his leadership had been instrumental in improving discipline as well as operational performance. Yet, when Warden completed his tour at Moody, some of his colleagues had mixed feelings about him. While most agreed with Hermes and McCoy that he had contributed greatly to improving the wing's warfighting capability and morale, a few still believed that he had caused the wing's failure in the inspection and thought him a bad leader.[30] As would happen throughout Warden's career, these widely divergent opinions probably resulted more from his personality than his ideas. Warden simply behaved and operated differently than most of his colleagues, and some viewed those differences with suspicion. Whether the stereotype is accurate or not, Warden did not fit the description of "your typical pilot":

> The mainstay of social life was the officers' club, and alcohol was the linchpin of camaraderie after duty hours. Fighter pilots have always loved games and competition, especially drinking games, and the officers' club environment provided the perfect venue for both. All clubs had a stag bar where women were forbidden to enter, and the penalty for even a telephone call from a wife was a free round of drinks paid for by the chagrined husband. "Happy Hours" on Wednesday and Friday afternoons offered drinks at half price, or less, through most of the evening. Dice games, "Horses," "4-5-6" and "21 Aces" were continuous as one pilot or WSO [Weapon System Operator] after another lost, then bought rounds of drinks to the point where it was common for a man to be behind, with several lined up in front of his place at the bar. As the evening wore on, dice games, darts, and "dollar bill" games soon progressed into more physical events, some carried along as part of the fighter culture from previous wars. Whole squadrons linked arms and conducted "MiG sweeps" of the bar area as they steamrolled over tables, chairs, and people in their path. Another game was for a small group of men to attempt to throw a buddy over the bar . . . Flying and drinking hard were expected among the peers of the fighter squadrons. Those who did not do both were suspect, and those who did were expected to be perfect the next day on the mission, following a fighter pilot's breakfast—a Coke, a candy bar, and a cigarette.[31]

Such behavior was alien to Warden. He was not one to tell anecdotes beginning "There I was at 20,000 feet . . . ," and he did not swear, brag, get drunk, or gossip about people. He never established the buddy-buddy relationship that pilots so often view as essential to a good wing. Warden was essentially a private man who valued his close family relationships, stressed the importance of good manners, and did not give way to his feelings. Yet he combined his social courtesy with intellectual outspokenness: he gave voice to his visionary opinions and his enthusiasm sometimes blinded him to the realities of available time and budget. Colleagues and superiors believed that he did not know when to stop pursuing an issue, that he did not always know how to present ideas tactfully, and that he could come across as being overbearing. While some welcomed his nonflamboyant character, his analytical skills, his drive, and the courage that he showed in thinking and acting in ways that challenged the mainstream, others thought that he was simply not a "people person." Everyone acknowledged that he was articulate and persuasive, but many found him too serious and aloof. Seldom inclined to small talk, he came to the commander's office mostly to obtain approval for an idea or a decision, and he visited the men on the flight line mostly to discuss what could be done better. At casual social functions he dressed formally and at military ceremonies he insisted on wearing white gloves and a saber regardless of weather and temperature. He was admired, loved, or ridiculed, depending on the situation and his audience.

Admittedly, during the Moody tour Warden took some initiatives that some considered eccentric in a warfighting wing. For example, he found some officers who shared his interest in military history and the group instituted periodic dinners with a military theme. On one such occasion he had Maj. David McDaniel put together a presentation that highlighted the career of General MacArthur, hoping to develop some historical awareness and interest among his men. The group that participated, over a third of the fighting crew, found it inspiring, while others merely found it odd for an air force officer to draw such attention to an army leader. Warden also had the briefing rooms decorated with quotations from famous military strategists; again most appreciated this, while a few found it distracting, odd, and improper.[32]

Many also thought that Warden suffered from the "Churchill syndrome": on any given day he would propose several ideas, some brilliant and some rather far-fetched, but he seemed unable to distinguish the good from the bad. Maj. Lester R. Moore, who was in charge of Standardization and Evaluation, remembered that he received so many suggestions from Warden on how to improve the wing that he had to separate all the incoming memoranda, notes, and messages into three piles: "crazy ideas," which he hoped would be forgotten by the end of the day; "strange ideas," which he hoped would go away by the end of the week; and "ideas with potential merit," to which he paid attention because Warden would probably persist in carrying them out.[33] One idea that Moore put in the first pile was the suggestion to arrange for F-4s to land on the highway outside the base. Warden noted that in war airfields would be attacked and the planes might need alternative landing strips: landing on the highway would improve survivability and the Europeans had practiced it with success. Moore countered that Moody was far away from the Soviet Union and other plausible threats; the local citizens would not look favorably on the interstate road's being closed for several hours; electrical cables and telephone lines would have to be dismantled; the pine trees would be damaged; and it amounted to an unnecessary security risk. Moore was understandably glad to see the suggestion go away by the end of the day.

Warden also made an impression, although perhaps not the one he would have wished, during a staff meeting at Moody with Piotrowski. Warden made a suggestion: alternative paint and camouflage schemes for the F-4. Warden noted that it was more likely that action would take place in the desert than in central Europe. Colors other than grey and green would make the plane less visible, and after examining a few sample color schemes presented by 1st Lt. Ahmed Ragheb, an American-born Egyptian pilot who was an impressive artist, Warden had concluded that pink was the best choice. It was hard for the audience to keep from laughing at the image of a squadron of pink aircraft: no one could imagine a pilot ever being willing to identify himself with such a color.[34] Piotrowski managed to remain serious and responded that "I have seen a lot of paint schemes in my life and this is certainly one of them."[35] With that the meeting came to an end.

Still, looking beyond such single events, Warden impressed people as a younger Billy Mitchell: a thinker at the grand scale; a rebel who constantly sought ways to improve himself and his organization without having the patience to explain his reasoning or seek consensus; a revolutionary who refused to take political and personal sensitivities into account in his eagerness to change things fast; and a gentleman of unfailing integrity.[36] It is astonishing that the same man could exhibit so many facets, reflecting a range of paradoxes. Yet Warden was no chameleon: he was always the same, but people who worked with him came away with different perceptions. Consequently, a few viewed this complex man as unfit for command,[37] while many believed that any weaknesses were marginal when compared to his strengths.

In the spring of 1984 Warden received orders to move to Decimomannu Air Base, located on the southern coast of Sardinia. It was not an impressive career jump, but as commander of Detachment 4, Fortieth Tactical Group, he would have considerable operational responsibilities and Warden was pleased. Privately Hermes had mixed emotions about Warden's leaving: he knew he would miss one of the most resourceful officers he ever had, but he had to admit that Warden was "high-maintenance." An officer who always pushed for change and demanded approval to embark on something new took a toll on the commanding officer and his wing. Still, at the end of the tour Hermes and McCoy gave Warden an outstanding efficiency report. They recognized that he had proved himself during troubled times; they were not intimidated by his insistence on change; and he had served them as a loyal and dedicated officer.

Moody marked Warden's last posting before his children moved out. About to turn eighteen, Betsy accepted a four-year ROTC scholarship to study economics at Mount Holyoke College in Massachusetts, although her father had offered to pay her tuition at the college of her choice. He actually tried to talk her out of joining the air force:

> He tried to explain that my ideas that everyone in the Air Force was a hero and a gentleman were not accurate and that I might be shocked by the language and behavior of some of the people in the Air Force . . . Once I made my decision, my father was very supportive and proud. At my graduation from college, he was our commissioning speaker and commissioned my ROTC class.[38]

John IV had developed an early interest in flying and decided to spend a year in preparatory school in Texas before entering the Air Force Academy. With the children away and her husband on an "unaccompanied tour," Margie commuted between her parents' home in Lake Forest in the outskirts of Chicago and Decimomannu in Italy.

Decimomannu, Italy: Commander of Detachment 4

As the commanding officer at Decimomannu, Warden reported directly to Col. Frederic A. Zehrer III, the Fortieth Group commander at Aviano Air Base, in the northeastern part of Italy, and indirectly to Gen. Charles L. Donnelly Jr. and Lt. Gen. Carl H. Cathey, respectively the commander in chief and the vice commander of USAFE, headquartered at Ramstein Air Base in southwest Germany. Decimomannu, or Deci, as most people called it, was a physically large air base with a great deal of air space and the most extensive instrumented air-to-air range in USAFE; it enjoyed good weather most of the year; and it had fewer flying restrictions than the large air bases on the European continent. Thus, it provided excellent conditions for air-to-air, air-to-ground, and low-level navigation operations for the Italian, German, British, and American air forces that underwent training there. The base was one of the busiest in the world in terms of take-offs and landings, since it operated from dawn to dusk every weekday, and at any given time the U.S. commander might host F-4s, F-15s, and F-16s from a variety of wings.

Warden was in charge of approximately one hundred men, of whom fewer than twelve were officers. His instructions defined his primary duties as:

> Direct USAF operations on a quadrinational base; serve as a principal on the allied commander's committee which provides direction for the entire base; improve tactical training opportunities; improve facilities used by U.S. Forces; represent USAF at a variety of official functions held in and around Cagliari, the capital of Sardinia; prepare for and

attend biannual quadrinational meetings; promote projects to improve the whole of Decimomannu and to build a more cohesive quadrinational operation; review performance reports and make recommendations for decoration of assigned USAF personnel; oversee operation of the Air Combat Maneuvering Instrumentation range and the Dart special target program; meet and escort visiting officers from USAF, allied and neutral countries.[39]

It did not take long for Warden again to earn a reputation for breaking with tradition. He quickly realized that the Italian support staff both on and off the base understood so little English that at least some knowledge of Italian was a prerequisite for operating effectively and doing business with the host nation. Thus, he made it compulsory for all officers and NCOs to take a two-week, high-intensity course in the Italian language. Warden led by example: he attended a language course in Milan, spent hours listening to cassette tapes, and insisted that his Italian secretary speak to him in her own language. He encouraged his officers and enlisted men to practice their spoken Italian as often as possible, suggesting the base institute an "Italian day" once a week on which they would answer the telephone and speak to their colleagues in Italian. The initiative had the added advantage of improving the relationship between the Americans and the Italians in the area. Many of Warden's men came to appreciate their new ability to converse with their hosts, but others, inevitably, considered the entire program a waste of valuable time.

Warden instituted another requirement that upset the base's daily routine: he insisted that all officers and enlisted personnel engage in organized physical training three times a week. It did not take long for opposition to form. Since Warden "would not listen to reason," some of the officers and senior enlisted men confronted him: they insisted that the regulations required only that they pass certain physical tests each year and that he had no right to demand any additional fitness training. Warden told the small group that while the air force established a minimum physical fitness requirement, it was both his responsibility and his choice to raise the standard in order to meet the higher command's goals. Again, he led by example, but, as with the language course, few welcomed the extra workload. Warden also insisted that his men show respect for the service by wearing the uniform properly. Decimomannu was hot most of the year, and far away from the prying eyes of the air force leadership, and in his opinion the men tended to dress too casually. Not surprisingly, they considered Warden's appearance overly formal.

The most important task that Donnelly had assigned to Warden was to examine the possibility of turning the base into one that could allow for accompanied tours. Unlike most bases in Europe, Deci lacked the infrastructure and

facilities to accommodate spouses and children, and as a result both officers and
enlisted men stayed only a short period of time before they were reassigned. This
meant that many left almost as soon as they had learned to perform their jobs
properly and were replaced by novices, which hampered the base's operational
efficiency. Warden thought it unnecessary for air force personnel to be separated
from their families when deployed on a noncombat tour. The Italian, British,
and German contingents deployed to Deci with their spouses, and he believed
that the Americans sent a bad signal by indicating that the local amenities were
not good enough for them. After some initial analysis he made the case for expanding the base's infrastructure to include postal services, better housing conditions, and other elements that would make it not only possible, but even attractive, for spouses to take an active part in the Mediterranean assignment. Warden's
team searched for acceptable housing, looked into options for having goods and
supplies delivered to the base, worked hard to get funding for setting up an exchange and a commissary outlet, and investigated the possibility of establishing
schools and kindergartens. While most American bases in Europe were "Little
Americas," deliberately segregated from the host community, Warden believed
he could find a middle way where all parties would benefit. In his report to
USAFE he recommended accompanied tours at Decimomannu.

> In response to a query from USAFE as to the suitability of Deci-
> momannu for an accompanied tour, we respond in the affirmative.
> The U.S. is the only one of the four user nations serving non-accom-
> panied tours. There are reasonably extensive military support facilities
> including an Italian commissary, a British BX, a German BX, and an
> infirmary on the base. The base is located within 15 miles of Cagliari,
> the capital of Sardinia, which has a population of about a quarter mil-
> lion. Consequently, there are all kinds of services including housing,
> department stores, and hospitals available on the economy. An accom-
> panied tour would be helpful from several aspects; most importantly,
> however, it would extend tours for the majority to two years and thus
> alleviate a severe continuity problem exacerbated by the fact that the
> other users are on three and four year tours. The accompanied tour
> should become a reality and start as soon as possible.[40]

Warden also devoted considerable time to "morale, welfare, and recreation" (MWR). He believed this area had been neglected, and initiated a project
that earned him a reputation for working around the bureaucratic system. The
enlisted men had complained that the three-meals-a-day schedule of the mess
hall was insufficient: the troops wanted a place where they could get food and
beverages on base outside fixed hours. Warden agreed, but initially Aviano told

him that there was no money available for such a snack bar, that financial regulations demanded advance planning, and that he would not be allowed to construct a new building on the base even if he managed to obtain the funding.

Determined to set up the facility, Warden convened a brainstorming session. 1st Lt. Richard D. Taylor offered to lead the effort, and Warden assigned him the task of designing and building an extension to an existing U.S.-owned building.[41] Taylor, not one to shy away from a challenge that included working around regulations, led a team of volunteers who secretly built and painted the annex in one of the hangars. They then had a truck transport the completed unit under the cover of darkness and before first light they had connected plumbing pipes, electrical cables, and wires from the existing building. Because the annex was painted the same color as the original building it looked as if they had simply found new use for an old structure. The following morning Warden invited the Italian base commander, Col. Bruno Servadei, and his wife to breakfast in the new facility. His guests were delighted and the *coup de main* was an immediate success. The snack bar became known as McDeci: it was an all-rank facility, run by the NCOs, which gave the men a place to eat on the flight line instead of having to travel to the dining hall. It was just one of those cases, Warden thought, where one acted first and apologized later, and at a remote base in Europe he could get away with such creativity.

Warden also established a library at Decimomannu, despite space constraints and predictable opposition from those who believed that air force personnel did not need such a facility. The library's initial holdings fit into a cardboard box; by the time Warden left, the library contained two thousand volumes and was growing. He also set up a twenty-four-hour cable television network, remodeled the dining hall, and improved the recreation center. Again, Warden needed both approval and funding from Aviano for these projects, which often slowed progress, but many of the problems were eased when Donnelly approved a local purchase authority for the chief of MWR.

Warden also sought to improve operations. He wanted to press for big-wing exercises, but settled on less ambitious projects since he lacked the authority to organize such an undertaking. He suggested measures to enhance the Air Combat Maneuvering Instrumentation (ACMI), since the existing configuration limited high-activity tracking to eight participants and constrained them to a thirty-mile-diameter circle; he sought approval to use flares, chaff, and electronic countermeasures in the air-to-air areas; and he initiated programs that integrated Airborne Warning and Control System (AWACS) aircraft in an intense combat area. At the time Warden observed:

> After taking part in operations at Eglin, Moody, and Decimomannu, I
> have become convinced that changes in organization and training could

lead to significant improvements in air-to-air proficiency. With respect to training, Decimomannu offers the ideal location for a complete air combat training center. A complete training center would take advantage of the latest developments in exercise physiology and would include an intense physical training program. It might also include a centrifuge to be used exclusively as an exercise device for general muscle training and for increased G-tolerance. There could also be a comprehensive academic program which would focus on enemy equipment, capabilities, and tactics. Video and computerized presentation could speed the learning process. For actual air training, the ACMI enhancement program would open vistas in multi-bogey practice and would provide superior reconstruction and debriefing of successful and unsuccessful tactics used in package missions.[42]

Cathey, who visited the base several times, seemed to have been pleased with what he observed, and Donnelly, whom Warden visited in Germany on several occasions, was reportedly very happy with Warden's achievements. Warden was perceived as aggressive and focused, and once again received favorable efficiency reports. According to Capt. Richard L. Boyd, who had worked with Warden at Moody and then when assigned to Deci, "he was simply loved by the Italians."[43] He was the first commander who had tried to integrate the base fully into the community, to some extent on Italian terms. They appreciated his taking the time to learn their language, which they viewed first and foremost as a sign of respect; they enjoyed his anecdotes; they applauded his insistence on wearing the uniform with respect and being formal at ceremonies; they welcomed his belief that everything was possible; and it even seems to have worked in his favor that he was somewhat eccentric and different from other U.S. officers. Unlike many of his American colleagues, who were bored or puzzled by his discussions of ancient and modern history, the Italians reportedly welcomed his affection for Thucydides and the Peloponnesian War. He was also considered an impeccable host: he dealt graciously with public figures, guests enjoyed his receptions, and he had a good relationship with the Italian commander.[44]

Yet, as always, Warden was not universally appreciated. He had undertaken his initiatives to improve the quality of the base as he defined it, but some of his colleagues argued that he did so "without looking too much into the rear-view mirror." Warden certainly had an uneasy relationship with the administrative headquarters at Aviano. As he was to do throughout his career, Warden insisted that while one had to comply with legal requirements, there was no reason to stay within bureaucratic constraints if the system was not working: one should simply develop a better system rather than complain and remain passive. After only a few weeks in the job he had become increasingly irritated by the difficulty of obtaining all the forms that the base needed for acquisition and procurement. He attempted to work within the system, first by making telephone calls and then by traveling to Aviano, but concluded that the continuous lack of "the right forms impeded the efficiency of operations."[45] He consequently had his staff develop provisional forms, which solved the problem in the short run but created tension between the detachment and the headquarters.

The physical separation between Decimomannu and Aviano also made it difficult to obtain support from civil engineering and contracting services. Because he considered working through "the bureaucrats" at Aviano burdensome, Warden secured approval directly from USAFE to establish a contracting office, giving up personnel slots in maintenance and transportation in exchange—actions that both military personnel and civilians felt subverted the chain of command.

The commander at Aviano, Colonel Zehrer, recalled that he had "several professional disagreements with Warden on fundamental issues," but added that he never thought that his detachment commander was insubordinate or in breach of protocol.[46] Most troubling to him was a sense that Warden was leading a "movement of independence." Zehrer was working hard to prevent Aviano Air Base from being closed down, while at the same time Warden was strongly advocating that the USAFE operation at Decimomannu should become an independent Tactical Fighter Training Group, reporting directly to the Sixteenth Air Force:

> This proposal would align the command structure with activity and responsibility at Decimomannu and relieve the Aviano Group commander of a responsibility unrelated to his primary area of concern. It would also recognize the responsibility the Decimomannu commander has for an extensive flying operation . . . It will remove needless bureaucratic duplication in performance reports, decorations, and other reports to higher headquarters . . . To become self-supporting, Decimomannu will require about 20 additional manpower slots.[47]

Zehrer told Warden not to pursue the matter: he was not opposed to Deci's gaining its independence, but this was not the right time to make that argument. However, Warden continued to press the case and Zehrer felt that "Warden had no respect for authority." It was clear to Zehrer that Warden had a special relationship with Donnelly, and at times he felt uncomfortable with the direct link and Warden's unconventional way of operating, but he also believed that Warden had done a great deal of good for Deci.[48] The basic friction between Deci and Aviano was partly systemic and partly personal.

Warden would have welcomed a longer stay at Decimomannu, but in the autumn of 1985 he was offered a place at the prestigious National War College

(NWC) in Washington, DC. His promotion to full colonel at the age of thirty-nine and his selection for the NWC three years later were strong indications that he was destined for higher command. The air force recognized him as a hard-working officer who was dedicated to the future of the service; he held the reputation of being a brilliant staff officer; and now he had received good efficiency reports for his tours at Eglin, Moody, and Decimomannu. These reports alone might well have earned him the opportunity to attend NWC, but the strong recommendation he received from Donnelly certainly helped.

In his "End-of-Tour Report" Warden included among "lessons learned" that it was "absolutely imperative that the commander, the majority of officers and selected NCOs speak Italian . . . The investment in time and money is well worthwhile."[49] He also argued that "we sometimes think that the American way is the only way. This is not the case. It is imperative that the commander and the officers at Decimomannu realize that the American way, in many cases, cannot be used."

Yet some drawbacks of his freewheeling approach appeared shortly after he left. Warden had initiated some worthwhile changes and brought many of them to fruition, but the limits imposed by a one-year tour meant that the complexities of implementation were left to others. Warden's successor, Col. Omar R. Wiseman, faced the challenge of following up Warden's many initiatives without being privy to the reasoning behind them. In doing so, Wiseman found that he was perceived as the "negative guy," since Warden had always been so "positive" about life in the region. Wiseman recalls that his greatest difficulties were unauthorized contracts and implementing accompanied tours. Wiseman disapproved of the plethora of provisional forms being used to obtain equipment and services, and practically upon his arrival he faced investigations about expended funds. After reviewing the paperwork and identifying the local contracting and civil engineering arrangements, an inspection team from Aviano concluded that there had been a questionable use of both appropriated and nonappropriated funds. Warden deserved credit for building the snack bar, refurnishing the dining hall, and providing a weight room, but in the view of the inspectors he seems to have been too creative financially in doing so.[50] Still, his practices did not provide the grounds for formal charges against him.

As Wiseman saw it, Warden had done little, if anything, to prepare the base to support dependents. He quickly noticed the difference between Warden's concept of "an effortless assimilation" into the Italian lifestyle and the "expectations of the families who arrived at Deci."[51] Wiseman thought that Warden had apparently believed that American families would welcome the opportunity to experience life in a Mediterranean country as much as he had, and that the details would sort themselves out once they arrived. In Wiseman's view the housing available for the U.S. families was substandard; the medical support system was inadequate; food and gasoline could not be delivered as promised; and Wiseman concluded that he lacked both the personnel and the money to make the necessary changes within the time available.[52] Again, according to Wiseman, Warden's enthusiasm for southern Italy was not shared by many of the U.S. officers, enlisted men, and spouses, who found the community distinctly primitive compared to their customary way of life. Warden's efforts to improve appreciation of Italy and of Mediterranean history had helped to show that the American military could appreciate other cultures, rather than being "ugly Americans," but generally speaking he had greater success in convincing Italians than Americans.[53]

5

THE ART OF AIR WARFARE:
THE AIR CAMPAIGN

Shortly after arriving at the NWC Colonel Warden, now forty-two years old, decided to write a book about how to design a coherent and unified air campaign. By doing so he hoped to provoke and reopen the debate on the true potential of conventional air power. His book, *The Air Campaign: Planning for Combat*, represented an attempt to understand the complex philosophy and theory associated with air warfare at the operational level by focusing on *how* and *why* air power could be used to attain the military objectives needed to win a war. Warden was on a quest, and therefore made no attempt to produce an objective study: he supported his case by juxtaposing theory, operational principles, and historical illustrations to create a practical guide to the most effective use of air power.

Operational Art
The NWC's senior-level program prepares selected personnel from the armed forces, the Department of Defense, and other U.S. government agencies for high-level command and staff positions. The curriculum was designed to expand and deepen the students' knowledge of national security and to sharpen their analytical skills. The core curriculum had changed in the two years before Warden enrolled: the commandant, Maj. Gen. Perry M. Smith, encouraged the faculty members and their students to focus on operational art.

Warden had initially considered devoting his book to the contemporary validity of Alexander the Great's operational approaches, recalling Fuller's belief that commanders in the Second World War could have avoided many mistakes if they had been acquainted with the classics on ancient warfare, but he realized that he had a unique opportunity to link strategic insight to his experiences with tactical air power. Moreover, the exercises in which he had participated at Eglin and Moody had convinced him that big-wing formations could play a key role in achieving local air superiority, and he wanted to explore historical examples to confirm the validity of his approach in different times and places.

As these elements came together he decided to focus his research on air campaign planning at the operational level of war: the dimension between the strategic and tactical levels that dealt with campaigns rather than battles. The concept was relatively new in the United States,[1] but it had started to take root when the Military Reform Movement introduced Maneuver Warfare and its Deep Battle concept in the 1970s and with subsequent publications such as Harry G. Summers Jr.'s *On Strategy: A Critical Analysis of the Vietnam War* (1984) and Richard E. Simpkin's *Race to the Swift: Thoughts on Twenty-First Century Warfare* (1985). The army had been the first of the services to incorporate it into doctrine when it revised Field Manual (FM) 100-5 in 1982, but Warden was adamant that the new AirLand battle doctrine did not deal adequately with air power's role in combat. A revision four years later discussed air power at greater length, but only at the tactical level.[2]

The AirLand Battle doctrine, FM 100-5, was a significant document with obvious shortcomings: it viewed air forces as supporting elements to a ground campaign that would be fought against numerically superior Warsaw Pact mechanized forces and would involve a front several hundred miles deep and wide in a Central European battlefield. American forces would abandon fixed defensive positions and strike the enemy's flanks, and then, covered by attack helicopters and aircraft, penetrate to the rear, interdict supply lines, and attack enemy command and control centers. Air operations would provide fire support for ground maneuver, and although planners would coordinate "air and naval support," the ground element would never support air operations. Nothing in the manual precluded the use of air power in an independent and decisive fashion, but the doctrine neither accounted for nor encouraged it.[3]

In Warden's opinion, the AirLand battle doctrine would allow the army to dictate key decisions, which could result in nothing more than a tactical, army-oriented ATO rather than an operational-level air campaign. While the new doctrine contained useful elements for ground combat in a cold war setting, he feared that the unique character of air power would be lost in the new warfighting paradigm. Because the doctrine made the corps commanders the lords of the battle, and allowed them the deciding voice, Warden also feared that the theater would become fragmented in a way that undermined the very strength of air power—the flexibility, mobility, and responsiveness that allowed it to attack any target in the theater.

In addition, Warden questioned its fundamental premise: that the sole objective of warfare is defeat of the opposing army and that a nation must therefore direct all resources of war toward that end. He believed that the rise of air power had changed the way wars should be waged by nations and fought by the armed services. In his view, nations take certain actions because their leaders, or their leaders' constituencies, decide to take them; therefore military campaigns should target the opponent's leaders to make them capitulate. While assisting and protecting ground or maritime forces was unquestionably a laudable mission, it circumscribed the independent potential of air power and kept it from achieving the operationally significant results of which it was capable.

Synopsis

The book first presents a generic framework for the overall analysis, defining the four levels of war—grand strategic, strategic, operational, and tactical—noting the lack of a coherent doctrine within the penultimate category. Warden believed that this level of war had been ignored for two reasons: it was considered difficult to deal with and it was regarded as irrelevant in an age where nuclear weapons "made the massing of armies, navies and air forces obsolete."[4]

Raising an issue that would characterize his strategic thinking, Warden next suggested that each of the four levels contained one or more centers of gravity: those characteristics, capabilities, or locations from which a nation derived its freedom of action, physical strength, or will to fight, or "the point where the enemy is most vulnerable and the point where an attack will have the best chance of being decisive."[5] Although the term has been the subject of many interpretations, and Warden's definition is debatable, to him a "center of gravity" was in essence a point against which a given level of effort would accomplish more than it would accomplish if applied elsewhere. The commander's most important task was to identify the centers of gravity correctly and strike them appropriately.

With this in mind the commander should decide on the most suitable military instrument for inflicting decisive blows: he "must avoid making an automatic decision that all his available services must participate equally (or conceivably at all), that one is *a priori* supreme and must be supported by the others, that all must be about the same business at the same time, or that an enemy action demands a reaction in kind."[6] Under certain circumstances, then, the commander should consider air power as the primary means of achieving political and military objectives—a highly contentious notion that called the premises of AirLand doctrine into question.

Air Superiority

In his book, Warden argued that air forces could perform three types of combat missions: air superiority, interdiction, and close air support. Underlying *The Air Campaign* is "the idea that air superiority is crucial, that a campaign will be lost if the enemy has it, that in many circumstances it alone can win a war, and that its possession is needed before other actions on the ground or in the air can be undertaken."[7]

Since the German attack on Poland in 1939, no country has won a war in the face of enemy air superiority, no major offensive has succeeded against an opponent who controlled the air, and no defense has sustained itself against an enemy who had air superiority. Conversely, no state has lost a war while it maintained air superiority, and attainment of air superiority consistently has been a prelude to military victory.[8]

Warden defined air superiority as having sufficient control of the air to conduct air attacks against the enemy without serious opposition and being free from the danger of serious enemy air incursions. He considered it a precondition for all other military operations,[9] which then meant "all operations must be subordinated—to the extent required—to its attainment."[10] Thus, in a reversal of the established order, maritime forces might direct gunboat fire against SAMs and commando raids might neutralize bomber units, seize airfields, and destroy radar sites; achieving air superiority was not merely the task of air forces—"thinking that air superiority must be obtained by air means alone seriously limits commanders in their quest for victory."[11]

Warden next presented a logical framework for analyzing how to achieve dominance in the air by focusing on three critical factors: "skilled personnel" (pilots, key aircrew, and technicians); "materiel" (aircraft, SAMs, manufacturing facilities, and supporting infrastructure); and "position" (the relative location and vulnerability of air bases, missile fields, ground battle lines, and infrastructure).[12] Although he devoted most of his analysis to the physical aspect of targeting, Warden also noted the importance of understanding the enemy's doctrine, warned against mirror-imaging, and urged planners to take advantage of inconsistencies in the enemy's strategy and doctrine.

Warden offered two absolutes: "if a single lesson can be learned in military history, it is that the key to winning battles is to have greater forces at the key location than the enemy does" and no simpler, or more often ignored, principle exists for air warfare than concentration of force.[13] As a theoretical basis for evaluating and planning at the operational level he identified five cases of war that demanded adjustments in the relationship between skilled personnel and materiel in conjunction with the vulnerabilities of airfields and rear areas.

In the Case I scenario both sides are vulnerable to attacks, but have the capability and will to strike each other's air bases and rear areas. The commander confronts a choice between emphasizing defense against enemy air attacks and concentrating on offensive operations. Warden cautioned against the standard compromise, which might stretch forces too thinly and thereby become the worst possible solution. While accepting that some situations justified defensive thinking, Warden argued that defense was "a negative concept" that by itself could lead at best to a draw,[14] while offense would maintain initiative, force the enemy to react, and place the enemy under constant pressure by carrying the war to his homeland. Thus, whenever politically acceptable, "the offensive course should be selected."[15] Moreover, unlike Clausewitz, Warden concluded that the two most important principles of war—mass and concentration—were most effective when applied in an offensive fashion: "In the Pacific war, we saw one side make the radical decision to fight a whole offensive campaign for air superiority. One side was innovative and determined in concentrating mass on an objective; the other made piecemeal attacks and reinforced piecemeal."[16]

The most common argument used against offensive action was that an enemy with a strong air defense system could cause high casualties, but Warden believed that such risks could be minimized by continuously reviewing and analyzing intelligence information and incorporating that information into war-gaming exercises. Indeed, he argued that ground-based defenses, whether antiaircraft artillery or guided missile systems, had never provided effective counters to an air offensive. If destruction of the ground-based defense system were unrealistic, Warden suggested that neutralization "through electronic suppression of key parts, through adequate disruption of the system's command and control, or through isolating the system from its sources of supply" would suffice.[17]

The Case II scenario represents the commander's ideal: his own bases are nearly immune from enemy attack, while he can attack all parts of his enemy's structure. According to Warden, such a situation provides the opportunity for "action so decisive that war can theoretically be won from the air."[18] Since air power is an inherently offensive weapon, the air campaign planner should capitalize on that intrinsic advantage by assaulting five air centers of gravity: equipment (numbers of aircraft or missiles); logistics (the quality and resilience of supply support); geography (location and number of operational and support facilities); personnel (numbers and quality of pilots); and the command and control structure (importance and vulnerability).[19] The priority accorded these centers of gravity would depend on individual circumstances. In some cases there might be a panacea: a target that, when attacked successfully, would lead to victory.

Warden further broke down the categories by focusing on vulnerabilities within the chain. For example, when analyzing "aircraft" as a center of gravity, Warden insisted that plans include airfields; the shelters in which the aircraft were located; the ferry routes, bridges, and railroads that enabled engines, airframes, munitions, and fire control systems to travel from the factory to the airfield; and the raw material and power plants that enabled the assembling of the aircraft in the first place. He applied the same logic to the other centers of gravity, emphasizing that such effects were not immediate: "patience and persistence are key."[20]

Warden identified command and control as the most critical center of gravity, and believed that the difficulty of measuring short-term success and the perceived risk had kept forces from attacking it.

> Command is the sine qua non of military operations. Without command, a military organization is nothing but rabble, a chicken with its head cut off . . . Clearly, command, with its necessary associated communications and intelligence gathering functions, is an obvious center of gravity, and has been from the earliest times: As the death of the king on the field of battle meant defeat for his forces, so the effective isolation of the command structure in modern war has led to the rapid defeat of dependent forces.[21]

Command elements could be attacked in the information sphere, the communication sphere, and the decision-making sphere, and attacks could "range from direct strikes at enemy command posts to complex operations to mislead the enemy and induce him to do something inappropriate."[22] In this context Warden highlighted the value of long-range bombers in the war against Japan, reinforcing his central arguments: "no government can long function when the enemy operates freely above it, that is when the enemy has air superiority . . . The mere possibility, however, means that the air superiority campaign must be given great thought—as an end in itself, or as a means to an end."[23]

Case III represents the worst scenario, in which the enemy can strike anywhere anytime, while friendly forces can hardly reach the front. For all the advantages of offensive operations Warden suggested that some situations required a defensive posture: for example, if not enough fighter-bombers were available to carry the war to the enemy or if the political leadership lacked the will for an offensive. The only possible goal in those circumstances would be to avoid defeat, and the key would be to inflict so much damage that the enemy would not be willing to pay the price of a Pyrrhic victory. Warden submitted that the history of air warfare proved that masses in the air could only be opposed by countermasses: attempts to defend with inferior numbers, or conversely, to attack with inferior numbers, had a notable record of failure. Other than strengthening air defense systems, especially by developing a sustainable warning and control structure, his prescription for success in defensive operations was to focus on two general principles: "The first principle is to concentrate forces, to confront the enemy with superior numbers in a particular battle, sector, or time. The second is to accept that it is impossible to defend everywhere and everything: He who tries to defend all defends nothing."[24] Again, the essence was to outnumber the enemy in any given engagement: "the difference between losing a little each day and losing a lot on a particular day is significant."[25]

In Cases IV and V, with both sides restricted to fighting over the front, either because of political restraints or because of physical inability to reach appropriate targets, air superiority was unlikely to be an end in itself. Instead, the objective would be to prevent "the enemy from interfering with ground operations over and near the front, while permitting friendly air operations over corresponding parts of enemy territory."[26] Consequently, tactical air-to-air operations would dominate. First, the commander could establish a fighter screen between the enemy bases and the front, which had the advantage of showing presence over enemy territory and providing local air superiority. However, this approach was immensely expensive: it was vulnerable to enemy attacks; it relinquished the initiative to the enemy; and friendly ground forces would be unable to take advantage of the favorable air situation. Second, the commander could conduct sweep operations: fighter aircraft establishing a corridor for the bomber fleet and engaging enemy air forces en route. Under the third option, close escort, fighters would stay close to the bomber fleet, responding only to direct enemy attacks, but Warden considered the sweep option more effective.

INTERDICTION

Warden defined interdiction as "any operation designed to slow or inhibit the flow of men or materiel from the source to the front, or laterally behind the front,"[27] and divided it into three categories:

> We may define distant interdiction as an attack against the sources of men and materiel, or, in the case of a warring party that has no industry, the ports or airfields where materiel provided from outside enters the country . . . Intermediate interdiction occurs somewhere between the source and the front . . . Close interdiction is interdiction in that area along the front where lateral movement takes place.[28]

He considered distant interdiction a possible "war-winning campaign" that could produce "decisive outcomes" throughout the theater, but identified close interdiction as the most useful when a battle was in progress.

All forces must establish lines of communication so that men, equipment, and supplies can reach the front, and commanders must place their forces between the enemy and their own logistical base. Warden suggested that these interposed forces were vulnerable and that effective operations against supply lines could induce the enemy to make peace even without major battles. Although interdiction had not been applied effectively in Vietnam, he believed that it had nevertheless made it difficult for the North Vietnamese and the Viet Cong to launch a general offensive, and had done so at relatively low loss rates for U.S. forces. Moreover, the interdiction operations during the Linebacker campaigns

(May 10–October 23 and December 18–29, 1972) forced the North Vietnamese to commit large numbers of people to defending and repairing the Ho Chi Minh Trail even in the absence of significant U.S. ground forces. To Warden, the telling argument for interdiction was that the North Vietnamese were able to succeed quickly as soon as air power operations came to an end.[29]

Warden broke down action at the front into six categories: own forces in retreat, static defense against an enemy offense, offensive operations on both sides, offensive operations against a static defense, a retreating enemy, and attacks against self-sufficient forces. He then provided historical examples of successful and unsuccessful interdiction campaigns for each category, asserting that combining an interdiction campaign with an offensive on the ground, all under the umbrella of air superiority, would inflict damage on the enemy, while "air is of marginal value in a fight against self-sustaining guerrillas who merge with the population . . . obviously, a force that needs little or nothing to exist or fight does not need the kind of supply lines that make air interdiction worthwhile."[30] Interdiction could be especially effective when the enemy was under pressure and needed to move major forces quickly, such as during a retreat, a pursuit, or a defense against a determined offensive. As with the air superiority campaign, Warden cautioned against expecting immediate results: "in the very short term, air cannot stop large bodies of men; interdiction takes time to work; and attacks on war production take even more time. Ground must be the key force if time is of the essence, and it is agreed that ground action can lead to the political objective significantly faster than could air action."[31] He cited the U.S. decision to invade Japan rather than wait for the results of the submarine blockade and the strategic bombing as a prime example.

For all the advantages of interdiction missions, Warden warned planners against being seduced by their effectiveness:

> Interdiction operations should not be done at the expense of something more important. That something more important almost certainly will be air superiority. A ground commander will demand interdiction in many instances before air superiority has been won. Interdiction missions, except under unusual circumstances, when the benefit clearly outweighs the risk, should not be attempted in the absence of air superiority. A commander does so at his peril, for he is likely to jeopardize his chances of ever winning it.[32]

CLOSE AIR SUPPORT

Warden defined the third combat mission, close air support, as "any air operation that theoretically could and would be done by ground forces on their own, if sufficient troops or artillery were available."[33] He contrasted close air support—

ground-attack aircraft directly assisting ground forces—with interdiction carried out by fighter-bombers and light bombers attacking infrastructure, supplies, and forces in transit in the depth of the theater of war. He acknowledged that close air support had proven successful in several battles, but laid out the reasons why he considered this mission highly overrated. Since ground commanders concentrated on the immediate battle and judged progress only by movement of lines on a map, they tended to favor close air support at the expense of the other two combat missions. In contravention of established doctrine, Warden argued that the air campaign would under some circumstances be more important than the ground campaign and that the ground commander needed to recognize that other missions should receive higher priority: air superiority was a theater necessity and any effort that did not contribute to it would be diversionary until air superiority was gained:

> If we think of close air support in terms analogous to the operational ground reserve, we tend to put proper value on a scarce and valuable commodity. We put it in terms both the airman and the soldier can understand. We also make it easier to comprehend that close air support, like operational reserves, is something to be used quickly and decisively. It is a shock weapon that is most effective when concentrated in space and time.[34]

Thus, Warden suggested that close air support was properly applied only "where an operational-level commander would want to employ his operational reserve and where bursts of power—as opposed to the long-term power of ground forces—are indicated."[35] He further insisted that a well-executed air campaign would prevent the enemy from ever coming near enough to engage friendly forces; thus, close air support had to be viewed as a last option.

OPERATIONAL RESERVES

Perhaps the most original aspect of *The Air Campaign* was Warden's advocacy of operational reserves. Airmen had traditionally dismissed the idea of holding back forces to exploit emerging windows of opportunity for three reasons: they believed that a unit not committed to the battle was not pulling its weight; they interpreted the principles of concentration and mass to mean using all resources from the opening moment of the war; and they viewed a sortie not flown as a sortie lost forever. To them, withholding air forces meant substantially reducing momentum. Soldiers on the ground viewed air reserves simply as lack of commitment. Warden, by contrast, argued that reserves could lessen the fog, friction, and uncertainty of war in two ways: fresh troops might break an enemy attack and restore the line of defense, or they might give the commander the resources to exploit an enemy error or weakness and lead to an offensive breakthrough. Thus, Warden claimed that reserve forces could create and exploit an entirely new battle, or at least a distinctive new phase, in the middle of a war. Success depended on avoiding gradualism: "piecemeal commitments . . . lose much of their ability to induce confusion and fear in the mind of the enemy. Adapting to a gradual change in a situation is far easier than to have to adapt to a sudden and massive change."[36] He viewed the impact of shock as more important than the physical effect of deployment and commitment of reserves. Warden suggested that air reserves were most needed against equal or stronger forces, submitting that operational and tactical reserves had played a key role in winning the Battle of Britain.

OBJECTIVES AND MEANS

Warden also explored the relationship between political and military objectives, noting that military objectives tended to fall into one of three categories: the destruction or neutralization of some or all of the enemy's military forces; the destruction of some or all of the enemy's economy and industry; and the destruction of the will to resist, either the will of the government or the will of the people. In addition to noting moral objections to direct attacks on civilians, he pointed out that historically populations had proven resilient to bombardment and instead he advocated an indirect approach to influencing popular will by inflicting military casualties or economic damage, or by presenting oneself as a liberator rather than a destroyer. Moreover, Warden cautioned that military objectives and campaign plans had to be tied to political objectives, "as seen through the enemy's eyes, not one's own,"[37] to ensure that the enemy received the right message. He also acknowledged that the very unorthodoxy of his view would prompt opposition: "They will do so with the best of motives, sincere in their belief that they are protecting against flights of fancy and against reckless adventures that may well lead to disaster."[38]

Once the theater commander had identified the military objective and chosen a conceptual plan to target centers of gravity, he had to select a key force to attain his objective:

> To understand the concept of a key force and the relationship among complementing forces, thinking about another art form—the concerto—is helpful. A composer writes the concerto to say something, to attain some objective. Having selected an objective, the composer decides how best to reach that objective. Should it be a piano concerto, a violin concerto, or a flute concerto? Only one will get him to the objective he has chosen; clearly, a piano cannot say what a violin can say, and vice versa. That he has chosen an instrument to be his key force does

not mean that the other instruments do not have roles. To the contrary, the other instruments are vital, for they provide the support that allows the key force to do things it could not do by itself.

During the course of the concerto, the key force will be the only instrument active at certain times; the rest are in repose, awaiting their turn. At other times, the key force is silent while the complementing forces bear the whole burden. The composer, and later, the director, has the task of orchestrating—not subordinating or integrating—his instruments so that each can do its job—whether that be as the key force or the supporting force. In the process, he does not try to make one instrument sound like another, or do another's job; rather, he uses each to do what it is naturally constituted to do and what only it is capable of doing. Orchestration, not subordination or integration, is the sine qua non of warfare.

If we carry the concerto analogy to the realms of warfare, we can say that a particular war, or campaign, or phase of a campaign could be a sea concerto if sea power were the key force. Likewise, we would say that a war or campaign was an air concerto if air forces had the dominant role. We also would say that the theater commander had the job of "orchestrating" his forces in such a way as to achieve his objectives.[39]

Critique

A close reading of *The Air Campaign* reveals that Warden was both less objective about air power's role in warfare than his supporters would argue and more objective about air power as a universal solution than first impressions might suggest. He believed that air power stood apart from other instruments of warfare because it could bring mass to a point rapidly, without regard for intervening terrain or ground forces. Yet, while the book makes the case for recognizing air power as an equal partner, and under certain circumstances as a war-winning instrument, Warden did not dismiss the importance of ground operations. He simply objected to their definition as "a priori supreme" and believed that dogmatic adherence to the mantra of "seize and hold ground" as the determinant of success presented the main obstacle to the full development of the potential of air power. In his view, major wars were rarely won by capturing territory, unless that territory included a vital political or economic center of gravity: "territory will be disposed of at the peace conference as a function of the political, military, and economic situation at the war's end."[40]

By arguing against the air force's prevailing doctrine of subordinating air power to ground forces, highlighting the crucial importance of air superiority and the value of operational reserves, and asserting that air power could win a war independent of ground force engagements, the book contradicted the prevailing wisdom of the mid-1980s. Warden's provocative arguments and somewhat selective interpretation of history made for conclusions that were highly contentious at the time and attracted extremes of both praise and condemnation. Supporters found Warden's thesis convincing and his approach valuable, since he provided insight, analysis, and prescriptions. Detractors dismissed the book as thoroughly biased—a piece of special pleading that left no fact unaltered if it could thus support the author's case. Despite these polarized opinions the book made an indisputable contribution to air power theory. The end of the cold war and the new technologies that entered the U.S. arsenal under the Reagan administration made Warden's wake-up call particularly interesting.

Warden—Theorist and Throwback

At one level *The Air Campaign* offered an informed, thought-provoking, and imaginative discourse on how operational art and the principles of war applied to the design and execution of a unified air campaign, and challenged conventional ideas about the role of air power in the conduct of war. At another level it was an air power manifesto in the tradition of air power theorists: Warden's line of reasoning shows a high degree of overlap and continuity with those of earlier visionaries. Indeed, almost all of his points had been argued before, but he succeeded in organizing a range of fragmented beliefs into a coherent philosophy about the conduct of an air campaign at the operational level of war. To some extent his "old" ideas suddenly seemed new because by the late 1980s the air force as an institution had seemingly forgotten them.

In arguing the importance of air superiority and that "war can be won from the air," Warden's most obvious predecessors were Giulio Douhet with *The Command of the Air* (1921), William Mitchell with *Winged Defense* (1925) and *Skyways* (1930), and Maj. Alexander de Seversky with *Victory through Air Power* (1942).[41] Douhet, Mitchell, de Seversky, and Warden believed that command of the air was a prerequisite for all other military operations; that in certain situations air superiority could ensure military victory on its own; that air power could be the supreme military instrument in ensuring national security; and that it was an inherently offensive instrument of force that amounted to a revolution in military affairs. They insisted on a sharp and violent application of force and downplayed the role of ground-to-air systems: the three pioneers because they did not comprehend their utility and Warden because he believed that countermeasures could render them ineffective. All four suggested that an airman should have complete control of an air campaign; they believed in centralized control and decentralized execution; they argued that naval forces were becoming ever more irrelevant; they supported the old adage that "the best defense is a good offense"; and they cautioned against committing aircraft to operations in support of ground and naval forces at the expense of air superiority or deep attack.

Perhaps the strongest similarity between Warden and the earlier air power theorists is that all of them strongly advocated the use of strategic air power. Paradoxically, however, Warden did not deal extensively with the topic in his book: he mentioned strategic attack as an important mission for the theater commander and implied that it could be a war-winning instrument under certain circumstances, but he did not develop a unified concept of strategic bombing until two years after he submitted the manuscript of *The Air Campaign*. Moreover, analysis of Warden's concept of strategic air power (discussed in subsequent chapters) reveals that his philosophy underlying targeting, and the targets he favored, differed from those of his predecessors. *The Air Campaign* might have benefited from a chapter on strategic air power as a separate combat mission, in addition to air superiority, interdiction, and close air support, but Warden had chosen to focus exclusively on the operational level of warfare.

In discussing whether Warden was a "theorist or throwback," U.S. air power analyst David R. Mets concluded that even if Warden's book did nothing more than synthesize old ideas into a single, highly accessible form, it would have much in common with Alfred Mahan's magnum opus, *The Influence of Sea Power Upon History, 1660–1783*: "Nothing new appeared in that book, but it had an enormous influence. Mahan synthesized old ideas into a compact and readable set of notions that had long been the basis for the success of Britain's Royal Navy and British sea power in general."[42] Indeed, it is not so much new facts that advance military thought as new interpretations of known facts, or the discovery of new mechanisms or systems that account for known facts. Here Warden contributed significantly. The early visionaries were just visionaries; Warden had both the technological basis and the theoretical underpinnings to make the arguments credible. It is difficult to distinguish clearly between the expression of ideas and their origin, but Warden clearly documented a planning logic and process that presaged today's concept of effects-based operations.

Another element also comes into play: while Warden was reasonably familiar with the air power pioneers, they had never captured his imagination. To a large extent he had developed the ideas in his book independently, on the basis of his operational experience and his intuition. Although Warden has stated that the *U.S. Strategic Bombing Survey*, as well as the thinking of Gen. Hayward S. Hansell's *The Air Plan That Defeated Hitler* "heavily influenced his writing,"[43] he nevertheless owed his greatest intellectual debt to Fuller and Liddell Hart rather than to any of the air power visionaries.

The basic strengths of Warden's work are obvious: the top-down, systematic approach and lack of jargon demystified a topic that had previously been examined only in tactical and technical terms, and the core set of arguments made for stimulating reading. Warden succeeded in making them credible and vivid and giving readers an overall understanding of air power as a reliable basis for action. The book is focused, engaging, and logically structured, and avoids excessive detail. For all of these reasons it attracted a far wider audience than doctrinal manuals ever had. Warden's approach to the analysis of air power seems to have been highly appreciated by those for whom the book was intended: combat officers dealing with operational-level issues.

Yet his methodology requires closer examination. Warden unquestionably belonged to the school of thought that adhered to general formulations, models, and identifiable links between cause and effect. His study was didactic and normative: that is, he sought to deduce either immutable principles or lines of historical trends as guides to the efficient conduct of air warfare in the future. Warden was convinced that military theory, as a mixture of art and science, could only be advanced by using reductionism to simplify complex matters. Like Mahan before him, Warden therefore tended to generalize, an inevitable byproduct of using semiscientific methods when theorizing; as with his predecessors, such a method permitted an overview that would otherwise prove elusive.

Thus, for better or worse, Warden's methodological approach bears a strong resemblance to that of Antoine-Henri Jomini, who spoke and wrote in the language of neoclassical rationalism. Both were committed to simplification and prescription: they sought to produce practical guides to the conduct of warfare rather than abstract philosophy on the nature of warfare, and to reduce the complexity of warfare to a small number of crucial factors, rules, and principles. In that process they shied away from the "null-hypothesis" test: they ignored those cases in which military experience did not conform to the predictions based on their formulas. Both deliberately used epigrams to express conclusions that exceeded the supporting evidence to ensure that their main arguments were heard. Consequently, their beliefs in recipes for success stood in contrast to the objective probability approach that characterized the works of Clausewitz.[44] It is worth noting, however, that Jomini's approach to the conduct of war has been remarkably durable: perhaps Jomini, rather than Clausewitz, can claim the dubious title of being the founder of modern strategy.[45] Whether one agrees with such a proposition or not, Jomini's works, aimed at the general public rather than the military experts, indisputably prompted a widespread and rigorous examination of ground warfare. Warden provided an equivalent for air warfare.

Perspectives

Undeniably, Warden's logic had flaws. He intentionally downplayed the interactive nature of warfare, primarily because he believed in the decisive character of overwhelming air power. While Warden argued that air power used offensively could reduce and almost negate friction at the operational level of war, some scholars assert that he was insensitive to Clausewitzian uncertainties.[46] Warden's belief that a modern force could obtain almost perfect information about the enemy's physical capabilities also influenced his preference for focusing on measurable physical effects rather than the intangibles of war, and again resembles Jomini's approach of using a deductive Newtonian process to search for enduring principles. Warden has also been criticized for not acknowledging the fundamental differences between conventional warfare and protracted revolutionary warfare.[47]

Others have assailed Warden for assuming that air superiority would automatically lead to great advantages on the ground, and questioned his main hypothesis, "no nation has lost a war with air superiority."[48] Vietnam was cited as an example against Warden's hypothesis, but he countered that criticism by pointing out that the United States did not lose the war until *after* it withdrew its air power.[49] The fact that Germany had air superiority throughout 1942 and still lost the war is used as another example, but it must be noted that Germany only had air superiority over its own territory: it could not reach the military and industrial heartland of the United States, Britain, or Russia. Moreover, the war was not over until 1945, and by that point the Germans had lost air superiority.

Another criticism relates to terminology. Some readers argued that by recognizing more than one center of gravity Warden defeated his own purpose: the logical consequence would be to disperse physical as well as mental forces, which in turn would weaken the principles of mass and concentration. In addition, opinions differ on what "center of gravity" means. Is it a strength, weakness, or vulnerability? Is it a weapon system, a capability, or a location? Should it be defined if it cannot be reached? Other critics objected to Warden's use of the term "air campaign": in their view there could be only one "campaign"—the joint military campaign—and everything else was an operation supporting that campaign. Others strongly believed that air forces were so fully integrated into the warfighting force as a whole that the concept of an independent air campaign made no sense. Yet there can be little doubt that the book was instrumental in prompting the air force to think seriously about the operational level of war and today terms such as "air campaign" and "center of gravity" are taken for granted in doctrines and operational planning documents throughout the Western world.

Perhaps the strongest, and most justifiable, objection to Warden's book relates to his use of historical examples to support his theoretical arguments. While many saw his use of history as one of the book's strengths, others found that he had been too selective: that he had arranged facts to support a preconceived argument or conclusion. The most damning review came from Niklas Zetterling of the Swedish National Defence College, who ultimately compared the book to "old Soviet style propaganda."[50] The Swedish historian criticized Warden's interpretation of history on six main counts: first, the author did not account for the range of factors that must come into play when determining the linkages between cause and effect; second, he did not objectively distinguish between decisive and supporting factors; third, he overestimated the effectiveness of air power whenever it suited him; fourth, he was selective in his examples, ignoring those that would lead to the opposite conclusion; fifth, he used references and quotations that were taken out of their original context; and, lastly, several of his facts were simply wrong. Zetterling presented a range of examples, including an eight-page appendix, that detailed what he believed were logical flaws and inaccuracies in Warden's use of history.

Zetterling's objections, though overstated, cannot be ignored, but history can be interpreted in many ways and Warden never claimed to be a historian, nor did he set out to develop the history of air power. He stated his intention openly: to lay out a set of ideas that, if applied, might help military planners achieve a higher probability of success. He used the social scientist's approach: convinced that his basic ideas were correct, he sought examples that would help illustrate his points. For Warden the crucial issue was applicability to the real world: if he could find enough evidence to make a case he would present it; he would not forgo a good argument just because there was no empirical evidence available. Warden had clearly subordinated details to strongly held ideas, and he did not share Leopold von Ranke's oft-quoted aspiration "only to show what actually happened."[51] He began his investigation with insight—a light dawning on his inner consciousness and intuition; the insight hardened into a conclusion; and he then mustered illustrations and proof.

Even if Warden could be criticized for some of his conclusions, the way he brought different components of air power into a larger picture was unique at the time. His systematic linkage of *ends* (political objectives), *ways* (strategies to attain those ends), and *means* (identifying specific targets to execute the chosen strategy) led many airmen to regard his work as an extremely useful guide to planning air campaigns and thinking at the operational level of war.[52]

Warden's support for operational reserves was, and remains, both contentious and important, and could have merited more attention in the book. Many airmen supported his stance, albeit for a reason to which few would admit: air reserves placed under the control of a ground officer, even on a temporary basis, would have little chance of being unleashed no matter how urgent the needs elsewhere—a situation highly frustrating to forces eager to join the fray. Perhaps most important, operational planners have found Warden's concept of assessing own and enemy strengths and weaknesses in terms of centers of gravity immensely useful. Although the Air Corps Tactical School pioneers had viewed the enemy as a system, and air force officers had long argued that close air support was not the most effective use of air power and that sweep was more effective than escort,

Warden restored such thoughts to the agenda, with additional insight. By doing so he began a process that led midlevel officers to think in terms of operational systems effects rather than mere tactics and destruction.

The Air Campaign certainly did not represent standard air force practice, but instead offered profound ideas to consider when planning for combat. The book suggested that the art of air warfare was something more than picking targets and matching them with the right aircraft and munitions. The book must therefore be assessed on its own terms: as a position paper, a springboard for thought by operators and staff officers concerned with planning operations. The real significance of *The Air Campaign* was that Warden introduced a way of thinking about air power separate from ground forces and the immediate battlefield that was largely ignored in the mid-1980s. Although cooperation between the air force and the army had led to several projects that emphasized how air operations could contribute to maneuver warfare and the ground campaign, few if any had thought of a unified air campaign as coherently as Warden. Rather than accept NATO's notion of establishing a central front and fighting outnumbered and on the defensive, Warden made the case for acting offensively and provided a framework for applying air power beyond tactical missions. His examination of air power at the operational level of war, and of the ways an air commander should plan, orchestrate, and structure an air campaign, provided officers with a conceptual framework for thinking about the practice of air warfare beyond the dominant cold war paradigm. As such, it represented a conceptual shift in attitudes about air power that manifested itself over the next decade.

It is therefore fair to suggest that in the context of the 1980s Warden broke new ground by presenting air power as the leading element of a military campaign. Air force historian Richard P. Hallion has noted that the book "had a profound impact on the American defense establishment":

> the clearest American expression of air power thought since the days of Mitchell and Seversky, though considerably more concise, cogent, and balanced . . . Warden's "The Air Campaign"—with its cautious, realistic, yet essentially hopeful appraisal of air power application—provoked widespread discussion, controversy, and review throughout the Air Force. It catapulted Warden into the first rank of modern air power theorists.[53]

In sum, Warden's ability to crystallize the concepts of operational air power and describe them elegantly brought him a reputation as a capable strategist. Over time he would refine his views, but the concept that he developed for Operation Desert Storm four years later was at the very least implied in his book long before such a war was contemplated.[54]

PUBLICATION

Maj. Gen. Perry M. Smith, the commandant at the NWC, was impressed when he read an early draft of *The Air Campaign*.[55] When he received the final version he commented, "this is the most important book on air power written in the past decade. Must reading for everyone interested in future combat. This is the book I wish I had written."[56] Warden received the college's USAF award for research and writing and Smith took it upon himself to have the work published by the NDU Press. Its president, Lt. Gen. Bradley C. Hosmer, agreed: "this book offers planners greater understanding of how to use air power for future air campaigns against a wide variety of enemy capabilities in a wide variety of air operations."[57] Since the publication process would take several months, Smith arranged for preliminary distribution of the manuscript to other air force generals, including a copy to Donnelly, who was still the commander of USAFE. In his cover letter he stated, "a John Warden does not come along every year . . . You ought to get John Warden over there and give him a wing, give him an opportunity. This guy has great potential to contribute, both operationally and intellectually, to the United States Air Force."[58]

Donnelly needed little persuasion. In a recent speech at the NWC he had discussed the importance of understanding how to use air power at the operational level of war, stressing that air superiority could be "thought of as a theater-level campaign in and of itself" and that there was unknown war-winning potential in "attacking enemy forces before they can be brought to bear in battle."[59] He ended his speech by saying that "as commanders in peacetime, it is easy to get caught up in day-to-day duties. Expand yourself! Force your thinking to higher levels. Communicate your ideas . . . I challenge you to think about the intricacies of how you would prosecute war, improvising as situations develop."[60] After reading the manuscript of Warden's book he offered to write the introduction:

> This book is the start of something very important—it integrates historical experience into a clear, visionary set of conclusions and guidelines for using air forces to achieve strategic goals in a war. This book is exceptional, because it is the first book that thoroughly covers the area between the selection of national objectives and tactical execution at the wing and squadron operations levels. A book of this type has been needed for a long time . . . I strongly recommend "The Air Campaign," because it provides the air commander the intellectual wherewithal needed not only to avoid losing, but to win.[61]

Donnelly had retained the high opinion he had formed of Warden in Spain, remembered his outstanding performance at the Pentagon, and had more recently observed his actions as a detachment commander in Italy. In essence,

Donnelly liked the way Warden operated, recognized him as an insightful thinker, and apparently believed he would not merely handle a wing well, but would excel when given such a responsibility.

Warden's fellow students at the NWC recognized his commitment to learning and paid him considerable respect in academic terms.[62] Again, however, he did not attract unqualified admiration: some observed that the colonel also had an inflexible side. He revealed this unmistakably when he led a group of students who visited South America as part of the end-of-the-year school trip. As the officers were about to visit Colombia, Panama, Honduras, Mexico, and El Salvador the college decided that they should wear suits rather than uniforms. Warden objected strongly, asserting that as a matter of professional respect and pride in serving their country the future leaders of the U.S. Armed Forces should wear uniforms when visiting senior military and political leaders. His was a lone voice and the decision remained. Warden felt even more aggrieved when the students were told to wear casual clothes when visiting a refugee camp: they would be taking a bumpy ride through the countryside in hot weather. Again Warden insisted that it was not appropriate for representatives of the U.S. Armed Forces to appear in t-shirts and jeans. He was voted down; as a result he was the only one to show up in a coat and tie in the middle of the jungle. While such examples should not be blown out of proportion, they explain why some found him academically gifted but personally eccentric, inflexible, and unrealistic. Yet, for all the advantages of his sojourn at Fort Lesley J. McNair, Warden was looking forward to getting back into the operational world, where he would get the chance to put some of the theoretical constructs into practice.

6

WING COMMANDER:

NINETY-THREE INITIATIVES

The combination of outstanding efficiency reports and personal endorsements from Gen. Charles Donnelly and Maj. Gen. Perry Smith led to Warden's being offered the vice commander position at the Thirty-sixth TFW, located at Bitburg Air Base in the Eifel area of Germany, with the likely prospect of advancing to wing commander within months. Warden was delighted at the opportunity: for a fighter pilot there was nothing more attractive than working with the premier F-15 wing in the heartland of Europe. Donnelly suggested that he try to convert some of the ideas from his book into operational realities for the wing, and noted that the initial assignment as vice commander would give him the required preparation time. As might be expected, Warden's initiatives met with resistance from both personnel at the base and higher command.

Vice Commander

Warden began his assignment at Bitburg on June 25, 1986. In an interview with the *Bitburg Skyblazer* shortly after his arrival Warden emphasized that a wing consisted of far more than fighter pilots at the sharp end of operations: "every member of the wing and the tenant organizations plays a critical role in the success of the mission. It is like the old adage—'for want of a nail, the shoe was lost. . . .' The guys flying the F-15s are like the knights on the horse, but somebody first has to put the horseshoes on the horse."[1] Col. Peter D. Robinson, the wing commander at the Thirty-sixth TFW when Warden arrived, agreed wholeheartedly; in fact, he had spent much of his time ensuring that the wing thought in those terms.

Warden's duties included preparing for inspections and exercises, dealing with the paperwork that found its way to the command section, and representing the wing commander whenever needed. Inspections obviously represented nothing new, as he had dealt with them both at Eglin and at Moody, but European air bases at the time underwent two types of major inspections: NATO Tactical Evaluations (TACEVALs) and USAFE ORIs. The timing of the two tended to coincide, creating an enormous challenge. Although the criteria were the same, the assessment results often differed for two reasons: the two inspection teams did not coordinate their activities well and they had different priorities. Thus, in preparing for no-notice inspections, commanders assigned to Europe had to march to two different drummers simultaneously. During Robinson's first inspection the two out-briefings had diverged so dramatically that he felt compelled to apologize to the wing for the disparity.[2]

Warden was aware of the dilemma, but he had confidence in his team. The first ORI took place on October 14–20, 1986, less than three months after Warden arrived. The wing scored "Excellent" on the initial response and "Satisfactory" in combat employment, survival to operate, and alert force readiness.[3] USAFE had lifted its prohibition on using Red Teams—a simulated enemy assigned to test security arrangements—and Warden had managed to reintegrate U.S. Special Forces and the Royal Air Force "Intruder force" into the wing's base-defense training program.[4] The ultra-light aircraft that the assistant director of operations, Col. Richard Maki, had introduced allowed for immediate and accurate airfield damage assessment, and previous training with the Intruders and special forces had clearly strengthened the base's defensive capability.[5] Col. Emery M. Kiraly, who led the TACEVAL team, was immensely impressed with Robinson and gave the wing a glowing report; Robinson, in turn, gave Warden much of the credit.[6]

The reports and statistics for the Thirty-sixth TFW show that Warden did what USAFE expected from a vice commander, that he was ahead of his time in his ability to use a personal computer, and that he had a special interest in war-gaming exercises. Robinson remembers Warden as "a loyal, responsible and creative subordinate who had the ability to think conceptually," but also as someone who did not always accept "the limits of his own authority."[7] He noted that Warden could be very persistent when he had set his mind to something, but that he did not lose his drive, focus, and determination when told his ideas could not be put into practice. According to Col. George K. Muellner, the director of operations, Warden's strength as a vice commander was that he thought deeply about the operational art of air power and encouraged younger officers to view their profession in those terms.[8] It was evident to all of his colleagues that Warden enjoyed discussing strategy and that he had a strong interest in modern and ancient military campaigns. During his early months at Bitburg he received the call sign "Genghis," an obvious reference to Genghis Khan, "the emperor of all emperors."

Warden observed that the fighter pilots had retained the competitive drive that he had witnessed during his initial training in the late sixties and early seventies. The fighter pilot culture of the mid-1980s was multifaceted; many believed that the three most important criteria were flying skills, flight discipline, and unit cohesion. According to USAF historian C. R. Anderegg:

> A fighter pilot who was adept at maneuvering and controlling his jet was said to be a "good stick" or to have "good hands." Those who were less adept were referred to as "ham fists" or "hamburgers." Every fighter pilot aspired to be the best in the squadron. The highest compliment was to say a pilot was a good stick . . . Ones with good hands usually presented an air of humility, but beneath the humble exterior roiled competitive souls who viewed any losing effort as abject failure . . . The attitude was, "I am good, and I know it. I can learn anything quickly and well. There is no challenge too great, and no task I cannot master. I prefer that you teach me, but if you will not or cannot teach me, then I will teach myself. I seek only one reward: someday someone will say of me, 'good hands.'"[9]

Although he did not fly as often as some commanders, Warden used the opportunity at Bitburg to upgrade himself as an F-15 flight leader and as a mission commander. He completed the program without difficulty and was accredited as a mission-ready F-15 pilot. Interviews with contemporaries reveal that he was considered a "competent pilot": he did not receive the ultimate compliment of being known as a "good stick," but neither was he thought to have "ham fists." His year as vice commander passed without controversy, but it proved to be the calm before the storm.

A two-star general had warned Donnelly that it would not be in USAFE's best interest to assign Warden wing command responsibilities, but the four-star remained certain that Warden would perform outstandingly well.[10] He had great confidence in Warden and expected him to practice long-range missions, make sure the squadrons were able to launch *en masse* and, most important of all, test the approach of using F-15s in big-wing formations. By contrast, when it became known that Warden would be the next wing commander, TAC sent an officer to Bitburg with the unofficial mandate of "keeping an eye on the colonel."[11]

Warden's own ambitions were clear: he would provide the Thirty-sixth TFW and USAFE with a proven concept of operations for fighting in superior numbers and winning. He was convinced that the practice of pitting small numbers of highly capable fighters like the F-15 against very large numbers of enemy bombers and fighters was a recipe for disaster. In addition, he planned to improve the professionalism of pilot officers, paying special attention to making them more familiar with military history and encouraging them to view themselves as officers as well as pilots. His time as vice commander, combined with his previous operational experience and theoretical studies, gave him faith in these objectives, and he was convinced that many other areas would benefit from systematic consideration. The wing was in good shape, but he believed there was room for improvement; where the old aphorism advises "if it ain't broke, don't fix it," Warden adhered to "if it isn't broken, look harder."

Controversial Wing Commander

On August 13, 1987, Warden assumed full responsibility for seventy-two F-15s and some five thousand personnel. According to the job description, the wing commander

> commands and directs administration, training, and employment of the 36th Tactical Fighter Wing, whose primary mission is to prepare for and conduct air superiority operations. Commands three tactical flying squadrons. Coordinates staff activities pertaining to administration, operation, intelligence, materiel, comptroller, planning, and programming to assure accomplishment of mission. Monitors and directs tactical flying activities. Administers flying safety program. Flies and participates directly in unit combat employment exercises to ensure combat effectiveness and to evaluate performance, equipment, tactics, and techniques. Is a mission ready F-15 pilot.[12]

It was evident from the outset that the new commander had devoted considerable thought to many issues and that he planned to make many changes in a short period of time. At his staff meeting on his first day in office, an occasion normally confined to a mere exchange of niceties, Warden presented a list of projects that he believed the wing should implement. The meeting lasted several hours, as the officers reviewed administrative and operational matters in detail. Over the next month Warden refined and expanded these ideas. Under the credo "we trust people" he identified eight core values: emphasize quality, reward good work, venerate the customer, debureaucratize, decentralize, create teams, be honest, and reduce regulations. He then listed twelve focal points: base appearance, communications, maintenance, medical care, operations, post office, quality of life, resource management, safety, security, services, and survival and reconstitution. From these eight core values and twelve focal points he derived ninety-three initiatives, complete with titles, descriptions, and allocations of responsibilities, which he published in an eighteen-page memorandum issued on September 27, 1987. The introduction stated:

> Over the last month, we have discussed a number of goals and projects which will help the wing move toward new horizons in efficiency, quality

of life, customer service, job satisfaction, operational effectiveness, and ability to carry the battle to the enemy should we be called upon to do so. What follows in the next pages is the result of the many discussions we have had on the goals and the projects.

Think of this as a campaign plan for the coming years. This plan, like any good plan, does not tell people how to do their job, nor does it attempt to lay out everything that the wing will be doing for the next twelve months. Rather, it provides the tone of our operations and highlights those projects we have corporately agreed will keep the wing growing. And grow we must! The world is too tough and too competitive to permit anything or anybody to rest on the laurels won in bygone years. The commercial grave yards of the world are filled with companies that stopped growing because they thought they had found perfection. Perfection is illusionary; it is valid for a fleeting second before someone else develops something even better. The company, country, or military unit that does not grow, that does not search everyday for a better way to get the job done, is doomed. Let us lead the way in growth and innovation.

Some of these projects will take years to reach fruition. Others we have already begun. Some will take money not currently available, and others will require us to establish new priorities. While we are working out the new priorities, I ask everyone to pursue each of these goals and projects aggressively and as ardently as your personal resources will permit. Please also make sure that none of your own projects conflicts with the thrust of this campaign plan. The projects part of this plan is organized alphabetically by project name. At the end of each description, you will find the organization or organizations primarily responsible for it.[13]

Warden declared that he wanted his wing to be the best in USAFE: an objective that could become reality if the leadership worked with a clear vision related to operations and to the quality of life on the base. The initiatives included administrative matters such as "Christmas decoration" (project 11), "promotion ceremonies" (project 58), "snow removal" (project 71) and "street and building names" (project 75) as well as operational elements that dealt with the "flying schedule" (project 35), "mass launch" (project 46), and the "Red game plan" (project 60). He distributed the list to the entire wing so that everybody would have a broad picture of the commander's intent.

Although Warden had discussed several of these projects with some of the command staff, the list that he presented surprised superiors and subordinates alike. The number of projects affecting each individual was smaller than it seemed, and many of the projects would not consume much time, but many in the wing perceived them as overload. While the value of each project was debatable, most agreed that each had its merits—it was just that the amount was disheartening. More important, many in the wing felt alienated because they had not been involved in the decisions. To make matters worse, Warden promulgated the list of changes and later added other tasks without consulting his staff, which led to both confusion and resistance. Warden also failed to identify the priorities among the projects. These contextual issues, rather than the substance of each project, meant that the list was ridiculed—and the wing commander with it.[14]

OPERATIONAL ISSUES AND DOCTRINE
Warden was determined to improve what he saw as conceptual flaws and inadequacies in the wing's approach to warfighting, insisting that willingness to take some tactical and operational risks was essential to better prepare for war. In fact, he thought it negligence of duty not to push new ideas. Specifically, he wanted to demonstrate large-formation tactics at the wing level and use the results to convince NATO to change its doctrine regarding air defense and air superiority. Since European Command, USAFE, and the Thirty-sixth TFW in Bitburg had nothing resembling an air campaign plan that he considered sufficiently offense-oriented, he set out to develop one. Believing that this accorded with Donnelly's intentions, he established exercises and daily training that focused on high-altitude ingress, long-range missions, and big-wing tactics in the form of large packages of fighter aircraft deployed *en masse* to attack and destroy Warsaw Pact air power.[15] In his view:

> The operational commander's duty is to ensure that he masses superior forces at a particular time and place. That he is inferior in the theater does not relieve him of this duty. In fact, it is the essence of generalship . . . What counts is the numbers when the two forces meet in actual battle . . . Practice is a necessity. So is creating the mind set of "fight in superior numbers and win." The fighter pilot has a tendency to plunge bravely into the fray, but such action can be wrong. Audacity may lead to defeat . . . The political slogan of "fighting outnumbered and winning" has no place at the operational level of war.[16]

Warden wanted to do with F-15s what he had previously done with F-4s, and since the mission of the Thirty-sixth TFW was air-to-air rather than air-to-ground operations, he concluded that he would not face the inspection problems that he had experienced at Moody. Warden still maintained that although the Warsaw Pact outnumbered NATO on a theater basis, the alliance would not necessarily be outnumbered at a tactical level—provided NATO applied the principles of mass and concentration of effort in terms of large wing formations. He stated that within a year the Thirty-sixth TFW should develop the capability to launch the entire wing for "mass combat missions," and told his pilots that they should assume that a combat wing formation consisted of fifty-six aircraft. The goal was to launch the aircraft for defensive as well as offensive operations in the minimum time and with minimum communications. On a separate, but related, issue Warden wanted to be able to scramble the entire wing in the event of a crisis, rather than merely a few aircraft.

The squadrons immediately responded that this was impossible: such a formation would be too dangerous because of likely midair collisions and would be too difficult to lead and control. They argued that the essence of air-to-air combat was the ability to react swiftly to enemy action and that such huge formations would take too long to redirect on short notice. Warden's knowledge of the controversy over the Battle of Britain, and of the actions of Air Marshals Hugh Dowding and Trafford Leigh-Mallory, enabled him to refute most of the arguments and reinforce his suggested approach. He often referred to his book:

> for the side for which the force ratios become more favorable, loss rates will fall more than the ratios would indicate. The change in loss rates, either positive or negative, is not linear; it is exponential. Furthermore, no point of diminishing returns for the larger force seems to exist. That is, the larger the force gets, the fewer losses it suffers, and the greater losses it imposes on its opponent.[17]

Warden's insistence on huge modern fighter force formations in Europe was unprecedented, and skeptics became opponents when he added that he disagreed with the established view that NATO would necessarily be on the defensive in the first days of a European air war.

To begin practicing the new techniques he insisted that at least a third of the wing participate in an air-to-air exercise scheduled for November 1987 in Incirlik, Turkey. He received approval from higher command, including the added funds for the deployment. Warden chose flight commander Maj. Frank Gorenc as his project officer, and the two worked closely together to make the exercise possible. Gorenc, a future brigadier general, found it an overwhelming logistical task simply to bring the aircraft into theater and back, let alone get them airborne in large formations. He recalled that the initiative encountered considerable opposition from his peers, but that Warden had a clear idea of the objectives and inspired him to work out the details of coordinating the exercise. When they could find no units willing to play the Red Team, Warden told Gorenc to arrange for the wing to play both sides. Gorenc was impressed by Warden's unambiguous commitment to an entirely new initiative, and recalled that Warden was always a step ahead and held the course no matter how vehement the opposition.[18]

QUALITY OF LIFE

Challenging the flying community stirred up professional controversy, but much of the criticism eventually directed against Warden related not to his operational ideas, but to administrative issues. To improve the quality of life on the base Warden wanted to improve postal services and the accessibility of medical care (in accordance with the command surgeon's goal). He encouraged his airmen to develop better nutritional habits and was thoroughly convinced that physical fitness produced mental alertness and readiness. Despite the fallout he had encountered from some of his men in Italy, he insisted that officers "participate in a physical training program during duty hours at least three days each week" and that all other personnel be given time to exercise.

Warden had long felt that fighter pilots identified first and foremost with being pilots, and only second with being military officers. He believed this created an atmosphere of selectiveness and even snobbery, and although it promoted bonding at the fighter squadron level, it hobbled team building for the wing as a whole and for the air force as an organization. The attitude of some pilots almost undermined discipline and respect for the profession. Warden therefore sought wider integration of the pilots into the rest of the wing. To promote this he reduced the flying day to six hours on at least three out of five days a week and encouraged pilots to wear flight suits only when they were flying a mission. He also offended most officers by insisting that they follow the official dress code for the officers' club, which required a coat and tie after 1600, rather than the customary Wranglers, flight suits, or fatigues. He was merely enforcing a USAFE rule with which he agreed, but the result was contrary to his intent: many officers decided to use one of the three squadrons' own clubs or simply to head home, in effect boycotting the officers' club.

Warden also introduced a formal promotion ceremony, with sabers down, at the flight commander level. While the air force sometimes held a ceremony when an officer became a squadron commander, Warden believed that formalizing the promotion at the next level down would increase the new commander's sense of responsibility. Some appreciated the additional attention given to the event, but others found the ceremony unnecessary and burdensome. Objectives such as "have best looking fighters in the Tactical Air Force" also became an easy target for jokes.

The most controversial change that Warden implemented was to abandon reserved parking spaces—an action he had taken to remedy a serious parking problem on the base. Warden had studied the issue and believed the existing system had two problems: it identified one person as more important than another, and at any given time many of the reserved spaces were vacant because of shift arrangements, holidays, or temporary work outside the base. He therefore directed his staff to implement the change immediately. He did not consider the issue complicated or highly significant: the new system would simply reward those who came to work early and offer "equal opportunity." Col. Jeffrey G. Cliver, his vice commander, told him in private that he might want to reconsider his decision because it would stir up emotions unnecessarily,[19] but Warden had made up his mind and would not be swayed from his position. Not surprisingly, non-commissioned officers resented losing their privileges overnight without any explanation, and so did senior officers, who had become used to the convenience of parking close to building entrances in a windy and rainy part of Europe.[20]

Within a few weeks of taking command Warden also angered the church community by turning down a proposal to renovate the chapel. As he saw it, fewer than two hundred people attended services, the building presented no safety problems, and the funds would benefit more people if used for other purposes. This decision, insignificant for many, provoked opposition among a group that had supported his decisions about parking spaces and dress codes. Moreover, many of these actions were not among the original ninety-three initiatives, adding to the sense that the new commander would constantly and arbitrarily impose new rules.

Finally, Warden wanted to provide home mail delivery for on-base families and establish one-day service for local mail, which would make Bitburg's system the best in USAFE. The headquarters reluctantly accepted Warden's proposal, but the first weeks went badly: no system had been worked out for the delivery routes, the apartment buildings did not yet have individual mailboxes, and mail simply disappeared. Some even objected that their mail was no longer private because letters were placed in open mailboxes. People began to grumble about the new system even before it had been fully implemented. A project intended to make life easier for air force spouses instead produced frustration—in another group that had welcomed his previous initiatives.

All these elements, not devastating individually, came together early in Warden's tenure. Cliver later noted that the problem arose because Warden "told airmen to do things without telling them why, and he would not necessarily inform their bosses about the changes, nor necessarily bring it up at staff meetings."[21] The wing believed that their commander made decisions without consulting others and that there was no consensus behind his initiatives. Most military officers try to anticipate their superior's wishes, but with Warden "the status quo was always in flux."[22]

The opposition that formed during those initial weeks solidified, and Warden was caught in a vicious cycle where many of his actions were automatically questioned or derided. For example, USAFE ordered each of its wings to arrange a "safety day"—a mandatory stand-down. Warden's approach was to gather officers and men at one of the main buildings and give a pep talk from its roof-top. He described the wing's purposes and how its mission related to the overall international situation; how the wing could perform exceptionally well if it fol-lowed a few rules of thumb; and how it should deal with safety requirements. The topic was a serious one and he delivered the speech well, but a few members of the audience found it strange to have their commander address them from the top of a building; he seemed detached from the rest of the group.[23] In Warden's view, most people found "safety days" to be boring and predictable: if people were to benefit from the time investment, something about the event had to be different and memorable. To give the occasion extra flair he had invited cheer-leaders to entertain the crowd; this, too, was poorly received by a few, as some of the dyed-in-the-wool traditionalists in his audience believed that it turned the occasion into a circus. People, of course, remember a circus.

A firm belief in his mission, combined with sheer willpower, energized Warden, but a few members of the wing viewed the actions that seemed to have an impact on them with suspicion. Warden was to some degree aware of the dissension, but believed it represented a relatively small group that would be won over as they began to see the advantages. Preoccupied with the big picture of what needed to be done, he nevertheless underestimated the importance of the seemingly trivial interpersonal niceties necessary to create synergy in the wing. That Warden had not served as a squadron commander and not attended the prestigious Fighter Weapon School at Nellis AFB might have raised questions about his credibility. Some may also have been jealous of a fast-burner with an obvious four-star patron.

OFFICIAL DOUBTS

In fact, Warden no longer had high-level support: Donnelly might have given him the necessary vote of confidence, but he had retired five months before Warden became wing commander. In May 1987 Gen. William L. Kirk replaced Donnelly as the European commander in chief, and although the two generals respected one another, they had very different leadership philosophies. While Donnelly was an open and well-respected leader who enjoyed extravaganza, Kirk had established a solid reputation as a premier tactician and first-rate pilot; few, if any, questioned his knowledge of operational matters and his ability to com-mand. Donnelly treasured his relationships with senior military officers and dip-lomats and the social gatherings that brought them together, and often hosted congressmen and foreign leaders alike to discuss procurement and policy, whereas Kirk was quintessentially the "operator's operator." He had shot down two MiG aircraft and was generally known for having "revolutionized the way air power used electronic warfare during Vietnam."[24] At the Pentagon he had implemented the Top Secret "Teaball" project that developed a system for detecting and identifying enemy aircraft.[25] During his second Pentagon tour he played a critical role in creating the Aggressor Squadrons, which greatly improved the Red Flag exercises, and as deputy chief of staff for operations at USAFE from July 1982 to July 1985 he initiated the Warrior Preparation Center.[26] He had then replaced Lieutenant General Piotrowski as the commander of the Ninth Air Force. Now he had returned to Germany for what would be his last assignment before retirement.[27]

When Kirk took up his new duties he knew little about Warden other than that Donnelly had nominated him as the next wing commander of the Thirty-sixth TFW. Kirk read Warden's efficiency reports and discussed the candidacy with Lt. Gen. Thomas G. McInerney, who had replaced Lt. Gen. Carl H. Cathey as USAFE vice commander in September 1986. In that position McInerney acted as the point of contact for most wing commanders who wanted to communicate with higher headquarters. McInerney had discussed air power with Warden on several occasions; he thought favorably of big-wing tactics and held the colonel in high esteem.[28] Others with whom Kirk talked were less complimentary, but nothing of substance emerged to make Kirk countermand the appointment.

A few weeks into Warden's tenure General Kirk flew to Bitburg to visit his new wing commander. Warden gave him a windshield tour of the base in the commander's car, and Kirk liked what he saw until they headed toward the officers' mess. Kirk noticed that they circled the building several times, searching for a parking space, and he asked Warden why there was no reserved space for the commander. Warden responded that he viewed the wing as a team where no one had special privileges. Kirk was appalled: the notion of equality was ideologically commendable, but when it was taken to such extremes he considered it counter to military practice, resulting in loss of respect for senior officers and men. As it happened, the day was rainy and Warden had to leave the general at the entrance for several minutes while he parked. He later provided Kirk with the "commander's brief," in which he proclaimed his vision for the Thirty-sixth TFW and his view of how it related to the overall missions of USAFE and the air force. Kirk acknowledged his broad perspective and positive attitude, and appreciated most of what he heard about operations, training, and tactics, but he also noticed what he considered "a number of strange ideas about how to approach warfare." Some were "at odds with long accepted NATO doctrine" and others were a bit "academician" in nature.[29] When he left the base he was apprehensive about some of the changes that Warden suggested, but he told Warden only to "fix that parking space thing."[30]

When Kirk returned to his headquarters he was unsure what to make of this wing commander. He believed that he was "bright with exceptional forward looking abilities," but that his operational concepts might be too aggressive compared to NATO's established mission of air defense: he suspected that Warden did not show sufficient respect for proven and accepted doctrinal elements that could not be changed overnight in the sensitive cold war era.[31] Besides, Kirk did not see it as a wing commander's job to think of NATO strategy and new tactics; the wing commander was supposed to focus on the execution of plans and concepts given to him by higher command. But this Kirk could live with. His biggest concern was Warden's leadership style.

The USAFE inspector general was receiving complaints from Bitburg and the USAFE chief master sergeant told Kirk that the enlisted men were deeply unhappy at the changes being forced upon them. In their view, they had lost privileges, had new routines imposed on them, and had to work far harder than before without understanding why. Rumors about flight suits, fatigues, and strict dress codes added to Kirk's doubts. It seemed that Warden's authority was being questioned by the very men he was supposed to lead—an unacceptable situation for the premier F-15 wing. The two met next at the commander's conference in Ramstein, but Kirk did not inform Warden that he was concerned about the Thirty-sixth TFW. However, his skepticism was reinforced when he returned to Bitburg for a second visit shortly afterwards: Warden had not "fixed the parking space thing" to his satisfaction, although he had modified it. If he could not trust his wing commander in such minor matters, how could he trust him on larger issues?[32]

Reports from his deputy chief of staff for operations, Maj. Gen. Robert L. Rutherford, and his deputy chief of staff for plans and programs, Brig. Gen. Buster C. Glosson, only reinforced Kirk's concerns.[33] Glosson had recently been assigned to Moody, where he first replaced Colonel McCoy as the vice commander and then Colonel Hermes as wing commander, and had received the impression that Warden had performed poorly as director of operations.[34] Kirk told Glosson to visit the base and report what he saw. Warden gave Glosson the wing presentation, which included the initiatives under way. Glosson raised no objections to any of the ideas, and before going to one of the squadrons to fly he very explicitly told Warden that he was there just to fly, that he had always hated higher headquarters spies, and that whatever he saw at Bitburg would stay at Bitburg, although he would certainly tell Warden as a matter of courtesy if he saw anything that needed to be addressed. However, Glosson returned to the headquarters and reported that he was unimpressed with Warden's command.[35]

Part of the difficulty was that while complaints found their way to the inspector general, compliments did not. Many of Warden's initiatives had produced indisputable benefits. For example, because jet exhaust had blackened the aircraft shelters, Warden arranged to have the walls sandblasted and painted white, which improved the working environment considerably. Bitburg's self-service store for individual equipment, such as boots, gloves, and other personal gear, also an innovation at the time, was applauded and even featured in a Pentagon newsletter; Warden calculated that it reduced waiting times for personal items by over 50 percent.[36] Warden also arranged for an extensive system of television monitors that gave decision makers real-time oversight of the flight line and the hangars. This improved coordination between primary and secondary command posts during exercises, and helped security police and the fire department to respond to real incidents. He oversaw upgrades to physical fitness equipment and made real progress in enhancing base appearance. Even the parking situation and the mail system improved after the initial problems.

However, convinced that Warden's strengths did not lie in commanding a fighter wing, but rather in strategic planning, Kirk initiated a personnel action to have him transferred to the Air Staff.[37] He called upon Maj. Gen. Richard M. Pascoe, the Seventeenth Air Force Commander, to whom the Thirty-sixth TFW reported, and told him to inform Warden of the change of plans. Pascoe had visited Warden's base on several occasions, and although he saw potential trouble spots the situation had not worried him.[38] He and Kirk had never discussed Warden's record as a wing commander, and Pascoe seems to have received the impression that Warden was being reassigned because his expertise was needed elsewhere. In early November Pascoe told Warden that he would soon be sent to the Pentagon because an important project needed his attention. Warden was unconcerned at the time; he was told that he would lead the wing's huge air-to-air exercise in Turkey before signing out, and as far as he knew Kirk had voiced no major objections to his command. Indeed, the move was presented to him as one that would increase his chances for promotion.[39]

Interestingly, the exercise at Incirlik scored a tremendous success and vindicated Warden's advocacy of big-wing formations. Warden succeeded in testing some of his important ideas: twenty-four F-15 aircraft flew in an air superiority formation, and the pilots who participated in the exercise saw the advantages immediately.[40] Typically, the formation operated at 20,000 to 40,000 feet against simulated enemy aircraft. The exercise had required considerable coordination, but those who took part were overwhelmed, and many who had initially protested now asserted that the air force should have taken this approach a long time ago. Several officers later commented that this exercise had played a major role in the wing's success in the Gulf War several years later.[41]

In retrospect, the controversy over big-wing formations seems odd. Big strike packages had been used in Vietnam, but a decade after U.S. troops withdrew from Southeast Asia such an approach was simply not even considered in the European theater, where operational change was glacial at best. The Bitburg wing had been performing tactical air defense missions for decades and no one had thought much about whether the basic concept might be fatally flawed in the face of a large Soviet attack. Lt. Col. William R. Looney III, who was poised to take over as the Twenty-second Tactical Fighter Squadron commander at Bitburg and who later became a four-star general, characterized Warden's contribution to large formations as "ground-breaking." In his view, Warden was the first to provide the intellectual insight and courage to execute the concept in Europe: as far as the F-15 was concerned, "the massing in the air started with Warden at Incirlik."[42] Looney praised Warden for having the vision to go beyond the confines of accepted doctrine and the tenacity to implement his ideas despite misgivings and reluctance from all levels. Maj. Frank Gorenc, Warden's project officer, who would later fly F-15s in Desert Storm, also insisted that Warden had prepared the air force for the big-wing formation concept that first manifested itself in combat in 1991 and then found its way into U.S. doctrine. At a time when the air force thought in terms of two-ships, or four-ships at best, Warden had stood up against opposition and had the vision and courage to explore new territory.[43] His allocation of air assets based on boxes five miles wide and five miles deep was innovative, and he used the opportunity to have the wing practice high-altitude ingress as well. After the exercise Warden arranged awards for those who had participated and morale at Bitburg peaked.

During the same timeframe, November 16–23, Bitburg underwent USAFE's Unit Effectiveness Inspection. The wing received the overall rating of "Satisfactory": within the twenty-six areas tested it received two "Outstanding," eight "Excellent," fifteen "Satisfactory," and one "Marginal" (social actions).[44] Warden was gratified: he had successfully introduced a new concept and the wing had met the conventional measurement criteria.

A Stigma of Failure

With the exercise behind him, Warden tried to learn more about his next assignment. He soon realized that his new position was far down in the chain of command and that there was no hint of urgency about his taking the job: Lt. Gen. Harley A. Hughes, chief of Plans and Operations, did not even know that he was coming.[45] The assignment was definitely not a step toward flag rank, since he would only have the responsibilities of a division chief. Warden was puzzled; he called McInerney, who told him the truth. It was Kirk's last tour, he wanted it to end quietly, and he was uncomfortable with Warden's "rocking the boat" and experimenting with a range of new ideas at his most important U.S. base in Europe. Thus, Kirk had basically decided to have him removed as a wing commander.

It was not unusual for wing commanders to be relieved of commanding duties,[46] but it should be noted that Warden was not "removed for cause": the wing had experienced no accidents during his tenure and he was not regarded as irresponsible. Most telling of all, he was encouraged and allowed to take a third of the wing to Turkey for a very unusual exercise. No MEI, ORI, or TACEVAL took place during his tenure as wing commander and, with the exception of one internal exercise in which the wing scored "Marginal," no local exercises or unit effectiveness reports received lower grades than "Satisfactory." The monthly USAFE readiness statistics for the period indicated no problems, and the mission-capable rates fluctuated between 78 and 84 percent. The number of non-judicial punishments was unremarkable: according to the USAFE History Office, "none of the statistical scores or inspection ratings indicates that Colonel Warden performed below standard."[47]

Although many generals who knew about his actions questioned Warden's leadership, there was no widespread feeling that his performance was so poor that it required reassignment. His immediate superior, Major General Pascoe, seemed supportive of Warden throughout the period, stating that he "conceived, developed and validated squadron size air superiority formations" and that he had "broad knowledge of air power employment from details to international impact." Moreover, "during exercises, major inspections, and while hosting dignitaries, he is the prime source of stability," being "rational and calm in all endeavors": Warden "maintains professional demeanor through positive attitude." The report indicated that the wing became more responsive and more capable during Warden's tenure. McInerney, Kirk's vice commander, agreed with Pascoe's assessment and had personally received a favorable impression when he visited the wing.[48] Thus, while Warden doubtless realized that there were elements of tension in the wing that needed to be fixed, he genuinely believed that he had the overall support of the senior leadership. His efficiency reports, written after the reassignment, stated the following:

> Colonel Warden has made extraordinary improvements in every area of his wing. An innovator without parallel, he has conceived and created procedures and techniques unique in the Air Force in areas as diverse as mobility, individual equipment issue, intelligence debriefing, postal service, command and control, and tactics. He has improved quality of life markedly. He has brightened his base, instituted massive recognition programs, started perhaps the biggest self-help project in the command, and engendered a wonderful and pervasive sense of pride. Morale is at a new high at Bitburg—and it shows in such areas as maintenance where aircraft mission capable rates are the highest they have been. In the operation area, he conceived, tested, and validated tactics that add significant new forces to the NATO arsenal. He also developed and began installation of a base-wide

television system that promises to make combat command far easier and more effective. One of the most capable officers in the Air Force, he is more than ready to take on the higher command and staff positions.[49] [Major General Pascoe]

Colonel Warden has worked extraordinary results at Bitburg in a remarkably short period of time. He has grasped the essence of the CINC's desire to improve quality of life, and in place after place has created model programs. He wrote the proposal that has put the post office under wing control—and then put his post office in the forefront of service to the customer. I toured the self service individual equipment issue he created—and wondered why it had not been done years ago across the Air Force. Customer service, base appearance, tactics, and quality of life have blossomed under his command. His potential is unlimited.[50] [Lieutenant General McInerney]

Colonel Warden has made significant contributions to this command and to NATO. Seeing the opportunity to combine the principles of mass and concentration with the technological superiority of the F-15, he led a third of his wing to Turkey where he developed and validated the procedures needed to make his idea a reality. The result was a major step forward in the employment of fighter aircraft. He is unquestionably an outstanding tactician. I agreed to curtail his tour—and did so only because his new position is so important. Move him to higher responsibilities as quickly as possible.[51] [General Kirk]

Such reports, of course, cannot be taken literally. Reviewers tried to avoid putting condemnation in print; much of the real meaning lay between the lines; what was not committed to paper was often more important than what was; and the language contained specific "codes" that readers had to understand. Warden's report seems to have been intentionally vague: Pascoe did not provide statistics to back up the achievements he cites, McInerney focused on administrative rather than mission command issues, and Kirk does not mention Warden's leadership capabilities—these all could be interpreted as warning signals. Kirk's statement that his tour was cut short because "his new position is so important" probably harmed Warden, since it mentioned no specifics; in any case, no position could be more important than commanding the premier F-15 wing in the air force. Moreover, being labeled an "innovator" might not have been helpful. What appeared on the surface to be positive comments may actually have damned Warden by the absence of praise for certain key qualities and achievements.

Ultimately, Warden was reassigned because Kirk had a different philosophy of how to run a wing, and it was his prerogative and duty to act upon his best judgment. As Kirk saw it, the reports he received indicated problems, and although the individual incidents were minor, they were too many for a leader who did not favor rapid change. Kirk concluded that Warden did not instill confidence and that his demonstrated leadership showed major deficiencies.[52]

Some contend that Warden should have recognized the dangers, been more accommodating and more flexible, and avoided interfering with well-established routines. In fact, Warden did not undertake his changes merely to make a point and his reasons seemed so obvious to him that he did not consider his actions radical—or understand why anyone else should. To him, the ninety-three initiatives simply represented an attempt to formulate his commander's intent, but he seems to have ignored relative priorities and conveyed the impression that he considered all initiatives equally important. Added to this, he came across as someone who was convinced that he was right about most matters and he could be as stubborn about a peripheral issue as on a matter of global strategy.[53] It might be argued that Warden did not appreciate that he had to choose his battles. Unfortunately, the daily minutiae were what mattered most to many of his subordinates, and they perceived Warden as incapable of relating to their everyday concerns. This, in turn, marginalized the effectiveness of his beneficial contributions and his intellectual capabilities;[54] indeed, to a certain extent his self-assurance, intellect, and insight were perceived as intimidating.[55]

Fundamentally, Warden neglected the public relations dimension of his command. In retrospect it seems that he was unable to convince his subordinates and superiors that he had their best interests at heart: he had developed his ideas in isolation, he was convinced that he had the correct answers, and he lacked the patience to bring everybody else to the same conclusion.[56] His working methods and leadership style were diametrically opposed to the standard practices of the air force, and at no point in his career did this clash of cultures become more evident.

A successful assignment as wing commander was viewed as essential for officers destined for flag rank: a "make or break." The previous ten wing commanders at Bitburg had all seen promotion during or shortly after their tenure. Although Warden's report was confidential and very few had access to it, it did not escape notice that a promising wing commander had been removed from his post early and sent to a mediocre staff position. As a result, airmen throughout the USAF, particularly at Tactical Air Command, thenceforth came to regard Warden as a failed wing commander, and disparaging opinions, hypotheses, and anecdotes would follow him throughout his career. Many in the fighter community dismissed him as "an intellectual maverick who did not fit in."[57] Major General Smith, who admired Warden's grasp of theory and strategy, summed up why he believed things went wrong:

When he became a wing commander, he really ripped it in a number of senses. He tried to initiate major changes in a very short period of time, and it was so disruptive to the wing that the wing undercut him in many ways . . . I think he struggled within the fighter community. A lot of fighter pilots and fighter people see him more as a kind of intellectual and less as a kind of operational sweaty suit kind of a guy. When he is on track for something, he is very hard to move; very hard to move. That is an unfortunate quality. When you are a commander of people, you have got to be flexible . . . When you do change management, you should do it incrementally, not because you don't need to do things fast, but you need to bring the people along . . . That, I think, is a part of his personality that worked against him as a commander . . . I think a lot of people would say, "If you cannot succeed as a commander in a military service, then you do not deserve to move to higher positions," because that is the real test of leadership . . . I think some people can feel threatened by John Warden. John Warden is an intellectual giant. I mean, I love to interact with him, and sometimes he is dead wrong, but he is tough to take on because he is really well read and very thoughtful. He knows how to read, and he knows how to write, and he knows how to pull people together in certain ways. He has a lot of negative characteristics, but he is a "one in a generation" kind of individual, and some people are just intimidated by someone like that . . . When you really challenge some of the politics and doctrines that are well established within an institution, you are oftentimes considered to be not only wrong but disloyal. Maybe that explains some of the emotion and the heat relating to the Warden story.[58]

The Thirty-sixth TFW's history journal states that the change made Warden "available for further duties at the Pentagon,"[59] but a retired three-star general said it most succinctly: "It simply does not matter what happened—the fact is that the Air Force as an institution viewed Warden as a failed wing commander."[60]

His return from Bitburg represented the lowest point in Warden's career: he had been removed from an important wing commander position and assigned to an unimpressive staff job in the Pentagon. Warden registered the setback, and immediately began to look for a way out of the predicament.

7

AIR POWER THEORY: CREATION, LOSS, AND RECOVERY

Shortly after Warden returned to the Pentagon to take up an assignment that did not seem especially promising, Lt. Gen. Michael J. Dugan and Maj. Gen. Charles G. Boyd gave him a unique opportunity to rectify his personal situation. The two general officers discovered that Warden had the ability to advance ideas and concepts that would reinvigorate air force thinking by focusing on the operational art of war, air strategy, and the independent use of air power. With that mandate in mind, Warden was placed in charge of the Directorate of Warfighting Concepts in the summer of 1988. He created an intellectual atmosphere that encouraged the explicit linkage of air power as an instrument to national security objectives. In the process the divisions under his control conceived, developed, and promoted ideas that defied the air force's prevailing view of air power as an adjunct to ground forces.

Struggle for Power: SAC vs. TAC

Warden's new assignment at the Pentagon was to prepare for Constant Demo, an air base operability exercise scheduled for 1991. His task was to study the damage a Soviet attack would inflict on Bitburg Air Base and then suggest defensive measures that would improve the base's chances of survival. It seemed that the task envisioned a repetition of the Salty Demo exercise conducted at Spangdahlem Air Base in the spring of 1985, which had demonstrated the importance of concealment and deception in the face of a large-scale attack. The after-action report stated that even moderate air and ground attacks could dramatically reduce a wing's capability to generate sorties. Since then the air force had improved resilience at its air bases, but Warden maintained that the whole exercise missed the point: the key issue was not whether the Warsaw Pact could destroy one tactical fighter wing and its air base, but whether it could neutralize the entire command, control, and communications system in Central Europe by taking out several wings at the same time. He therefore insisted on broadening the scope of the exercise to include several bases so that preparations would focus on the operational aspects of a full air campaign waged against NATO. Warden was also adamant about another issue: if the objective was to neutralize seventy-two aircraft, the enemy could paralyze the entire wing by attacking the fuel system or the electrical system on which it depended. Thus, one or two bombs could make a crucial difference if the chain of resources were properly identified.

Constant Demo was an important project, but Warden received little attention until Dugan replaced Hughes as the deputy chief of staff for Plans and Operations on March 1, 1988.[1] Dugan supported Warden's proposal of enlarging the exercise, and as the two began to discuss the wider potential of air power, Dugan found Warden a kindred spirit. Although the air force was respected for its tactical, technological, and managerial skills, Dugan was concerned that it had lost its own identity and the unique contribution that the full range of air power could make to warfighting.[2] He believed that the creative air power thinking generated at the Air Corps Tactical School in the latter half of the 1930s had disappeared with the cold war, and that the reason stemmed largely from the rivalry between TAC and SAC.

SAC had gained the upper hand by 1954, when President Eisenhower defined Massive Retaliation as the national military strategy to counter the growing Soviet threat. Because SAC was responsible for nuclear-armed bombers and intercontinental ballistic missiles, as well as for air-to-air tankers, it was considered the prime force for fulfilling the mission of nuclear deterrence. Consequently, it received most of the funds, built a promotion system in the air force that favored its own, and came to view itself as the tip of the nuclear spear. Its powerful leader, Gen. Curtis E. LeMay, let it be known that he considered TAC and other parts of the air force of secondary importance.

When President Kennedy took office in 1961 he modified Massive Retaliation and adopted a policy of Flexible Response, which included the use of conventional forces and offered alternatives to total nuclear war. The change in national policy gave TAC an opportunity to demonstrate its relevance and its role gained momentum during the war in Vietnam. Many in the air force believed that strategic bombing had failed to deliver a decisive blow and viewed support of ground operations as air power's most useful contribution in Southeast Asia. If counterinsurgency were to be the mission of the future, SAC would become increasingly irrelevant.

After Vietnam the air force revised its doctrine and technology, and with it fighter pilots began to replace bomber pilots in the most important leadership positions. From 1978 to 1984 Gen. Wilbur Creech led TAC from being the junior to the senior partner. However, the army still played the dominant role, and when Creech became TAC commander he feared that unless TAC demonstrated its commitment to close air support the army would take over the mission, depriving TAC of many of its tactical aircraft and possibly its *raison d'être*. Rather than confront his army colleagues on the issue, or explore a division of responsibility that would meet the needs of both services, Creech sought close cooperation. He later recalled that it was of paramount importance to return to the "roots of supporting the army because we had really drifted away from that."[3] As he worked with the army, especially with Gen. Donn A. Starry at the Training and Doctrine Command (TRADOC), Creech came to believe that if TAC deferred to the army on close air support, the army would accept the importance of other missions, such as air superiority and interdiction. TAC and TRADOC established the Air Land Force Application Agency to formalize the relationship, and in the process Creech became a strong supporter of the AirLand Battle doctrine:

> The AirLand Battle was conceived as a very broad battlefield, including the air supremacy battle, the deep battle, and against follow-on forces; that is, air superiority and interdiction became newly important to the Army along with their traditional focus on close air support. And Air Force capabilities to wage that high battle and deep battle were not only acknowledged, those missions and the Air Force assets needed to carry them out were now strongly endorsed in the new doctrine. They became a matter of the concerns of both services and for both to champion in the joint arena . . . And that, in fact, happened. We got more support from the Army in those aspects than we ever had before.
>
> The Air Force has its own doctrinal warriors who play "Roland at the Pass" against any change in their traditional and largely parochial ways of thinking about air power and its application: but we gave up little, and it was all in the right cause. . . . we did agree that the joint commander, who usually is an Army general, could dictate when and where air power would be applied, but that was always the case anyway. We also agreed to give the Army ground commander a "stronger vote" and greater participation in the allocation of air, but not any kind of decision or allocation authority. And that was always a de facto fact of life as well. . . . Those Air Force naysayers were overcome as well, but it was neither a brief fight nor an easy one. This was a fight I took on with relish, because it has a decidedly better flavor to it than our previous go around with the Army during the Howze Board grasp to take over the entire mission from the Air Force.[4]

Thus, the concept of air power as a war-winning instrument had disappeared from the agenda. Moreover, it was perceived as a counter to the Goldwater-Nichols Department of Defense Reorganization Act of 1986. To reduce the interservice rivalry that supposedly undermined warfighting effectiveness, Goldwater-Nichols had placed a strong emphasis on joint activities. It centralized operational authority in the chairman of the Joint Chiefs of Staff rather than the individual service chiefs, and designated the chairman as the principal military advisor to the president, National Security Council, and secretary of defense. It also streamlined the operational chain of command from the president to the secretary of defense to the unified commanders, again at the expense of the individual services.

When Gen. Robert D. Russ became the commander of TAC in 1986 he took the emphasis on interservice cooperation very seriously, stating that "tactical aviators have two primary jobs—to provide air defense for the North American continent and support the Army in achieving its battlefield objectives."[5] He emphasized that the mission of tactical air forces was to support the army:

> Everything that tactical air does directly supports Army operations. Whether it is shooting down enemy airplanes, destroying a tank factory, attacking reinforcements or killing armor on the frontline, tactical air's objective is to give friendly ground forces the advantage on the battlefield . . . The Army tells us their scheme of maneuver and what effect upon the enemy they want us to create, we then provide the appropriate tactical air to achieve their objectives. Most recently, our discussions have focused on the need for both close air support and air interdiction/battlefield air interdiction on the lethal, dynamic battlefield of the 1990s as described in the AirLand Battle Doctrine.[6]

Creech and Russ had undoubtedly elevated the importance of TAC, and they contributed significantly to improving the air force's inventory of technologically superior weapons and its air-to-air tactics, but they had been unwilling to think of air power beyond the tactical level of war. TAC may have been so busy fighting for its institutional life from 1945 to 1975 that its leaders lacked both the inclination and the incentive to understand air power in its broadest sense. Yet the reduction of options for the conduct of national security strategy was perhaps the most damaging outcome of an organizational structure composed of separate baronies that viewed the scramble for funding, personnel, and systems as a zero-sum game.[7]

TAC spent considerable time on refining specific mission capabilities, such as close air support, interdiction, defensive counterair, and air refueling—capabilities that the air force could offer to a joint force commander. As an institution, however, TAC did not think in terms of a comprehensive air campaign that could achieve strategic objectives without resorting to nuclear means. Indeed, at the time there was no real debate on the employment of air power: TAC and the unified commands focused more on preparing air forces for deployment than on considering how to use the forces when they arrived, and SAC for its part tended to focus on the first few hours of attack without devoting much thought to operations that would last several days, or might be conducted by conventional means.

Thus, the air force of the late 1980s was a divided service that lacked an overarching and cohesive identity. Dugan believed that the SAC-TAC division had prevented air power from reaching its full potential: airmen understood tactics superbly, but very few thought in terms of a comprehensive and unitary campaign plan that could achieve strategic results. As deputy chief of staff for plans and operations, he was determined to change this mindset.

Project Air Power

Dugan found Warden's book, *The Air Campaign*, "original, refreshing, focused and easy to read"; he believed it expressed a coherent foundation for thinking about air power at the operational level of war. As the two officers began to discuss air power, Warden told Dugan that his experience at Bitburg indicated that neither the higher command at USAFE nor the tactical commands at the wing level thought about air power in terms of operational art. It was time, he argued, to start thinking beyond the tactical level of war. Dugan concluded that Warden had "an exceptionally good grasp of strategic thought," which he noted was "a rare commodity among airmen."[8] He decided to make the colonel his personal assistant and let somebody else take care of Constant Demo. Dugan then told Warden to write a position paper that described the purpose of the air force and how the service could improve itself.

Warden's response was "Project Air Power," formulated as a one-page memorandum suggesting why and how the air force could develop a coherent air power strategy that included an overall statement of its mission. He proposed that the air force establish a directorate that would allow him to develop, expand, and promote these ideas to the service, the Joint Staff, and the defense community at large.[9]

Dugan liked the assessment and directed Major General Boyd, who became the director of plans in May 1988, to implement the suggestions. Boyd soon agreed that the colonel was the right man to spearhead the effort to advocate for air power as the leading military instrument.[10] Although they did not view it in those terms, Dugan, Boyd, and Warden initiated a process that reinvigorated air force thinking about air strategy, the independent use of air power, and the operational art of war.[11]

In July 1988 Boyd appointed Warden as director of the Deputy Directorate for Warfighting Concepts (XOXW). The new directorate was staffed by approximately eighty officers assigned to five divisions: Doctrine (XOXWD), Strategy
(XOXWS), Requirements (XOXWR), Long-Range Planning (XOXWP), and
Concepts (XOXWC).[12] These divisions had strong connections with the Department of Defense, Congress, the national intelligence agencies, the Joint Staff,
and a range of think tanks. The directorate included officers from each of the
USAF's major commands, and in essence constituted the intellectual core of the
Air Staff. It was designed to give Warden maximum room to maneuver: he had
considerable latitude to focus on issues he considered important and he was given
a reasonable budget. From this base he could launch ideas and interact with the
larger military-political community in Washington.

Dugan, Boyd, and Warden defined the new directorate as a countervailing
force to the AirLand Battle concepts that had gained wide acceptance among the
leaders of TAC.[13] They recognized that air power should support surface forces in
certain circumstances, but they feared that if the air force did not begin to think
beyond tactical applications, the army would invariably play the deciding role
and compel the air force to conform to the army plan of action.[14] Warden even
asserted that the mission of the air force should not be "to fly and fight," but "fly
and win."[15] In early August he identified the goals for the new directorate:

1) Define the air force in terms the public can understand;
2) Develop a coherent theory for employment of air forces in support
of the military strategy that supports national goals. Explain the theory
simply and succinctly to policy makers and public alike;
3) Write doctrine consistent with theory, directed at war-fighting, exciting to read, and useful in action;
4) Build understanding across air staff and air force of operational level
of warfare through focused professional military education and multi-
media presentations;
5) Develop full range of operational level tools;
6) Link strategy, assessment of political, technological, and economic
trends to create force structure appropriate for next quarter century;
7) Institute programs within the deputy directorate which help members of the group broaden their knowledge and experience;
8) Think smart, think long.[16]

Warden then translated these goals into a core set of ideas: think about
strategy in offensive terms as opposed to static defense and attrition; think of air
power as a national instrument and not merely as tactical support for surface
forces; think in terms of effects rather than number of sorties and degree of

destruction; think about education and doctrine in terms of system warfare and campaign objectives rather than merely getting bombs on target; and think about how to organize the air force in order to accommodate the goals cited above.

In addressing his staff Warden insisted that "We are not responsible or beholden to TAC or SAC. Our charter is to think, and we can think any kind of thoughts that we want to think, and it is okay. In fact, that is what we are supposed to be doing."[17] In the immediate aftermath of the Goldwater-Nichols Act Warden also feared that joint operations had become an end in themselves. He therefore challenged his five divisions to contemplate air power in terms of what it was and what it could be, the reasons for using it, how and when to employ it, and how to sell it. He insisted that they were going to bring the air force "back into prominence."[18]

In keeping with his charter, and sheltered by his superiors, Warden encouraged discussions and tolerated dissent.[19] Dugan had recommended that all officers in the XO read *The Air Campaign*; Warden in turn encouraged his divisions to criticize and improve the book's arguments.[20] While *The Air Campaign* had formulated a coherent philosophy for the operational level of war, Warden now sought to define a theory for the strategic application of air power that in turn would serve as an intellectual underpinning for the air force mission. He made it clear that he expected his team to come up with ideas that the senior leadership would reject: "If ninety percent of the ideas are not sent back as unrealistic and even ridiculed, then we are not doing our job: our job is to keep pushing the envelope."[21]

Warden sought synergy between two groups: his own team and a few retired air force generals who he believed could advance the cause of new conceptual thinking. In a memorandum to the latter group, which included James Ahmann, Richard Lawson, and Perry Smith, he stated that "It strikes us that we are doing a disservice to the Nation by not capitalizing on all our capability and by not making sure that members of the defense community and the public at large know what the air force can offer an air-maritime power like the United States. We want to rectify the situation."[22]

Initially Warden and his ideas received only a cool reception from the majority of his staff. While most who worked in the directorate eventually came to appreciate him, some almost worshipping him for his vision and courage, they were not easy to win over: in the summer and autumn of 1988 he was perceived as engaging himself in projects outside his territory. The Strategy Division in particular, which was known for its "skunk works" and generally considered the intellectual javelin of the Air Staff, thought Warden too aggressive, too ambitious, and overly fixated on what air power could accomplish independently. Many of Warden's subordinates found it difficult to balance his views and intentions with the give-and-take considered necessary to implement closer cooperation with the army; they had grown used to thinking in terms of compromises to push programs through the system.[23] Several also disagreed with his belief in the strategic role of air power, and some expressed skepticism about what had become his perhaps most cherished notion: the Five Rings Model.

The Five Rings Model

Warden had articulated the basic idea for centers of gravity in *The Air Campaign*, and many of the arguments echoed those of the Air Corps Tactical School, but by the summer of 1988 he arrived at a much more reasoned concept. In an essay called "Global Strategy Outline," he provided an air power theory, created a framework for planning, and developed an alternative force structure with implications for both professional military education and air force doctrine.

Warden portrayed the enemy as a system with certain centers of gravity, suggested that air power could be the most effective instrument for changing the system into one that met U.S. objectives, and asserted that adversaries would make concessions when they realized the heavy cost of continuing a war. He returned to the fundamental issues of defining the objectives of war and then developing a strategy that would fulfill those objectives in the most cost-effective manner. In the process he drew a high-level picture that defined the centers of gravity, concluding that a nation-state could be defined in terms of five "Strategic Rings":

> For a modern state to wage modern war, it must have a command structure at the civil and military levels to give it direction; it must have (or have access to) the industrial facilities needed for war production; it must have an infrastructure capable of providing for internal distribution, transportation and communication; it must have a populace capable of supplying soldiers and workers—not actively opposed to the war effort—and the agricultural system needed to feed itself; and it must have fielded military forces. These elements can be thought of as concentric circles with the innermost being the most critical. . . . Cost or pain can be imposed on an enemy by doing—or in some cases threatening to do—the following: destroying the enemy's command structure, which may range from the highest civil command to an appropriate level of the military command; destroying enough of his war material base that he is unable to support forces in the field; destroying or damaging enough of his infrastructure that necessary movement of goods and services becomes impossible; imposing sufficient hardship on the population that the people become either unwilling or unable to support the war effort; and destroying or incapacitating

enough of his fielded military forces that he is unable or unwilling to continue effective offensive and defensive operations.[24]

The Five Rings Model, graphically presented as concentric circles, reflected the relative importance of the target-sets contained within a nation-state. He labeled the bull's-eye "the command ring." It consisted of the state's national leadership: the aggregate of individuals who possessed the power to initiate, sustain, and terminate wars. The objective of most wars, Warden insisted, was to induce the command structure to make concessions. This structure functioned as the nation's brain: it gave the state its strategic direction and helped it respond to external and internal challenges. If an enemy's spinal cord could be severed, disconnecting the brain from the rest of the body, then the appendages—the nation's military forces—could only twitch and wither with no coordinating function. Typical targets in this circle were the nation's leadership and its connections, including communication devices, propaganda, media, and various organs for internal control, such as security forces and intelligence networks.

The circle surrounding this inner core he identified as the state's "critical war industry": the key production centers. This second ring included energy facilities, such as oil, gas, and electricity, as well as research facilities and industries. Warden asserted that if a state's essential industries were damaged, the state would become incapable of employing modern weapons and thus would make major concessions. Even a large state had a relatively small number of key industrial targets. Of these, power production and petroleum refining were fragile, but he acknowledged that those targets might be located deep inside enemy territory and be heavily defended.

The third circle contained the state's "infrastructure," primarily industry and transportation links such as roads, bridges, and railways. For both military and other purposes a society needed to move goods, services, and information from one point to another: "if this movement becomes impossible, the state ceases to function."

The fourth circle represented "population and agriculture"—the citizens of the state and its food sources. As he had done in *The Air Campaign*, Warden stressed that it was difficult to attack the population directly: "there are too many targets and in many cases, especially in a police state, the population may be willing to suffer grievously before it will turn on its own government." Instead, he favored indirect attacks through psychological operations, designed to undermine the morale of the populace or lower its support of the war effort and the ruling regime.

The final ring was the state's "fielded military forces." In Warden's view, "Although we tend to think of military forces as being the most vital in war, in fact they are means to an end. That is, their only function is to protect their inner rings or to threaten those of an enemy." In short, Warden postulated that attacking the leadership meant attacking the source and cause of the problem, while military forces were nothing more than symptoms.

From this model he deduced that if simultaneous attacks were launched against multiple target-sets within each of the five rings, the effect on a modern nation-state would be exponential. The individual and collective disruption of several subsystems through massive and continuous aerial attacks and the mutual reinforcement of all these disruptions were likely to cripple the entire national infrastructure, thus inducing strategic paralysis. This approach challenged the established notion of viewing strategic results as a sum of things attacked and destroyed, or even as a product of weighted values. In Warden's view, failure against one target, and perhaps even a target set, would not negate the entire effort because the cumulative effect would remain.[25]

The order of the five rings explained not only the relative importance of the centers of gravity, but also their vulnerability to attack. The outer ring contained numerous widely dispersed targets, all of which could return fire; destroying them would therefore be extremely costly. The fourth ring, population, presented a tremendously difficult target—physically, psychologically, and legally. Deliberately attacking a nation's population would violate national policy and would trigger adverse domestic and international political repercussions. Moreover, the fourth ring presented many targets and striking them would yield few benefits. The third ring, infrastructure, offered a large number of targets that individually might be vulnerable; eliminating them collectively would produce significant results, but they would be difficult to destroy. In other words, attacking the third ring would yield a relatively low return. The second ring offered a more attractive target set: hitting a few vital targets in key production areas could disrupt entire sectors of an enemy's war economy and his ability to continue the conflict. The second ring, therefore, offered the possibility of engaging relatively few targets with high return. Finally, enemy leadership presented the most important and vulnerable target of all: obliterating a few hardened bunkers could potentially decapitate a regime in a single raid. The small number of targets in the inner ring would be difficult to hit, but successful attacks on them would allow for very high return.[26] Stated differently, effects on the inner rings were the most important and those on the outer rings the most immediate.

This theoretical construct, Warden believed, was highly applicable to the real world. He insisted that a strategic commander should force an enemy to make the concessions desired as rapidly and as cheaply as possible. He concluded that air power would have far more to offer if the air force had a well-defined strategy:

The Navy's maritime strategy is a very good statement of Navy capabilities to operate against enemy strategic rings and is especially apropos for an air-maritime nation like the United States. Airland battle doctrine is the Army's view of how to fight against land armies only. It is just above the tactical level in concept. The Air Force has not articulated how it fits into the big picture. Its association with Airland battle is only a small part of what it can and should do. Its capabilities, however, clearly mark it as the tool of primary importance for an air-maritime state. Air forces have capabilities not possessed by other forces and they should be employed to exploit those capabilities. They are theater and global level weapons which can be employed anywhere in a matter of hours or days. They are mobile and can be concentrated for the offense or defense. They can operate successfully against air, land, or sea forces. Because of their mobility, they can be used at the time and place of their owner's choosing; they are not constrained to a limited sector or to the point an enemy may choose to mass forces. They can circumvent enemy ground and air forces to strike deep behind the lines. They alone of the forces can operate easily against all of the strategic rings. Air forces have more capability to affect the outcome of most wars than do land or naval forces—because of their ability to engage or protect every strategic ring. The only thing they can't do is occupy territory—which should not normally be a primary goal for an air-maritime state such as the United States.[27]

Warden then argued that the air force needed an overarching mission. That mission should encompass conducting global operations against enemy strategic rings to force concessions demanded by grand strategy; exploiting and enhancing the inherent mobility and range of air forces; avoiding peripheral engagements and geographic constraints to the maximum possible; and supporting sea and land forces when doing so would not conflict with operations that would be more decisive and less costly in time, blood, and treasure.[28]

Warden believed that the Global Strategy Outline provided coherence to air force thinking and could serve as an effective tool for evaluating the organization and its force structure. The immediate implication was that the air force should move away from an organization that was separated into "tactical" and "strategic" communities. He also suggested that the new force structure should rely on highly mobile forces that were not intentionally or irrevocably tied to fixed bases or geographic regions: the air force "should be able to operate from as large a percentage as possible of the world's thousands of air strips—until such time as it is possible to conduct operations world-wide from bases in the United States itself."[29]

Warden's essay alluded to a targeting philosophy that would later become known as effects-based operations. Rather than focus on destroying and killing, Warden saw an air campaign in terms of degrading, delaying, disrupting, harassing, isolating, and neutralizing. Generally speaking he recommended that planners think in terms of creating chaos, confusion, and paralysis. He also emphasized the importance of viewing the military instrument together with political and economic dimensions, and noted that air power could have both a destructive and a constructive role. Warden also favored eliminating enemy means rather than undermining morale; the psychological effects would follow from physical deprivation.

In Warden's view, the lethality of modern air weapons, coupled with the freedom of maneuver, range, precision, and sustainability of air attack, had revolutionized warfare. The synergy between long-range global air power and precision weaponry made earlier visions of the future attainable. Only air power, Warden insisted, could strike anywhere in the world, at any time, hitting multiple targets in a way that ground forces advancing along a front or naval forces steaming at sea could not. In the air power era, neither armies nor navies should be considered the primary instrument of securing victory in war.

The theory possessed a rare combination of elegance and rationality; it could be explained in simple terms; and it seemed to simplify complex problems. Importantly, Warden connected this systems approach with the objective of the overall air campaign, which in turn was part of the larger war: to convince the enemy leadership to do what the United States wanted it to do.

Dugan and Boyd found the outline exceptionally useful as a starting point for linking air power to national security. Since only Warden voiced such views at the time, his ideas became the basis for XO's thinking about air power. After a policy review by the air force public affairs office, he "went public" in early March 1990 at a symposium sponsored by the Military Operations Research Society.[30] He also circulated a revised version of his paper as a memorandum called "Centers of Gravity: The Key to Success in War."

The new version included a comprehensive exposition of his Five Rings Model, defined as a descriptive model of modern combatants.[31] Warden had added an explanation of how he envisioned the same approach for the operational level of war. The first operational ring consisted of the military commander himself and his command, control, and communication system. The second was logistics, and included the essentials of combat such as ammunition, fuel, and food. Infrastructure, in the form of "roads, airways, seaways, rails, communication lines, pipelines and a myriad of other facilities needed to employ fielded forces," was the third ring. Support personnel who operated the logistics and the infrastructure systems comprised the fourth ring. The last ring included fielded military forces in the form of aircraft, ships, and troops. Warden again asserted that as a general rule a campaign focused on the fifth ring was likely to prove the longest and bloodiest for both sides, although "sometimes it may be necessary to reduce the fifth ring to some extent in order to reach inner operational and strategic rings."

At the operational level the impact of coherent operations would overwhelm the opponent's ability to command and control his forces, denying him the ability to respond to U.S. operations, and forcing him to execute uncoordinated preplanned actions:

> The focus of war operations must be against the enemy leadership whether civil or military. To affect the enemy leadership, we must understand what the enemy looks like conceptually. If we accept the idea that an enemy is conceptually a leader in the center surrounded by centers of gravity, we can think more clearly about how to affect the enemy leadership. By thinking in these larger strategic and operational level terms, we simplify our tasks enormously. We may not have to find and destroy thirty thousand tanks if we can destroy the few hundred fuel or ammunition distribution points. We may not have to destroy the few hundred fuel distribution points if we can immobilize an entire society by destroying dozens of electrical generation systems. And we may not need to destroy dozens of electrical generation systems if we can capture or kill the enemy leader. Our task is to look and work as close to the center of the enemy's operational and strategic rings as possible. When we have identified where the real centers of gravity lie, we must then decide how best to strike those centers. If we go through the process honestly and rigorously, we can be confident that we have crafted a good campaign that will lead to realization of the political aims of the war.[32]

Targeting the leadership directly during the opening moments of a war, using the principles of mass, concentration, and the offensive, represented the core of Warden's thinking, but by urging the military to move beyond Clausewitz and ground-centric warfare Warden provoked controversy. He contended that forcing the national leadership to produce desired policy changes should be the primary aim and that this should guide the employment of air power. The military strategy should produce the instantaneous effects of "a shot through the head" rather than a slow bloodletting.[33]

Warden had defined a theory, but now he wanted to prove that the theory applied in the real world. War-gaming, scenario analysis, and various simulations were the closest available approaches to verification short of war. The opportunity to conduct extensive war-gaming exercises presented itself in early

1989: during another reorganization of XO, the Checkmate Division and the Mission Area Analysis Division had merged to become the Force Assessment Division (XOXWF) under Warden's directorate. Checkmate had by then developed an excellent reputation for its expertise on the Soviet order of battle, doctrine, and warfighting concepts. The officers assigned to the division represented a mixture of operational, logistical, and analytical backgrounds. By early 1989, when the Soviet threat had all but disappeared, Dugan and Boyd had thought about disbanding the division, but Warden convinced them that he could use it as a think tank:

> I wanted to use it as the division that would allow me to look at operational level concepts. I wanted to identify some examples of centers of gravity, then I wanted to develop the plan to attack those things. I was thinking about the division as being kind of the connection between the almost ethereal world of long-range plans and strategy and so on and the operating world. How do you convert these general principles into operational concepts which then can be executed at a tactical level? I did not formally do away with [the red/blue scenario], but the task that I gave them was that they could no longer put much attention on it.[34]

Thus, the Force Assessment Division became part of XOXW, although Air Staff officers continued to refer to it as the Checkmate Division, or simply "Checkmate."

Warden instructed Checkmate to look beyond AirLand Battle doctrine and to focus on potential trouble spots, paying special attention to the Persian Gulf. A contractor who had worked hard to improve combat models, Terrence Colvin of Synergy Inc., was immediately impressed by Warden's ability to think creatively and listen to new ideas.[35] Colvin and his colleagues introduced Warden and his group of officers to "the art of modeling," which forced them to examine more rigorously which targets to attack and in what sequence, how to match these targets to sortie compositions, and finally how to quantify the effects they wanted to achieve. This effort went hand in hand with Checkmate's war-gaming exercises, and both efforts focused on effects rather than attrition.

To test his centers of gravity theory Warden also encouraged the Checkmate team to start with the "Soviet Operational Level Fuel Depot Interdiction Study."[36] Although the intelligence community maintained that fuel was not a center of gravity, Warden told the Checkmate group to study the vulnerability and significance of petroleum, oil, and lubricants (POL) depots in East Germany, and investigate whether crippling them would slow or even halt a Soviet advance into West Germany. Warden was primarily concerned with the Persian Gulf, but thought the example would carry weight with the army.

According to intelligence reports, the Soviet Union had six months of fuel supply buried in hardened storage buildings in East Germany, and consequently it was not realistic to attack all the storage facilities. The challenge would therefore be to examine how the fuel would get from storage to the military forces and their tanks at the front. Checkmate concluded that if the United States shut down one or more of three output manifolds at one of twenty-five fuel depots that each supported a front (corps in Western terms), the Soviet front would run out of fuel in three to five days. Even better, as soon as the front commander became aware of the problem, he would probably begin rationing his fuel supplies and this would slow his forward movement. Not all fuel supplies would be destroyed, but the lack of oil would force the commander to await resupply rather than advance. A hundred F-16 sorties could have a devastating effect on Soviet operations simply by hitting a single depot in the distribution system. Thus, Checkmate confirmed that POL was an important center of gravity that should be attacked systematically.[37]

Warden's team brought these conclusions to Gen. Crosbie E. Saint, the commander in chief of the U.S. Army in Europe and the Seventeenth Army. General Saint was delighted, and commented that this was exactly how he thought air power should be used. He asked Checkmate to extend their analysis to Warsaw Pact ammunition depots, but this project came to a halt with the Iraqi invasion of Kuwait, and by the time the resultant conflict ended, all interest in analyzing the now-defunct Warsaw Pact had evaporated.

The Fuel Study and others convinced Warden that the Five Rings Model and its systems approach allowed for a method that would increase the effectiveness of air and ground operations. Warden pointed out that in the Second World War German production increased as bombing raids increased, but that effective strikes on oil facilities and on the German transportation network meant that much of this production went literally nowhere. Furthermore, the strategic air campaign tied up thousands of troops and antiaircraft weapons in the defense of the Reich that could have been used elsewhere.

The thinking behind the Fuel Study, like that in the Global Strategy Outline, presaged the concept of effects-based operations, and the Joint Warfare Analysis Center later explored a broader set of projects of the same type.[38] Warden further increased the value and effectiveness of such exercises by having officers within his directorate critique the exercise plans: this method not only identified the weaknesses and strengths, but also exposed his officers to new concepts and encouraged them to think creatively.[39]

While the critics of air power seemed obsessed with costs and production numbers, Warden believed that the Five Rings Model illustrated the linkages among societal elements and showed that planners could not look at one aspect in isolation. The model became a marketing tool and the basis for a strategic air power theory. In the course of developing his theory Warden came to the definite conclusion that strategic air warfare was *the* form of warfare. Although viewing the enemy as a system was not new, Warden at least suggested a coherent model that focused on the societal rather than merely the mechanical aspects of a system.

Warden explored the matter extensively with some of his most capable subordinates, initially Lt. Cols. David A. Deptula, Lonnie Dale Turner, and John Piazza. The group soon became convinced that technological progress, in the form of stealth and precision, made it possible to attack the centers of gravity simultaneously at the strategic level of war. By contrast, serial warfare could only engage each ring and its components in turn. Striking all the decisive points of each ring and of the entire system at the same time would create so much confusion and disorder in the enemy system that any reaction would be ineffective, and the enemy state would rapidly suffer either total or partial paralysis. Warden's team stressed that long-range aircraft and precision targeting made it possible to translate the theory effectively into practice. The new approach meant carrying the war to the enemy's state organization (system warfare) rather than to the enemy's armed forces (military warfare). Destroying the best targets would render the enemy's strategy and decision making irrelevant.

Warden continued to refine the concept with his own staff, and encouraged them to improve it further. They, in turn, lectured before diverse audiences, from the U.S. Army Command and General Staff School at Forth Leavenworth and the Air War College at Maxwell AFB to a range of think tanks in academic and political environments.[40]

PROFESSIONAL MILITARY EDUCATION

The Global Strategy Outline and its Five Rings Model, published in May 1988, became the basis for many other XOXW projects. One of them dealt with improving the professional military education (PME) curriculum that was intended to make airmen knowledgeable about and conversant with the basis for their profession. Warden had already shown an interest in this topic at Eglin and Moody, and in the late 1980s the air force faced considerable outside pressure to improve its education program. In fact, Williamson Murray, an associate professor of military history with experience at Newport, West Point, and Maxwell, termed the landscape of PME "an intellectual desert": virtually every institution seemed to confuse appearance with substance and training with education.[41] After inspecting the war colleges, Murray concluded that the Naval War College had the best program: at least it graded its students throughout the course and provided them with "tools for self-education throughout the remainder of their careers" by placing a heavy emphasis on nonclassroom teaching. The National

War College suffered from guest speaker superfluity because of its location. The Industrial College of the Armed Forces was too narrowly focused on procurement, logistics, and mobilization, doing "nothing to prepare its students for the larger strategic and political issues involved in war"; and the U.S. Army War College was blighted by "an unimaginative curriculum . . . a rabbit warren of courses and lectures" with minuscule reading assignments. The Air War College was the weakest, lacking a serious intellectual curriculum and the resources for supporting more than "a simplistic course of study."[42] Murray might have overstated his case for effect, but clearly all was not well in the education system.

In November 1987 these findings led the House Armed Services Committee to establish a Panel on Military Education, chaired by Representative Ike Skelton (Democrat-Missouri). The Skelton committee concluded that the war colleges should place the study of war, strategic history, operational history, and the business of making U.S. strategy at the heart of their curriculum. Like Murray, the Skelton committee described the air force as by far the weakest of the four services. The committee found that both the Air War College (AWC) and the Air Command and Staff College (ACSC) had by far the highest percentage of passive learning in their curricula; both schools defined examinations as unnecessary and useless; the educational philosophy was to teach a little bit of everything the colleges thought the students should know; and the mission statements of both schools were too broad and vague to provide guidance for curriculum development. Alone among the PME schools, ACSC gave more weight to staff skills than to warfighting; three-quarters of the ACSC faculty moved directly from the resident course to their faculty positions; and the student/faculty ratios were about twice as high as those at the other services' colleges.[43]

The air force chief of staff, Gen. Larry Welch, determined to take action, ordered Dugan and Boyd to suggest an alternative curriculum, and they in turn tasked Warden's directorate. Warden, Lt. Col. David Tretler, and a small group that included Murray developed a proposal that followed the Skelton committee's recommendations. It defined the purpose of the AWC and the ACSC: "to produce officers with the values, understanding, perspective, and analytical skills essential to conduct successful aerospace warfare at the operational and strategic levels." Officers should be versed in the nature, purpose, and conduct of war; capable of commanding and staffing air forces at the operational and strategic levels in independent, joint, and combined operations; capable of rigorous analysis of military problems, as well as clear articulation of solutions to those problems; capable of organizing, training, and equipping air forces in peacetime so that they could execute their wartime tasking when called upon to do so; and versed in the broad range of organizational, managerial, political, doctrinal, and strategic issues facing air forces in peacetime. The service schools should teach the conduct of aerospace warfare, air force concepts and doctrine, challenges of command, the staff process, and joint and combined warfare. The proposal even set out the case studies that should be presented and how many hours should be devoted to each. As for the faculty, it should ideally include a mixture of prominent civilian scholars, tenured military professors, and soldier-scholars.[44]

During the autumn of 1988 and the early spring of 1989, Warden and Tretler briefed many senior officers and institutions on this proposed curriculum, which focused strongly on strategy and history. Dugan and Boyd were very supportive, as were General Welch and Lt. Gen. Ralph E. Havens, the commander at the Air University, and the majority of his faculty members. When the new secretary of the air force, Donald B. Rice, took office in May 1989 he, too, reacted favorably to the proposal, and Gen. Jack T. Chain, the SAC commander, was pleased with the main outline.[45] The curriculum that Warden and Tretler proposed was not accepted in total, but the AWC and the ACSC began to devote attention to strategy, operational art, and the purpose of their profession. When Havens died later that year, Rice and Welch ensured that Boyd became the new commander at Air University. According to Rice:

> We handpicked General Boyd to go down there and shape the place up in dimensions having to do with greater understanding of air power and its role and how you think about it, how you plan for it, and what kind of doctrine ought to support it . . . We have an institution that is made up of people who attach themselves, in their minds, to a type of airplane or maybe a command that had not been very well structured for the conduct of warfare and not to the broader purpose that air power brings to the table and offers to the national security and to the options available to the National Command folks.[46]

The suggestions for educational reform met surprisingly little resistance from a conceptual standpoint, although not much was done to put the recommendations into practice. The least enthusiastic reception came from TAC. General Russ commented that he did not see the effort as particularly relevant to real-world operations. He later stated: "I am a professional fighter pilot, and getting a PhD is a nice thing to do, but it has nothing to do with flying and fighting airplanes."[47] Some even suggested that in the fly-and-fight culture of TAC it was considered "unmanly" to develop one's intellect.[48] Whether education was unmanly or not, Warden was adamant about the importance of teaching officers to understand their own history and to move beyond the perception that their only mission was "to fly and fight," which essentially excluded most airmen, since only a small percentage of the air force consisted of fighter-pilots.

The PME project went hand in glove with another project that Warden initiated. Shortly after he arrived in the Pentagon he observed that the navy displayed huge paintings of its admirals and of sea battles, and that the army honored its tradition with paintings, photographs, and sculptures of heroes and campaigns. By contrast, the air force seemed to lack awareness of its past: offices might contain the odd picture of aircraft and previous chiefs of staff, but they were not especially inspiring or motivating. Warden wanted to showcase airmen who had succeeded because of their thinking about air power rather than excelling only at command and organizational matters. Billy Mitchell and George Kenney were the obvious candidates. Warden attempted to obtain large portraits of both, but soon discovered that the air force's archives did not even have decent photographs of them. Lt. Col. Thomas K. Kearney managed to find only an old oil painting of Kenney at the Air University in Alabama and a photograph of Mitchell at the Mitchell Museum in Wisconsin. Warden arranged to have photographic copies of each enlarged into portraits in the style of oil paintings and hung in the offices of the chief of staff, the XO, and XOXW, as well as in the hallways.[49] By drawing attention to these individuals, and developing the PME proposal, Warden hoped he would stimulate airmen to become more appreciative of strategic air power and its contribution to victories in the past.

AIR FORCE DOCTRINE

The importance of doctrine for military services has always been a contentious subject. Pilots, in particular, rarely took it very seriously. Traditionally they knew their tactical manuals inside-out, but the nature of war and of aerospace power, the principles of war, and the different levels of war did not really matter to them; doctrine did not provide instructions for how to operate aircraft and put bombs on target. In the late 1980s general officers tended to convey the attitude that doctrinal work was boring and a useless intellectual exercise.[50] Warden, however, took it very seriously and was pleased that the Air Force Doctrine Division fell under his jurisdiction.

Warden decided that his team should completely revise and reorganize the edition of Air Force Manual (AFM) 1-1, *Functions and Basic Doctrine of the United States Air Force*, which his predecessor, Col. Alan L. Gropman, had published in 1984. His team played an active role in revising AFM 1-1 and provided input to contingency plans that fell under the different regional commands and joint doctrine publications.[51] Warden wanted the new version to be less oriented to cold war conditions, and to make a strong case for conventional strategic operations. Most important, and predictably, he wanted the new manual explicitly to recognize and actively use terms such as "operational art," "the operational level of war," "centers of gravity," and "campaign," noting:

> A campaign is a series of related military operations aimed to accomplish a strategic or operational objective within a given time and space.

A major operation is simply a shorter term, more limited version of the same thing. The essence of operational art is campaigning—combining and sequencing individual battles, engagements, and movements into a scheme or pattern that ties their effects together to achieve a broad common goal.[52]

Tretler, who had worked with Warden on the PME proposal, suggested many improvements and coordinated inputs to the new doctrine. *The Air Campaign* served as a key starting point for debate and refinement. The new version of AFM 1-1 stressed the importance of air superiority and emphasized the key characteristics of air forces: speed, range, flexibility, precision, and lethality. To meet the needs of a joint force commander, the updated air force doctrine also defined the terms "independent," "parallel," and "supporting operations."[53]

The new version, not surprisingly, paid little attention to close air support. Despite protests from the army and TAC, Warden maintained that the worst way to allocate air power was to respond to the immediate needs of individual division commanders who focused only on their restricted battle zone. Realizing that it would be impossible to convince the air force and the army to abandon close air support as a mission, Deptula suggested a substitute: "battlefield air operations." These operations were intended to have a direct impact on the on-going ground battle, which distinguished them from battlefield air interdiction, but the ground commander would not choose the targets, which distinguished the mission from close air support.[54] Battlefield air operations would attack "tactical reserves" in the close rear area and the movement to and from front-line ground formations. Thus, air power could directly attack enemy troops and equipment in close proximity to the engagements: Warden envisaged that these attacks would take place five to ten miles from the front lines, which would reduce the need to coordinate directly with the on-going battle. They would leave the engagement to the army or the marines, while dealing with enemy forces that were about to engage. This had several advantages: it would reduce the likelihood of "friendly fire," and at such distances the enemy forces tended to be concentrated, which in turn would increase air power effectiveness. Battlefield air operations would also prevent the enemy from accumulating reinforcements.

Importantly, battlefield air operations constituted "direct attack": air operations against enemy ground forces regardless of the presence of friendly ground forces. Thus, they were not necessarily a prerequisite for ground engagements: they could under certain circumstances achieve the joint force commander's overall campaign plan on their own.

Battlefield air operations represented an attempt by Warden and some of his staff to formally define the ability of air power to engage and destroy an adversary's fielded military capabilities and to think operationally rather than tactically, focusing on higher-level coherence rather than single engagements. Its opponents considered it pure parochialism. Gen. Merrill A. McPeak, commander of Pacific Command, told Warden that it was a good idea, but that he would not support it in public because it contradicted the official air force line that close air support was its first priority.[55] General Russ did not find the concept particularly interesting.[56] As it happened, the term never found its way into the revised doctrine, because TAC had succeeded in inducing the U.S. Army to include "air interdiction," "battlefield air interdiction," and "close air support" in its AirLand Battle doctrine, and these terms were also used in recent joint publications. Warden was therefore forced to accept that it was preferable to retain the established terminology for the time being. Even so, the very existence of such a debate was noteworthy, because Warden and others successfully advocated direct attacks rather than interdiction and close air support during Desert Storm—an approach that Deptula later summarized as: "We are not preparing the battlefield—we are destroying it."[57]

The draft version of the new AFM 1-1 presented throughout the defense community in the summer and autumn of 1989 reflected a far more ambitious view of the capabilities of air power than did the 1984 doctrine. Warden recalled that the effort to include new ideas in the manual made satisfactory progress, but the Doctrine Division had to make many compromises. According to Tretler and Turner, who worked on inputs for joint publications, many of Warden's ideas found their way into both air force and joint doctrine, but some of the more extreme elements, such as the Five Rings Model, were left out and some of the statements about independent air power were toned down. Tretler and Deptula later asserted that the systematic and deductive thinking helped officers who had previously been uninterested in doctrine and the theoretical aspects of air power to examine the purpose of air operations more systematically. Perhaps most important, the new manual stimulated the air force as an institution to discuss the operational level of war, centers of gravity, and independent operations.

However, XOXW's initiative to create a new AFM 1-1 found itself competing with an effort being conducted at the same time by a team from Air University. Col. Dennis M. Drew was driving an independent doctrine process from the Center for Airpower Development, Research, and Education (CADRE), and by late 1989, under instructions from the chief of staff, the Warden proposal was withdrawn in favor of the Air University version. Warden was unhappy with CADRE's taking over the process, but his superiors noted that the decision had been made and he resigned himself. When Boyd became the commander of Air University in January 1990, Warden thought at first that he would return the responsibility for doctrine to the Air Staff, but to his disappointment Boyd became an advocate of his new organization's continuing the work. The new manual was put into final form that month, but publication was delayed by bureaucratic turf battles and continual minor modifications.[58]

While doctrine was important, Warden also made sure that members of his team reviewed the contingency plan for the Persian Gulf region, Operations Plan (OPLAN) 1002-90, and the plans for the other regional commands, all of which were consistent with the AirLand Battle concept. Warden's representatives, who advocated moving beyond what they considered a fixation on close air support, reported to the Pentagon that the regional commands tended to build contingency plans that reflected their existing force structures rather than tailoring them to meet the situation and determining how to deal with possible threats. It was also becoming increasingly obvious that OPLAN 1002-90 subscribed to a cold war mentality and that the Pentagon's information on Iraq was "woefully out of date."[59] Warden's directorate did not succeed in making concrete changes, but at least it ensured that air power received a wider hearing.

The Air Legion

The ideas about air power theory, PME, and doctrine that Warden's directorate initiated and advocated helped airmen think more clearly about their own possible contributions to national security. However, it was when Warden and some of his key staff suggested restructuring the air force organization into composite wings that he attracted considerable attention from the senior leadership, drawing both praise and condemnation.

In December 1988 Warden and Lieutenant Colonel Turner convened a three-day meeting with a small group from the Air Staff to discuss the organization of the air force. In his opening statement Warden postulated that the trends of Glasnost and Perestroika would lead to a new world situation in which the large-scale forward base structure in Europe could no longer be justified. After presenting his air power theory and the five rings, and stressing the central role of strategic air power, Warden raised the basic question: How should the air force reorganize itself to ensure rapid and decisive power projection at any point in the world?

Although the participants agreed with Warden's basic premises, they claimed that the Soviet Union would continue to pose a military threat for the foreseeable future. Turner recalled that whenever he thought the group was about to make progress somebody would disrupt the discussions by protesting that "This is just stupid . . . we're wasting our time."[60] Warden and Turner dismissed the group after one day and spent the next day together, exploring different ways to structure air force formations. They concluded that the air force could exert considerable combat power if it relied on the equivalent of fifteen normal wings in active service and ten normal wings kept in reserve. The issue then became: How should the air force organize those twenty-five wings to optimize its power projection capability? The answer, Warden thought, was composite wings. Unlike the current structure, where most fighter units were constituted with only a single type of aircraft, a wing should control most of the aircraft necessary to accomplish its mission on its own. It should thus consist of a combination of different aircraft and those aircraft should operate together on a day-to-day basis.

This solution ran strongly counter to over thirty years of established practice. For organizational and logistical reasons, the air force had been structured around a range of wings, located either in the United States or at forward bases in Europe and the Pacific, each of which had a unique capability. If a crisis occurred, the regional commander responsible would request certain forces from each of the four services. The deployment would be more or less in accordance with a specific contingency plan, which in turn was based on the cold war containment doctrine. After the combatant commander had initiated all the requests to the different organizations, the forces would arrive in theater according to a preestablished schedule and only then—over the next few days, weeks, and months—would they train together in preparation for their mission. Thus, the forces did not train in peacetime as they would fight in wartime.

Warden believed that by focusing exclusively on its own capability, each wing developed a mindset that related only to tactical-level application of air power. Wings had no responsibility for planning at the operational level: they basically received plans from higher headquarters and delivered sorties. This structure was useful in a cold war setting, both in terms of a heavy presence in Europe and sensitive execution plans, but the future would hold a stronger focus on regional crises and such unpredictability required a more flexible ability to respond and to project power.

The composite wing idea was straightforward: wings should incorporate a mix of aircraft, for example, bombers, fighters, reconnaissance, airlift, and refueling aircraft. These forces would train together on a daily basis under one commander. If the need arose the joint commander would request complete composite wings with multiple capabilities rather than specific aircraft with individual capabilities. Each composite wing would have different combinations of aircraft and a mix of personnel expertise, which, in turn, would allow the air force to respond appropriately to the full spectrum of conflicts. The wings, which would include the necessary maintenance and logistic teams, would also be ready to deploy at short notice.

Warden's group argued that the mixed-wing concept had several advantages over the old system: an operational rather than a tactical focus; greater flexibility to respond to different types of crises worldwide; greater force projection capability; and an operating team whose members knew each other well. Moreover, it would complicate the enemy's strategy. When challenged that these ideas did not match the principle of mass, Warden responded that technology, through precision, more than made up for the difference. Mixed wings would improve deployment, training, and employment, and a composite force structure would reduce the artificial distinction between "fighter wings" and "bomber wings." Warden was convinced that the ideal application of air power required that the service categorize its missions as nuclear and conventional rather than strategic and tactical:

> We should not distinguish between tactical and strategic forces. The "tactical" fighter bombers of today are fully capable of attacking every enemy strategic ring—and should be used to do so whenever possible. Consider the Libyan operation: by any measure, it was a strategic operation designed to affect the state's high command and it was certainly conducted over "strategic" distances. It serves us poorly to think of "tactical" air forces as being limited to "tactical" missions. The word itself tends to drive our thinking down to a very low level with very small objectives. Air forces are big picture weapons which have war winning capabilities.[61]

Warden also insisted that each wing be led by a one-star general rather than by a colonel, as was the standard at the time; this would increase the wing commander's authority relative to his two- and three-star army counterparts. In addition, he wanted the commanders of the composite wing to play an active role in both the planning and execution phases of an operation.

After reviewing the new concept with Dugan and Boyd, Warden became convinced that it had merit. He needed a memorable title to promote it, and decided on "Air Legion." The Roman Empire had used its legions to dominate the continent: now the U.S. Air Force, the world's premier aerospace power, dominated airspace. Although the composite wings philosophy was only one element of the larger picture, it became a catchphrase for thinking about change. The concept, advertised on t-shirts, bumper stickers, and watches, drew considerable attention over the next few months.

The Air Legion had several novel elements, but it was not new per se. TAC had formed the Composite Air Strike Force (CASF) in response to the Korean War, and by the mid-1950s had begun testing a quick-response force that could deploy a command element and its communication units together with fighter-bombers for both conventional and nuclear attack missions, as well as transport, tanker, and tactical reconnaissance assets.[62] Capitalizing on the responsiveness of the CASF, the Department of Defense activated U.S. Strike Command in 1961 as a unified command composed of elite ground troops and tactical fighter units; Strike Command became Readiness Command in 1972.

However, the CASF was formally deactivated in July 1973, and Readiness Command was dissolved in 1987.

The most common argument against reorganization was that the air force already conducted extensive dissimilar air combat training during Red Flag and other exercises. Warden's team remained unconvinced:

> Red Flag represented an interesting paradox. On one hand, Air Force units were required to be combat ready to fight together at a moment's notice, but the majority of Air Force units trained separately, not as a mix, on a daily basis. Only at Red Flag and similar exercises did they train as they would fight by integrating the different systems and capabilities needed in actual combat. The average pilot only attended one Red Flag exercise in a three-year tour and this new-found combat capability dwindled quickly after he returned to the normal training regimen within his unit. The Air Force was not organized to train as it would fight.[63]

The team contended that the exercises had a high degree of artificiality and that only if men and machines worked together on a daily basis would the wings develop the right team with the right spirit and the necessary *Fingerspitzengefühl*, an instinctive understanding of how each team member should act in a given situation.

The Air Legion was first presented in six handwritten slides, and Warden assigned Piazza and Deptula to extend the project. They built their case on the basis of geopolitical changes, prevailing operational requirements, and the recent evolution of logistical support. First, the declining Warsaw Pact threat to NATO would almost certainly lead to force reductions in Europe. Conversely, policy makers would support a military force sized and shaped to meet emerging challenges. If Warden's directorate could present the air force as the key military instrument of the future, it would gain the necessary advantages in the upcoming budget battles.

Second, the composite organization would allow a cohesive warfighting structure that optimized the use of air power. It would streamline the command chain, and the logistical and intelligence communities would become integrated parts of the combat force. If the air assets were collocated under one commander who had the authority to deploy and employ them in a fast and coherent manner, the air force would become the first line of defense and offer a viable political option for crisis management.

Third, the most common argument against a composite wing solution was cost-related: many feared that putting multiple aircraft in one wing would drive up the support costs dramatically. Once again, Red Flag proved something of a paradox: its logistics structure had the highest operational readiness rate in the air force, even though it supported numerous types of aircraft and capabilities. Warden therefore asked experts at the RAND Corporation's Project Air Force to study the costs of organizing Air Legions.[64] RAND concluded that costs could actually be reduced if the air force eliminated some obsolete routines in the process. Warden's team used RAND's results as they sought to convince the air force that the technological advances in command, control, communications, intelligence, and space, coupled with improvements in reliability and maintainability of equipment, meant that composite wings offered a way to ensure the balance between operational effectiveness and logistical efficiency.

Warden believed that the composite solution would have another positive effect. As he had noted, officers defined themselves first by their community, such as operations, intelligence, or maintenance, and second by their specific functions, such as F-15 pilot, target acquisition officer, or depot inspector. Composite wings might replace this tribal orientation with a sense of identification with the wing's overall mission.

Warden's team had acknowledged from the beginning that the Air Legion idea could be blocked by a single decision maker who might not like or understand it. They expected high-level opposition, if only because of bureaucracy's intrinsic resistance to change. Warden, Piazza, and Deptula recognized that they needed to build a sense of ownership for the concept throughout the different layers of the air force. They decided that they would first create a working group of action officers from across the Air Staff, with Warden's directorate at the center. This would allow the core group to develop the concept using input from experts from logistical, operational, personnel, and research environments. The core group would examine the advantages and disadvantages of the new structure, identify issues that would require further exploration, and prepare memoranda and presentations. They would also keep Boyd updated on both progress and obstacles. Meanwhile, the action officers would work closely with a few retired generals, think tanks in the aerospace industry, and RAND to establish a solid foundation and network for the composite idea. After completing a lower-level sanity check they would establish a working group composed of two-star generals from each of the key functional areas of the Air Staff: areas that already shared ownership of the idea. Finally, they planned to brief three- and four-star generals, including the commanders of European, Alaskan, and Pacific Commands and of TAC, the chief of staff, and ultimately the secretary of the air force.

The first two groups became strong supporters from the very beginning. The close cooperation with RAND strengthened their case by helping them to focus on logistical aspects. Meanwhile, defense industry representatives developed analytical models, war games, and simulations to illuminate command, control, and intelligence issues.

However, the third step proved more difficult than anticipated. In May 1989 Dugan replaced General Kirk at USAFE and the new director of Plans and Operations, Lt. Gen. Jimmie V. Adams, told Warden that neither he nor the TAC commander, General Russ, believed in the Air Legion concept. It was for the unified commander in chief to decide what he wanted for any given scenario, and then the air force would provide him with the air assets he deemed necessary. This system had worked for years and Adams considered it inappropriate for a colonel publicly to advocate ideas throughout Washington that the senior leadership did not support. Despite this, Warden and his team continued to argue their case. By the end of June Adams was so annoyed by Warden's constant insistence on changing the organization and mindset of the air force and by his freewheeling style that he issued a decree: no one was to present any briefings outside the Pentagon without his approval. This obviously imposed a burden on an organization whose charter to plan the future of the air force required it to present scores of briefings each month.

Shortly afterward, Adams attended the annual air power symposium at the Air University. The action officer organizing the event, well aware of the Air Legion project, decided to add "composite wings" to the agenda and identified it as an XO project. Thus, when Adams arrived at Maxwell he found himself leading that particular session. In the process he had to discuss and defend the concept before an audience that included both active duty and retired generals and industry leaders. Russ was reportedly not pleased, and Adams himself was furious. When he returned to the Air Staff he called Warden, Deptula, and Piazza into his office and let them know in no uncertain terms that their campaign for composite wings had to stop: "I want you three to drive a stake through the heart of this idea! Turn it off! You started it, now go out and tell people you were wrong. Kill this idea . . . it has absolutely no redeeming value for the Air Force."[65] No one had ever berated Warden so loudly, and he put the project on hold—for the moment.

In the meantime Donald Rice had become the new secretary of the air force. During his tenure as president and chief executive of the RAND Corporation from April 1972 to May 1989 he had come to the conclusion that the single biggest problem the air force had was its inability to think conceptually. A navy officer could discuss maritime power and the six-hundred-ship fleet; an army officer could describe the purpose of his profession at length; but "when you poke a person in a light blue suit, they talk about their airplanes and their command. They do not talk about air power."[66] After spending his first months in the job preparing for committee hearings on Capitol Hill, Rice became increasingly interested in developing better options for deploying and employing air power.

In September Rice and Welch agreed that they needed to establish a working group to answer the following question: "Given the future constrained fiscal environment, and evolving geopolitical changes, how do we craft air force units to meet likely contingencies—becoming lean and mean, ultra responsive, and the Service of choice for the NCA [National Command Authority]?"[67] As it happened, Deptula, who had just been assigned to Rice's policy staff group, suggested that the working group might wish to examine some of the ideas developed by the Air Staff. Rice called upon Boyd for inputs and then directed a study team to report directly to him and Welch. He wanted broad new thinking that included examining alternative structures for the air force, and the composite idea sounded tempting. While Deptula would address the issue for the secretary's office, Boyd placed Warden and Piazza in charge of the Air Staff's effort. Over a six-week period the group worked intensively to improve the composite wing concept, but for "political reasons" they changed the name from "Air Legion" to "Air Battle Force" (ABF).

The main arguments were that the new design would allow for "cohesive warfighting structure benefits" in the areas of planning, training, and employment.[68] The ABF would enable an expanded wing to conduct counterair operations, interdiction, close air support, reconnaissance, refueling, airlift, and other operations. Decision makers could tailor the force to the particular problem at hand: "I'll take seventy-two of these, forty-eight of those and twelve of those"— and could take them all from the same ABF. The new structure would offer numerous advantages: "operational level impact on the war; optimize the use of airpower; flexibility/ability to respond; train like you will fight; force protection capability; force package from single base; ABF [commander] is battle commander (broad mission type orders and tailored to the threat); ability to reconstitute; optimized for tomorrow's world; complicates enemy strategy."[69]

When Welch heard the presentation on October 11, 1989, he was unconvinced, but he thought that some of the ideas should be developed further. He suggested that it might be useful to establish an "expeditionary" force as an interim measure, and told Warden, Deptula, and Piazza to give the presentation to Russ. To prepare themselves, Warden and Deptula first briefed Brig. Gen. Michael E. Ryan, TAC's deputy chief of staff for plans, and then Maj. Gen. Joseph W. Ashy, TAC's vice commander. The generals did not endorse the proposal, but neither did they oppose it.

The XOXW working group expected a large audience when they met with Russ on October 30, 1989, but the TAC commander had decided to deal with the issue together with only his vice commander and his executive officer, then Col. Gregory S. Martin.[70] Warden, Deptula, and Piazza made the best case they could, but it was clear that neither of the two generals was enamored of the ABF concept. Russ termed the ABF "a very interesting exercise," but asserted that the current level of composite forces and dissimilar training was sufficient to get the job done and that the organization that the Warden group had proposed was no more than a land-based aircraft carrier with significant vulnerabilities. Russ also pointed out a practical problem: few bases were large enough to accommodate this kind of organization, and logistics would be difficult with such a wide variety of aircraft. "Most importantly," he said, "You assume you know what you will be tasked for . . . We do what the CINCs tell us they need." He continued,

> We did not know what forces were wanted or were needed. We did know that the list of forces that you normally identify for a contingency is always wrong. In other words, you never send exactly what you have planned. In fact, one of the lessons I have been emphasizing to people for many years is that your plan is good for one purpose, and that is: to get you into the practice of putting things together and making it happen; but when you actually have a contingency, I can guarantee you; I can say without a doubt, 100 percent, that you will never send in toto the number of forces and the types of forces that you have in your plan. It just will not happen.[71]

Overall, as Warden's group recalled, Russ saw no problems with the existing organization: "TAC is the best organized, the best trained and the best led it has ever been, and I do not see any need to make any changes."[72] Ashy agreed: "TAC had been doing operations successfully for over ten years, so why change that?"[73]

Russ apparently believed that Warden and his team had performed an academic study and that they were tinkering with his organization. Now that he had expressed his viewpoint he expected Warden to drop the matter. General Welch, for his part, was nearing the end of his career and was never entirely convinced of the utility of the new structure. Still, he admitted that the project had raised some important ideas and he agreed with the slogan "air power should hit the enemy like a vicious thunderstorm, not like a sprinkling of raindrops."[74] Thus, although Rice supported the composite force idea, it did not gain the necessary endorsement from four-star generals at the time. Generals Dugan and McPeak, respectively air commanders in chief for Europe and the Pacific, strongly approved of the idea but did not press for its adoption.

Warden's goal was to change the air force mindset, and the Air Legion was only one instrument that he used to "push the envelope" of thought. Warden and Deptula sought a "new image of airpower and its capability to 'create effect' on the enemy," suggesting "Think of the Air Force in terms of its ability to fight and produce operational level results—not in terms of numbers of aircraft and sorties."[75] The senior leadership finally accepted the composite wing idea when Dugan replaced Welch as air force chief of staff in June 1990:

> We are looking at new concepts for our organizational arrangements—
> composite force structures—units and combinations of units made up
> of different kinds of aircraft capable of projecting airpower over all
> distances long and short . . . units assigned to a single commander and
> capable of carrying out such missions as close air support, defensive
> counterair, and battle area interdiction and other missions as necessary
> with its own assets.[76]

When McPeak in turn replaced Dugan later that year he expressed the
same view: "the Air Force should consider creating tactical wings that reflect the
mix of aircraft required to fight as an integrated unit . . . forces should be organized the way we intend to fight."[77] During November and December 1990
McPeak called on Warden several times to present new ideas on how to implement composite forces and ultimately approved Warden's proposal by establishing two composite wings: one at Mountain Home AFB in southwestern Idaho,
which was dedicated to long-range strikes; and the other at Pope AFB, adjacent
to Fort Bragg, North Carolina, which would be associated with the army and
would deploy together with ground forces when necessary. The new structure fell
short of the Air Legion's original scope: McPeak reduced both the numbers and
the composition to fit his own preferred structure,[78] but Warden's group had
succeeded in reintroducing a concept that had been abandoned for decades. In
1991 Secretary Rice reported to Congress that:

> internal restructuring focuses on streamlining the Air Force to increase
> organizational efficiency from the flight line to Air Force headquarters.
> One innovative initiative is the creation of composite wings that in-
> clude—at one base, under one commander—all the resources needed
> to form composite force packages. One wing commander will have all
> the necessary resources to execute "mission type" orders, significantly
> reducing command, control, and communications (C^3) problems.[79]

The composite wing philosophy, which to some extent followed from the
Air Legion, never established itself in the air force. Still, according to Welch, it
was the forerunner of what would later become the Air Expeditionary Force: not
in form or function, but in prompting the air force to extend its thinking beyond
the static cold war structure.[80]

THE AIR OPTION

Warden's directorate undertook another important project that helped move the
USAF out of its cold war orientation by changing how the biennial Defense
Planning Guidance (DPG) reflected the air force's potential contributions. The

DPG represented the secretary of defense's strategic plan for developing and employing future forces. It included both the formulation of defense strategy and guidance for key planning and programming priorities to execute that strategy, and reflected military advice and information provided by the Joint Staff and each of the services. Typically, in preparing for the DPG, each service would present the Office of the Secretary of Defense (OSD) with its projections of the most plausible future threat scenarios and what forces it would need to meet such threats. The OSD then used the DPG to define the major weapon programs and budgets for each service.

When Warden examined the existing document he observed that, in broad terms, the answer to each threat scenario came down to a choice between reliance on the "Land Option" or the "Maritime Option," with the air force playing a secondary or tertiary role. His Long-Range Planning Division was obligated to provide input to the DPG, and in early 1989 he asserted that there was a third option for crisis management: the "Air Option," which allowed for swift deployment and employment that would deter, halt, and even defeat an enemy from the air. Actions could range from retaliatory air strikes, such as Operation El Dorado Canyon (the attacks against Libya in April 1986) to an operation in which the Soviet Union threatened to attack, or attacked, the Persian Gulf region. Warden sought to convince the leadership that its inputs to the DPG should showcase the unique characteristics that air power could contribute to national security. Turner and Deptula, who led this project, stressed the advantages of air power in both economic and military terms. In an era of diminishing defense budgets, the "Air Option" was affordable and it strengthened the American economic and technological base. From a military perspective, air power had the ability to reach a conflict area faster and more cheaply than other forms of power, and employment of air power typically put fewer people at risk.

As Warden's group presented the case for global power projection, they used many of the same arguments as for the Air Legion concept, but they highlighted four trends. First, deterrence would remain the fundamental mission, but smaller forces would be adequate for confined threats. Second, the future would require lighter and more agile forces than the NATO structure. Third, force projection rather than force presence would be crucial. Finally, each service would perform the specific functions best suited to it, rather than merely contributing to parts of the broader tasks that had resulted in missions being diffused across the Department of Defense. Consequently, the core air force missions would be:

> nuclear deterrence (fundamental mission); aerospace control and employment (strategic defense, air and space superiority); projection of air power (ability to attack targets globally and timely deployment); attack of surface forces (more likely in conjunction with allies); air

movement of national influence (more than movement of military forces); and global surveillance and reconnaissance (essential national asset).[81]

At a fundamental level, Warden's team described air power in a new world order. Their major argument asserted that air power would assume greater importance in the national defense equation as forward basing decreased, that the international situation was becoming more complicated and less predictable, and that rapid response had become increasingly important. Thus, air power had a significant role to play across the spectrum from nuclear deterrence to disaster relief. Ten days before Iraq's invasion of Kuwait, Warden made a remarkably accurate prediction:

> The most likely kinds of wars that we will fight will be the kinds that are intended to stop offensive behavior on the part of a country that is working its own agenda, that is trying to steal something from us or from some other country, or in some way or other is doing something that is entirely unacceptable to us, not because we are the world policemen, but because it interferes with very legitimate U.S. interests. These wars that we conduct to stop offensive behavior on the part of other states will be characterized by sharp, decisive action on our part, designed to reach a conclusion as quickly as possible, and to do so with few or no U.S. casualties—and I might add with the least number of casualties to the enemy state consistent with the political and military objectives that we have set for ourselves.[82]

The impact of the Air Option initiative on planning documents is difficult to assess, but during the latter half of 1989 and the first half of 1990 the secretary of defense and the secretary of the air force increasingly referred to the "aerospace option" when discussing military capabilities, and over time the DPG and the Quadrennial Defense Review (QDR) began to incorporate what air power could achieve separate from supporting action on the battlefield proper.[83] According to Maj. Gen. Ronald J. Bath, who was closely involved with the subject for several years, the basic ideas pursued by the "Wardenites" found their way into the QDR in the late 1990s; "their footprints were all over the documents."[84] He stated: "Warden was the vanguard of a new air force and his ideas are embedded throughout the USAF's organization and doctrine beyond the 1990s, although many of his ideas have evolved far beyond what he foresaw and others have been left mainly untouched."[85]

The Air Option apparently helped the air force to define its own role and make it more conscious, as an institution, of power projection. Indeed, the slogan developed by the Warden team was that "global air power *is* power projection."[86] Warden was convinced that air power could, in essence, seize territory by controlling access to that territory and movement across it.[87] If taken to an extreme not contemplated at the time, the Air Option meant that a country could be occupied from the air, revisiting the air policing that the British conducted in the 1920s and 1930s in the Middle East and North Africa. Such activities, of course, became a reality throughout the 1990s over Iraq and the Balkans.

In predicting that the future would entail smaller conflicts along the periphery rather than a large war in Europe Warden's group maintained that the air force should be able to conduct two simultaneous contingencies. Their recommendation relied on twenty-four USAF fighter wings, twelve active army divisions, and twelve aircraft carriers. XOXW presented the "two concurrent regional contingencies" philosophy to the Joint Staff, and the initial proposal served as a basis for national force structuring over the next decade. The concept encountered considerable opposition from the overseas commands, because it implied reducing forward bases, but the Joint Staff adopted it and expanded it into national policy.

A VIEW OF THE AIR FORCE TODAY

In the summer and fall of 1989, noting the lack of a position paper that identified the problems within the air force rather than the symptoms, three of Warden's subordinates wrote a paper titled "A View of the Air Force Today." The principal author, Lt. Col. Michael V. Hayden, and his two collaborators, Cols. Jeff Watson and Jeff Barnett, offered a provocative and constructive criticism of the air force leadership, expressing concern that the lack of a central vision was costing the service its long-term relevance.[88] It argued that the air force identified itself with air weapons and rooted itself in commitment to technological superiority, with the consequence that aircraft and systems, rather than missions and roles, had become the primary focus:

> The lack of an overarching strategy to integrate its constituent parts has fostered an unusual conservatism within the Air Force. With an inclination to focus on the parts (systems and commands) rather than the whole (mission and strategy), other than in the application of new technology to exciting ways of doing business, there is a tendency to view innovation as a threat rather than an opportunity. . . . We ultimately have to admit that we have failed to communicate a coherent strategic vision from which we and Congress can draw the meaning and justification for various Air Force programs. It is our contention that we have failed to fully communicate such a vision because the

current "culture" of the Air Force makes even the development of such a vision difficult, if not impossible. . . . some 40 to 50% of the Air Force junior officers have reported consistently that they "think of themselves as specialists working for the Air Force rather than as professional military officers."[89]

The authors suggested that the way forward was to focus on "operational art." This meant, first, identifying the unifying thread that ran through all of the service's warfighting tasks; second, viewing air power as a tool at the operational level of war; third, understanding the service's rich heritage—exemplified by Gen. George Kenney, who "viewed airpower as an integrated whole and applied it with imagination"; and fourth, reasserting the commitment to joint operations. Although Warden was never closely involved with the writing, all three authors have stated that he encouraged them to express their real concerns and that he served as an "air power mentor." They also recalled that Warden encouraged his men to think seriously and critically about the purpose of their own profession and its role in national security.[90]

The document was highly controversial, and many senior airmen disliked the effort altogether. However, both Dugan and Boyd praised the paper and Dugan ensured that it was distributed among a select few within USAFE. The "underground paper" was closely held and has never been published in its entirety, although excerpts were printed in *Inside the Air Force* in May 1991 and Carl H. Builder, senior analyst at the RAND Corporation, summarized it in his book *The Icarus Syndrome* three years later.

Global Reach—Global Power

From an intellectual perspective, the culmination of XOXW's doctrinal and educational influence was "Global Reach—Global Power": a set of briefings which was turned into a white paper that defined how air power could be used to achieve national objectives and suggested a path toward an integrated view of the USAF and its use of air power. First published in June 1990, the paper was expanded after Operation Desert Storm: the second version differed from the first more in style than in content, which reflects well on the visionary nature of the first report. It has since been circulated to a wide audience inside and outside the air force.

"Global Reach—Global Power," as published in June 1990, boldly asserted that air power in the modern world offered a hitherto unknown degree of leverage and power. The paper's concise and powerful message, supported by the leadership, provided a clear directive for airmen, while at the same time serving as a doctrinal, budgetary, and force structure blueprint.[91] It offered a perspective on how air power's unique characteristics—speed, range, flexibility, precision, and lethality—contributed to national security in a rapidly changing world. It broke the linkage between specific aircraft types and mission areas, emphasizing that "U.S. forces must be able to provide rapid, tailored response with a capability to intervene against a well-equipped foe, hit hard, and terminate quickly. The implication for U.S. force structure is a requirement for fast, agile, modernized conventional capabilities."[92] In the Persian Gulf area, or deep in other theaters, long-range bombers could threaten or strike targets in the crucial first hours or early days of a conflict, and in fact might be the only assets capable of doing so.[93] The bomber's extended reach meant that the United States could project power and enhance presence in a very short time, and at a lower cost than other options. According to Builder, the document marked a watershed in air force history:

> It came from the highest level of Air Force leadership as a statement of its perceptions and policies; it served to fill, partially, the apparent vacuum identified in *A View of the Air Force Today* about the fate of the Air Force as an institution; its short title, *Global Reach—Global Power*, caught on as an apt motto or slogan for the Air Force and its role in the future; [and] it was decidedly up-beat at a time of fiscal bleakness and institutional uncertainty. At the very least, it was a soothing and reassuring balm to a troubled Air Force constituency. At best, it was a bold bid to define the Air Force's central role in the future of the nation's security.
>
> Most of all, it is about current Air Force capabilities and air power attributes—not so much about what they should be as about what they are. Strikingly, it presents a perspective of the nation's interests and security needs which are extensions of the past, but projected into a future world environment that is admittedly, uncertainly different. It briefly declares priorities only with respect to Air Force people and technology—aspects whose importance is not reinforced elsewhere in the document or supported by its balance. It declares the attributes of air power that should be revered and preserved. It devotes most of its attention to restating the traditional spectrum of Air Force missions.
>
> Perhaps the short title of the document will be its greatest, most durable contribution. Global Reach—Global Power captures something that seems new and pertinent to air power in the future. Air power has finally achieved evident and routine global reach—not just through the aerial refueling of bombers, fighters, and airlifters, but also through the reach of intercontinental ballistic missiles and global nets of spacecraft. And the desire to apply such power anywhere on the globe, if not simultaneously globally, seems to be independent of the uncertainties about the changing world and the nation's interests.[94]

Deptula, one of Warden's key action officers, was the paper's primary author. With Warden's full support, he had moved from XOXW to the office of the secretary of the air force in September 1989, and the two remained in close contact. Deptula brought Warden into the effort when he discussed the white paper project with him; he also asked Warden to think about a catch phrase and a position paper. After a few days Warden offered, among others, "Global Reach—Global Power." Deptula, after generating his own ideas and soliciting input from several different sources, considered the phrase the "best of breed" in capturing the essence of how air power contributed to national objectives.[95] He used it as the title for Rice's briefing, and Rice, too, liked it.

Warden offered three pages of notes for the position paper. Deptula used the main arguments along with his own, and led the effort to expand the ideas originally outlined by Rice into a fifteen-page manifesto. Warden had significant input and undoubtedly furnished insights, but what made it such a powerful document were Rice's vision and determination, Deptula's ability to translate some of the more abstract ideas into clear and forceful writing, Christopher Bowie's analytical skills in cutting to the heart of issues, and Col. John W. Brooks's editorial talent.[96]

In contrast to the then-current focus on the aircraft carrier as the key platform for rapid force projection, the paper advocated long-range, land-based air power projection. Although it emphasized the need to think jointly, it implied that a reassessment of the role of the aircraft carrier in long-range strikes against deeply located land targets was long overdue. It urged defense planners to rethink what large, expensive, and manpower-intensive carrier battle groups actually brought to the table.

"Global Reach—Global Power" made both politicians and military officers aware of what air power could contribute in the event of a crisis. According to air force historian Richard P. Hallion, it "attracted immediate attention within the national defense community, provoking an immediate debate between air power modernists and sea power traditionalists, particularly over its recognition that land-based air power now constituted the dominant form of national presence and power projection."[97] In addition, when Iraq invaded Kuwait the paper presented a rationale for what air power could contribute beyond supporting ground operations; read in retrospect, it set forth many of the attributes of land-based air power made manifest in Desert Storm.[98] The document also provided the conceptual basis for a later white paper, published in 1992: "Reshaping for the Future." The latter suggested moving away from the "old, artificial distinction between tactical and strategic weapons and organizations." Acting on its recommendations, the air force dismantled SAC, TAC, and the Military Airlift Command and reassembled their constituent elements as Air

Combat Command (fighters, bombers, reconnaissance aircraft, C³ platforms, some air-lifters and tankers, and intercontinental ballistic missiles) and Air Mobility Command (the majority of air-lifters and tanker assets). Ironically, some of the uniformed leadership misunderstood this attempt to reflect an integrated vision of air power, and instead caused the air force to exchange a divide between strategic and tactical for one between "power" warriors and "reach" warriors.

WORKING RELATIONSHIPS

The late 1980s were in many ways a period in which the USAF regained its own theory of operational and strategic operations, a recuperation that had started in the mid-1980s and manifested itself in the 1990s. By developing and presenting a persuasive air power theory Warden's group of airmen helped identify a mission statement relevant to a period of transition and played a leading role in rediscovering the lost art of operational and strategic air power. Warden's directorate articulated how air power could contribute to national defense, challenged the existing structure by reintroducing the "composite wing" philosophy, formulated a new PME curriculum, revised the air force's basic doctrine manual, and provided significant inputs for the original "Global Reach—Global Power" white paper. "Global Reach—Global Power" was, arguably, the USAF's most important statement on its role in national security since it became a separate service in 1947.

It is difficult to assess Warden's influence on the intellectual and conceptual development that the USAF underwent in the timeframe of 1988–1990, but at the very least he served as a catalyst and provocateur. Both Dugan and Rice acknowledge Warden's importance as an intellectual force,[99] an assessment confirmed by Rice's speechwriter, Ellen Piazza:

> Warden's ideas were reflected in all major speeches that Secretary Rice gave for as long as he was working in the Air Staff. Whenever I was preparing a speech I would contact Warden and we would discuss what arguments should be made for the various audiences, be it industry groups, business leaders, the senate, the USAF or other air force organizations throughout the world. He was the most forward thinking officer in the Air Staff. He was very generous with his time and he was willing to share his ideas without thinking about getting credit for it. He was driven by clarity of purpose and an unerring ability to see over the horizon.[100]

Warden's indirect link to the secretary of the air force, through Deptula and Ellen Piazza, and his direct link to other general officers energized most of his subordinates, but did not please Lieutenant General Adams, who believed that Warden circumvented the chain of command inappropriately.[101] The strained relationship would play itself out over the next few months. According to David Halberstam, by the summer of 1990 Warden had already earned a reputation as "Right Turn Warden," because "if he had a compelling idea and a superior rejected it, he simply took a right turn and went to the next higher level. Failing there, he would take yet another right turn and go to the next higher level, infuriating in the process a long line of his superiors."[102] Warden simply believed that major changes required major steps, and in support of his ideas he would operate in the twilight of the feasible as a matter of principle: "Real exploitation of air power's potential can only come through making assumptions that it can do something we thought it couldn't do . . . We must start our thinking by assuming we can do everything with air power, not by assuming that it can only do what it did in the past."[103]

In fact, Warden generated "crazy ideas" as well as acknowledged insights. For example, he directed Col. John W. Roe, who headed the Long-Range Planning Division, to develop a plan for how the USAF could prepare itself for a possible war scenario five hundred years in the future. Roe decided this assignment was not worth the effort, and prayed that it would go away. When Warden later commented that he was saddened by the lack of progress, Roe explained that, for all practical purposes, "he had been asked to stand on the deck of Santa Maria in 1492, preparing to sail west, and to foresee electricity, computers, television and rubber tires."[104] Much work was needed on more pressing issues. Moreover, the project would create such a high "giggle factor" that Warden would lose credibility; Roe warned Warden that his many initiatives had stirred up considerable controversy and this project would merely add to it without generating anything of value. Warden reluctantly agreed to table the effort. But, as Roe observed, "the process that produced those ideas was the same that resulted in some of his best ideas, and in all fairness, he generated a remarkable number of both."[105]

While his men at Bitburg had perceived him as someone who could not relate to their daily concerns, in XOXW Warden developed a constituency that thought very highly of him and his ideas and was willing to take risks to support his actions. He learned the names and backgrounds of all his subordinates, and assigned them to projects according to individual potential.[106] Many admired him because he did not hesitate to express his reservations about the system, and in promoting fresh and innovative ideas he stimulated his subordinates to examine the service's basic doctrines.[107] In the Pentagon he established a reputation for intellectual openness, creativity, and energy. He cared deeply about important air power ideas and was willing to debate and refine them with anyone who showed an interest, regardless of rank.[108]

But Warden did not win everyone over. He seems to have inspired tremendous respect and dedication among those who worked with him on a daily basis, particularly those who were part of his team on a given project or with whom he exchanged ideas, while those who saw him only from a greater distance seem to have perceived him as obsessively intense and humorless. The intellectually inclined among his staff found Warden "mentally stimulating" since he challenged them to think: through brainstorming and analysis he created an environment uniquely conducive to developing alternative ideas about air power and strategy.[109] To some this was the epitome of ideal leadership: they were given a legitimate mandate to criticize existing patterns and promote institutional change.[110] To others, questioning the current organization and operational procedures amounted to disloyalty.

In leading XOXW Warden emphasized that individuals from all divisions would work together, and he assigned team members on the basis of individual expertise, knowledge, and interests. His division chiefs were given a free hand in addressing their tasks rather than detailed orders. He held monthly sessions with as many as possible, while chiefs and key project officers would meet weekly. His "loose-rein" leadership style brought out the best in some, but he paid less attention to administration and motivation, simply assuming that everybody would exhibit his own level of energy and dedication to the job. Moreover, Warden did not always delegate tasks explicitly, and consequently his subordinates developed some rivalry over gaining control of interesting projects. The less interesting work was left largely untouched, which prompted some skepticism about Warden's management by "chaos theory." Warden expected his staff to be competent self-starters who needed very little supervision, but many officers did not fit such a description.

Subordinates recall that sometimes Warden seemed a genuinely caring leader and at other times seemed to view his staff merely as implementers of his ideas. The comments were reminiscent of T. E. Lawrence's description of Royal Air Force Marshal Hugh M. Trenchard as a great man who was unaffected by all the little people around him, who were not as brilliant as he, and who tried to hinder or help him in his work.[111] These admittedly subjective impressions help to explain why Warden often failed to convince both subordinates and superiors that he had their best interests at heart.

As in his previous assignments, Warden proved controversial as the Director of Warfighting Concepts, becoming known by names that ranged from "Saint John" to "Mad John."[112] Yet he rose from the ashes of Bitburg, found his milieu, and established himself as the Pentagon's premier authority on air power strategy. The air campaign plan that he suggested in response to the Iraqi invasion in August 1990 did not represent a sudden leap of creativity, but the embodiment of a process that had been ongoing for more than two years in the Directorate for Warfighting Concepts. When Iraq invaded Kuwait he had the ideas and the team that made a crucial difference.

8

INSTANT THUNDER:
VICTORY THROUGH AIR POWER

The planning to liberate Kuwait originated with Warden's group of air power advocates in the Air Staff. They suggested an effects-based, war-winning air campaign concept that sought to paralyze the Iraqi regime and its leadership. Their proposal, Instant Thunder, stood in sharp contrast to the existing contingency plans for the Persian Gulf, in which air power was viewed as a ground-supporting instrument. Not surprisingly, Warden's initial concept created widespread controversy, especially among the leaders of TAC, who developed an alternative concept far more in line with the accepted AirLand Battle doctrine. Disagreements over issues central to air power may help explain why Gen. H. Norman Schwarzkopf thought highly of Warden's ideas, why Gen. Robert D. Russ and his planning group at TAC categorically rejected the same ideas, and why Lt. Gen. Charles A. Horner had very mixed feelings about the Air Staff's planning effort.

Background: The Contingency Plan for the Persian Gulf
In the fall of 1989 Gen. Colin L. Powell, chairman of the Joint Chiefs of Staff, asked General Schwarzkopf, commander in chief of Central Command, to update the off-the-shelf plan for a scenario in which Iraq threatened and then invaded both Saudi Arabia and Kuwait. Schwarzkopf responded in April 1990 by issuing an outline of what became OPLAN 1002-90, describing how the United States would deploy and use its military forces. The contingency plan was based on the premise that U.S. forces would have sufficient time to deploy prior to an invasion and that air power would support army ground forces as they closed with the enemy.

Schwarzkopf and his staff viewed air power as the means of gaining and maintaining air superiority to protect the ports of entry, as a force multiplier for defensive ground operations, and as a participant in a land-dominated offensive that would restore preconflict international borders.[1] In accordance with AirLand

Battle doctrine, the plan divided the main operational scheme into three phases: deterrence, defense, and a ground-based counteroffensive. The first phase would seek to dissuade Iraq from attacking through a show of force: deployment of aircraft and, if necessary, demonstrative strikes against a few high-value targets. The second consisted of counterair operations to establish air superiority and an interdiction campaign to delay, disrupt, or destroy attacking enemy troops. The third phase would begin when the fighting capability of the enemy army had been reduced to a level in which the force ratio favored American troops: air power, in the form of close air support would then work in tandem with the ground forces to counterattack and push the enemy back within its borders.

Lieutenant General Horner, commander of Central Command Air Forces (CENTAF), assured Schwarzkopf in April 1990 that he could deploy on short notice and that air power could prove very effective, either by interdicting the Iraqi second echelon and its supply lines, or by playing a defensive or offensive role in conjunction with ground forces. Horner had been the deputy chief of staff for plans at TAC from May 1985 to March 1987 and in that capacity had worked closely with the army's TRADOC. He thought that the new AirLand Battle doctrine was a useful step in the context of joint operations, but he did not view it as governing the employment of air power: it simply represented how the army at Fort Leavenworth thought they would fight a force-on-force land battle.[2]

Horner suggested several elements that Schwarzkopf should consider: he elaborated on combined Saudi-American operations and advocated that the air forces receive border-crossing authority early so that they could attack the air defense system in southern Iraq, engage follow-on forces, and disrupt supply and infrastructure in the rear area. Most important, during the counteroffensive Horner planned to move away from traditional close air support operations to "PUSH CAS." He would give all aircraft counterair or interdiction missions: "I want them always hitting a target, and then if the army needed them, we would divert them. . . . If there was no divert requirement, no meeting engagement by tanks on tanks, then I would just continue that sortie, and it would go on and strike a valid target; go back and land, rearm, and go again, so I always had my air employed."[3] As for supporting ground operations, Horner noted that he would "build a hose and point it where the ground commander sees that it is needed."[4]

Horner also suggested that he could conduct retaliatory strikes to demonstrate American resolve if Iraq used chemical or biological weapons. He referred to punishment, deterrence, and quid-pro-quo targeting, and he referred to high-value Iraqi assets as "strategic targets." Schwarzkopf liked this notion, but Horner regretted using the term "strategic" the moment he uttered it: he believed it made no sense in a non-nuclear setting.[5]

Schwarzkopf's second draft of OPLAN 1002-90, issued in July, contained no major changes from the previous outline.[6] The updated version relied on a defensive posture; it did not include Horner's retaliatory option and it did not envision large-scale offensive operations. It also did not include anything that resembled a strategic air campaign.[7] In preparation for the Internal Look command post exercise to be held that month, CENTCOM and CENTAF planners devoted most of their time to examining logistical problems and maintenance issues, identifying command and control relationships, and formulating a scheme for moving assets into theater in a timely manner.[8]

The Internal Look scenario involved Iraqi forces attacking Kuwait, consolidating their position, and then invading Saudi Arabia along two routes. Horner's CENTAF staff generated a plan with six objectives: defend rear areas and maintain air superiority over the battlefield; suppress forward-deployed enemy air defenses; conduct close air support for friendly troops; conduct interdiction to delay and inflict loss on the advancing enemy; conduct offensive counterair against the southern airfields; and conduct reconnaissance of the enemy rear, command and control, and lines of communication.[9] Horner approved a target list that comprised eleven categories and 218 targets, most of them in southern Iraq, Kuwait, and northern Saudi Arabia. However, CENTAF admitted that it lacked sufficient imagery or information to prosecute half of those targets.[10] The simulated National Command Authority allowed cross-border strikes only in the last two days of the exercise, which reflected the prevailing sensitivity over offensive operations against an enemy's homeland.[11]

As CENTCOM and its component commands focused on Internal Look, the concentration of Iraqi formations on the Kuwaiti border indicated that a real threat might be developing. At 1400 EDT on August 1, 1990, the secretary of defense, Richard B. Cheney, summoned Powell and Schwarzkopf to the Pentagon for an update. Schwarzkopf characterized the Iraqi threat as a bluff aimed at extorting higher oil prices; he believed that Iraq merely sought the forgiveness of debts from Kuwait and other Arab states. He acknowledged that Iraq might attack two islands, Warba and Bubiyan, as well as a few ports in Kuwait and the disputed oilfield of Rumalia, but he did not believe that Iraq would invade the entire country. He reviewed OPLAN 1002-90 with Cheney and Powell and explained that since he had no forces in the region he would need several weeks to deploy sufficient assets to deal with the Iraqi war machine even if the president, Congress, and the Arab states sanctioned the commitment of forces.[12]

U.S. RESPONSE TO IRAQI AGGRESSION

Iraq's full-scale invasion of Kuwait, launched at 1800 EDT on August 1, thus took the American political and military leadership by surprise. CENTCOM ordered CENTAF to prepare for deployment to Saudi Arabia through its Rapid Reaction Plan 1307-88, a package of aircraft comprising twelve F-16s or eight

F-15Cs, two E-3 AWACS, one RC-135 Rivet Joint, and three KC-10s. The greatest fear was that Saddam Hussein might order his troops into Saudi Arabia and capture the critical oil facilities in the northeastern areas. The fighter-bombers would be sent to deter the Iraqis from acting upon such a temptation. The plan anticipated arrival in theater within forty-eight hours and operational readiness within ninety-six; it also envisioned sending another package with the same composition, in effect preparing for the implementation of OPLAN 1002-90 should it be deemed necessary.[13]

At 0800 on August 2 President George H. W. Bush convened a meeting of the National Security Council (NSC), which Cheney, Powell, and Schwarzkopf attended. Schwarzkopf explained it would take three months to mass enough combat power to defend Saudi Arabia against an Iraqi attack, and another five to seven months if he were ordered to liberate Kuwait. Later that day Cheney told Powell that he needed "practical military options to lay before the president": he would like more imaginative plans, especially one that allowed for powerful retaliatory strikes. Remembering the "Air Option" and "Global Reach—Global Power," Cheney urged the chairman to prepare "a serious air campaign" that would "hurt Iraq."[14]

The next morning, Schwarzkopf drove his staff mercilessly. His main objective was to produce a deployment plan for the defense of Saudi Arabia in accordance with OPLAN 1002-90: he was dissatisfied with CENTCOM's progress overall and was distinctly unhappy with the air power portion. Schwarzkopf turned his frustration at his director of operations, Maj. Gen. Burton R. Moore, and then called upon his air commander for help. Horner arrived in Tampa that evening and recalled that the atmosphere was very tense:[15]

> General Schwarzkopf and I listened to their briefing and he felt it was terrible. Since General Schwarzkopf was upset about that, I suggested to him, about 11 o'clock at night, to give me a chance to build the briefing and give it to the President. He would present the briefing about what ground operations would be involved if we got into it with Iraq over the defense of Saudi Arabia while I built the air portion of that briefing. We worked until about 3 o'clock in the morning. The slides were dripping wet when we got on a C-21 and flew to Washington.[16]

In the briefing delivered to Bush, Cheney, and Powell at Camp David on August 4, Schwarzkopf declared that he would need five divisions to defend Saudi Arabia. For the short term, he proposed a defensive delaying action with no amphibious assaults, airborne operations, or use of special forces. Horner then explained that to defend Saudi Arabia air power could try to defeat the lead elements of the Iraqi forces, but he recommended a basic strategy of attacking and defeating follow-on forces by first cutting off their logistical support, especially food, water, fuel, and munitions.[17] He stated that air power should support Schwarzkopf's scheme of maneuver: the basic plan was to weaken the attacking elements and make sure they lacked the logistics support they needed to press the attack against Riyadh.[18] He also mentioned the possibility of conducting "punitive air strikes against Iraq" if U.S. forces faced Scuds armed with chemical warheads.[19]

The briefing centered on the defense of Saudi Arabia, but Schwarzkopf also mentioned that if he were ordered to liberate Kuwait he would prefer an attacker-to-defender ratio of five-to-one. With nine Iraqi divisions in Kuwait this meant that Schwarzkopf wanted forty-five divisions. Since such a force was unrealistic he suggested that air power could pave the way for ground operations, showing a slide that stated: "Must have heavy air attrition prior to ability to wage successful offense."[20] He also stated that U.S. formations would need eight to ten months to prepare for such an offensive.

The presentation was well received, and the next day Cheney traveled to Jeddah, Saudi Arabia, to persuade King Fahd to accept the deployment of U.S. forces. Cheney told Schwarzkopf to accompany him, and Schwarzkopf in turn told Horner to join them. The Saudi regime quickly accepted the U.S. offer and Cheney ordered Schwarzkopf to initiate deployment. He also directed him to develop an "offensive option that would be available to the president in case Saddam Hussein chose to engage in further aggression or other unacceptable behavior, such as killing Kuwaiti citizens or foreign nationals in Kuwait or Iraq."[21]

Schwarzkopf returned to the United States with Cheney, leaving Horner in charge in theater and instructing him that his primary tasks were to receive deploying troops and to develop an ATO for defending Saudi Arabia following OPLAN 1002-90. He also informed Horner that he would have the Pentagon look into some strategic targets—the retaliatory strikes that Cheney insisted on: "Chuck, you are going to be tied up over here, and your staff is coming over here, so in the interim I am going to have the Joint Chiefs of Staff look at a strategic targeting plan."[22] This made Horner uneasy: "Sir, the last thing we want is a repeat of Vietnam, where Washington picked the targets! This is the job of your Air Force commander."[23] Schwarzkopf promised Horner that he would undertake preliminary work only and then hand the matter over to him. While Horner believed that the commander in chief would keep his word, he remained suspicious of any Washington involvement in choosing targets.

THE WONDERFUL TELEPHONE CALL
Warden was unaware of any of these events. When Iraq invaded Kuwait he and his family were on a cruise in the Caribbean, celebrating his son's graduation from pilot training. They were south of Cuba, on their way back to Miami, when

he heard about the invasion on "Ocean News." Margie recalled his immediate comment: "Stupid, stupid Saddam—this means war."[24] Although he took part in the obligatory family activities for the rest of the trip, his mind was elsewhere: unable to get back to the Pentagon until August 5, he stayed in his cabin and thought about how he could develop an offensive strategic air campaign that would force Saddam Hussein to withdraw his troops from Kuwait.[25]

Warden feared that the collection of operational and conceptual plans at the Joint Staff, CENTCOM, or CENTAF included no option for a strategic air campaign. He was further convinced that OPLAN 1002-90, as tested in July 1990, lacked the "nucleus" of an air campaign plan and that CENTAF's plan consisted of no more than a series of air strikes intended to roll the enemy back.[26] He suspected that CENTAF had neither gone beyond discussions about interdicting the second echelon and sample retaliatory strikes nor given full attention to an independent, or even semiautonomous, air campaign that would precede the ground battle.[27] As he saw it, CENTAF had no plans for attacking the enemy's "jugular."[28] Moreover, Warden reasoned, it was highly unlikely that the deliberate planning process would yield any plan with a strategic outlook.[29] He was utterly convinced that conventional thinking would merely produce a ground-oriented campaign focusing on Iraqi ground forces.

When he arrived at his office on August 5 his suspicions were confirmed. He spent his first day back at the Pentagon receiving updates on the crisis and thinking about how to approach the situation. After talking with Col. Michael M. Dunn, the leader of the Strategy Division, he concluded that the Joint Staff had done nothing beyond starting to look at the occupation in terms of a limited cold war scenario. All planning seemed to center on the deployment of forces rather than concepts of operations. Air forces were mentioned only occasionally, and then only in connection with defending an area. Warden decided that "the field was open" and that he was free to make his own suggestions.[30]

Warden believed he now had the opportunity to provide the military commanders with a swift, lethal, air-oriented campaign plan focused on the Iraqi leadership. He would use the Five Rings Model to explain his rationale for targeting. He knew he had the right team for the task and the concept already existed in his mind's eye; developing a plan would be a matter of adapting generic air power theory to the specifics of Iraq. The real challenge would be to bring such a plan to the attention of Schwarzkopf or Horner, neither of whom he knew personally. The senior-level officers with whom he had contact were all in the Air Staff, an organization that the Goldwater-Nichols Act of 1986 explicitly excluded from the combat chain of command.

At a staff meeting on the following day, Warden told the director of plans, Maj. Gen. Robert M. Alexander, "I do not have any idea how it is going to come out, but we are going to put something together anyway and see what happens."[31]

Alexander agreed that it was always good to have options. He was familiar with the idea of an air offensive: he had supported Warden's quest for promoting the Air Option and as a bomber pilot he understood the concept of strategic targets. Thus, on his own initiative and with support from his immediate superior, Warden ordered key members of his directorate to begin selecting target-sets for a stand-alone, war-winning air offensive based on the Five Rings Model.

Warden also contacted Deptula, who had been given access to CENTAF's deployment plan. Both men were troubled because it seemed that the CENTAF staff was preparing for defensive operations only: the plan called for neither fighter-bombers nor the stealthy F-117s, and F-111Ds were preferred to F-111Fs, which were capable of delivering precision-guided munitions (PGMs). Alexander noted that Warden quickly recognized that "We needed to get the proper forces inbound with the right priority."[32] Warden and Deptula believed that the invasion of Kuwait presented them with a mission where their shared vision of "Global Reach—Global Power" could prove its value, but first they would need CENTAF, CENTCOM, or the Joint Staff to give them a hearing.

As it happened, while Warden and Deptula were seeking ways to influence the planning process, Schwarzkopf had become increasingly dissatisfied with his own staff's suggestions for the retaliatory air strikes that he had ordered them to investigate.[33] They proposed using cruise missiles and even discussed the possibilities of threatening to use nuclear weapons or blowing up the dams north of Baghdad. The first course of action would do little more than anger Saddam Hussein; the second and third options would pose serious political problems.[34] Schwarzkopf asked Powell whether the Joint Staff could provide him with a serious air campaign plan, but Powell responded that it lacked the capability to do so.[35]

The two army generals agreed to contact the Air Staff: Gen. Michael J. Dugan, who had become the air force chief of staff in July 1990, had proclaimed that air power could achieve impressive results independent of ground forces if only given the chance.[36] At 0800 on Wednesday, August 8, Schwarzkopf telephoned Dugan, but because Dugan was away the vice chief of staff, Gen. John M. Loh, took the call.[37] In a ten-minute conversation, Schwarzkopf explained that the overloaded CENTCOM and CENTAF staffs could not spare the resources for additional planning, and asked if Loh had a team that could provide him with strategic targets for retaliatory strikes in case Saddam Hussein did something "heinous." Schwarzkopf wanted a plan that would strike deep into Iraq and damage or destroy targets of great value to the Iraqi leadership: "We cannot go out piecemeal with an air/land battle plan. I have got to hit him at his heart! I need it kind of fast."[38] As Loh remembers the discussion, Schwarzkopf wanted a "broader set of targets that dealt with the infrastructure of the country" rather than merely "close air support, battlefield interdiction [and] a few long-range targets."[39] Loh responded that he would be more than happy to help.

General Loh would normally have asked Lieutenant General Adams to prepare a response, but Adams was out of town. Loh then had to decide whether to contact the directorate of plans, which was responsible for long-range planning, or the directorate of operations, which was responsible for current operations. Since Alexander had mentioned to him that the planning directorate had already started to think about an offensive air campaign plan, Loh sent the request to Alexander.

Loh also spoke with General Russ. The TAC commander agreed that the air force should respond to Schwarzkopf's request, but insisted that Horner be included and that TAC lead the effort. Loh was uncomfortable with Russ's demand, but chose not to argue with him for the time being. Loh next contacted Gen. Jack T. Chain, the SAC commander, who immediately offered to send some of his people to help. Finally Loh informed Dugan about the conversations, and Dugan in turn called Schwarzkopf to ensure that the air force fully understood the commander in chief's needs. Schwarzkopf told him that he wanted an air option that could be executed on short notice, and that it should be coherent, independent of ground forces, and strategic in its focus.[40]

As Dugan saw it, such an air option could either be planned by TAC, under the supervision of Russ, or developed by the Air Staff, under the leadership of Warden. Having been Russ's deputy director for operations he feared that the TAC commander and his staff would think only in terms of supporting ground operations, or interdiction at best, rather than strategic air operations. Warden, by contrast, could devise something "conceptually better" and do so "in a shorter timeframe." Dugan also thought that the Pentagon environment had certain advantages over Langley AFB. Most important, he had "extreme confidence in Warden."[41]

Warden was thrilled to respond to "this wonderful call from Schwarzkopf." Schwarzkopf may not have distinguished between retaliatory targets and strategic targets, or retaliatory air strikes and a strategic air campaign plan, but Warden certainly did.[42] Whether or not Schwarzkopf or Loh used the term "strategic air campaign," to him the assignment to plan for strikes deep into the Iraqi homeland in fact meant building a full-blown strategic air campaign.[43] Warden seized the opportunity: as air force historian Richard G. Davis has noted, "The man and the moment met and jumped as one."[44]

THE NO. 1 PROJECT IN THE AIR FORCE

Remembering his experience at Bitburg, where he had been criticized for keeping decision making to himself, and inspired by Tom Peters's *Thriving on Chaos*, Warden decided to approach the forthcoming work using the principle of "open planning."[45] He wanted to involve many people in brainstorming sessions, and since the assignment was a massive and complex undertaking that had to be compressed into a very short period of time, he wanted to bring together personnel with a variety of backgrounds.

Warden first met with his planning team, a group of some thirty officers and enlisted men, on August 8.[46] The briefing took place in a cavernous old room (designated BF 922B) in the Checkmate office suite located in a subbasement of the Pentagon. Standing against a backdrop of maps that covered the shabby walls from floor to ceiling, Warden told the men assembled there that they had been given a historic opportunity: this effort was not an exercise, but a serious attempt to match military power to national objectives, and real lives could be at stake. Warden noted that it was important to design a quick and decisive campaign plan: the air campaign had to be violent and intensive because that would shorten the war and thereby limit casualties and damage. He also jotted down objectives, tasks, and potential target-sets on the whiteboard.

After Warden had provided broad guidance, the team sought an operational title for the plan: a phrase that would explain the concept and also be catchy. When some suggested that a campaign plan featuring a gradual buildup might present a better option, Lieutenant Colonel Kearney, Warden's assistant, replied that the last thing they wanted to do was to repeat the Rolling Thunder strategy. Warden responded: "That's exactly it: it's not Rolling Thunder—it's Instant Thunder!"[47] Warden thought this name provided both a good description and a persuasive selling point: the title as well as the content would imply rejection of a gradual escalation of air attacks that would allow the enemy time to recover and adapt. His plan would be called "Iraqi Air Campaign Instant Thunder."

Warden's directorate had spent several months exploring how best to apply air power in an independent fashion, and over the two previous days the team had investigated how the core set of ideas could be applied against Iraq. The first proposal was therefore ready for internal review in a matter of hours. On the afternoon of August 8 Warden presented Loh, Alexander, and Maj. Gen. Charles A. May Jr., who substituted for the absent Adams, with a plan that included political objectives, military objectives, military strategy, assumptions, five strategic and operational rings with corresponding target-sets, and the USAF weapon systems that would be used to attack those target-sets.

Warden's team had derived the political objectives from the president's speeches, press conferences, and newspaper articles, and formulated them as "withdrawal of Iraqi forces from Kuwait; restoration of Kuwaiti sovereignty; unimpeded flow of oil; and protection of American lives."[48] The corresponding military objectives were to force the withdrawal of Iraqi troops from Kuwait, degrade Iraq's offensive capability, protect oil facilities, and reduce Saddam Hussein's effectiveness as an Arab leader.

Against the background of these political and military objectives Warden emphasized that air power should be used against Saddam Hussein and his regime rather than against the Iraqi people or ground troops. To demonstrate resolve, the United States should apply air power in an offensive, intensive, and aggressive fashion rather than piecemeal, and the campaign should take advantage of advanced technology such as stealth and precision. U.S. strengths would be applied against Iraqi weaknesses and the strategic air campaign, if executed as suggested, could induce the Iraqi leadership to withdraw its forces, eliminating the need to target anything in Kuwait. This strategy was based on several assumptions: Iraq would act without substantial allies; the air campaign would cause selective impairment rather than massive destruction; and American losses, Iraqi civilian casualties, and collateral damage would be held to a minimum. If the air campaign succeeded in keeping casualties low the U.S. population would support the effort and the Iraqi people might even come to view the American action as being in their best interests.

Warden then moved on to the target categories and introduced his Five Rings Model at the strategic and operational levels. The strategic rings consisted of the leadership (Saddam Hussein and military and civilian C^2 systems), essential industry (oil, electricity, chemical plants, and a nuclear research facility), infrastructure (railroads, ports, highways, and civilian and military airfields), population (Iraqi people and foreign workers, targeted through psychological operations (PSYOPS) only), and fielded military forces (strategic air defensive and offensive capabilities associated with Iraqi missiles carrying chemical warheads). He emphasized the importance of focusing on the inner ring, arguing that Saddam Hussein was the source of most of America's problems with Iraq. Since killing Hussein from the air would require extraordinarily good luck, Warden hoped instead to isolate him from his forces and his people by attacking leadership facilities and their communication lines—targets that provided linkages between the highly centralized decision-making elements and the Iraqi population, security forces, and fielded military forces. Neutralizing these systems would upset and discredit the regime while simultaneously reducing its capability to command and control military operations. Even if Hussein survived he would be weakened: he might lose his capability to govern and he might be overthrown. Television and radio stations would be targeted and their output replaced by coalition broadcasts emphasizing that the attacks were directed against the regime and not the Iraqi people.

Moving from the inner ring to the next, Warden emphasized the interdependence among certain targets. Successful attacks against the Iraqi power grid would disrupt every type of information flow within the country. By hitting the electrical network, Warden hoped to gain political leverage over the Iraqi population. "Putting out the lights" in Baghdad would have an added psychological impact; back-up generators would quickly prove inadequate once the national grid had ceased to function. The collapse of the electrical network would also have a considerable impact on the military apparatus: radar installations and communication centers, which depended on computers, were particularly vulnerable. Warden also preferred to reduce oil production available for Iraqi consumption by 70 percent rather than lay waste to the oil fields. He viewed chemical weapons as a more likely threat than biological attacks, especially if they were combined with Scud launchers.

Warden emphasized that Iraq's industry and infrastructure should be damaged only to the extent necessary for victory and so that Iraq could easily repair them after the war with American help.[49] His preference for avoiding long-term destruction reflected his certainty not only that the war would be short, but also that U.S. bombing would be so accurate that it could obliterate parts of a facility while purposely leaving other parts intact. In Warden's view, the new precision and lethality of air weapons meant that for the first time the United States could strike directly and decisively at the strategic heart of the enemy with non-nuclear weapons. Airfields constituted the most important target-set in the third ring for the time being. Air superiority was the key to success; bombs would leave craters and mines behind and render the airfields unusable.

As for the fourth ring, population, it should be subjected only to psychological warfare. Such a campaign was of the utmost importance to increase the impact of the physical attacks, and the physical and psychological pressure would be linked by a scheme for "information warfare."

In the most controversial portion of his presentation, Warden stressed that air power should not be directed against the Iraqi army and its artillery and tanks, and he stated explicitly that a ground campaign would not be necessary to liberate Kuwait. Still, Warden's team identified the air defense system as a target-set because it provided tracking information for Iraqi fighter aircraft and would enable Iraq to launch SAMs against U.S. aircraft. Disrupting this flow of information would fragment the Iraqi air defense effort, forcing the missiles into autonomous mode and leaving interceptors virtually helpless. Thus, attacks on the first, second, and fifth rings would ensure pressure on Iraqi information nodes throughout the operation.[50] The listing of the five operational rings provided further details within corresponding categories: joint commander, war supplies, infrastructure, support personnel, and fielded combat forces.

The final segment of the presentation listed weapon systems that would achieve these effects: fourteen to thirty-two B-52Gs (for area and mining operations); forty-eight F-15Cs (to complement the Royal Saudi Air Force fighters); an unspecified number of F-117s, F-111Fs, F-15Es, and F-16s; Volant Solo EC-130E (an aircraft designed to conduct broadcast missions for PSYOPS); and an unspecified aircraft for unconventional operations if deemed necessary. During these early stages of planning Warden envisioned F-117s hitting targets throughout Iraq and air-launched cruise missiles striking targets in the north.

The Checkmate planners believed that timing and sequence of strikes could have a major effect on success. Their campaign would attempt initial strikes on all major targets within the first forty-eight hours, beginning at night by attacking air defenses. Warden knew of studies that identified a direct relationship between the intensity of operations and the psychological impact on fielded troops: widespread damage over a short period of time was likely to be more unsettling than the same damage over a longer period of time. If the phenomenon applied to trained troops it would probably also hold true for civilian leaders.[51]

Instant Thunder, as presented on August 8, made the case for applying intense and unremitting pressure on Iraq to inflict national paralysis. Such paralysis, Warden argued, would diminish the power of the Iraqi regime to the extent that it would either acquiesce to U.S. demands or be toppled. In essence, the plan's operational approach was to "conduct powerful and focused air attacks on strategic centers of gravity." The air offensive would involve "round-the-clock operations against leadership, strategic air defense," and electrical targets with the aim of achieving "strategic paralysis and air superiority."[52] Physically, it was important first to overcome the system's ability to withstand and compensate for losses—especially challenging because of the robust design of military systems—and then to repair lost capability after the conflict.

The overall concept could hardly have differed more from OPLAN 1002-90. It identified air power, rather than land power, as the primary instrument of force; it focused on how, why, and when air power could achieve specific effects rather than mere destruction; it had a strategic orientation; it could be executed in days rather than months; it promised quick and decisive results; and it focused on the regime rather than on the battlefield.

Loh, Alexander, and May were greatly impressed with the scope and coherence of a plan delivered on such short notice. Loh approved the thrust of the briefing and instructed Warden to expand the skeleton into an executable strategic air campaign plan. He also told him to deliver the presentation to Schwarzkopf within the next two days and then uttered some of the sweetest words Warden had ever heard: "This is the No. 1 project in the Air Force. You can call on anybody anyplace that you need for anything."[53] The colonel took those words literally.

DIVIDED OPINIONS

While Warden and his team continued to focus on the substance of the plan, Alexander sought to build a constituency by persuading various organizations to take part in the planning process from the beginning. He received little encouragement. Concerned that CENTAF was not in the loop, he called the Ninth Air

Force at Shaw AFB, only to learn that most of its members were preparing to deploy, that those left behind were overworked, and that the Tenth Air Force, a reserve unit that was supposed to substitute for the departing Ninth Air Force, had yet to show up. Alexander was told, "If we haven't got anybody, we can't make them available."[54]

THE INTELLIGENCE-PLANNING DIVIDE

However, the greatest obstacle during the first two days of planning was the tense relationship between the Air Staff planners and the intelligence community. Alexander asked Maj. Gen. James R. Clapper Jr., the assistant chief of staff for intelligence, for help, but Clapper considered it inappropriate for a single service to become involved with planning independent of CENTAF. He made it clear that the Air Staff had no place in the chain of command and paid little attention when Alexander told him that the request came directly from Schwarzkopf: Clapper was used to people claiming that they had top cover whenever they wanted something out of the ordinary. Moreover, he believed that the target list that CENTAF had prepared for Internal Look responded adequately to Schwarzkopf's alleged request.[55]

When Alexander called a second time, on instructions from Loh, he stressed the urgency of the request and Clapper gave in, offering Col. James R. Blackburn, the director of targets at the Air Force Intelligence Agency. Yet when Blackburn and Warden met it was obvious that the two men could not agree on how to proceed. First, Blackburn objected that the group lacked clear direction in the form of a "commander's intent." Second, he believed that Warden did not appreciate that intelligence officers needed weeks to produce a target list that could serve as the basis for execution. Third, he considered Warden's effects-based thinking unrealistic. For example, the intelligence database did not have sufficient information to identify all the stations and links that would have to be destroyed to prevent the Iraqi leader from broadcasting on television and radio. Moreover, given the size of Iraq, the United States did not have the resources to stop the entire flow of information and communication. Fourth, Blackburn objected to Warden's insistence on trying to quantify things that were not measurable, such as how many sorties would be needed to achieve 80 percent degradation of a specific target-set. Blackburn believed this would be guesswork at best; for example, "You do not have a 70 percent leadership. We cannot measure the flow of conversation or the flow of command and control messages."[56] Fifth, although Saddam Hussein was the military commander, Blackburn questioned whether he could be targeted directly, because Executive Order 12333 prohibited the targeting of individuals. Sixth, Warden insisted on using a unique target identification system developed by Deptula, who was already working to turn the concepts generated by the Warden group into executable operational reality.

The international intelligence community had an established coding system: each target in the worldwide database was designated by a basic encyclopedia number (BEN) consisting of ten alphanumeric characters assigned sequentially as the targets entered the database. To the uninitiated these thousands of numbers appeared random, and they were impossible to remember. To Blackburn's fury, Warden insisted on using letter identifications according to the Five Rings categories so that the operators would know from the outset what target they were discussing: leadership targets fell in the "L" series, the "E" series designated electricity targets, "O" oil targets, and so on.

Blackburn was especially troubled by Warden's disregard for existing routines and systems. Like most intelligence officers, Blackburn considered it entirely unacceptable to work intelligence projects outside the chain of command. He also feared that Warden's effort would gain independent momentum by taking control of other organizations and individuals, and that carefully designed formal networks would be undermined. In particular, he objected to the group's receiving input from various intelligence agencies, because he believed this resulted in unsound conclusions that did not benefit from skilled intelligence fusion. Yet, despite his reservations, Blackburn announced his support for Warden's effort on August 9. Two days later, at Warden's insistence, Blackburn moved from Bolling AFB into the Pentagon, where he set up a supporting cell of thirteen intelligence officers. Over time the two colonels established a reasonable working relationship, but they never developed mutual trust, and Warden believed that Blackburn continually undermined his operation.

PREPARING TO BRIEF SCHWARZKOPF

Warden's group worked around the clock to develop the presentation for Schwarzkopf, and most of its members found that the Five Rings Model provided a common focus and purpose. Warden told his staff that for every target they selected they would have to answer the key question: how does attacking this target influence the leadership? He encouraged his team to think systematically, but creatively, of targets within the Five Ring Model's target-sets, and he ensured that weapon system experts were assigned to Checkmate to match the appropriate assets to the targets.

During the first forty-eight hours of the planning effort Warden relied primarily on three men: Deptula, who now worked for the secretary of the air force; Lt. Col. Bernard E. Harvey, who had assisted in the strategic planning leading to Operation Just Cause against Panama (1989) and was assigned to the Strategy Division; and Lt. Col. Ronald Stanfill, who had been part of the team that planned Operation El Dorado Canyon against Libya (1986) and was now assigned to the Checkmate division. Deptula concentrated on relating the overall purpose of the plan to the effects it sought to achieve, Harvey took the lead on intelligence-related matters, and Stanfill was responsible for weapon systems.

On the morning of August 10 Warden met again with Loh, Alexander, and May to give them a quick update on the plan that he would deliver to Schwarzkopf later that day. He asserted that if Schwarzkopf accepted the Instant Thunder concept by August 12, including a change in the deployment flow, the plan could be executed by August 18.[57] He further suggested that this would leave his division enough time to implement a deception plan: a formation of forces would apparently attack straight ahead into Kuwait while the real attacking force would aim for Saddam Hussein's leadership in central Baghdad.[58]

The plan that Warden prepared for Schwarzkopf differed from the first draft only in minor details. The title changed from "Iraqi Air Campaign Instant Thunder" to "Instant Thunder: A Strategic Air Campaign Proposal for CINCCENT." Because Schwarzkopf had requested a strategic air campaign, the new version deleted the operational rings and their associated target-sets. It also left out the graphic showing the five concentric rings, because Maj. Gen. Michael E. Ryan, the deputy chief of staff for operations at TAC and a classmate from the Air Force Academy, had seen an early draft of Instant Thunder and bluntly advised Warden to get rid of the rings because they were "an academic bunch of crap."[59] Ryan commented that he "liked everything [about the brief] after the last slide . . . [it was] the biggest disinformation plan I have ever seen in my life."[60] Finally, the new version devoted more attention to assumptions and objectives, including a brief war-termination scenario and an outline of courses of action.

The new version also incorporated a general target list of eighty-four targets, a summary of capabilities, a deployment and execution flow, a deception plan, and more ideas about PSYOPs. The psychological campaign now sought to discredit Iraqi propaganda: planners targeted foreign workers in Iraq to "neutralize" their support of Saddam Hussein's military initiatives and unspecified "Iraqi audiences" to lessen their opposition to U.S. actions.[61]

The unified strategic air campaign plan was bold both conceptually and technologically. The keys to success would be the hitherto unproven combination of stealth and precision, which in turn redefined the principle of mass. The revised plan highlighted two weapon systems: the B-52G and the F-117A. The first would employ long-range standoff munitions and general-purpose bombs, while the second would carry GBU-27, which could penetrate bunkers with unprecedented precision and power.

Loh, Alexander, and May were comfortable with the plan, and both Rice and Dugan, who had been briefed over the phone, thought that Instant Thunder was exactly what Schwarzkopf needed at this point. Rice had argued from the start that only defending Saudi Arabia was "too myopic," that the plans developed by CENTCOM were "intellectually inadequate," and that the Air Staff was obligated to present Bush, Cheney, and Powell with "the range of options that were available to them."[62] Both Rice and Dugan thought that the Five Rings Model served as a useful stimulus to thinking and that the leadership should at least consider the concept Warden proposed. They also believed that Instant Thunder was more than a category of target-sets: it provided a rationale for which targets should be struck and why, as well as an objective framework for dealing with the problem at hand.[63] Moreover, they believed that only Warden's group was thinking in those terms. Lt. Gen. George L. Butler, the director of strategic plans and policy in the Joint Staff, had heard a full presentation the day before and he too expressed his approval: "Excellent, excellent! This is the exact opposite of what we did in Vietnam! This is what we want!"[64]

General Schwarzkopf: "Shit, I Love It!"

When the Air Staff team arrived at MacDill AFB General Moore told them that the meeting with the commander in chief would be low profile. The only other CENTCOM officer present would be USAF Lt. Gen. Craven C. Rogers, Schwarzkopf's deputy commander.

Warden began his presentation by listing what he assumed would be the four political objectives sought in a war with Iraq, namely: "immediate, unconditional and complete withdrawal of all Iraqi forces from Kuwait; Kuwait's legitimate government must be restored to replace the puppet regime; committed to the security and stability of the Persian Gulf; and protect the lives of American citizens abroad."[65] The only real difference from the previous draft was that "committed to the security and stability of the Persian Gulf" replaced "unimpeded flow of oil." The campaign objectives reflected the previously defined military objectives: "raise to [an] unacceptable level the cost to Iraq of remaining in Kuwait; isolate forces in Kuwait from an incapacitated regime; and disarm the Hussein regime" (since it was politically incorrect to state that they were targeting Saddam Hussein personally). Warden made certain that Schwarzkopf recognized the deliberate links between the political and military objectives and their relationship to the campaign's target-sets.

What Warden had termed "assumptions" in the first presentation to Loh were now presented as five planning considerations: pit U.S. strengths (air power) against Iraqi weaknesses (a rigid air defense system); concentrate air power against the Iraqi regime and its mechanisms of power rather than against the Iraqi people and soldiers in Kuwait; eschew massive destruction and instead strive for the selective destruction of key targets with pinpoint accuracy; minimize civilian casualties and collateral damage through stealth and precision; and minimize U.S. losses by not engaging forces on the ground. Warden emphasized that a quick and decisive air campaign against the regime, combined with extensive PSYOPS that would leave the population and the soldiers occupying Kuwait unharmed, might mean that Americans would be viewed as liberators rather than conquerors. The overall goal was to inflict "paralysis and shock": the selective destruction would allow the United States quickly to restore Iraq's industry and economy, which in turn would result in good relations and consequently the free flow of oil at acceptable prices—a national end-state objective.

Warden also stressed the importance of envisioning a war-termination scenario even at this stage of planning. In this context he noted that it might prove counterproductive to target the Iraqi ground forces *en masse*, because if Iraq were left too weak neighboring countries might well subject it to attacks after the war. Concentrating on the ground forces in Kuwait would undermine the strategic focus because destroying Iraq's huge complement of artillery and tanks would take a long time. Besides, attacking the Iraqi army would lead to unnecessary casualties and focusing on Kuwait might well lay waste the country in the attempt to restore its autonomy. Warden suggested, however, that if Iraq should invade Saudi Arabia the United States could strike Iraqi formations with forces deliberately held in reserve.

Warden openly stated his belief that the strategic air campaign alone could paralyze the Iraqi regime to the extent that it could no longer engage in offensive operations. The regime would be unable to manage its economy, support and resupply the troops in Kuwait, or defend itself from air attack. He admitted that there was no guarantee that the plan, if implemented, would result in the fall of Saddam Hussein, but the national objectives would be met: Saddam Hussein would have neither offensive power nor any strategic defense. Equally important, he would not have a nuclear program or biological program—he might still be in power, Warden admitted, but he would not pose a threat to any other country.[66]

The five strategic rings had been transformed into five columns, but the target-sets were the same as those presented to Loh on August 8. Warden described the linkages between strategy and tasks in logical terms: destroying a few key elements of Iraq's electricity distribution system would plunge much of Baghdad into darkness; eliminating a half-dozen key POL facilities would have immediate effects on the military and civilian sectors; interdicting several key transportation nodes would impede reinforcement and stop operations of Iraqi forces in Kuwait and along the Iranian border; and degrading the telecommunications system and Saddam Hussein's internal control forces would isolate the dictator from the populace. The psychological impact on the Iraqi people of unremitting air attack would be a powerful sign of the bankruptcy and impotence of the Saddam Hussein regime.

Warden strongly emphasized that the planners thought in terms of systems: the goal was a synergistic degradation of the entire Iraqi command and control system, in which friction, confusion, and uncertainty would combine to make defenses ineffectual. The attacks against the strategic air defense network would ensure air superiority, while the attacks against the strategic offensive capability and nuclear, biological, and chemical (NBC) research facilities would reduce the short- and long-term threat that Iraq posed to its neighbors. Although NBC production and research facilities had to be eliminated, Warden cautioned against destroying Iraq's oil production capability because this might prevent Iraq from paying its war debts and building a prosperous society after hostilities ended.

He then moved to the necessary force structure. The weapons experts in Checkmate had suggested that thirty F-117As, thirty-two F-111Fs, forty-eight F-15Cs, twenty-four F-15Es, seventy-two F-16s, twenty-four F-4Gs, eighteen OA-10s, six EF-111s, thirty-six F-111D/Es, seventy-two A-10s, five AWACS, and more than twenty B-52Gs would suffice. He stressed the importance of acting sooner rather than later.

Warden devoted a considerable portion of the briefing to PSYOPS. The dual objectives were to separate the regime from international and domestic support and to increase support for the United States among the Arab nations. Such operations had to be coordinated with other governmental agencies and be consistent with national policy directives. The concept of operations stated that the PSYOPS messages would support "each military strike," that U.S. broadcasts would replace Iraqi ones, and that military action would end when Iraq complied with the wishes of the international community. The American forces would need help from the intelligence agencies to develop and implement the plan; they would also need to contact the resistance movement—and if no resistance movement existed they would have to create one. For this they would need double agents, insurgents, and military dissidents.

Toward the end of the presentation Warden described how the campaign would unfold, suggesting three waves of attacks during each twenty-four-hour period. Importantly, Instant Thunder sought to prevent Iraq from executing air strikes against U.S. forces. After the first morning air superiority would be attained and within six to nine days all target-sets would be destroyed or neutralized. He envisioned twelve hundred sorties, of which seven hundred would be bombing sorties flown within the first twenty-four-hour period; a total of nine hundred sorties would be flown each day for the rest of the campaign.[67] The combination of stealth and precision, Warden stated, would allow the United States to attack the leadership and its command, control, and communications apparatus prior to attaining air superiority in the conventional sense. He then suggested two options for air superiority: the first was to maintain combat air patrols with F-15s south of Baghdad, moving north only if the Iraqis took to the air; the second was to conduct a prestrike offensive fighter sweep, destroying aircraft on the ground and in the air. The latter, he argued, would drive Iraqi air forces into an autonomous mode by the first morning of the war.[68]

When Warden ended his forty-minute presentation Schwarzkopf expressed immense enthusiasm:

> Do it! You have my approval, 100 percent. This is absolutely essential. I will call the Chairman today and have him give you a directive to proceed with detailed planning immediately. I have already briefed the President on a lot of elements of this, but lots of folks are leaning backwards saying it was too hard to do. You have restored my confidence in the United States Air Force. CENTAF cannot do planning. Their CC/VC are gone and the staff is trying to flow forces. Do it where you want. It is up to the Air Force. Shit, I love it! We are dealing with a crazy man and he is going to lash out. We cannot afford not to have options to fall back on. He will attack Saudi Arabia, do something nasty to the hostages. After you do this, we will drop leaflets on his front line forces and tell them they are out of business. If they do not believe it, let them try to call home, your ass is next. If we invade Kuwait, they will destroy it. This might leave Kuwait intact. . . . I am with you. This will lower losses.[69]

Most of Schwarzkopf's questions focused on when the plan could be executed and what changes in the deployment flow would be necessary in order to implement the planned offensive: it was important to have an executable plan by August 22. He indicated that he favored the removal of Saddam Hussein from power and that his immediate concern was weapons of mass destruction.

Schwarzkopf also liked the suggestion that the war could be over in six to nine days, but was concerned that when attacked, Saddam Hussein would surrender and that the United Nations or the United States would order operations to halt before they had achieved sufficient destruction. The CINC agreed that it would be desirable to hit as many high-value targets as possible across a broad spectrum of target-sets, so that if the war ended early the air campaign would have inflicted at least a minimum level of damage on all the target-sets identified.

Schwarzkopf wanted more detail about the logistical aspects of the campaign and told Warden to return in a few days with a plan that would be ready for execution. Alexander, fearing that this might force Warden's team to move to a level of detail beyond their expertise, intervened: "We are going to have to take this to TAC and let TAC get to work on this." Schwarzkopf, however, disagreed and told Warden: "I want you to do it."[70]

As Schwarzkopf was leaving the briefing room Warden said: "General, you have the opportunity now to carry off the most brilliant operation that any American general has executed since Douglas MacArthur went ashore at Inchon." Alexander was appalled by what he found an "outlandish comment" that could only be intended as flattery, but Schwarzkopf seemed to relish the comparison: "He smiled broadly, puffed out his chest, and strode confidently from the room."[71] In fact, Warden was absolutely sincere, believing that the general had a historic opportunity. In any event, Schwarzkopf later recalled, "I felt a hell of a lot better after I left the briefing room than when I entered it. Warden turned on the proverbial light bulb."[72]

Both Rogers and Moore had private reservations about some of Warden's promises, especially that air power could achieve such unprecedented results so rapidly, but overall they were pleased with the plan, not least because their superior liked it. Life around "Stormin' Norman" was far easier when he was happy, and Moore recalled that Schwarzkopf had been exceptionally unhappy with his own staff in early August 1990.[73]

It is obvious in retrospect that Schwarzkopf considered Instant Thunder a retaliation option to be executed if Saddam Hussein continued his aggression in any way, while Warden saw it as a stand-alone, war-winning campaign that should be executed no matter what the Iraqis did. The point is critical: whereas Schwarzkopf wanted an *air option*, Warden offered him a *military solution* to the problem presented by the Iraqi regime and believed that Schwarzkopf shared that view. Schwarzkopf may have noticed that Warden's rationale for attacking the regime differed from his own, but this did not matter because he liked the target-sets, the intensity of the attack plan, the short duration of the campaign, and the anticipated paralyzing effect on the leadership. Most important, he could now offer Secretary Cheney "serious air power" on short notice, with the added possibility of decisive results. Thus, Schwarzkopf opened the door for the air campaign planning almost unintentionally: his interest in a strategic campaign was prompted less by his belief in air power than by the paucity of ground force options.[74]

TAC'S OPPOSITION AND ALTERNATIVE PLAN

Not everybody liked Instant Thunder. While Warden and his team worked to refine their plan, General Russ and his planners at TAC, who had received an early version of the proposal by fax, expressed strong disapproval on conceptual grounds and would have preferred that the plan never see the light of day. The new concept could potentially disrupt a very complex deployment plan, and this upset officers who were themselves working almost around the clock. Russ demanded that Warden's group come to TAC's headquarters prior to presenting Instant Thunder to Schwarzkopf.[75]

Warden had strongly opposed sending Instant Thunder to Russ in the first place and had no wish to meet Russ at this stage; he feared that the TAC commander and his team would try to dilute the strategic emphasis. When Loh decided that Russ should see the plan before Schwarzkopf, Warden protested vehemently and suggested that he show the briefing to Dugan instead: after all, it was the chief of staff who had been given the task of helping CENTCOM. Dugan learned of the dispute and decided that Warden should go directly to Schwarzkopf, in effect bypassing Russ: he was confident that Warden had something useful to offer and time was of essence. Warden saw this as an important bureaucratic triumph.

General Russ objected strongly to Instant Thunder—and to Warden— because he believed that the plan was not in the country's best interest. While Warden recommended that the air force bring its assets into theater as soon as possible, Russ preferred holding them back, fearing that the newspapers would report the increased activity: "I did not want for us to get so far ahead of the decision makers that it would be picked up and publicized and that action by itself would trigger something."[76]

Russ also opposed having the Air Staff perform the planning without in-volving the air commander who would be responsible for executing it.[77] The approach reminded him of Vietnam, where he had flown 242 combat missions, of which 50 were over North Vietnam. Like most military men, he had been appalled by the way President Johnson and his team had micromanaged the ef-fort and he was greatly troubled by the possibility that Warden would pick tar-gets from Washington and then feed them to the planners in theater:[78] "What starts as a little bit of help from the Pentagon soon leads to more and more 'help' and pretty soon you get the President in on it. . . . Then you have people in the White House sitting on the floor trying to figure out what targets they are going to hit. That is just the wrong way to fight a war!"[79] He shared the common belief that the theater command, the "flight suit people," ought to plan and execute wars, while the Air Staff should confine itself to the political-military elements of the war.[80] Whereas Warden distinguished between advice from the Pentagon on the west side of the Potomac and interference in planning details from the White House on the east side, Russ treated the entire capital area as a single entity that was unwelcome in the planning process.

Russ's third criticism was that Warden presented Instant Thunder as a victory-through-air-power scenario:

> One of the things you learn as TAC commander is to be sensitive with the Army and other services. . . . I had a gut feeling that there was a group of hair-on-fire majors in Washington that were going to win the war all by themselves. They were going to have the Air Force win the war. . . . I have been in the Joint arena too long watching these things, and everybody has got to do something.[81]

JOHN A. WARDEN, Jr., Sales Representative, Harrisburg, Pa. Born Apr. 28, 1913, San Antonio, Tex. Texas A&M (BSEE, '36). Began as Student, Phila., 1937. Has served as Service Rep. in Trenton, Harrisburg, Phila., Camden, N. J., and Baltimore, and as Asst. to Const. Supt. in Richmond, Estimator, Phila., Local Serv. Mgr., Baltimore. Present job, 1954. WW I vet.

JOHN A. WARDEN, JR., IN OTIS NEWSLETTER. © *OTIS HISTORY ARCHIVE*

CADET JOHN A. WARDEN, PHOTO FROM THE USAF ACADEMY YEARBOOK, 1965. *USAF PHOTO*

CAPT. JOHN A. WARDEN WITH HIS WIFE, MARGIE, AND THEIR TWINS, ELIZABETH KATHLEEN AND JOHN A. IV, AT TORREJON AFB, 1972. *USAF PHOTO*

COL. JOHN A. WARDEN,
WING COMMANDER FOR
THE THIRTY-SIXTH TACTICAL
FIGHTER WING, BITBURG,
GERMANY, AUGUST 1987.
USAF PHOTO

COL. JOHN A. WARDEN
DEVELOPED THE FIVE RINGS
MODEL IN THE SUMMER OF 1988,
AND IT BECAME A CONCEPTUAL BASIS
FOR INSTANT THUNDER AND IN
TURN THE FIRST PHASE OF
OPERATION DESERT STORM.

Col. John A. Warden in Checkmate, designated BF 922B, Pentagon, August 15, 1990. *Courtesy of David A. Deptula*

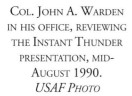

Col. John A. Warden in his office, reviewing the Instant Thunder presentation, mid-August 1990. *USAF Photo*

Lt. Col. Bernard E. Harvey, Col. John A. Warden, Lt. Col. David A. Deptula, and Lt. Col. Ronald Stanfill (left to right). The team is going over the Instant Thunder plan during a refueling stop in Greece en route to Riyadh, August 18, 1990. *Courtesy of David A. Deptula*

Lt. Col. Bernard E. Harvey, Col. John A. Warden, Lt. Col. David A. Deptula, and Lt. Col. Ronald Stanfill (left to right) in the Royal Saudi Air Force HQ when the quartet arrived in Riyadh on August 19, 1990. *Courtesy of David A. Deptula*

LT. COL. DAVID A. DEPTULA (RIGHT) GIVING THE AIR COMMANDER, LT. GEN. CHARLES A. HORNER, AN UPDATE OF THE PLANNING EFFORT IN THE SPECIAL PLANNING CELL (THE BLACK HOLE), RIYADH. *COURTESY OF DAVID A. DEPTULA*

MAJ. GEN. THOMAS R. OLSEN, LT. GEN. CHARLES A. HORNER, BRIG. GEN. BUSTER C. GLOSSON, GEN. H. NORMAN SCHWARZKOPF, AND LT. COL. DAVID A. DEPTULA (LEFT TO RIGHT) IN THE BLACK HOLE ON JANUARY 16, 1991, WHEN DEPTULA BRIEFED SCHWARZKOPF ON THE INITIAL ATTACK HOURS BEFORE ITS LAUNCH. *COURTESY OF DAVID A. DEPTULA*

Col. John A. Warden (left) with Secretary of the Air Force Donald B. Rice (middle), and Secretary of Defense Richard B. Cheney (right) in Checkmate, February 1991. *USAF Photo*

Secretary of the Air Force Donald B. Rice, Col. John A. Warden, Dr. Zalmay Khalizad (RAND), and Undersecretary of Defense Paul D. Wolfowitz celebrate the Gulf War victory in Checkmate on February 28, 1991. *USAF Photo*

COL. JOHN A. WARDEN (FRONT ROW, CENTER) AND MANY OF THE OFFICERS AND OFFICIALS WHO PARTICIPATED IN THE CHECKMATE PLANNING PROCESS BETWEEN AUGUST 1990 AND MARCH 1991. THE PHOTO WAS TAKEN ON THE STEPS OF THE RIVER ENTRANCE TO THE PENTAGON, EARLY MARCH 1991. *USAF PHOTO*

COL. JOHN A. WARDEN SERVED AS THE SPECIAL ASSISTANT FOR POLICY STUDIES AND NATIONAL SECURITY AFFAIRS TO VICE PRESIDENT DAN QUAYLE FROM JULY 1991 TO JULY 1992. *WHITE HOUSE PHOTO*

Col. John A. Warden and Vice President Dan Quayle. *White House Photo*

Col. (ret.) John A. Warden after a presentation at the USAF Academy, 2002. *USAF Photo*

Russ had reservations about dropping bombs on Baghdad without having ground forces in place, because he believed Iraq might well respond by invading Saudi Arabia. Further, he found it unacceptable to suggest that a plan could be executed within days when it did not account for the electronic warfare measures required to gain air superiority. He therefore sent Brig. Gen. Larry L. Henry, his electronic warfare expert, to the theater to investigate.

Russ also believed Schwarzkopf had asked for several air power options: Instant Thunder represented only one approach. In the absence of a clear statement of the "commander's intent," the air force could at best provide a set of options from which Schwarzkopf could choose: "Just to sit down and develop a strategy without any sort of guidance is very difficult at best. . . . I had not received any guidance that said, 'here are the political problems. Here is what we can and cannot do,' or anything of that sort. None of that was provided to me."[82] Russ also said that "In this case it did not appear that coming up with a plan was absolutely urgent in the next day or so" and he felt uncomfortable about suggesting a plan when there were no "ground rules in which we are operating."[83] He apparently believed that the plan would be executed under political constraints that had yet to be defined.

Finally, the TAC commander considered the campaign plan too violent: he believed Instant Thunder advocated bombing Iraq into oblivion, and such an implication would not be in the best interest of either the air force or the country.[84] The American public would not support an all-out war and one "couldn't just go in there and start a massive attack to win."[85] He was not ready to take part in a plan that might put "the United States in the position of starting World War III" with a preemptive attack that could cause uncontrollable chain reactions.[86] A better option for Schwarzkopf would be an air campaign that demonstrated resolve, or relied on a gradual escalation that would allow Saddam Hussein the time and opportunity to "reevaluate his situation and back out while there is something to save."[87]

Thus, on August 9, Russ ordered his deputy chief of staff for plans, Brig. Gen. Thomas R. Griffith, to develop an alternative to Instant Thunder. He told his staff to "work with the Army" and make sure it was "joint in nature because it would not go through the Chairman if it was not joint."[88] Griffith in turn gathered four of his best colonels to examine Warden's concept in detail. The TAC planners, following accepted doctrine, concluded that the United States could not ignore the immediate threat posed by the military power that occupied Kuwait. They characterized Instant Thunder as lacking "tactical perspective":[89] it failed to commit forces to holding a defensive line on the Saudi/Kuwaiti border and it omitted integration with ground forces in general. Griffith was convinced that it would be too much of a gamble to start bombing before U.S. ground forces were in place.

TAC first proposed an intensive air campaign plan to repel the Iraqi forces at the border and at the same time strike troops throughout the Kuwaiti theater of operations. Russ agreed on the need to attack the ground forces, but emphasized that they needed a clear alternative to the massive use of air power against strategic targets. Russ told the team to look into "a demonstration of power": for instance, an attack on Osirak, the heavily defended nuclear reactor outside Baghdad, would send the message that "We have the strength to take out anything in your country at any time and at any place that we want to, as demonstrated by what we did here."[90] Russ saw this as a unilateral one-time option, "an initial statement," that the State Department could exploit.[91] As Russ subsequently stated:

> My idea was this: First of all, it shows the tremendous capability that we have. It shows we have the ability to knock out anything we want, at any time we want. In fact, you could even lead this attack by saying that unless you do such and such, we are going to wipe out so and so, and then carry that threat through. Secondly, the results of an attack like this would do what I believe world opinion wanted; to rid the nuclear weapons capability in Iraq. By taking down the reactors, people would breathe a little easier and say "well, even if we do not attack anymore, we have gotten rid of the nuclear reactors for another ten years . . ." The overall objective was to demonstrate to Saddam Hussein that we had the ability with airpower to operate anywhere in his country, at any time and destroy whatever we wanted. And we were going to demonstrate that by going against his most heavily defended target; wipe it out and not lose anybody. That was the idea.[92]

The alternative plan went through several forms, but by the late evening of August 10, when Schwarzkopf had already accepted the thrust of Instant Thunder, TAC had agreed on the "CENTCOM Air Campaign Plan" (see Appendix 2). TAC's planning team considered their option superior because it was "politically correct" and it accorded with the joint doctrine and contingency plans for the region. It recommended that the United States establish a "deterrent posture" in the region based on "active defense" and "visible offense." From that premise the planners advocated two possible strategies. If Iraq attacked Saudi Arabia they suggested that Schwarzkopf "conduct offensive operations to defend Saudi Arabia": "establish air superiority through a comprehensive counter-air campaign; attack and destroy all means to conduct chemical operations; support ground scheme of maneuver of ground force commander; and interdict critical items of re-supply to Iraqi field forces." Alternatively, if Iraqi formations neither attacked Saudi Arabia nor withdrew from Kuwait, TAC recommended that Schwarzkopf "conduct offensive operations to preclude stalemate and liberate Kuwait" using a strategy that would "demonstrate our ability to conduct offensive operations against Iraqi targets of our choosing; escalate as required until all significant targets are destroyed; and keep up the pressure until Iraqi power has diminished to the point that regional stability has been restored." Many of the target-sets were the same as those in Instant Thunder, but the priority was reversed: military forces were of primary importance and "strategic targets" were at the bottom of the list.

The plan had both tactical and strategic components. The former encompassed destroying armor and artillery ("massive air strikes against the Iraqi ground forces"[93]), while the latter involved demonstrating resolve ("demonstrative attacks against high-value targets [and then] escalate as required until all significant targets are destroyed"[94]). The plan stated that "this strategy allows time and opportunity for Hussein to reevaluate his situation and back out while there is still something to save."[95] The air effort would essentially concentrate on targets "that reduce his ability to project power, [i.e.,] field armies [and] infrastructure to support offensive operations."[96] Griffith asserted that the strategic portion would gain the Iraqi leader's attention: for example, U.S. aircraft could attack the nuclear research center, then pause for perhaps twelve hours, attack one or two more high-value targets, pause again, attack three more facilities, and so on. The advantage of the new plan, TAC argued, was that it gave Schwarzkopf a range of options, whereas Instant Thunder was solely a strategic air campaign plan based on overwhelming power.

Beyond the differences over content, the animosity that Russ and his planners felt toward the Air Staff's involvement stemmed from their deep-seated belief that the established chain of command should plan all campaigns. If inputs were required from the outside, however, they should come from the warfighters at a major command, such as TAC, rather than from the administrators at the Air Staff. There was also a human dimension: Russ could not accept that Warden, of all people, should be spearheading the effort.

General Powell: "I Want Smoking Tanks"

When Warden returned to the Pentagon on the evening of August 10 he was told that Powell wanted a briefing the following morning. He received a fax of the alternative plan as he was preparing for the meeting. After spending a few seconds reading the slides he concluded that the TAC alternative was useless. He did not like the gist of TAC's proposal: as he saw it, the TAC plan was simply a replay of Rolling Thunder. Besides, there was no reason to bother; Schwarzkopf had already approved the Instant Thunder concept.[97]

Before going to Powell's office in the Pentagon, Warden instructed his staff not to get "bogged down in tactical details," but to remain focused on the "strategic levels." They were to produce an "executable" product that would be a "strategic, political-military campaign—pure Clausewitz," wherein "every bomb is a political bomb."[98] Warden also told them that if they succeeded the campaign would "go down in the history books [as a] classic strategic victory."[99]

Warden presented Powell with the same briefing that he had given Schwarzkopf the day before. The audience was much larger. Powell had invited, among others, Adm. David E. Jeremiah, the vice chairman; Lt. Gen. Michael P. C. Carns, the director of the Joint Staff; Lt. Gen. Thomas W. Kelly, the director of operations; and Lt. Gen. George L. Butler, the director of plans. Warden was accompanied by Loh, Alexander, May, and several of his own planners.

The presentation unfolded without major interruptions and afterwards the chairman applauded the effort: "Good plan, very fine piece of work."[100] Powell was as concerned as Schwarzkopf about what needed to be done to have the plan ready for execution by August 22 and asked many questions about logistics and the deployment flow. The discussion went smoothly until Powell asked the obvious question: "OK, it is day six and the strategic campaign is finished. Now what?" Warden declared firmly that it would most likely induce the Iraqis to withdraw. "This plan may win the war. You may not need a ground attack. . . . I think the Iraqis will withdraw from Kuwait as a result of the strategic air campaign."[101] He asserted confidently that the conscripts in the foremost positions were likely to return home and might try to overthrow the Iraqi leader.

Powell disagreed with this view of the desired military goal and stated in no uncertain terms that he wanted "to finish it: destroy Iraq's army on the ground."[102] While he acknowledged that the strategic air campaign would cut out "the guts and heart," he also wanted to deal with "the hands":[103] "I won't be happy until I see those tanks destroyed. I do not want them to go home—I want to leave smoking tanks as kilometer posts all the way to Baghdad."[104]

Warden opposed this suggestion, and said so. He believed the United States should refrain from attacking the Iraqi troops, and instead subject them to PSYOPS and then use them to topple the Iraqi regime. At the very least he thought attacking the ground forces took time and energy away from the important goal: "General, one of the things we really need to be careful about is that if there is some action on the ground, you cannot re-role the strategic air campaign. We made that mistake in World War II, and we do not want to do that again."[105] Some generals might have been appalled by such audacity, but Powell let it pass.

Kelly, however, asserted that "air power has never worked in the past by itself. This is not going to work. Air power cannot be decisive."[106] Loh, for his part, feared that Powell and Kelly would insist on conducting Instant Thunder "in conjunction with ground operations."[107] Attempting to keep the focus on strategic targets rather than the Iraqi ground forces, he and Alexander strongly supported Warden's arguments.[108] Loh told the chairman that "It is a highly integrated plan like the Bekaa Valley but more massive than Linebacker,"[109] but Powell said that if they were going as far as implementing an offensive air campaign—something more than mere retaliation—they had to go all the way: they could not "just sit and wait for results like we had to do after Hiroshima."[110] He agreed that the strategic air campaign should not be diluted and that it had to be a sustainable effort, but he could not "recommend only the strategic air campaign to the President."[111]

Powell was thinking beyond Schwarzkopf's retaliation concept and playing with the idea of using air power in an offensive fashion to liberate Kuwait, but he fundamentally disagreed that this could be done without directly targeting Iraqi military forces in Kuwait and southern Iraq.[112] Saddam Hussein would not be allowed to walk away without penalty; therefore air power had to destroy Iraqi armored units occupying Kuwait.

The disagreements were settled when Admiral Jeremiah suggested that the United States carry out the strategic air campaign first and then focus on the ground forces. Warden assented: his group could plan for a strategic air campaign against the leadership as suggested, and if it became necessary to continue beyond the strategic attacks they could transit into an operational-level air campaign that systematically destroyed Iraqi tanks and armored personnel carriers in Kuwait. At the end of the two-hour-long meeting, Powell endorsed further planning, but insisted that they make the campaign joint, that there be an Instant Thunder Phase II to deal with the attrition of Iraqi ground forces, and, finally, that Warden put together a short version of the plan that Powell would soon present to Cheney and possibly the president.[113]

Warden returned to his office with mixed feelings. He was more than pleased that Powell apparently liked the proposal and that they were to continue the planning, but he also realized that Powell thought in terms of force on force, which contradicted the idea of concentrating the full effort on the enemy's "inner ring."[114] Although Warden was not overly keen on transitioning into a joint setting, he felt gratified that his team was to all intents and purposes now an extension of the Joint Staff, which *de facto* "legitimized" further planning.

It could be argued that Powell absorbed the entire concept and expanded it, suggesting the structure of what was to become a comprehensive offensive strategy: use air power strategically and then against ground forces to prepare and shape the battlefield for a ground campaign.[115] Alexander later recalled that Powell had merely been humoring the airmen by not openly disagreeing with their contention that the Iraqi army would leave Kuwait as the result of Instant Thunder.[116] Powell noted in his autobiography that "Warden's approach could destroy or severely cripple the Iraqi regime. But we also needed an air plan to help drive Saddam out of Kuwait, if it came to that."[117]

Instant Thunder had made its presence felt, but Warden realized that he now had to devise a plan for attacking Iraqi ground forces in Kuwait in order to sell the strategic air campaign. In preparing for the follow-up presentation to Schwarzkopf, Warden's team continued to work predominantly on the strategic campaign, but they also initiated "the operational-level campaign," which would include "direct attack on the Iraqi army in Kuwait itself."[118] Warden put his deputy, Col. Emery Kiraly, in charge of what became "Instant Thunder Phase II: KTO [Kuwait Theater of Operations] Operations Against Iraqi Army." The follow-up phase responded to Powell's instructions, but Warden did not put his heart and mind into it. Lt. Col. Phillip S. Meilinger in the Doctrine Division also considered Phase II a diversion and offered an analogy that Warden applauded: he described the original Instant Thunder as an "aerial Schlieffen Plan," in which it was all-important to "not weaken the right." In other words, the planners should not dilute the strategic air campaign by diverting assets to attack ground forces.

When three of the colonels who had worked on TAC's alternative plan arrived later that morning, asking Warden's opinion of their plan, he simply told them "It has been decided not to use that."[119] They then inquired how they could contribute; Warden told them that Kiraly would appreciate some help on Instant Thunder II. The TAC trio saw their mission as "putting some tactical sense into the plan," but they also felt that "Warden had a plan, and he was not going to listen to any outside changes or inputs."[120] They had been sent to Checkmate against their wishes, and although they provided some useful input they never established a good working relationship with Warden's team. In fact, they were referred to as the "TAC spies," since they continually kept Russ and Ryan updated on Checkmate's efforts.[121]

GENERAL DUGAN: "KEEP THE EMPHASIS ON A STRATEGIC ATTACK"

On August 12 Lieutenant General Adams, the director of plans and operations, returned to the Pentagon. His absence had allowed Warden direct access to Loh, and Warden had used that opportunity to the fullest. Adams had been kept informed by his deputy, Major General May, and he knew that Russ—his close friend, mentor, and former superior—disliked Instant Thunder and the Air Staff's involvement. Thus, when Adams returned, he was openly angry with Warden for having injected himself into the planning.[122] He was skeptical about Warden's running the planning effort for professional and legal reasons: he thought Warden was "ahead of his own headlights" and that he was walking in the middle of the air commander's lane.[123] When told that Schwarzkopf had called for help Adams could not quite shake the suspicion that Warden had orchestrated it on his own: "I have been tasked by John Warden before so if it happened [it] would not surprise me."[124] Warden swore that he had not arranged "this wonderful call from Schwarzkopf." In any event, Adams believed that Warden had a "talent for trouble," that he could not fully "trust him with an order," and that it was his responsibility to keep Warden under control and make sure that Horner was not blindsided.[125]

When Adams later met with the senior Joint Staff generals he stated that he was quite concerned about the Air Staff's interfering with CENTAF's planning process, but he was told that neither the Joint Staff nor CENTCOM could do the planning. Adams then expressed reservations about the Air Staff's working alone rather than jointly. To improve organizational relations Kelly informally deputized Adams as the "Joint Staff J-3 for Air," which semiofficially defined the Warden group's status as an appendage of the Joint Staff and placed Adams in charge of a planning effort he disliked in the first place.[126]

With the administrative issues settled, Adams told Warden to give him a complete presentation. Not surprisingly, it went poorly, especially because Adams insisted on asking questions about tactical and technical details, such as tanker altitudes and radio frequencies. Adams made it clear that he found large parts of Instant Thunder superficial, and that he thought the plan was too theoretical and promised too much. He told Warden to stop committing himself to a timeframe needed to achieve the results he predicted: "What I cared about was that there was an overall approach and if it took four times as long I did not care. . . . I did not have a better number, I just felt like it made the Air Force look too tall. I felt like it would be a hard sell in the joint arena, because we thought we were king."[127] Warden remained unshakable in his belief that the campaign would achieve results within the six to nine days he had postulated from the outset. He therefore continued to make this claim when he presented the plan to various officers and officials. Indeed, he thought six days was more realistic than nine days, and was not shy about saying so.

Adams also stated that it made no sense to ignore the Iraqi ground forces. He suggested that Warden divide the campaign plan into two phases: first attack the Iraqi army, and then, with leftover air power, execute the strategic phase. Warden insisted that such a proposal was counter to the orders from Schwarzkopf. Besides, completely destroying the Iraq army might allow for a power vacuum in the region that was counter to the desired end-state articulated by the president. Adams responded that their job was to provide options and that nothing was set in stone. Warden shot back that "[We] don't want to do a half-assed strategic air campaign," to which Adams replied "Right, but [we] don't want to leave those Iraqi forces in place to kill 200,000 soldiers."[128] Adams ordered Warden to look into the possibility of executing the two phases simultaneously, to provide him with ideas for how air power could destroy the Iraqi ground forces, and to make the whole operation a joint effort.

Adams also pointed out that to enable early execution they needed to account for all aspects of an air campaign, such as tanker support, logistics, sortie rates, and a range of limiting factors. He concluded that the plan could not be executed in the short term and that Warden had grossly underestimated the time it took to arrive at a complete ATO.[129] Thus, just when Warden felt he had overcome TAC's objections he discovered that his own superior directly opposed the very concept that Schwarzkopf had asked for. Still, he was not overly concerned, because he knew he had the support of Rice, Dugan, and Loh.

Major General Alexander, the man between Adams and Warden in the chain of command, found himself in no easier position: Dugan and Loh had tasked him to do a job of which he knew his immediate superior disapproved. When Adams returned to the Pentagon he virtually "placed Alexander in the penalty box," telling him that he was no longer needed. Alexander later recalled that "it was almost a punishment session for the [Warden] team the next couple of days with Adams,"[130] yet Warden remained undeterred, because he believed Schwarzkopf had fully endorsed a strategic air campaign plan.

Even so, Warden could not ignore the guidance from Powell and Adams. He instructed his team that Instant Thunder Phase II should have four components: gain air superiority in Kuwait, target Iraqi systems designed to deliver chemical weapons, attack Iraqi C^3 and military support systems in Kuwait, and target Iraqi armored forces in Kuwait.[131] The corresponding target-sets were Iraqi air defenses, corps and division C^3 nodes in Kuwait, corps and division military support structures, lines of communication, and tanks and artillery.[132] Warden never believed that Phase II would have to be implemented. "My own vision of how the war ought to be conducted was one that deliberately avoided destroying the army in Kuwait because I wanted to use the army in Kuwait to go after Saddam."[133]

Warden suggested to Adams that he would brief Schwarzkopf in depth on the strategic portion, and only if the commander in chief asked questions about the Iraqi army would he present Instant Thunder Phase II. Adams accepted this, albeit reluctantly, and recommended that Warden prepare for questions about the possibility that Iraq could retaliate with an offensive into Saudi Arabia in response to attacks on Baghdad. Warden countered that Iraqi forces would not want to expose themselves by moving south beyond their ability to supply themselves effectively; however, in case the issue arose, he drafted a separate slide: "What If: Iraq attacks Saudi Arabia in response to Instant Thunder?" His team calculated that ninety-six A-10s, forty AV-8Bs, thirty-six F/A-18s, thirty AH-1Ws, and seventy-five AH-64s would suffice to stop the Iraqi forces.[134] Warden believed that these aircraft and helicopters should be kept in reserve, an instantiation of the "operational reserves" concept that he had suggested in *The Air Campaign*. These reserves would allow the United States to sustain the momentum of the massive, concentrated strategic attacks, while at the same time making it possible to add fresh forces at a given point if deemed necessary.

Throughout the week Warden's directorate continued to develop Instant

Thunder and conducted an extraordinary effort to gather information from all possible sources. According to the registration book, more than four hundred people came to Checkmate between August 10 and 17 to provide input or gather information. To improve the plan, Warden's team drew on organizations and individuals with access to special knowledge of Iraq and its regime. They consulted the National Intelligence Council as well as key members of the Central Intelligence Agency (CIA), thanks largely to Lt. Col. Richard Stimer and Capt. Steve Hedger, both of whom worked for Warden and had developed a range of intelligence contacts over the previous two years. In a military system such contacts usually require formal applications, but Warden's team simply initiated the contacts they thought appropriate. They cut through the bureaucratic quagmire to finish the plan for Schwarzkopf and in the process turned informal networking into a veritable art form.

When Warden briefed Dugan on August 14 the chief of staff observed that attacking the production centers and infrastructure might not be essential: he saw the leadership targets as the most important in influencing Saddam Hussein and his regime. Therefore the entire effort should be directed at the inner ring. He also wanted an encompassing study of the chemical warfare issue, since he saw chemical weapons as the biggest threat posed by Iraq. He offered to set up a Red Team that would view the plan and its effects through Iraqi eyes, and he told Warden to search for innovative thinkers who were experts on Iraq and could enlighten them about the way Arab culture viewed the conduct of war. Dugan believed that Saddam Hussein cared nothing about military or economic targets, only about himself, his family, and his mistresses, but he wanted to know "what kind of targets will play on Arab culture." Finally, he asked Warden to look into options for inducing the Iraqi troops to return home. He stressed the importance of strategic attacks, noting that the "army mop up is a tactical thing for the on scene commander. . . . keep the emphasis on a strategic attack, do not allow diversion of effort to operational and tactical concerns about the Iraqi army in Kuwait. . . . press hard on planning for Instant Thunder. . . . be bold and imaginative."[135] Dugan's comments strengthened Warden's determination to push uncompromisingly for strategic attacks.

In the meantime it became apparent that parts of the initial Instant Thunder slide program had somehow found their way to the National Command Authority. On August 14 Schwarzkopf presented Powell with some thoughts on an offensive air plan whose focus and target-sets closely resembled the essence of Instant Thunder. The following day Powell reviewed the concept with Cheney, who approved it.[136] Later that day Schwarzkopf outlined an offensive option for the president that was apparently based on slides and notes from the Instant Thunder presentation. The option called for an effort that would incapacitate or discredit Hussein's regime, eliminate Iraqi offensive/defensive capability, and create conditions leading to an Iraqi withdrawal. Schwarzkopf evidently saw Instant Thunder as one element of a multiattack, multiphased overall campaign plan that would culminate in a ground offensive; after the strategic air campaign, air attacks would be directed against the Iraqi forces and a ground attack would follow.

Immediately after the briefing President Bush gave a speech to the Pentagon employees in which he compared Saddam Hussein to Adolf Hitler. Some of the phrases he used in the speech had been included in the Instant Thunder slides. Schwarzkopf's option for a substantial offensive air campaign, developed by Warden's group, might well have provided the Bush administration with the extra confidence that resulted in such aggressive rhetoric as early as mid-August.[137]

Secretary Rice, who was kept informed about the planning progress, received a full presentation of Instant Thunder on August 15. He asked many questions, but declared that he was more than pleased with the plan. Indeed, Schwarzkopf had told Rice that he was comfortable with the Air Staff's support, and Rice observed that Cheney was becoming increasingly content with the air force, most likely because of the Instant Thunder effort.[138]

Major General Moore called Warden personally to inform him that Schwarzkopf wanted the updated version of Instant Thunder on August 17. Moore supported Warden's effort and there seems to have been no animosity between the CENTCOM planners and the Air Staff. Dugan, for his part, had called Schwarzkopf in advance to say that he believed Instant Thunder was a good conceptual plan and that he supported its thrust. He personally believed that it would be useful for the president to have such an option and that it could be executed in the short term. He also said that Horner needed to be involved "because there is going to be some head wind with it." Schwarzkopf acknowledged his concerns and said he knew "how to handle all that."[139]

Warden was told that the upcoming presentation for Schwarzkopf would have a much higher profile than the previous one. It would be sponsored by the Joint Staff through Maj. Gen. James W. Meier, its deputy director for National Military Command Systems (J-36), who had been selected as the liaison between the Joint Staff and the Air Staff. He had already received a presentation of Instant Thunder on August 12 from Deptula and was, at best, a reluctant supporter. In preparing for the briefing to Schwarzkopf he made life difficult for Warden's group. Whereas Adams had ordered Warden not to deal with details that belonged to the level of an ATO, Meier argued that such details were required at this stage: "There is not enough detail here! You cannot expect to take this thing to the CINC! I mean, the CINC wants a war plan! He wants to know what the details are! This just is not adequate for a four-star."[140]

Meier demanded so many changes that Warden's men thought they might have to delay the briefing. As they worked throughout the night Warden became increasingly frustrated and during one confrontational session he expressed his anger: "Well, now, look, General. This is what we were tasked to do by the CINC. This is what we have put together, and this is how it ought to be presented."[141] It was a "very long night," but Warden finally persuaded Meier to accept a scheme that encompassed a notional attack plan for the first twenty-four hours, including sortie rates, time over target, mission numbers, and types of aircraft.[142] When Meier asked who should make the presentation Warden recommended that the two-star confine himself to giving an introduction. Meier must have found it insulting to have a colonel tell him what to do and suggested they draw straws. Warden retorted that this was one of the most ridiculous ideas he had ever heard. After some discussion Meier gave in and said he would limit himself to some remarks "worthy of a two-star."[143] Warden would be allowed to give the whole presentation, except for the intelligence portion, which was reserved for Blackburn.

The last thing Meier said before he left the office was that Warden should bring only a "minimum number of people," but when Warden realized that they would travel to Tampa in a large airplane he interpreted that to mean about fifteen people with the skills needed to answer Schwarzkopf's and the CENTCOM staff's questions. Moreover, Warden wanted to reward the hard work of the Checkmate team by letting them attend what he considered a historic meeting.[144]

GENERAL SCHWARZKOPF: "YOU HAVE GOT ME SO EXCITED WITH THIS"
While the first briefing had been given at a conference table, with paper copies handed around, the second was formal and was attended by many of Schwarzkopf's senior staff. Meier began his opening remarks, but Schwarzkopf quickly brushed him aside, saying, "I want to hear the Colonel."[145] Warden confidently opened with a slide stating: "What it is: A *focused, intense* air campaign designed to incapacitate Iraqi leadership and destroy key Iraqi military capability in a *short* period of time and it is designed to leave basic infrastructure intact. What it is not: a graduated, long-term campaign plan designed to provide escalation options to counter Iraqi moves." The Instant Thunder material had two components: thirty slides that bore the Joint Staff emblem (see Appendix 1) and a 180-page unfinished operational order.[146] Warden repeated many of the arguments that he had made on August 10 and emphasized the links between the political, military, and campaign objectives; the desired effects that they sought; and the target-sets according to the Five Rings. Blackburn then presented each of the eighty-four targets, divided into ten target-sets by coordinates and functional description. Schwarzkopf had so far expressed no enthusiasm, but when Blackburn showed him the first satellite photo of a real target and discussed how that target would be struck, "the tide turned."[147] Blackburn gave an excellent presentation before giving the stage back to Warden.

Warden reemphasized the importance of maintaining the strategic focus and directly attacking the Iraqi regime from the opening moments of war. Referring to the target-sets, he explained once more that the strategic air campaign would inflict paralysis and shock upon the Iraqi nation: the regime would be unable to communicate with its security apparatus, military forces, and population. Attacks on electrical power plants would deprive the regime of its means to conduct effective operations. Strikes on refined oil distribution and manufacturing sites would further paralyze domestic and military internal movement. The reduced railroad capacity would complicate the movement of goods and services, and the destruction of NBC research facilities and military research, production, and storage facilities would reduce the long-term regional threat posed by weapons of mass destruction by limiting Iraq's offensive capability.[148] In emphasizing the need for air superiority, Warden argued that the destruction of the Iraqi air defense system would leave the country helpless. Thus, the first two days of the execution plan required a major suppression of enemy air defense (SEAD) operation, which called for the use of high-speed antiradiation missiles (HARMs) to neutralize or destroy Iraqi surface-to-missile sites.

Warden stated that the plan required thirty fighter-bomber squadrons, four bomber squadrons, and one special squadron with F-117s in addition to command and control elements. Rather than recommend attacking with three waves on the first night, as he had done in the first presentation, he now briefed the operational plan built by Deptula, which suggested two attacks: the first an hour after sunset and the second an hour before sunrise. The pilots would fly twelve hundred sorties the first full day and nine hundred on each of the succeeding five. Despite Adams's insistence that he not specify the duration, Warden reiterated that he believed the objectives would be achieved in six days. The attack would be massive, but Warden suggested that seventy-five to a hundred sorties should be held in reserve during the first night to deal with any Scud sites capable of launching chemical weapons. Unlike the previous version, this plan focused on using aircraft from all services and the integration of allies: among the most obvious, Saudi Arabia would participate in combat air patrol and the British would attack airfields.

As for deconflicting airspace, the air force would fly in western Baghdad and south-central Iraq; the navy in eastern and southeastern Iraq; and the marines in south-central Iraq. For all practical purposes this arrangement constituted route packages, a forbidden philosophy after Vietnam, but it seemed the most practical solution. Moreover, Warden did not see that it would pose a problem, because this time a unified air component commander would direct all operations and the attacks would last only a few days.

Warden not only described the target categories and effects, but also provided details about the weapon systems that would create the effects, the

sequence of events, the number of forces and their capabilities, the time of execution, and the importance of air superiority and SEAD—all of which his staff,
guided by Deptula's operational perspectives, had built into an attack flow plan
for the first forty-eight hours. Warden believed there would be little movement
in theater once the Iraqi regime was incapacitated, but he acknowledged the
possibility of Scud attacks against Tel Aviv and Saudi Arabia. If Iraq invaded
Saudi Arabia the United States would have an operational reserve for air-to-
ground strike missions: air power could stop any ground advance with only
minimal impact on the strategic air campaign.

As in the first presentation to Schwarzkopf, the colonel emphasized
PSYOPS as a critical element of the plan, noting that physical attacks alone would
not sufficiently alienate the Iraqi people from the regime to prompt them to take
action against it. He also mentioned disrupting the economy in a way that would
allow it to be restored quickly, postwar considerations, and other areas of concern
such as munitions distribution, tanker availability, and the need for a very simple
and straightforward aerospace plan.

Warden proclaimed that Instant Thunder had engendered "extraordinary
joint integration and coordination," which was a slight exaggeration, and he ended
his presentation by estimating that if Schwarzkopf did not change the deployment flow the air campaign would be ready for implementation by late September.[149] Schwarzkopf then asked about an early execution without changing the
flow, and Meier and Moore responded that the United States could draw on
other assets in Europe and that going in by mid-September posed only acceptable risks.

When Schwarzkopf asked how many men he would lose in the effort,
Warden replied, "We do not have any precise figures as yet, but in my professional judgment, we are looking at ten to twenty aircraft the first night."[150] Rogers,
Schwarzkopf's deputy, suggested it would be higher, but Warden asserted that he
believed he was being conservative rather than optimistic. Losses would be low
because the Iraqi air defense system would be attacked massively within the first
fifteen minutes of the war, resulting in confusion and paralysis. He then stated, "I
am a volunteer to fly the lead aircraft in the lead raid."[151] Discussing air superiority, Warden predicted that the Iraqi air force would be driven into autonomous
mode by the first morning.[152]

Warden also mentioned that if Iraqi ground forces started to move against
Saudi Arabia—although he thought this unlikely—the plan included keeping
some forces in reserve that could halt such an assault. He emphasized, nevertheless, that the strategic air campaign had to be given full priority. Warden used the
aerial Schlieffen metaphor, illustrating it with his hands, and when Schwarzkopf
told him that he did not like the analogy, Warden countered: "But it is a Schlieffen
plan rotated into the third dimension."[153]

Maj. Gen. Robert B. Johnston, Schwarzkopf's chief of staff, suggested "a more gradualist campaign so that we allow them to respond to our initial activities." Warden was mortified by the comment, but Schwarzkopf said he liked the aggressive approach, and his statement terminated any hint of gradualism.[154] When Rogers criticized Warden for basically having ignored the massive ground forces in Kuwait, Schwarzkopf responded:

> I am not worried about ground forces in Kuwait. . . . This is what makes the U.S. a superpower. This uses our strengths against their weaknesses, not our small army against their large army. . . . Our air power against theirs is [the] way to go—that is why I called you guys in the first place. . . . You have got me so excited with this.[155]

Warden mentioned that he had a scheme for how to deal with the Iraqi ground forces, but Schwarzkopf never asked for an elaboration, and thus Warden never presented Instant Thunder Phase II. Schwarzkopf did ask, however, "What would you have to do if we wanted our airplanes to operate freely over the battlefield in Kuwait?" Warden replied that they would simply have to destroy the Iraqi air defense system.[156]

The presentation and subsequent discussion lasted two hours. At the end Meier asked Schwarzkopf what else they could do for him. In response, the CINC pointed at Warden and said, "Go to Riyadh with at least one other. I am sending you to Riyadh, to Horner—to brief him. To hand off [the plan]. My intention is to continue to plan, to refine it to [the] point of execution."[157]

Schwarzkopf had already concluded that if he were ordered to liberate Kuwait he would eventually need a ground campaign, preceded by devastating air attacks against Iraqi forces. OPLAN 1002-90 advocated this strategy and Horner had already told him what air power could accomplish. Schwarzkopf also knew that U.S. forces would have to ensure air superiority over the battlefield prior to conducting such air-to-ground attacks and Instant Thunder had the virtue of being compatible with his own staff's plans for ground operations.[158] Instant Thunder would thus perform a dual function: it could serve both as a retaliatory option, as requested by Cheney, and as the first phase of a larger war effort.[159] The CINC reached a decision during Warden's presentation: if the president ordered him to conduct an offensive to liberate Kuwait he would present the political leadership with a plan consisting of four phases: a strategic air campaign to establish air superiority over Iraq and incapacitate the Iraqi regime; a subsequent air campaign to establish air superiority over Kuwait; a series of air strikes against Iraqi tanks, artillery, and troops in Kuwait that would reduce the enemy's operational efficiency significantly; and finally a ground campaign that would secure the liberation of Kuwait.

Lieutenant General Horner: "Wonders Never Cease"

In the meantime, Horner, who had been in Riyadh since August 6, was still preoccupied with getting forces into theater. He feared that Iraq might attack Saudi Arabia at any time, and his staff worked day and night planning how to defend against such an attack. By mid-August Horner had two air options. The "D-Day ATO," which would impede an Iraqi advance into Saudi Arabia, emphasized air attacks on Iraqi logistics while available ground forces waged a war of maneuver. The "Punishment ATO" envisioned limited retaliation strikes against the Iraqi homeland.

Horner did not consider a comprehensive bombing of Baghdad, but he was already aware of Instant Thunder. To keep the air component commander informed, TAC had faxed Horner a copy of both Instant Thunder and the TAC alternative. Horner could not believe his eyes: TAC and the Air Staff were developing air campaign plans without knowing what he wanted and without knowing the specifics of the situation. Of course he wanted ideas about how to apply air power, but sending him bullet points was not his way of planning an air campaign. He looked at the two messages for a moment, then scribbled a note to his deputy, Maj. Gen. Thomas R. Olsen: "Do with this what you will. How can a person in an ivory tower far from the front, not knowing what needs to be done, write such a message? Wonders never cease."[160]

Adams had called Horner to inform him that the Air Staff had no intention of usurping his planning functions and meant only to suggest targeting.[161] Horner responded that his directions were clear: his mission was to defend against the Iraqis if they chose to cross the border into Saudi Arabia and he was not charged with developing an offensive campaign plan. He was open to ideas, but for the moment he believed the Air Staff was working "the wrong plan."[162] General Adams had also sent Col. Steven G. Wilson from the Air Staff into theater as a "peacemaker" to "smooth the way for Warden's visit."[163] Prior to his departure, Adams had told Wilson that Horner would pay careful attention, although he would "ask a lot of questions," do "a lot of screaming," and pretend "not to listen."[164] Wilson felt that he was being thrown into the lion's den for no good reason and spent as many hours as he could with Deptula prior to his departure to gain a complete picture of Instant Thunder.

Col. Samuel J. Baptiste, CENTAF's director of combat plans, who was present when Wilson presented the plan to Horner on August 14, recalled that Horner "flicked through the first few pages rapidly, indicating very little pleasure and then he threw the briefing at me."[165] After objecting harshly several times, Horner told Wilson that he was not interested in giving priority to "strategic targeting" because the imminent threat was on the Saudi border.[166] Nor did Horner like the terms used in the plan: "center of gravity" was a "college boy term," "strategic" had "nuclear" connotations, and "Instant Thunder" smacked of Vietnam.[167] More important, Horner felt that the concept did not amount to a plan: it merely called for bombing Baghdad and hoping to win, and hope was not a good basis for planning. Wilson's understandable inability to explain the plan fully may have increased Horner's doubts about Instant Thunder's viability.

When Warden and his briefing group arrived in theater five days later, Wilson warned them that the Air Staff involvement had put Horner in a foul mood and that the general's exclusive focus was on a defensive plan. Warden did not take his warning fully to heart: Powell and Schwarzkopf had endorsed the effort and Warden believed that he would win Horner over as soon as he was given the chance to explain the logic behind Instant Thunder. He had heard that Horner liked to be challenged and would fire many questions to see if the concepts had been examined from all possible angles. His personal objective was to ensure that Horner would approve the thrust of the plan and would keep him in theater.[168]

The team Warden brought with him to Riyadh consisted of Lieutenant Colonels Deptula, Harvey, and Stanfill, the three men most closely involved with developing the content of Instant Thunder. Major General Olsen welcomed them shortly after they arrived in theater on August 19. He suggested that Warden explain Instant Thunder to key members of the CENTAF staff; he would then arrange for a meeting with Horner the next day. In addition to Olsen, Baptiste, and Wilson, the CENTAF leaders attending the meeting were Brig. Gen. Patrick P. Caruana, STRATFOR commander; Brig. Gen. Larry L. Henry, director of the electronic warfare cell; Col. James Crigger, director of operations; and Col. John A. Leonardo, director of intelligence. Warden prefaced his briefing by saying that Schwarzkopf had requested and endorsed Instant Thunder; that the planning effort had been joint, albeit led by Checkmate; and that the plan was offered in the spirit of "if it makes sense, use it; if not, chuck it."[169]

Among the general officers, Olsen was the most positive and Henry the most skeptical, but all those present agreed that Warden's team brought something useful to the table.[170] Caruana recalls that Instant Thunder had "tremendous appeal. . . . we were impressed by what was an encompassing plan." Still, he had to admit that it was "too abstract" and he agreed with the assessment by Crigger and Baptiste that although Instant Thunder included many praiseworthy elements, CENTAF was for the moment fully occupied with forming a viable plan for the defense of Saudi Arabia.[171] Olsen concluded the meeting by saying he was glad the Air Staff planners were in theater; their help was much needed and he hoped they were prepared to stay.

The next morning the CENTAF staff presented the newly arrived team with its D-Day plan, an all-out defensive plan to blunt an Iraqi attack into Saudi Arabian oilfields.[172] The airmen discussed the pros and cons and then returned to Instant Thunder. When Warden asked if the CENTAF planners had any ideas for improvement, Crigger, who acknowledged that Instant Thunder included a breadth and depth of target-sets that the theater planners lacked, offered several tactical suggestions.[173] Again, the atmosphere seemed positive. Olsen had arranged for Warden to present Instant Thunder to Horner in the afternoon, a meeting that would constitute the finale to twelve days of hectic planning.

Horner had mixed emotions about the entire effort. He was angry that the Air Staff was building a plan without involving him; he had told Wilson and Baptiste in clear terms that war plans should not be developed in Washington. He had also learned a little about Instant Thunder from telephone calls with Russ, Adams, Ryan, and Dugan, and he knew that TAC was not thrilled. In theater Olsen told Horner that he thought the plan had something to offer and that they certainly needed more capable airmen in theater. By contrast, Henry had warned him that the plan was incomplete.[174] Schwarzkopf had expressed great enthusiasm for the plan, but told Horner to do what he thought appropriate.[175] Horner expected a good discussion, but Warden would certainly have to prove himself. The general saw the occasion as a job interview: if the colonel performed well, he would hire him; if not, he would send him home.

The presentation went badly from the outset. Warden had been told that the meeting would start at 1400, so when Horner arrived at 1355 Warden was in another room and the general had to wait for the colonel. There were no formal introductions or greetings. When Horner sat down, Warden placed a box of candy in front of him, explaining that the sweets and the bags on the floor, which were filled with skin lotion, chap sticks, sunscreen, lip balm, and razor blades, had been sent by Adams, who believed that such items were in short supply in theater. Warden thought this friendly gesture could be a good icebreaker, but Horner perceived it as demeaning and his grimaces revealed his displeasure. "I don't need any of this shit," he stated, and then pushed the box aside and ordered Warden to "proceed."[176] Warden recalled that "the warmth of the briefing did not improve after that."[177]

Warden presented the same briefing that he had given to Schwarzkopf three days earlier. He began the presentation by explaining the need for an offensive air campaign, but Horner became impatient, telling him to "skip the basic air power lecture" and get to the essence. Warden felt the tension, speeded up, and gave the briefing with few interruptions.

Horner, a fighter pilot through and through, followed up with several combative comments and questions. When Warden suggested that the United States act sooner rather than later, Horner insisted that Saddam Hussein was "bunkered up" and that time was on the U.S. side. As for Warden's praise of stealth and precision, Horner was reluctant to have F-117s with laser-guided weapons serve as the backbone for an offensive air campaign, since the aircraft had not been tested properly in combat. The F-117 had been used in Operation

Just Cause in December 1989, but Horner thought that it had performed poorly and had found the after-action reports discouraging.[178] He strongly criticized Warden's emphasis on PGMs; the real point was "precision delivery of munitions" and he stressed, "It does not matter what kind of bomb you use as long as it hits the target."[179] Horner also told Warden to stop talking about strategic and tactical targets: "Targets are targets."[180] As for cruise missiles, Horner said they had small warheads and that including them was an attempt to sell weapons and justify the military budget. When Warden suggested route packages for the different services Horner thought the colonel was out of his mind: "Do not deconflict by route packages. We did that in Vietnam; we will never do that again."[181] And when Warden emphasized the need to complement the strategic bombing campaign with PSYOPS, Horner insisted, "That's a theater-level responsibility, and it's concentrated in the Army."[182]

Horner told Warden that Instant Thunder had some good components. The leadership and command and control targets were interesting, but he was skeptical about "getting Hussein."[183] "I have trouble with the basic premise, severing the head from the body. . . . If you're trying to institute a change in his government, you can't leave this to chance."[184] Horner observed that if the United States wanted to kill Saddam Hussein it needed to make sure that it had enough information and, as a minimum, the air campaign would have to destroy the Iraqi command and control apparatus. Warden admitted that he did not yet have enough information about the complexity of the command and control system, and Horner commented that it was the responsibility of CENTAF, not the Air Staff, to get the information. Warden also noted that it might be difficult to achieve complete destruction and that it would be sufficient to "isolate [Saddam] for a while,"[185] but Horner countered that if he went down that avenue he needed to know who the likely successor would be. At one point Horner stated that "it sounds like a decapitate the snake plan. I do not see it as a slick plan, but as a hit-him-in-the-face plan."[186]

Horner further noted that although attacking central Baghdad would produce advantages in the short term, it would have repercussions for U.S.-Arab relations for the next two hundred years. Moreover, did Warden know when sufficient supplies would reach the theater to support such a campaign? What would happen if the Iraqi regime did not collapse after a five- or six-day campaign and CENTAF had used up its logistics in theater? Warden mentioned that the plan could be executable by mid-September and Horner thought he greatly underestimated the amount of work that was required to develop the ATOs for such a campaign.

Horner concluded that Warden had done an "academic study" and now CENTAF had to "make it reality."[187] He understood the strategic portion of Instant Thunder, but he remained unconvinced: lives were at stake and he was not going to gamble on the success of strategic operations. In his opinion, the plan lacked depth and he was very uneasy with the way it ignored the Iraqi ground forces on the Saudi border. Warden emphasized that strategic attacks on the Iraqi regime should be the centerpiece of the plan, but Horner countered that Iraqi forces could be in Dhahran in eight to twelve hours and such a threat could not be ignored: the ground threat was real and was his major concern at the moment. He simply could not design an air campaign plan that did not include attacks on ground forces. CENTAF's planners would need to rethink both the targeting philosophy and the timeline. When Warden again referred to Schwarzkopf's acceptance of the plan, Horner said he believed Instant Thunder could even be counterproductive, since it might trigger an Iraqi attack on Saudi Arabia.

Warden had presented the slide "What If: Iraq attacks Saudi Arabia in response to Instant Thunder" during the briefing with a caption stating, "Combining Instant Thunder and battlefield air operations can stop ground advance," but the claim had not allayed Horner's concerns. Warden could have returned to this slide and explained in detail to Horner why he believed that a nation under strategic attack could not organize and launch a substantial offensive on the ground. He could also have presented the Instant Thunder Phase II briefing, titled "An Operational Air Campaign Against Iraqi Forces in Kuwait," and explained that Checkmate had studied the threat from the Iraqi army and had developed options for dealing with the ground forces. But he chose not to raise these issues for three reasons: he feared that such a discussion would divert attention from the strategic portion of Instant Thunder, he did not believe in targeting ground forces, and Schwarzkopf had told him to deliver the same plan he had presented three days ago.

Warden confidently repeated that he did not see the ground threat as important: "General . . . you are paying entirely too much attention to those tanks. You are worrying too much about those tanks. . . . You are being overly pessimistic about the ground war, Sir."[188] These comments shocked the group. It was not accepted protocol for a colonel to address a thee-star general in those terms. Deptula recalled that everybody "took a deep breath and held it . . . you could hear a pin drop."[189] All expected Horner to throw the colonel out of the office and terminate the briefing, but the commander turned slowly to Henry, almost smiling: "I am being very, very patient, aren't I. . . . I am being very, very tolerant, aren't I. . . . I am really being nice not to make the kind of response that you all would expect me to make, aren't I?" Horner and Henry talked as though Warden were not in the room and the colonel felt that the generals were being "condescending." Warden apologized and Horner accepted his apology, but Warden soon realized that the briefing had run its course.

Horner was looking for an airman who would be flexible in "give and take," who knew the art of teamwork, and whom he could fully trust: as the air commander, he would leave it up to his chief planner to work out the details. His immediate assessment was that Warden did not suit the description. Horner separately asked each of the three lieutenant colonels if they could stay in theater, and they accepted, but by deliberately not including Warden in the invitation Horner in effect told the colonel to leave the theater as soon as possible. Warden departed immediately. The two men would never meet again.

Horner summed up his misgivings:

> When you are sitting in D.C., it is easy to think about and talk about different things, but when you are over here and your pink ass is on the line, that changes the way you think and what your priorities are. . . . Our goal is to build an ATO and execute this. . . . It should be open-ended. . . . Our goal should be to gut Iraq. You cannot do it with air alone."[190]

Horner believed it was irresponsible of Warden to ignore the Iraqi army, and although he liked the idea of going after the leadership as one element of an overall plan, he concluded that Warden never suggested a successful way of doing it: "It's one thing to have a vision, it is another thing to have the foresight to make that vision a reality."[191] Thus, Horner dismissed the Instant Thunder plan: it did not pass the "common sense" test—it was "incomplete" and "embryonic."[192] In his memoirs, *Every Man a Tiger*, he elaborated further:

> The briefing, unfortunately, started off poorly, the problem being that Colonel Warden had built it for a different audience than those like me who have been studying the Persian Gulf theater for years and airpower for decades. . . . That meant there was a lot of boilerplate up front. . . . Patience is not my long suit, and I do not like being talked down to, so I waved Warden off from his preparatory material and told him to get on with his main points. Where I had expected intelligence (and Warden was certainly intelligent), I was getting a university academic teaching a 101 class [the first course for undergraduates in their first year]. At every question I asked that dealt with the Iraqi ground forces, he would dismiss my concerns as unimportant. Even if he was right (which I greatly doubt), he would have been wise to forgo the temptation to treat me like a boob. The commander on the scene may well have been a boob, but he does not like to be treated like one. Warden's problem, I have come to realize, was partly due to personal arrogance. Soon, as discussions became increasingly disjointed, the room grew tense. One thing was clear: John Warden and I looked at the problem of air campaign planning differently. He viewed it as an

almost Newtonian science, with the targeting list being an end unto itself, while for me, air warfare revolves around the ATO, logistics, joint service and allied agreements, and the million and one little things that he never had to worry about back in the Pentagon. Sadly, I realized that his brilliance as a thinker would not carry through working with the team in Riyadh. . . . John Warden was too much in love with his own thinking, and too prickly to handle the give-and-take—the communicating—that Riyadh required. John Warden went home, where he did continue to support us by sending forward a flow of valuable planning and targeting information. But as far as I was concerned, he was out of the war.[193]

Although Horner did not like the way Warden presented his case he did appreciate the target-sets: "a solid piece of work" in which the Checkmate team could take pride. He acknowledged that Instant Thunder "contained elements of brilliance" and that Warden "had a way to rack and stack the targets so we could relate their importance to overall political objectives." Indeed, he was favorably impressed by Warden's having identified the political objectives and then tied the national strategy to the campaign that he laid out.[194] Still, he could not shake his feeling that Warden thought in terms of concentric circles to a fault and that there might be legitimate and higher priorities than going straight for the jugular: "If your army is getting overrun, who gives a shit what you take out deep. . . . just as there was genius, there was no common sense."[195]

Undoubtedly, the meeting was a clash of personalities as well as ideas, but at the heart of the matter the two fundamentally disagreed on the relative importance of strategic offensive operations. Horner saw the Iraqi ground forces as a real threat that could not be explained away and he worried that launching Instant Thunder prematurely might provoke an Iraqi ground attack that the coalition would find difficult to repulse. Warden believed that the impact of such an attack would preclude the invasion:

I made the point that it is highly unlikely that anybody is going to be able to organize themselves and launch any kind of dangerous offensive with little or no notice when the home front is falling apart behind them. People just do not do that. It is just not done; never has been done, and there is no reason to think that it is going to be now. Physically it is very difficult to do because of the lack of communications support, logistics support, opportunity to practice, etc. Despite all that, if it does happen, our recommendation is that we hold in reserve the A-10s, because we were talking primarily about A-10s. . . . Later we added the AV-8s, A-10s and some of the F-16s, which we do not need for the strategic operation; and in the event that the Iraqis launch a counter-offensive, we will use those airplanes that do not have strategic ability to attack the Iraqi advancing ground forces, and we are utterly confident that we will be able either to stop them or to slow them sufficiently so that they will not reach anything that has operational or strategic significance.[196]

In retrospect, each man felt that the other had dismissed his concerns out of hand. When Warden was asked later how he felt about the brutal reception he answered: "Like we had made a mistake someplace, that we had done something stupid; that there clearly had to have been a better way to have made the presentation. We felt that perhaps we had blown the whole thing, but had not lost all hope because [Horner] had kept three guys there who knew what the game plan was."[197]

Interestingly, both Horner and Warden thought that the other had failed to appreciate the lessons of Vietnam: Horner envisioned Warden's group sitting with the president and picking targets during Tuesday lunches in the White House, while Warden feared that Horner would not apply air power correctly. The CENTAF staff summed up Instant Thunder as "a good idea, but a bad sell"—a conclusion that is difficult to refute.[198]

Warden had definitely sunk to a low point when he returned to Washington. Some even believed that his influence had reached an end, but he concluded that the situation was not as bad as it seemed. He had injected his targeting philosophy into the planning process and the seed he had planted would come to fruition if he managed to use his directorate in the Pentagon as a supporting agency for the three men who had stayed behind. After all, Powell and Schwarzkopf supported the effort, and although he had wanted Horner's blessing he was convinced that the air component commander did not have the authority to derail the effort altogether.

What Warden did not know when he boarded his plane for the flight home was that Horner had already decided to establish a Special Planning Group with a mandate to develop an ATO for a strategic air campaign plan. That cell, in which Deptula became the chief planner, would ensure that much of Instant Thunder survived.

In the story of Instant Thunder a matter of chance became a matter of fact, as a few strong-minded and visionary individuals outside the established chain of command for war planning succeeded in grasping the flow of events and redirecting them through persistence, conviction, and vision. By taking a strategic view during a crisis and presenting an offense-oriented plan that targeted the Iraqi regime and its leadership directly, Warden and his team had filled a crucial void that nobody else seemed willing or able to fill.

9

CHECKMATE: SUPPORT TO THE MILITARY CAMPAIGN

When Warden returned from Riyadh he undertook a series of initiatives to draw into his circle people who could help in the planning process. This hand-picked group, which included midlevel staff from government and nongovernment agencies as well as military officers from all four services, represented many disciplines and became instrumental in supplying the air planners in theater with crucial information. In the process Warden's team established itself as an alternative to the formal wartime intelligence, planning, and execution structure, creating an informal resource that significantly influenced the development of the air campaign plan. Consequently, Warden's most important contribution to Operation Desert Storm—defining the debate on war strategy—was translated into an executable plan thanks to another effort of almost equal importance: he turned his directorate into a reach-back agency that helped the planners in Riyadh expand and complete the air campaign.[1]

Turning the Larva into a Butterfly

Warden left Riyadh on August 20 deeply discouraged, but he had not entirely lost hope: after all, Horner had chosen to keep Harvey, Stanfill, and Deptula in theater. However, the three newcomers did not feel welcome among the existing CENTAF staff, whose main task was to plan for the defense of Saudi Arabia and who apparently saw neither the purpose nor the urgency of a plan that Horner seemed to have condemned. Short on qualified people, computers, and time, CENTAF was unwilling to provide support for an offensive option that still had no mandate. The three lieutenant colonels felt like "exiles" and Harvey noted in his diary, "CINCCENT's positive attitude toward the plan and positive warfighting spirit is inverse squared of General Horner's negative attitude."[2]

The intelligence officers in theater and in Washington seemed to be deliberately undermining their efforts to develop an offensive option. Harvey recorded that the intelligence branch was boycotting them: the exiles were told that they were "mucking [around] in CENTAF's business," that Instant Thunder was "nothing more than an Air War College paper," and that it was just a matter of time before Horner would send them back to Washington as well.[3] Stanfill struggled to obtain basic information such as existing target lists, a map that identified the Instant Thunder targets, and even the target imagery folders that had been prepared for Schwarzkopf. Colonel Blackburn would not release the imagery for the eighty-four Instant Thunder targets and refused to depart for Riyadh because he felt compelled to ensure that Warden did not "ride rough-shod" over his targeteers.[4]

Harvey called Warden and told him that he was frustrated by the treatment they were receiving and that he thought Instant Thunder was doomed. Warden responded that he would dedicate his directorate in the Air Staff to serving as a supporting cell. The organization would provide the information the planners needed in theater and if necessary would operate around the clock. He emphasized the extreme importance of maintaining the strategic focus and encouraged the three airmen to call him whenever they needed anything.[5]

"INSTANT BLUNDER"

Horner, meanwhile, was "desperate to get the planning started before some other road show came into town with their version" and decided that the right man to develop an offensive plan would be Brig. Gen. Buster C. Glosson.[6] As the deputy commander of the Joint Task Force Middle East, stationed on the USS *LaSalle* in the Persian Gulf, Glosson had already told Horner that he was anxious to get off the ship and into action.[7] The two officers knew each other well and Horner placed Glosson in charge of the Special Planning Group.

When Glosson arrived in Riyadh on August 22, Brigadier General Henry told him that Horner had found Instant Thunder incomplete. As far as Henry was concerned, the plan should be called "Instant Blunder" because "six days' worth of hell in Baghdad" was not going to end the war: "Hitler made this mistake, did he not? 'We will go bomb the hell out of London, and they will quit.' Did not happen. Instant Blunder would have done the same thing."[8] Henry let Glosson know that he thought the Air Staff planners were a bunch of "academics" and that Horner had been right to send Warden home in a "body bag."[9] According to Glosson:

> As we drove to the Royal Saudi Air Force headquarters, Henry updated me on the lay of the land at CENTAF from the fertile soil to the "potholes and sink holes." In the sink hole category was an Air Staff briefing by Colonel John Warden, which Horner and Henry had seen the day before. Henry told me how Horner had picked apart many of the key assumptions just on practical grounds and sent Warden home. . . .

After dinner, Horner and I went back to his office at the Royal Saudi Air Force headquarters for a private meeting. The first thing on his mind was that the Air Staff back in Washington was trying to dictate to him how he was going to run the campaign.[10]

Horner gave Glosson five days to develop an ATO, stating that he could start with a blank sheet of paper or could use parts of the Instant Thunder briefing as he saw fit.[11] When Deptula presented Glosson with the plan he was pleasantly surprised and acknowledged that it was "a pretty good think piece. . . . The briefing had only 84 targets but that was 84 more than we had planning folders and photographs for at the time."[12] He was also quick to point out what he believed to be weaknesses: there was insufficient emphasis on counterair operations, the plan did not recognize the staying power of the Iraqi regime, and the idea of finishing the campaign in six to nine days was unrealistic. He wrote in his diary: "need air campaign for fifteen rounds not three; six days is dumb."[13] Two or three rounds, he argued, would end up with "just giving Saddam a bloody nose."[14] Glosson concluded that although "the Warden effort has merit, the people involved do not have any concern about Horner's position or desires. . . . they are all marching to their own drummer or have their own little agendas."[15] At the same time he decided that Instant Thunder would form the basis for further planning and that Horner's dismissal had been "an over-reaction to his resentment of Washington's interference and the way he had been treated by Warden."[16]

> When I arrived in Riyadh, I said, "Let me see any offensive plans that CENTCOM or CENTAF have for this region." I was told none existed. Then I requested any plans that TAC or the JCS might have. Again I was told none existed except for defense of Saudi Arabia and limited strike options against Iraq. Do you know what they provided me? Nothing. Zero. . . . Remember the situation: We were sitting there with no option for the President of the United States to execute. . . . The only input that I had on the 21st of August was the work that the Checkmate guys had done.[17]

Glosson next arranged for available resources, manpower, office space, supplies, and equipment—basically setting up the organization. Meanwhile, Deptula drafted an "attack flow" document that largely adhered to the original Instant Thunder philosophy. Deptula thus remained at the heart of the effort to plan a strategic air campaign.

Glosson overcame bureaucratic and physical obstacles to developing a strategic option and within a few days Lieutenant Colonels Deptula, Harvey, and Stanfill were exiles no longer. They convinced Glosson that an offensive should aim for the Iraqi regime rather than ground forces in Kuwait, and as they sought to remedy the problems that Horner had identified they stayed in close touch with Warden over the encrypted telephone system. Deptula quickly took the lead in modifying the target list, improving the force packages, and completing an attack plan.

While Glosson's task was to focus on deep strikes, Horner assigned his director of operations, Colonel Crigger, and his director of plans, Colonel Baptiste, to develop the accompanying scheme for targeting the Iraqi ground forces. This, in Horner's mind, would rectify the fundamental flaw of Instant Thunder. Since they had worked exclusively on the defensive plan, the two colonels realized that the only starting point they had was Instant Thunder Phase II. Harvey reviewed the plan with them and the CENTAF planners found it very useful; they adopted the title, format, and content.[18] When CENTAF was then told to develop an operational order (OPORD) they based it on the 180-page OPORD in Instant Thunder.

"DESERT SOMETHING"

Glosson presented the updated version of the offensive air campaign plan to Horner on August 26 under the title "Instant Thunder Concept and Execution." Horner was not amused and told him to get rid of the preposterous title and to use "Offensive Campaign Phase I" until Schwarzkopf came up with an official name. Horner added that it would be "Desert something."[19] Although Horner thought that Glosson had done well at eliminating some of what he considered the original version's flaws, he was appalled by the way Glosson presented it. Henry, who attended the meeting, later described the plan as "ill-prepared, poorly presented and violently executed."[20] The presentation reminded Horner too much of Warden; he noted that the terminology was typical of staff officers in the Pentagon and not suitable for the theater commander.[21] Horner ordered Glosson back to the drawing board and told him to stop using the term "strategic."

Glosson and Deptula worked through the night to improve the format of the briefing and the next day Horner was reasonably pleased with the plan, although he admitted that "the thrust of the briefing never changed."[22] The number of targets had grown from 84 to 127 and the air campaign would last from three to six days. Glosson emphasized that Phase I would "weaken resolve" and "induce fear," which he anticipated would "generate internal strife." Moreover, the destruction of "military capability" and the elimination of "government control" would "decapitate the Saddam regime."[23]

On August 27 Horner accepted the basis for a plan that closely resembled Instant Thunder. Two days later CENTAF published the first fully coordinated ATO, which remained the sole offensive option available to Schwarzkopf for several weeks.[24] Both Glosson and Deptula noted that all they did in terms of

Phase I planning after August 29 was "more of the same": they added targets and assets, but the philosophy remained unchanged. Deptula characterized what happened as a "CENTAF-ization" of Instant Thunder; the biggest difference was that PSYOPS were no longer included because Horner insisted that they fell outside his responsibility.[25]

To Warden and Deptula a reconstructed and reformed Iraq was the ultimate goal, and they believed that the ability to supply or deny assistance in restoring the oil and electric power industries would give the United States leverage over Baghdad. Instant Thunder thus showed both awareness of and sensitivity to civilian casualties and collateral damage. The OPORD "Offensive Campaign—Phase I," completed by Deptula and signed by Horner on September 2, noted, "civilian casualties and collateral damages will be kept to a minimum. The target is Saddam Hussein's regime, not the Iraqi populace. . . . Anything which could be considered as terror attacks or attacks on the Iraqi people will be avoided."[26] The planning in theater followed Warden's and Deptula's guidance that structures of cultural and religious significance to the Iraqi people should be spared. Moreover, to the extent possible, Iraqi industry and economy should be targeted with both military objectives and postwar recovery in mind.

To deal with Iraqi ground forces, Crigger presented Horner with a concept that would ensure air superiority over Kuwait and then degrade Iraqi ground forces, as described in Instant Thunder Phase II. Horner was satisfied, although he protested when Crigger offered a strategy that included pauses to regroup. He also told the colonel to assume that attacks would occur concurrently with the strategic operations.

Intelligence—"A Thorn in Our Side"

The greatest frustration for the planners in late August resulted from the lack of intelligence. Glosson's Special Planning Group had been ordered to provide Horner with an ATO by the end of the month, but Colonel Blackburn steadfastly refused to provide them with the imagery and photos that his team had prepared for the Schwarzkopf briefing. He claimed that the maps and analysis he had did not amount to "target folders" and were therefore not sufficiently developed for use. Blackburn was not swayed by Warden's argument that timely, imperfect data was more useful than perfect data that arrived too late. He wanted to follow established procedures, letting the different agencies in Washington do their jobs and then sending the products to CENTAF's intelligence branch. The three lieutenant colonels were equally frustrated with Col. John A. Leonardo, the CENTAF director of intelligence. Glosson lamented that the intelligence branches in Washington and Riyadh undermined his planning group: "I had never seen anything in my entire military service that was a parallel to the incompetence of CENTAF intelligence."[27]

What saved the planners in theater was that Warden's directorate managed to obtain information from a range of agencies outside the command structure. On August 22 Harvey sent a fax to Warden in which he requested intelligence data. According to air force historian Diane T. Putney, this initiated an extraordinary link between the planners in theater and those in the Pentagon that "would continue throughout Desert Shield and Desert Storm and significantly affect the development and execution of the air campaign."[28] In the process Warden gained both friends and enemies in the intelligence community: individuals appreciated his commitment to achieving results, while institutions believed that Warden was undercutting their authority. When intelligence officers insisted on "operating by the book" and "functioning as trained," Warden countered that when the existing system was inadequate one had to "act now [and] fix the system later."[29] Echoing Glosson's opinion, one of the Checkmate officers described the USAF intelligence group as "a thorn in our side"—whether Maj. Gen. James R. Clapper, the assistant chief of staff for intelligence; Brig. Gen. Billy J. Bingham, his deputy; or Colonel Blackburn, who operated with Checkmate on a daily basis.[30]

"PROPHET OF AIR POWER"

Less than two weeks after their arrival in theater both Stanfill and Harvey decided to return to the Air Staff. They were discouraged, found it difficult to work with Glosson, and concluded that they could be more useful to the planning effort from Washington. Horner for his part thought the two were "lightweights":

> I have little sympathy for the two who walked away from being in Riyadh in the only war they would experience in their career. If those two felt unloved then they were not tough minded enough to be there. A real warrior would have killed to be in Riyadh. It is no time to cut and run just because your ideas are being examined and rejected. I was whacking Buster Glosson from time to time, but I did not hear him whining.[31]

Deptula, by contrast, proved his worth, and both Horner and Glosson came to appreciate his dedication to achieving results. He succeeded by applying the approach of "if you want your ideas accepted, then convince your boss that they are really his ideas," and noted that "you can get a whole lot accomplished if you do not worry about who gets the credit."[32] Nevertheless, he encountered major challenges when he tried to implement the ideas that he and Warden had discussed throughout the previous months.

Certain members of the CENTAF staff did not understand the concept of "targeting for effects." Deptula viewed the enemy as a system, and by showing the connections among target-sets he tried to convince the planners that the campaign should focus on how to achieve general paralysis rather than physical annihilation. He therefore insisted that air power should attack several target-sets simultaneously, seeking to disrupt, delay, neutralize, deceive, or harass rather than destroy. When Deptula added that the United States needed to think in terms of hampering the leadership rather than being preoccupied with military targets, CENTAF's planners told him that targeting for effects basically wasted air power and produced an unfocused air campaign. They thought it was stupid to expend weapons on radio and television transmitters, and telecommunications in general, when solid infrastructure could be destroyed. Even Glosson protested at first—"What in the hell do you mean, 'targeting for effects'?"—but when Deptula explained the concept Glosson became the strongest supporter Warden and Deptula could have hoped for.[33]

Some of the CENTAF staff also took issue with Deptula's insistence that the ATO process begin with an attack plan. Normally, a team of officers received a target list and then selected a combination of aircraft, bombs, and missiles to destroy (or "service") the targets one by one. In Deptula's view, the ATO was simply an administrative vehicle to bring the plan to the unit for execution; generating an ATO was a "mechanical process" and not a matter of planning. He argued that if the coalition were to succeed at targeting for effects, the important task was to identify the overall objective of the attacks, and he proposed that this be done through the Master Attack Plan (MAP). Deptula pioneered the concept, which introduced timing and coherence for strikes that the ATO lacked. Each MAP would consist of a sequence of attacks during an individual twenty-four-hour period, and would include the time on target, target number, target description, number and type of weapons systems, and supporting systems for each strike package.[34] Thus, the MAP would drive the planning and provide a clear script for what would happen, when it would happen, and who would make it happen. The MAP would be entered into a computer system and combined with the air refueling plan, which contained schedules for tanker tracks, altitudes, fuel off-loads, and refueling.

Since many CENTAF staff members did not understand the philosophy behind Instant Thunder, Deptula took it upon himself, with help from Checkmate, to select weapon systems and build force packages: "The Instant Thunder brief laid out the air campaign 'strategy'; the MAP was the 'operational level' plan to that strategy; the ATO added details required for execution; and the flying units designed the tactics for executing the plan."[35] He would probably have been unable to implement the new approach without Glosson's support, since some of the CENTAF staff thought that Deptula was essentially "ignorant of the planning and ATO process."[36]

In the early days of the planning effort certain members of the CENTAF staff also took issue with Deptula's suggestion that the ATO include strategic attacks. They responded with the traditional assertion that there were only three types of missions: counterair, interdiction, and close air support, and if he could not think in those terms the attacks he advocated would simply not take place. Deptula had to settle for using the term "interdiction" to designate the sorties of the strategic air campaign, but he convinced Glosson to use the term "strategic" in briefings and in operational orders: "When we attack the Baghdad presidential palace, we are not interdicting anything; we are trying to go to the root of the problem here, direct attack. That is what strategic means."[37] Glosson, who had initially contended that "strategic" meant "nuclear," became a proponent of the term and allowed Deptula to insert it throughout the OPORD he was preparing for Schwarzkopf and Horner. Glosson also attempted to convince Horner that "strategic" was the right word to describe the air campaign and its target-sets. Horner could not believe that everybody was at ease with this term in a non-nuclear setting, but in his typical pragmatic way he concurred: "Alright. Just don't use it very often."[38]

A final source of controversy was Deptula's insistence on using the Five Rings Model in categorizing targets, following the numbering system that he and Warden had agreed upon, rather than the BEN system used by the intelligence community. Capt. John R. Glock, one of the intelligence officers assigned to the Special Planning Group, explained that they needed to use the BEN system simply because that was the way the intelligence community operated.[39] Deptula eventually prevailed on all counts, but it required great persistence and some in the CENTAF staff referred to him as the ProAP: Prophet of Air Power.[40] The Special Planning Group itself became known as the "Black Hole," because, according to Baptiste, "we would send people in, and they would never come out. We would never see them again because they would just stay there."[41]

"THE BEST AIR CAMPAIGN PLAN I HAD EVER SEEN"
Following instructions received from Schwarzkopf on August 31, Horner told Glosson that the Republican Guard should be targeted. The rationale behind the suggestion was that targeting the guard would weaken Iraq politically and militarily: the Republican Guard sustained the Iraqi regime and the occupation, posed an offensive threat to other nations in the region, and also had symbolic value as the pride of the regime. Weakening it would diminish Iraq's postwar position in the Middle East.

Warden opposed this tasking. First, it was a difficult target set to find—one that would require considerable intelligence and reconnaissance. Second, large numbers of strike aircraft would be needed to attack the dispersed forces. Third, since the troops were withdrawn to the Iraqi border they did not pose a threat to coalition forces. Fourth, sorties against the Republican Guard would occur at the expense of the more important leadership and C^3 targets. Fifth and finally, if the psychological campaign were conducted well the elite forces could possibly play a role in overthrowing Saddam Hussein's regime. Deptula agreed with Warden's arguments: "air power is subverted by ground force concerns," he complained.[42] However, he saw no reason to contest the issue: if Schwarzkopf and Horner wanted an attack on the Republican Guard, that was what they would get.[43]

A second change to the Instant Thunder target-sets came on September 2, when Horner told Glosson to include Scud missiles. Horner did not view the Scuds as militarily significant, but since attacks against Israel could prompt retaliation against Iraq, which in turn would threaten the cohesion of the coalition, he took the task seriously.

Schwarzkopf first received CENTAF's air campaign briefing on September 3, a week after he arrived in theater. The mission statement read: "When directed by USCINCCENT, the Joint Force Air Component Commander (JFACC) will conduct a strategic air campaign against Iraq to isolate and incapacitate the national leadership, destroy critical control centers, and neutralize Iraqi offensive military capabilities to include Iraqi forces in Kuwait and Southern Iraq."[44] Horner then gave a general introduction and Glosson presented a series of slides built by Deptula titled "Offensive Campaign Phase I," which included Concept to Execution (a flow chart diagram); Centers of Gravity (leadership, infrastructure, and military forces); Strike and Support Forces (assets available by mid-September); Attack and Flow Intensity (bar graph of strike and SEAD sorties for the first twenty-four hours); Attack Plan (specifying three to six days' duration); and Results ("decapitate Saddam regime" and "generate internal strife" to "change" the government).

Following the categories in the Five Rings Model, the target list identified Leadership (fifteen), Telecommunications (twenty-six), Electricity (fourteen), Oil (eight), Railroads (twelve), Military Production and Storage (forty-one), Strategic Air Defense (twenty-one), Strategic Chemical Warfare (twenty), Airfields (thirteen), and Ports (four). The ten target-sets and their 171 targets included the Republican Guard as well as five western Scud sites that fell in the chemical warfare category. Within the first twenty-four hours, more than 70 percent of the initial Instant Thunder targets would be struck and Glosson asserted that the campaign would succeed in six days.[45] He also pointed out the limiting factors, most of which involved weapon systems not yet in theater. As for F-117s, TAC had allowed eighteen to be sent to the theater and more might arrive at a later stage.

The OPORDs of August 17 and September 2 were remarkably similar.[46] Entire sections of the document that accompanied the briefing derived directly from the Instant Thunder OPORD prepared for Schwarzkopf on August 17, revealing the Air Staff plan as the basis for the strategic air campaign.

Following the presentation of the strategic portion, Colonel Crigger, CENTAF's director of operations, focused on the two succeeding phases, emphasizing how to roll back the Iraqi air defense system in Kuwait by attacking fixed and mobile SAM sites and antiaircraft artillery (AAA) systems. As air superiority was gained air power would concentrate on armored forces, command and control nodes, and logistical bases in Kuwait. Crigger emphasized that Phase II involved mainly SEAD operations that would focus on air defense artillery, multiple rocket launchers, and missiles, while Phase III, designed to prepare the battlefield, would seek to destroy 50 percent of Iraq's tanks, armored personnel carriers, and artillery.[47] These objectives would be achieved by 24 F-18s, 96 A-10s, 40 AV-8Bs, and 132 AH-64 and AH-1 helicopters.

Horner ended the briefing by saying that he viewed the air campaign as having two major parts: the offensive air campaign, which would gain air superiority and hit high-value targets such as Scuds and weapons of mass destruction, and the defensive air campaign, which would attack Iraqi ground forces threatening Saudi Arabia. The offensive and defensive plans were two sides of the same coin and it would be preferable to execute both at the same time. He also noted that Phase II made little sense: the air forces would easily gain air superiority in Kuwait and Iraq during Phase I.

Schwarzkopf responded that he wanted the air campaign executed serially in three distinct phases: he had reached this conclusion during Warden's presentation on August 17 and both Cheney and Powell had approved the concept on August 25. Aside from that, Schwarzkopf called it the best air campaign plan he had ever seen.[48] He was delighted with what he considered a broad range of options that could be "conducted as a stand-alone operation or part of a larger war."[49] Schwarzkopf told Horner and Glosson to fine-tune the plan, have the retaliation portion ready for execution by the middle of September, and be prepared to brief Powell in the near future.

"WALKING ON EGGSHELLS"
Deptula kept Warden informed on progress in theater from the outset, and he in turn provided Deptula with essential information, especially targeting materials. However, Deptula concealed his contact with Warden, because "at the very beginning General Horner and General Glosson were very averse [to] anything coming out of the Pentagon."[50] During the initial days in theater Deptula convinced Glosson that Checkmate could serve as a valuable reach-back organization; Glosson accepted the construct, since he lacked the resources and personnel in theater necessary to generate the analyses and data collection required for proper air campaign planning. He even noted, "we need to connect to the Pentagon and

Checkmate for support or we will fail."[51] Glosson had told Deptula to keep up the relationship, but he too feared Horner would object if he knew that the "airheads from Washington" were still in the loop. He therefore ordered that the inputs be addressed "Personal for Brigadier General Glosson" and that whenever possible the sender be deleted from the text.[52]

Warden gladly acquiesced and on September 1 he sent personally addressed messages to Glosson that included information and analyses on offensive counterair operations, SEAD, Scuds, and airfield attacks. Warden's team also identified limiting factors that CENTAF would need to overcome to facilitate quick execution of Instant Thunder and provided a status report on bringing more GBU-15s and GBU-24s to the theater. In fact, Glosson considered Checkmate so useful that he decided its role had to be made "official"; on September 4 he called Adams, whose agreement came with a warning:

> John's tendency is to get out in front of the process especially when he believes that the purity has been diluted in what he views as an air campaign, so you are working the real one and he is working the theoretical one, and he is always angry when the theoretical is not executed precisely as he has designed it . . . whenever Warden gets too heavy, thinking he is continuing to steer the log, then you tell me and I will just call him off.[53]

Glosson replied that he knew when to take Warden's advice and when to ignore it. From Adams's perspective, "The stick was in Saudi Arabia and however we could support we would do it. Now that did not slow John down . . . he is such a purist that he still believed that what he was doing was in fact going to be the real plan."[54]

Just as Schwarzkopf's call on August 8 had justified Warden's designing an air campaign, the telephone call from Glosson "legitimized" Checkmate as an ad hoc organization supporting the official planning group in Riyadh. Alexander, Warden's immediate superior, later described Checkmate as a planning cell that "became an umbilical cord back to CENTAF through Glosson."[55] With Adams's approval Warden invited air force and joint personnel to join the Checkmate group and began to keep longer hours.

Encouraged by Glosson's recognition, Warden sent him another comprehensive message on September 8. In it he addressed the level of attrition that would be achieved during the opening days of the war, ways to incorporate drones into the campaign plan, the projected effectiveness of PGMs, considerations regarding telecommunication connectivity, and ways to avoid damaging religious sites. Later, as more information became available in Washington, Warden also suggested how the planners could deal with chemical and biological sites. He continued to refer to the air campaign plan as Instant Thunder, although he knew the term was forbidden in theater, and to push for including PSYOPS in the air campaign.

Meanwhile, both Glosson and Deptula did all they could to prevent Horner from learning of Warden's continuing role; they deleted all references to Checkmate and Instant Thunder when they briefed the air component commander. They feared that Horner would order them to end contact with the Air Staff if he knew that Warden was still involved. Glosson confided to Deptula that he was "walking on eggshells" by requesting and accepting Warden's help.[56] However, unbeknownst to the planners, Horner was fully aware from the beginning that the "crazy man from Washington" was lurking behind the scenes:

> I heard that Warden was sleeping in Checkmate . . . There used to be a thing that we ran around the Pentagon called "Steering the Log." There are 10,000 ants on a log going down the Potomac River, each of them thinking they are steering the log. I said, "It is another case of the Pentagon steering the log theory."[57]

Horner had no intention of cutting off a source of such valuable information and did not oppose having a reach-back agency: to him there was a difference between sending detailed directions and targets from Washington, as had been the case in Vietnam, and supporting an operation that was directed from the theater and took real-world factors into account.[58] If Warden and his Checkmate had information that would help save lives he welcomed the inputs.

With support from his own superiors, especially Rice, Dugan, Loh, and Alexander, Warden devoted enormous effort to helping the CENTAF planning activity, still concentrating primarily on providing the planners with intelligence. In mid-September he renamed his organization "the Deputy Directorate for War Winning Concepts."[59]

THE CHECKMATE STRUCTURE

When Harvey returned to the Air Staff Warden placed him in charge of leading Checkmate's effort to collect information from a variety of intelligence organizations, including the Air Force Intelligence Agency (AFIA), the Armed Forces Electronic Warfare Center, the Defense Intelligence Agency (DIA), the National Security Agency (NSA), and the CIA with its National Photographic Interpretation Center. The CIA covered political and economic aspects, the DIA provided all-source intelligence and operational support to the unified commands, and the NSA provided signals and electronic intelligence. Charles E. Allen, the National Intelligence Officer for Warning on the CIA's National Intelligence Council, became perhaps Warden's most important intelligence source. Allen was "immensely impressed" by Warden and his Instant Thunder plan and considered it his task to support the planning in any way he could.[60]

In the absence of a central authority to coordinate interagency target intelligence and combat assessment in support of the theater commanders, Warden decided that Checkmate should serve as a "fusion center" that would gather intelligence, analyze it, and then distribute it in a timely manner.[61] When the planners in theater needed intelligence they worked around the problem of dealing with the established—and largely obstructive—intelligence hierarchy by calling upon Warden's group directly. This helped them in the short term, but worsened the relationship between the air planners and the forward-deployed intelligence community.

Warden's staff also established contact with the Office of Air Force History and with RAND; the former assigned a historian, Wayne Thompson, to Checkmate, and the latter assigned a Middle East expert, Zalmay Khalilzad. In addition Warden's directorate brought in David Roddy from the U.S. Geological Survey to help track the stationing of mobile Scud launchers. When Warden learned in early September that one building in Baghdad functioned as the focal point for the Iraqi telecommunications system he arranged for Maj. Mark B. Rogers to send the information to Riyadh, including suggestions for damaging the building directly, by bombing it, or indirectly, by cutting off its electricity. Rogers dubbed it "the AT&T building" and Deptula consequently included it in the MAP.[62] Warden also sought connections in both the Department of State and other parts of the Department of Defense, and he updated Rice, Dugan, and Loh on his progress every second day.

Glosson and Deptula came to view Checkmate as an all-important resource. The link with Checkmate became even more valuable to the overall campaign planning on September 12, when Horner assigned Glosson the responsibility for Phases II and III as well as Phase I. At this point Glosson's Special Planning Group took charge of planning all three phases in which air power would be used independently, while the CENTAF staff concentrated fully on developing the D-Day plan and a concept for supporting ground forces in Phase IV. Glosson and Deptula were gratified: now they could ensure the "strategic focus" of the offensive plan and would not have to battle CENTAF for resources. This also meant that Phases II and III would be kept on hold, for they viewed Phase I as far more important.

From mid-September on Glosson's Black Hole planning cell and Warden's Checkmate operated as a single team, with the former taking the leading role, but the latter retaining considerable initiative. Warden succeeded in having "chemical warfare" added as a target category. His initial analysis suggested eight sites associated with chemical research, production, and storage. Glosson and Deptula

in turn incorporated these facilities into their list and expanded the military production and storage target-set to include many more targets associated with the
development, storage, or launching of chemical warheads.[63] The Checkmate staff
also acquired and studied numerous intelligence reports that related to biological
and nuclear targets and ways to deal with them, and passed DIA information
about critical biological production and storage facilities to the Black Hole. Horner
later characterized this information as the most important input CENTAF received from Checkmate.[64]

On September 13 Glosson briefed Chairman Powell on Phases I, II, and
III, although he focused overwhelmingly on the first two days of the strategic air
campaign plan. He essentially repeated the briefing given to Schwarzkopf ten
days earlier: 174 targets would be attacked in less than a week and he anticipated
that the Iraqi regime would be paralyzed as a result. The chairman's main concern
revolved around time of execution, and both Horner and Glosson told him that
they could be ready for action by September 15. Powell left no doubt that he was
impressed with the plan, and at that point Powell and Schwarzkopf decided that
if it came to war an offensive air campaign would lead the effort.

This endorsement represented a great victory for Warden's vision: he had
essentially introduced a strategic air campaign, and this triggered exploration of
how air power should be used. The combination of Deptula in the theater and a
reach-back agency in the Pentagon ensured that much of the Instant Thunder
philosophy survived. Deptula became the architect of the MAP and the keeper of
the flame; at the same time, Horner was willing to let the "larva" (Instant Thunder) develop into "a butterfly" (Desert Storm).[65]

Dugan Dismissed

Just as the strategic air campaign concept was declared ready for execution, Warden and his team experienced a setback: General Dugan had made comments to
the press about the decisive role of air power that led to his forced resignation.
The chief of staff had insisted on being open with the press from the day he took
office, and when he traveled to Riyadh to visit the troops he allowed three journalists to accompany him. On the way to the theater Dugan handed each of
them a copy of Warden's book. Rick Atkinson of the *Washington Post* read it and
on the return trip he asked Dugan a range of questions about air power's role if it
came to war. On September 16 the headlines in the *Los Angeles Times* and the
Washington Post, respectively, read "U.S. War Plan in Iraq: 'Decapitate Leadership'" and "U.S. to Rely on Air Strikes if War Erupts":

> The Joint Chiefs of Staff have concluded that U.S. military power—
> including a massive bombing campaign against Baghdad that specifi-
> cally targets Iraqi President Saddam Hussein—is the only effective

option to force Iraqi forces from Kuwait if war erupts. . . . He ought to be at the focus of our efforts. . . . If push comes to shove the cutting edge would be downtown Baghdad. This would not be nibbling at the edges. . . . If I would want to hurt you, it would be at home, not out in the woods someplace . . . We are looking for centers of gravity that air power could take on that would make a difference early on. . . . when you finally get down to violence, in my view, it is the only option . . . I just do not see us conducting a big ground invasion. . . . Our nation has pursued for decades the policy that has substituted machines and technology for human lives. I think especially in this environment we will continue that policy.[66]

Dugan also told the journalists "Israeli sources" had advised him that to really hurt Saddam Hussein the United States ought to "target his family, his personal guard, and his mistress."[67] He made the comments for two reasons: he wanted to provide substantive underpinnings for President Bush's increasingly aggressive rhetoric, and he thought that the public should know how the military could liberate Kuwait without too much bloodshed. He stated afterwards, "I think what I told those reporters was useful to the American public, useful to the Department of Defense, useful to the President. I think I was very consistent with the President's policy at that time."[68]

Powell, however, was extremely upset by Dugan's statements. Since early September he had complained to Schwarzkopf about the way air power was being portrayed as the "answer to the problem" and said that he felt the Air Staff wanted to make the campaign "an Air-Force only show."[69] Powell suggested "Air thinkers will drive us down the wrong road."[70] From the beginning he had let it be known that he believed ground troops would be needed to occupy Kuwait, and that if the campaign were not joint it would not happen. He had also warned Dugan against taking journalists with him on the trip. The only person more upset than Powell was Cheney.

Warden, apparently the only airman who immediately recognized the potential consequences,[71] called Dugan to inquire if the story had been "deliberately planted" for reasons that he did not know. His action indicates the closeness of the relationship between the two: it was highly unusual for a colonel to telephone a four-star about such a sensitive matter. Dugan assured him that he was comfortable about what he had said. In his opinion, the articles did not reveal any sensitive information. Warden remained worried: tacitly planning to kill Saddam Hussein was one thing, but officially targeting individuals would bring the White House and the Pentagon into conflict with international law. Dugan countered that the United States had targeted Admiral Yamamoto, Colonel

Qaddafi, and Manuel Noriega, "so it was not antithetical to U.S. operations to 'target individuals.'"[72] Saddam Hussein was, after all, wearing a military uniform.

When the National Security Advisor, Brent Scowcroft, stated on television that Dugan was not in the chain of command and did not speak on behalf of the government, some still hoped that Dugan would escape punishment for the comments. The evening the news broke Warden, on his own initiative, developed a position paper for the chief's defense and a deception strategy to avoid linking the comments to the actual air campaign plan. However, his initiatives proved irrelevant, because the next day Cheney relieved Dugan of his duties. Cheney stated nine reasons for his decision

> General Dugan's bad judgment; the discussion of operational plans and a priority listing of targets; acting as the self-appointed spokesman for the JCS and the CINC; the setting of a bad example, especially for USAF personnel; the cavalier treatment of casualties; the citing of an intent to break the executive order banning participation in assassination; the potential revelation of classified information about the size and disposition of American forces; denigration of the role of the other services; and raising sensitive matters of diplomacy, including obtaining targeting information from Israel.[73]

Dugan had certainly been indiscreet, but many in the air force believed that firing him was an overreaction. Dugan left a note pinned to his desk: "To the men and women of the Air Force: Your mission—providing airpower and spacepower to the nation—is essential and enduring. I bid you a fond farewell with my head high, my Mach up and my flags flying. Good luck, good hunting, and Godspeed to the greatest Air Force in the world."[74]

Warden had lost his strongest supporter, but the incident left him with another concern: the Bush administration had dismissed Dugan, but it had not discredited or denied the strategy. He had to assume that Saddam Hussein followed the U.S. news, and therefore that Instant Thunder was compromised. Warden ordered two of his team, Lt. Col. Allan Howey and Maj. Roy Sikes, to develop a deception plan that could be leaked to the Iraqis if necessary. Their scheme, which they named Instant Angus, presented a strategy to isolate the regime from its people and military forces. Rather than target the capital itself, the bombing would focus on bunkers, airfields, and communication centers outside Baghdad. Instant Angus showed forty nonstealthy aircraft attacking central Iraq, mostly conducting SEAD operations to prepare the way for F-16 follow-on forces. The deception plan had an additional goal: if Saddam Hussein chose to use hostages as human shields, it might contribute to their being put at irrelevant sites. The plan retained 10 to 20 percent of the real targets to make it realistic and incorporated some historical anecdotes that would be typical of Warden in case Iraq had done some research on the colonel: Howey included some references to Fuller's "Plan 1919" and used the term "strategic paralysis" to describe the objective. The deception plan was sent to the theater on October 5, but was never used.[75]

Dugan's unfortunate trip to Riyadh did have one positive aspect. Glosson had asked Warden before the chief of staff's visit if he could assist the CENTAF team to acquire target imagery. The colonel did not have to be asked twice: he told his staff to collect the best imagery that could be found in the capital and then load it onto pallets on Dugan's aircraft.[76] Adams, who had accompanied Dugan on the trip, experienced first hand the lack of intelligence available to the wings.[77]

DECOYS: IMAGINARY AIR ARMADA

In late August retired Col. Owen Wormser, a freelance defense consultant, presented Warden with information about a highly classified program designed to create an unmanned vehicle that could mimic various airplane radar cross-sections. Warden showed immediate interest and began to review an electronic warfare concept that called for drones to simulate aircraft attacks—another deception tactic.[78] In gaining air superiority, it would make sense to launch a series of drones in advance of SEAD packages: the drones would look like aircraft on Iraqi radar screens and as the Iraqis activated their SAMs they would have to turn on their radars to fire. When the radars revealed their positions U.S. HARMs would destroy them to free up the medium-altitude range for nonstealthy aircraft. Since the air force inventory contained nothing appropriate, Warden had told Lieutenant Colonel Stimer to look into the possibility of producing drones in a short timeframe, and one manufacturer had responded that it could meet detailed specifications.

Warden raised the issue of using drones with Glosson and Henry on September 3, but the generals showed little interest. Henry was working the tactics that supported the strategy behind the MAP. Having studied the Iraqi air defense system in detail, including radars, SAMs, command and control arrangements, and AAA, he had a hand in integrating all electronic warfare assets into a unified SEAD effort, which in turn was incorporated in the air plan that sought to defend Saudi Arabia and ensure air superiority over Iraq and Kuwait. Henry rejected Warden's suggestion of using drones because he already had navy Tactical Air-Launched Decoys (TALDs) available in theater.[79] In fact, he found Warden's intervention irritating, recalling that the colonel was trying to help too much.

Warden could not be sidetracked by what he viewed as CENTAF's intransigence and he continued to insist that the plan incorporate drones. He discussed the matter extensively with Loh and Adams and both generals responded that they could supply the assets if Horner requested such drones. A few days later Warden sent Deptula an analysis that projected the air force and the navy could lose over twenty aircraft to SAMs in executing the strategic air campaign, even if the TALDs were used. Warden suggested a solution: generating deception targets through air-launched BQM-35 and ground-launched BQM-74 target decoys.[80] In a point paper Warden outlined the following "employment concept for BQM-74":

> Various options; Use to deceive enemy as to real axis of attack; use to soak up SAMS (when Israelis employed these drones in Bekaa Valley operation, Syrians fired multiple SAMS against each drone); use to bring emitters on the air for subsequent HARM attack. Drones as equipped present a radar cross section roughly the same as an F-15. Probably need to have enough in air in approximately same area to make enemy think at least a four ship involved. Probably need about two "four ships" to convince enemy a serious attack is under way.[81]

Deptula passed the analysis to Glosson, and Henry now showed some interest in "the imaginary air armada," but explained that the limited range of the drones would reduce their utility. Warden, becoming ever more impatient, called Glosson again, insisting that he officially request drones. When Glosson failed to respond Warden decided to order BQM-74s from Northrop himself, although he lacked the proper authorization.

On September 14 Adams heard about the procurement through the office of the assistant secretary of the air force for acquisition. Adams thought Warden had gone too far this time: "I have had it with John Warden. His string has run out, and I am getting rid of [him]. I just cannot put up with this anymore. He is undermining my authority as the XO. He is undermining the authority of the Chief and everybody else that is in his chain of command."[82] It was neither the first nor the last time that Adams considered having the colonel reassigned, but he never acted on his impulses, partly because he realized that Warden was too integrally involved in the planning and partly because Warden had the obvious support of Secretary Rice and General Loh.[83] When Warden later reflected on all the times he had infuriated Adams, he had to admit that his personal "survival was improbable from a statistical standpoint."[84]

Warden remained undeterred, and he next called Deptula to tell him that he would very much appreciate it if the Joint Staff were to receive a request for sending drones to the theater. Deptula in turn made the case for a certain number of drones, trucks, radios, and other supporting equipment to Major General Moore, CENTCOM's director of operations, and Moore found the idea excellent. Within the next few days the Joint Staff received a formal request for drones and Deptula incorporated BQM-74s into the MAP. Following the official request from CENTCOM Warden contacted then-Maj. Gen. Michael Ryan at TAC, who helped find qualified personnel to test the drones at a navy facility in California. Col. Jesse T. McMahn from the secretary of the air force's acquisition office took care of the administrative side, and Warden assigned Rogers from his office to make sure that the drones would be used in accordance with the Instant Thunder philosophy.[85] In early October, after successful tests, Stimer had forty drones and sixteen launchers delivered clandestinely to Saudi Arabia.[86] As the creator of the MAP Deptula already knew how he wanted to incorporate the drones into the plan. By skillfully reinforcing Henry's electronic warfare expertise, Deptula was so successful in turning Henry's initial opposition into support that the decoy program later became known as "Poohbah's Party," in reference to Henry's nickname.

Even so, Henry remained less than enamored of Warden's involvement. "I cannot tell you the syndrome of the Washington experts calling in advice," he recalled: "Every day there was someone in Washington and somebody from somewhere. Sometimes they just showed up with the next hot widget to try, not unlike what I thought Warden originally did when he called me about drones."[87] Another CENTAF member noted, "There were factions back in Washington that were trying to run things, just like Vietnam."[88]

Although sources disagree about the origins of the decoy program, Putney concluded that "the idea for the strike originated in Checkmate"[89] and the *Gulf War Air Power Survey* stated:

> The Instant Thunder briefing makes clear that the Checkmate conception provided for a mass SEAD attack on Baghdad at the opening of the campaign—one that would mislead the Iraqis into believing that the Coalition was beginning the war with a major raid on the capital. . . . The final result was a plan that attacked the heart of the Iraqi defenses; it aimed to break the connections between the nodes in the KARI system and to swamp the defenses.[90]

GLOSSON BRIEFS THE PRESIDENT

On October 6 Powell ordered Schwarzkopf to brief the president on his strategy: "Your air offensive plan is so good that I want these people to hear it . . . But you cannot just brief the air plan. You have to brief the ground plan too." The tasking made Schwarzkopf uncomfortable: he was happy to have Glosson present the air campaign plan, but he had no confidence in his own ground plan. He ordered his chief of staff, Major General Johnston, to tell the president that "we do not have capability to attack on ground at this time. Need additional heavy corps to guarantee successful outcome."[91]

Cheney and Powell responded positively to Glosson's briefing on October 10. Glosson noted "Cheney seemed in favor of a strong, strategic air campaign," and Powell's main concern seems to have been that he made the air campaign look too easy: "Tone it down. I do not want the President to grab onto that air campaign as a solution to everything."[92] Powell told Glosson to "go through the plan much faster and not be so convincing."[93] On October 11 Glosson gave a thirty-minute presentation to President Bush, Vice President Dan Quayle, Secretary Cheney, Secretary of State James A. Baker, National Security Advisor Scowcroft, White House Chief of Staff John Sununu, General Powell, and other national leaders.[94] Again Glosson focused on the first phase and gave a brief outline of the next two. He described how CENTAF would obtain air superiority and the essence of the targeting strategy; he sketched out the attack plan for the first twenty-four hours, indicating 822 attack sorties; and he presented a map of Iraq with acetate overlays that graphically illustrated the first day's attack sequence and objectives. Glosson left no doubt that CENTAF planned to target central Baghdad during the first wave. The number of targets had by now reached 218 as intelligence on Iraq improved, but the target-sets remained the same as in the September briefings.

Glosson argued that the strategic air campaign would ensure that the Iraqi leader would lose the ability to communicate with his people effectively and to command and control his forces; he would have significant problems reinforcing Kuwait and he would most likely have to deal with disruption throughout the country.[95] Glosson's "Results" slide asserted that Phase I would both "destroy military capability" and "disrupt government control," which would "reduce confidence in government" and then "decapitate Saddam regime."[96] Secretary Baker objected to the latter phrase, suggesting that "incapacitate regime" be used instead. Glosson replied that the phrase merely indicated the difficulties Saddam Hussein would have in controlling his armed forces and his people and that the country would be in disarray.[97] No one in the room could doubt that the focus was on the Iraqi regime, that the methodology was targeting for effects, and that the objective was strategic paralysis.

Glosson also offered a concise presentation of Phases II and III. While Phase II focused on gaining air superiority over Kuwait by eliminating the Iraqi air defense system and neutralizing the SAM and AAA threats in the Kuwaiti theater of operations, Phase III would first deal with the Republican Guard stationed in southern Iraq and only then attack regular Iraqi ground forces throughout Kuwait. The concept of operations (CONOPS) for Phases II and III consisted of three missions: roll back the Iraqi air defense system; attack enemy armor, C^2, and logistical bases; and conduct an interdiction campaign against reinforcing units.[98] After the presentation President Bush sought Glosson's opinion on whether Saddam Hussein could "rise up out of the rubble on national TV and say 'Here I am.'" Glosson answered he might stand tall "but not on his television and radio networks," but Powell interjected "We have to be careful not to lead people to expect that Saddam will be eliminated personally in Phase I."[99]

One of President Bush's immediate concerns was that attacks against leadership targets, such as the Royal Palace, would also damage targets of historic and religious significance. Glosson replied that they would do everything they could to avoid such damage, and assured the president of the accuracy of precision-guided weapons. Checkmate's estimates of relatively low civilian casualties had strengthened both the resolve of the planners in theater and Glosson's confidence in the strategic air campaign.[100] Warden believed wholeheartedly in stealth technology and maintained that the F-117 was perfectly suited for the mission, since it would attack the most critical targets at night, when workers had left the buildings. He therefore concluded that any collateral damage would result from misidentified targets rather than technological malfunctions. Powell acknowledged that Glosson had certainly impressed the White House audience and that the U.S. national leadership was "very comfortable with the air plan."

By contrast, the briefing on the ground campaign went poorly. Schwarzkopf presented a campaign plan that sent American forces north, straight into the Iraqi defensive line, and predicted ten thousand American casualties, of whom more than two thousand might die. Scowcroft and Cheney expressed disbelief and puzzlement at the plan, and Bush summed up his concerns by asking: "Why not do Phase I, II, and III, and then stop?"[101] Glosson would have loved to affirm that U.S. forces could liberate Kuwait without a ground invasion, but Powell beat him to the punch: "Phase I will devastate him, it will be massive; I do not know how he will deal with it. Phase II will make it more difficult for him, and Phase III will be additive—but you will have no assurance or guarantee we would get him out of Kuwait. Because we cannot guarantee he will leave Kuwait, we must be prepared to do Phase IV."[102] Cheney, Scowcroft, Powell, and Schwarzkopf all argued that the United States needed to double the number of forces in the region to secure victory, and Schwarzkopf was ordered to devise a more imaginative and solid plan over the next days.

Bush later acknowledged that he would have been comfortable going to war with the plans from October had Scowcroft and Powell not advised against it:

> Brent warned that we might eventually have to follow through with ground troops to liberate Kuwait, and if we pounded from the air too soon, before our forces were ready, there could be public pressure to stop all fighting and turn opinion against ever launching a ground campaign. That might leave Saddam in Kuwait—and us without a military option.[103]

The air planners realized that the presentation to the president had given them both a major victory and a setback: the National Command Authority had now decided that, if it came to war, air power would play the leading role for the first days and weeks. However, Schwarzkopf would receive another corps to conduct the ground campaign, and, in the planners' opinion, such a deployment meant that the United States had committed itself to sending those ground forces into battle. Glosson recalled afterwards that he could have made the ultimate air power argument in the White House if he had prepared attrition models showing how air power would decimate Iraqi ground forces in Phase III:

> When I briefed Powell, we did not have more than a thumbnail sketch of phases II and III of the campaign . . . I had not requested the Checkmate guys to do the modeling for me on the specific attrition based on our attacks of Republican Guard and other KTO units . . . I did not include that as part of my briefing. In all fairness to everybody, I screwed up.[104]

Checkmate's Contribution to Phases II and III

During the trip to Washington, DC, Glosson took the time to visit Warden in Checkmate and make it known that he appreciated his support. When Glosson told him about the outcome of the October 11 meeting, Warden was distinctly unhappy with the decision. The United States was ready to win the war with air power; Arab divisions could even be used if it proved necessary and desirable from a political perspective. Why should that victory be delayed because the U.S. Army wanted twice as many men on the ground to prepare for a large-scale ground attack when no such attack was needed? As Warden saw it, more men on the ground simply meant more targets for the Iraqis and thus more casualties.

Glosson told Warden that the strategic air campaign plan was complete: from now on, they need only fine-tune and update it. Since Phase I would no longer require much attention, he asked Warden to start thinking of models and ideas for dealing with the Iraqi ground forces in Kuwait. Both men saw this mission as an opportunity to demonstrate how air power could destroy tanks and artillery, thereby avoiding a massive ground campaign and saving thousands of lives.

KILL THE WHOLE IRAQI ARMY

Although Glosson contacted Warden about inputs for Phase III only after he had briefed the president, the colonel had already started to think about the subject because another factor had come into play. In late September Secretary Rice had requested RAND to produce a computer simulation of an offensive air campaign plan against Iraqi ground forces. While RAND was conducting its analysis, Warden told Major Sikes to analyze what air power could achieve when directed against ground forces in Phase III,[105] and to focus on the regular army rather than the Republican Guard. Although he was still convinced that the strategic air campaign would lead to an Iraqi withdrawal, and that bombing troops might even reduce the possibility of overthrowing the regime, he reasoned that it would be useful to quantify the likely destruction of Iraqi forces in the field. Initially Sikes found the task impossible: to destroy the "last tank and last platoon" would be like "trying to find a needle in a haystack." Moreover, how could pilots distinguish between operable and inoperable equipment?[106] Sikes did not know how to define "destroy the Iraqi army" and Warden had given him many other tasks, all with top priority, so in the short term he chose not to pay much attention to this assignment.

RAND's "Gulf Crisis Analysis," presented on October 6, concluded that the strategic air campaign was necessary, but not sufficient, to ensure Iraq's withdrawal from Kuwait; that it would not cause a popular uprising or a coup and thus would leave the regime in power; and, furthermore, that the Iraqi army would fight a ground war even if the regime were undergoing strategic attack.[107] Thus, RAND supported the view that a ground war was necessary to ensure victory. The immediate implication was that the air power strategy should involve heavy bombing of the deployed Iraqi troops at the same time as the strategic air campaign attacked the regime in Baghdad. RAND suggested that Saddam Hussein probably did not understand the potency of air power, but did understand the consequences of being defeated on the battlefield.

Warden, naturally, disagreed with the findings, contending that the research team did not appreciate the value of strategic paralysis and the effect of PGMs aimed at the heart of the regime. He presented his air power theory and challenged RAND's assumptions, arguing that the think tank held a preconceived notion of territory as the most important element of war and that this notion underlay the flawed conventional belief that clashes on the ground would be necessary to ensure victory. He also criticized RAND for basing their scenario on a cold war mentality and thought that they underestimated the importance Saddam Hussein placed on the Iraqi economy while overestimating the value of ground forces. The RAND researchers found that Warden could not substantiate his arguments and continued to focus on tanks rather than on the regime.

Despite RAND's conclusions Warden urged General Loh to have faith in the strategic air campaign and gave five reasons why the plan should be executed sooner rather than later: "Iraq grew stronger in Kuwait; the weather would begin to worsen in the foreseeable future; events involving Israel could crack the Coalition or deny Coalition forces the option of acting on the preferred time schedule; Iraq's nuclear weapons program would give Saddam Hussein more diplomatic leverage; and Iraq could preempt Coalition actions by launching conventional or terrorist attacks."[108] Besides, if Iraq conducted a partial withdrawal, action would become more difficult from a political standpoint.

The RAND briefing had put pressure on the air force to analyze how air power could play a direct role in weakening the Iraqi army. Warden realized on October 10 that unless the U.S. political and military leadership were convinced that air power would be effective in Phase III there might not even be a Phase I. Both Loh and Adams explicitly told Warden to use his intellect and resources to develop a response; Adams directed him to determine how much air power was required to "kill the whole Iraqi army."[109]

Glosson's request therefore coincided with orders from within the Pentagon, and Warden's Checkmate team took the lead in producing analyses for Phase III. They were tasked to answer two interrelated questions: how long would it take to render the Iraqi ground forces inoperable, and what would be the best application of air power to achieve that goal? Since the answers would provide the guidelines for a ground offensive, the calculation was important to Schwarzkopf in choosing his D-Day, and the tasking presented Warden with the chance to extend the argument for air power as the supreme instrument for liberating Kuwait.

Warden talked with Sikes again and made it clear that he considered this a high-priority task. He decided that Sikes should base his attrition-rate analysis on four assumptions. First, the only ground forces it should consider would be the regular army in Kuwait. Warden believed that the carnage would frighten the elite forces to such an extent that they would not want to join the fight. In any case, those forces, positioned in the rear as they were, posed no immediate threat, and he still believed that the Republican Guard might lead the effort to overthrow the Iraqi regime if given incentives to do so and might even help to rebuild Iraq after the war. Second, history showed that a ground formation lost its combat effectiveness when it suffered between 20 and 40 percent degradation. Third, the designated aircraft would be A-10s, F-15s, and F-16s, and they would conduct daylight missions using unguided bombs. Fourth, Sikes should assume a 95 percent target acquisition rate; in other words, that the pilots would drop a bomb on their designated targets 95 percent of the time.[110]

Over the next few days Sikes—together with Ross Ashley, a computer software development contractor, and Kim Campbell, an intelligence analyst—arranged for a range of calculations to be aggregated into "a larger-than-life Excel spreadsheet" that matched types of aircraft and munitions to targets, generated graphs showing the progression of bomb damage over time, and projected the number of days required to achieve various levels of destruction, including the 95 percent goal.[111] Sikes anticipated that the Iraqi army in Kuwait, except for the forces in Kuwait City, could be annihilated in less than two weeks if the weather permitted a thousand strikes per day. On October 14 Warden stated "it appears entirely feasible to destroy almost the entire Iraqi army in Kuwait from the air—with the exception of Kuwait City."[112] Warden knew that attacking troops in the city could cause civilian casualties, but beyond that he predicted that the Iraqi army could be reduced to an inoperative state with few American losses in less than ten days. Once he began to focus on the attrition of ground forces he anticipated results for Phase III as optimistic as those for Phase I.

On October 15 Sikes presented Warden with an analysis indicating that one day would be needed to deal with the SAM sites in Kuwait, and another nine days were required to destroy the Iraqi armor, artillery, and troops in Kuwait according to predefined criteria. Warden was so excited about the project that on the following morning he told his Checkmate team that the Phase III study was "the most important work in Washington now."[113] Checkmate analysts assumed that PGMs would be used to eliminate armor and artillery while cluster bombs would be used against troops in the open.[114] Warden told Sikes to develop a presentation for Alexander, who in turn found the effort so impressive that he feared some decision makers would decide the United States should conduct Phase III operations only. Warden responded that they had to insist on conducting Phase I first, if only because it was a prerequisite for establishing air superiority: as he had stated in his book, no other portion of a campaign should be executed before air superiority was achieved.

As the work progressed, Sikes and Campbell presented their results to Rice, Adams, Alexander, Clapper, and RAND. On October 20 they briefed General Loh on Phases II and III. Loh pointed out that "Iraqi troops are neither concealed nor camouflaged; no natural concealment; lack of fortifications; strained supply lines; harsh ground environment (water and food); and good flying weather (visibility and clear air)."[115] Sikes stressed one of Warden's major points: that there should be an "operational reserve capability of 80 sorties each day available for strategic campaign maintenance or use for interdiction operations in southern Iraq." The ultimate results predicted were that the "Iraqi army in Kuwait is effectively destroyed; re-occupation should be met with minimal resistance (would be desirable—and may be possible—by Kuwaiti / Arab ground forces); [and] near certain achievements of presidential objectives (without significant casualties of U.S. ground forces)."[116]

For the next three months Sikes became the point man for Phase II and III analyses and briefings.[117] He and Warden briefed several generals in the Air Staff on their results using various combinations of acquisition and attrition rates. Warden himself briefed Adams on an air campaign that would last twenty days: six for the first phase, one for the second, and less than two weeks to destroy the Iraqi ground forces. He defined five target categories for Phase III: airfield support facilities, command and control centers, armor and armored

personnel carriers, personnel, and trucks. Artillery was not yet a priority, because it posed no threat to coalition ground forces. Infantry was also considered
low priority, because it would be time consuming to kill men spread over a large
area and because the Iraqi soldiers could do little damage without equipment.
Besides, with supply lines damaged, the troops would be deprived of food and
water. However, Warden still insisted that this strategy would allow the national
security objectives to be met without a ground war.

Adams asked many questions, found the answers satisfactory, and praised
the effort; he told Checkmate first to present the campaign plan to Loh, then
send it to Glosson in the Special Planning Group, and finally inform the Joint
Staff. Overall, Loh was pleased with the presentation, but he wanted Warden to
examine the impact of friction and a range of uncertainties. What if chemical
weapons or terrorist attacks came into play? What if Iran intervened? What if
they lost a hundred aircraft on the second day? Warden discussed the attacks
conceptually and logically, but Loh believed that the presented model was not
"sophisticated" enough. Warden retorted that there was nothing sophisticated
about destroying ground forces in open terrain.[118] He also pointed out that he
did not consider the air campaign a prelude to the ground campaign; instead, he
sought to present a safer and more efficient alternative to a ground attack, and if
it came to a ground campaign he insisted that Arab forces would be adequate to
execute it. Loh found the argument compelling and encouraged further planning, adding that it might be useful to include photographs so that decision
makers could visualize what they planned to bomb.

When Warden began to focus on Phase III he devoted particular attention
to how operational-scale formations, such as divisions, corps, and army groups,
would react to heavy losses over a short period of time. His personal experiences
from exercises and his studies of operational art at the National War College had
convinced him that large units simply could not withstand such profound shocks.
He also believed that organizations at the tactical and operational levels would
respond differently. At a tactical level, a platoon of soldiers might literally fight to
the last man, depending on motivation and capability, while at the operational
level an organization depended so strongly on complex internal communication,
direction, and support that it would begin to lose its ability to fight when it
experienced losses that on the surface would not be overwhelming for a tactical
unit. Thus, a corps that lost some of its communication equipment and personnel would find it difficult to coordinate the activities of different regiments, artillery, reconnaissance, and other assets; it would also be seriously hampered if it
lost some of its fuel or its leadership. Warden assumed that 25 percent attrition of
equipment and men at the operational level would render the larger entity ineffective even if most tactical units remained intact:

It appears entirely feasible to destroy almost the entire Iraqi army in Kuwait from the air—with the exception of the forces in Kuwait City. Historical experience, however, suggests that most armies will either surrender, retreat, or be withdrawn when casualty rates approach 25%. Nothing suggests that the Iraqi army in Kuwait would choose to accept tens of thousands of casualties—not to mention destruction of virtually all of its armored fighting vehicles, command centers, and supply dumps—when there was nothing to be gained by doing so . . . Our conclusion from this analysis is that the special conditions of climate and terrain make destruction of the Iraqi army in Kuwait a feasible operation in a week to ten days. Total American losses in this permissive environment will be numbered in the tens.[119]

To verify his assumptions, Warden presented the modeling methodology to Trevor N. Dupuy, a retired army colonel whom he knew from his previous assignment in the Pentagon. After reviewing the issue with Dupuy he concluded that 50 rather than 25 percent would cover every case and that such a loss in a relatively short period of time would virtually guarantee the disappearance of operational-level effectiveness. Warden therefore decided to use 50 percent attrition as the criterion for defining Iraqi forces as inoperable. After these discussions Dupuy wrote an article for the *Washington Post* in which he questioned some of the military advice the White House was receiving and predicted a short war: while the Joint Staff informed the president that he had to expect that three to thirty thousand Americans would die in the first twenty days of a war, Dupuy argued that the first number was "close to the mark, but a little high; the figure of 30,000 is ridiculously high."[120]

On October 22 Warden sent his Phase II and Phase III predictions to Glosson in Riyadh, including the comments from Loh. The brigadier general liked the analyses and agreed to the 50 percent criterion: Lt. Col. Joe Purvis, one of the ground campaign planners, had already informed Glosson that according to army doctrine a unit was considered nonoperational when degraded by 50 percent. Warden's analysis strengthened Glosson's conviction in the number and he penned in his notebook: "I'm going to decree that we will attrit enemy ground forces 50% (people, armor, and artillery)."[121]

However, before he presented the study to Schwarzkopf and Horner, Glosson needed to bring a range of other assumptions into the calculations and he used Checkmate's work as the baseline for expanding the planning process. Just as he had found Instant Thunder narrow in its focus and too optimistic, he believed that Warden was overly optimistic in his assumptions about successful sorties. Most important, models would have to include the Republican Guard:

Schwarzkopf had identified the elite forces as a center of gravity and Horner had pointed out that the CINC was "obsessed" with those forces. Warden again insisted that the Republican Guard should not be attacked *en masse* in Phase III, but he had no choice but to obey Glosson's direction. He and Sikes calculated that it would take about thirty-six hours per division to render guard forces inoperable. Phase III was now conceived as having two parts: attacks on the Republican Guard and attacks on the regular army. Glosson told Warden to take the new parameters into account while he and Deptula worked on making the presentation acceptable to Schwarzkopf and Horner.

The Black Hole and Checkmate were about to make history by planning for a mission in which air power would directly destroy half of the enemy army before friendly ground forces would engage it. Some of the senior general officers in theater insisted that the coalition would need sixty days' worth of munitions before the start of operations, but Checkmate's computer analyses revealed that with sixty days of munitions the USAF could hit every potential target many times. The computation was not difficult, but only Warden and his Checkmate group were examining the issue. As a result, Glosson decided that Warden had so much valuable data that he asked him to send somebody to the theater with the detailed modeling results who could also serve as a planner; he recalled, "We did not have the analysis to back up our assertions."[122]

Warden and Deptula discussed whom to send: they wanted someone who had a good grasp of the strategic air campaign plan, had reasonable knowledge of Phase III, and would strengthen the link between the Black Hole and Checkmate. Deptula suggested Major Rogers, who was also a good friend, and Warden agreed. Rogers departed on October 27. Since all military transportation required CENTAF approval, and it was unlikely that its staff would welcome more "help from the Air Staff," Warden decided to send Rogers on a commercial flight.[123]

The plan that Rogers brought to Glosson did not take into account the latest intelligence reports, which indicated that the Iraqi troops were digging in and implementing camouflage techniques. After he reviewed the details with Deptula and Rogers, Glosson had them inform Warden that he liked what he saw, particularly the photographs that accompanied the target categories, but he wanted a few changes. For example, Glosson wanted the analysis redone to assume that one out of four aircraft would fail to find its target, and that only two of the other three aircraft would hit their targets. Warden thought Glosson was unrealistically pessimistic, but he complied. It became the standard working procedure for Glosson and Warden to agree on what to do and for Sikes in Checkmate and Rogers in the Black Hole then to settle the details over secure phone lines. Rogers was surprised to find that the intelligence branch in theater still refused to help in the planning effort. He concluded that the only way to improve the intelligence was to work with Checkmate officers who had contact with individuals in the different intelligence branches in Washington, and, once more, the informal structure superseded the formal to a large degree.

On October 27 Glosson again asked Warden what it would take to paralyze the Republican Guard. Warden replied that he considered that mission "a diversion of effort," but when Glosson insisted he estimated that it would probably take less than two days to destroy each division. Warden then suggested that Phase III could focus on the regular army and Phase IV could deal with the Republican Guard. Glosson responded that he would like both ground forces to be dealt with in Phase III and requested Warden to develop a model in which the Republican Guard was attacked before the regular forces. Warden disliked the request, but immediately agreed to help.[124]

On October 29 Warden presented Phases II and III to the new chief of staff, Gen. Merrill A. McPeak. McPeak was known for saying that the airman's best days came when he could devote all his energy to flying close air support, because that meant air power was saving American lives. Moreover, he proclaimed "he was not an airpower advocate like Mike Dugan."[125] Warden had already briefed him on the strategic air campaign, and although McPeak was both enthusiastic and complimentary, he showed greater interest in employing air power directly against ground forces.[126]

Warden made it clear that the outcome would give the Iraqi troops three options: retreat north, surrender in place, or suffer annihilation.[127] Whatever they chose to do, Arab ground forces could deal with the bedraggled troops and American soldiers would not have to cross the border. Checkmate's analysis indicated that the United States might lose sixty-six aircraft in the process of attacking artillery, armor, personnel trucks, airfield command and control, airfield support facilities, and area targets. Assuming a 75 percent target acquisition rate, air power would ensure a 95 percent destruction level within fifteen days if the Coalition could fly a thousand sorties per day under clear weather conditions. Warden identified the four target-sets needed to achieve 95 percent destruction and specified the length of time that would be required: bridges (three days); artillery (nine days); armor (nine days); and troops (nine days).[128]

Warden's was the first briefing McPeak had heard since officially assuming his new responsibilities, and although the proposal lacked a comprehensive description of the forces, and the precise location of the forces and some critical nodes were still unknown, he thought favorably of the ideas presented. After the presentation he dismissed Adams and Alexander so that he could talk with Warden alone for ninety minutes, reviewing the details again.[129]

In the meantime RAND provided feedback on Checkmate's Phase III analysis, criticizing both the assumptions and the methodology that Warden had used. In RAND's view the planners had underestimated the number of sorties required to destroy tanks, armored personnel carriers, and trucks. The RAND team considered the suggested acquisition rate for some weapon systems unrealistically high, and thought that double-berms around equipment would complicate target acquisition and that friendly aircraft attrition would be higher than Checkmate had modeled. Moreover, intelligence reports did not support Checkmate's assumptions about known target locations; Warden's group had not sufficiently accounted for overkill; terrorist attacks had to be incorporated into the assessments; and, finally, the planners had overestimated the destruction of artillery as a result of damage to trucks used to tow the guns and transport munitions.[130] Warden remained unconvinced, but RAND's overall critique, combined with Glosson's warning that his assumptions were too optimistic, led Warden to take a more cautious approach, and his willingness to let others review the plan led to his embracing a very convincing argument.

By contrast, the planning for Phase II proceeded quietly: Checkmate provided data, analysis, and suggestions, and in the Black Hole Deptula added and subtracted information as he saw fit. For example, when Henry considered the tactics to achieve air superiority over Iraq and Kuwait he relied on reports that had been developed by the navy's SPEAR (Strike Projection Evaluation and Anti-Air Research), an organization that had become involved through Checkmate. SPEAR provided operational intelligence for the navy, but rather than have only intelligence officers collect and analyze information, SPEAR used officers with operational experience. Warden had established contact with Capt. Mike "Carlos" Johnson, the leader of SPEAR, when he realized how much the think tank had to offer: Johnson's men knew in detail how the Iraqi air defense system worked. SPEAR characterized the Iraqi air defense system, KARI, as a "system of systems" that encompassed more than four hundred observation posts, seventy-three radar reporting stations, and seventeen interception centers.[131] By October the SPEAR team had developed good knowledge of how to eliminate critical nodes within the system and Checkmate made certain that the analysis was given to the Black Hole planners: Warden assigned one of his own subordinates, Maj. Richard King, to serve as liaison between Checkmate and SPEAR, and King kept Deptula up to date.

Checkmate's plan for Phase II, gaining air superiority over Kuwait, recommended destroying twenty-six SAM sites, including radars, crews, and missiles capable of launching SA-2 and SA-3 missiles, and suggested that air power could destroy all of these sites in one day. After the attacks, the Iraqis would still possess AAA and shoulder-held, infrared, heat-seeking SA-7s, but the medium-altitude airspace would be secure. Glosson was very pleased with the inputs and directed Henry to "revise and use Checkmate's Phase II products."[132]

PREPARING THE BATTLEFIELD

By November 2 Sikes and his colleagues had completed a scheme for reducing the fighting capacity of regular forces and the Republican Guard by 50 percent. Checkmate now suggested that it would take twenty-three days to reach 50 percent attrition.[133] Combined with further modeling, this conclusion eased the concerns in theater about a possible munition shortage.[134] Since Checkmate's estimate did not take into account the increase in U.S. forces that had occurred in the meantime, Glosson now stated that he thought it would take seventeen days, rather than twenty-three, to reduce Iraqi forces to 50 percent.

When Horner received a comprehensive presentation of Phases I, II and III on November 7 he was generally pleased. However, he told Glosson to focus more on artillery as opposed to tanks in Phase III; not to "poke the Army in the eye" by overselling how much havoc air power could cause against ground forces; and to use the term "Preparing the Battlefield" rather than Deptula's preferred phrase, "Destroying the Battlefield."[135]

All these planning elements came together for Schwarzkopf by mid-November. The national leadership had approved Phase I, the strategic air campaign plan, on October 10 and 11; Glosson and Deptula had converted Phases II and III from concept to substance; and Schwarzkopf's ground war planners had devised a two-corps attack plan for Phase IV that Washington found acceptable. On November 14 Horner, Glosson, and Henry took part in the comprehensive briefing on the strategy for the coming war that Schwarzkopf presented to all major commanders in theater. The briefing identified the three centers of gravity as the Iraqi regime, weapons of mass destruction, and the Republican Guard. Schwarzkopf asserted that the United States had three strengths: better air power capability, superior technology, and well-trained leaders, while Iraqi strengths were the size of its ground forces and its chemical weapons. He then identified five battlefield goals: attack Iraq's C^2 system and leadership; achieve and retain air superiority; sever Iraq's supply routes; destroy Iraq's NBC capability; and destroy the Republican Guard. With reference to the final goal he left no room for misunderstanding: "We need to destroy—not attack, not damage, not surround—I do not want them to be an effective fighting force anymore." He stated that the coalition should be ready to execute by mid-January and outlined four phases that should be executed sequentially, as formulated during his discussions with Warden August 17, 1990: "Phase I: Strategic Air Campaign; Phase II: Air Superiority in the KTO; Phase III: Preparation of the Battlefield; and Phase IV: Ground Attack."[136]

During the meeting Maj. Gen. J. H. Binford Peay III, commander of the 101st Airborne Division, asked the obvious question: "If we can bomb them to 50 percent in three weeks, why don't we take another three weeks and the other 50 percent for good measure?"[137] Schwarzkopf, however, insisted that boots on the ground were needed. The presentation revealed a fundamental and persistent mindset: air power could destroy ground forces, but it would take U.S. ground forces to complete Iraq's defeat. Still, Schwarzkopf would allow air power to take the lead: he would let it paralyze the regime in Baghdad and reduce the number of Iraqi ground forces by half before he would allow American ground forces to close with the enemy on the battlefield.

PSYCHOLOGICAL OPERATIONS

The November briefing was important in another respect: it marked the point when CENTCOM stopped considering PSYOPS at the strategic level. When Warden had presented the Instant Thunder plan to Schwarzkopf in August he had insisted that PSYOPS were of utmost importance. In preparing the briefing he had called upon Col. Daniel W. Jacobowitz, the director of PSYOPS in the Department of Defense, who was more than willing to contribute to the plan. Jacobowitz recognized that "psychological operations" had become a tainted term after Vietnam; as far as he knew, Warden was the first officer to make a real effort to integrate PSYOPS into the war plans rather than see it as a separate ingredient that would be added at a later point. Indeed, Jacobowitz found that the entire concept of targeting for effects, strategic paralysis, and targeting the regime ensured that psychological and physical operations would function in unison.[138] One statement that they crafted for the Instant Thunder operational order found its way into the CENTAF OPORD that Horner approved on September 2: "Psychological operations are inherent to this operation and will be as important as strike operations. Every mission will have critical political and psychological overtones, every bomb will have a psychological impact as well."[139]

On September 19 Schwarzkopf approved the overall CENTCOM PSYOPS plan, called "Burning Hawk." By this time responsibility for the psychological campaign had been transferred to Col. Anthony Normand of the army's Fourth Psychological Operations Group. Checkmate shared its analysis with Normand, emphasizing that the enemy was the corrupt dictator and his regime, not the Iraqi people. Burning Hawk developed four objectives: undermine the morale and combat effectiveness of Iraqi troops; foment desertion; educate Iraqi forces about the law of armed conflict; and encourage the overthrow of Saddam Hussein's regime.[140] The coalition would attain these objectives through radio and television broadcasts, leaflets, and other media. But Burning Hawk focused only on the tactical level of operations and the troops in Kuwait, and Warden realized that the concept of PSYOPS as an integral part of the strategic air campaign had lost momentum.

It soon became clear that the Joint Staff did not see the urgency of including PSYOPS in the campaign plan. Different parts of the plan disappeared in various branches of the Pentagon and the White House, and Warden expressed frustration about the lack of progress in Washington.[141] He was told that the immediate problem was that Executive Order 12333 prohibited the United States from targeting individuals. Worried, Warden wrote a letter to General Loh on November 1, stating that "as far as we can tell, there is no psychological operations campaign to accompany the strategic bombing operations. . . . It might be very useful if you asked General Schwarzkopf if he could use any help on strategic war psyops which he had earlier identified as a necessity if we were to win the war."[142]

It was not until December that Schwarzkopf demanded a PSYOPS plan, but he did not seek involvement from Washington. Horner, however, recognized that the Saudi leadership did not want a high-profile campaign that encouraged revolt against the Iraqi leadership, since that could possibly encourage the Saudi population to follow their example: "We could never get it off the ground because the Saudis wanted to be in control of it, and they really were not interested in trying to persuade people to rebel against their government. I think that is the bottom line. I think they also wanted to downplay the role of the Americans in the PSYOPS campaign."[143] PSYOPS became a very sensitive issue that no one was prepared to champion. When Warden and Deptula suggested targets in Baghdad, especially statues of the Iraqi leader, their requests were denied. Similarly, Washington only reluctantly approved preparations for a few leaflet drops on Baghdad and minor use of the EC-130 Volant Solo aircraft to broadcast messages encouraging civilians and soldiers to overthrow their leader.

WAR TERMINATION PLAN

From the day Warden first defined his air power theory in mid-1988 he had favored campaign planning that viewed military forces as the means to an end, and insisted that ultimate success did not consist of winning the war, but winning the peace for which the war was fought. This imperative had influenced his design for Instant Thunder, and later he and Zalmay Khalilzad, RAND's Middle East expert, prepared a war termination plan in the form of a peace treaty. Warden provided an outline in September and Khalilzad developed the main substance. The study was titled "Winning the War—and the Peace: The Termination of Hostilities with Iraq":

> Given Iraqi conduct, some might feel justified in demanding not only that Iraq withdraw from Kuwait, allow its former government to return, commit itself not to reinvade, and release the hostages, but also that Iraq agree to pay reparations and accept Nuremberg-style trials for its leadership as preconditions for ending the war. But insisting on the latter two conditions is likely to prolong the war: the Iraqi leadership

would be much more likely to fight on rather than accept what amounts to unconditional surrender. Such a degree of resolve may oblige us to occupy Iraq—thus increasing substantially the costs, casualties and duration of the war. Threats such as reparations and trials might have some useful deterrent value in affecting some Iraqi actions in Kuwait before war breaks out—but insisting on them after war begins might well become counterproductive. Because of this concern, the proposed Post War Armistice Agreement with Iraq has not dealt directly with the issues of reparations and trials. Instead, we have approached these issues indirectly and ambiguously—leaving them to be settled between Kuwaiti and Iraqi governments.

The idea of forcing Iraq to pay reparations is enticing: however, Iraq is not in a financial position to pay larger reparations—unless it commits its income from oil sales for an almost indefinite future. Imposing reparations will delay to the point of danger Iraqi's recovery from the effects of war and also from the effects of Saddam Hussein's gross mismanagement of the economy over the last decade. Since our aim is a long-term peace and movement of Iraq toward a stable, non-aggressive, and democratic government, it is imperative that we eschew reparations that may block realization of our real interests in the area. No one needs an impoverished Iraq that becomes a hot bed of revanchism . . .

On the disposition of the Iraqi heavy equipment—armored vehicles, artillery and other weapons—in Kuwait, we should demand that it be left behind. It is possible such a demand might increase the incentive of officers in the field or the leadership in Baghdad to fight on. However, it is likely to be a marginal factor in affecting the Iraqi incentives to fight on.

As far as the future stability of the region is concerned, U.S. and allied attacks will seriously weaken the military and economic power of Iraq and humiliate its leadership. The full range of potential internal and regional consequences of such a development are very difficult to predict. Some weakening of Iraq and punishment for its aggression can increase regional stability. Iraqi military preponderance and the absence of a balance of power in the Gulf contributed to the invasion.

Conversely, while some weakening of Iraq is in our interest, the total destruction of Iraqi power is not; a militarily devastated Iraq would be unable to balance the Iranian threat. This in turn might encourage Iran or some of Iraq's other neighbors to become aggressive and might result in the dismemberment of Iraq. This will almost certainly increase regional instability.[144]

Checkmate distributed the document in November, and both Khalilzad and Warden worked hard to bring it to the attention of the right people, but nobody saw a war termination plan as their responsibility. It is one of the ironies of Operation Desert Storm, and of Operation Enduring Freedom and Operation Iraqi Freedom more than a decade later, that the United States devoted so many months to planning the campaigns and so little time to defining postwar objectives.

CHECKMATE: AN INVALUABLE RESOURCE

Arguably, the war would have taken a different shape and produced different results had Checkmate not inserted itself into the planning process. The first days of the Special Planning Group were the most crucial for Glosson and his men in theater, and at that time Checkmate was their only source of data and plans. Moreover, Washington still looked toward a ground-focused campaign in which air power would merely add firepower to the battlefield, and Checkmate was the only organization that provided the U.S. political and military leadership with an alternative strategy. In retrospect, those who worked closely with the air campaign planning acknowledge that Warden made a significant contribution. Deptula, who wrote the MAP for every day of the war, insisted that there was no significant difference between Instant Thunder and Phase I from a philosophical and conceptual standpoint: there were adaptations and alterations, but the only real changes resulted from five additional months' worth of intelligence.[145]

Generals Dugan, Loh, Moore, Adams, May, Alexander, and Glosson all confirmed that the plan executed in Desert Storm was a version of Instant Thunder.[146] Glosson acknowledged that he had an executable option in mid-September in no small measure because of Warden's efforts: "Without the work that Checkmate did, that option would never have existed."[147] He later praised Warden's initiatives in the following terms:

> All I had to do was call [Checkmate] and say, I need this analysis done; I need you to contact this country, this contractor, I do not know enough about this . . . I could not have dreamed of such support . . . I would hope that history will be very kind to John Warden. I have told more than one group of people that the greatest compliment I can give John Warden is to say that if I had been given the task he was given and the short period of time that he was given, I would like to think that I would have been as successful as he was in covering the spectrum and placing as much thought provoking information down as he did, as quickly as he did. I cannot pay him any higher compliment . . . His effort was phenomenal . . . I question whether that could have been done anywhere else on the face of the Earth . . . Nobody has ever done

more or better work in any shorter period of time under the constraints that they were under. The ground work in putting some conceptual ideas together and husbanding an unbelievable amount of intelligence information and focusing on critical target sets was very impressive.[148]

Even Adams was impressed: "John had built a significant network of experts to really help lay out those details, and Buster Glosson used them almost every day, calling back, faxing back, or sending a message back."[149] Warden concluded that the arrangement "worked out well" and that a "symbiotic relationship" developed between the officers in Riyadh and USAF headquarters in the Pentagon. However, he unambiguously characterized Checkmate as a supporting effort: "We did not tell them how to run the war. We provided information."[150]

Checkmate undoubtedly made a substantial contribution to the planning of Operation Desert Storm, but although Warden provided an environment that encouraged independent thinking about the air campaign plan, others often played the primary role in turning his ideas into reality. Indeed, it was Deptula who was able to mold Instant Thunder, along with his own ideas, into a plan that Horner and Glosson could accept. Without Deptula's conceptual insight, operational perspective, and flexibility, and his central role in the planning, many of Warden's ideas would never have been implemented. Warden and Deptula functioned like the two sides of a brain: Warden was the creative and artistic right side, while Deptula was the scientific, operational-detail-oriented left side. The two complemented each other; the effectiveness of each would have been greatly limited without the other. Time and again Warden would develop a design with rough edges by focusing on qualitative and dynamic complexities, while Deptula converted those inputs into realistic, operational, and quantitative action plans.[151]

Glosson also played a major role in the air campaign. He was sufficiently clever, pragmatic, charismatic, and determined to convert Checkmate's products into a format acceptable to Horner and to drive a winning concept into execution. Both he and Horner brought their own technical, tactical, and operational skills to the equation, and they had the necessary leadership qualities to make the most out of the data that came from Washington.

IMPRESSIVE ACCOMPLISHMENTS

From late August to mid-October, Warden's team provided data and ideas for fine-tuning and improving Phase I, and from mid-October 1990 to mid-January 1991 Checkmate took the lead in producing the analyses that supported the assertion that air power in Phase III could reduce the Iraqi army to 50 percent before the start of the ground offensive. Warden initiated and developed Instant Thunder, which broke completely with the prevailing AirLand Battle doctrine and the existing contingency plans; he convinced Schwarzkopf and the national leadership of the importance of beginning the air campaign with strategic bombardment, which stood in sharp contrast to the alternative plan developed by TAC; and he established and directed an informal fusion center that passed information and analysis to the theater at a time when the formal structure proved inadequate on several counts.

Thus, in late August, when Horner had concluded that Warden had "flunked his interview" and Lieutenant General Adams believed that the Air Staff had "washed its hands of the project," the colonel rebounded.[152] Warden's resolution to continue pressing for an air campaign, despite the rough treatment from Horner and lack of enthusiasm from Adams, exemplifies his character: resilience under disappointment, persistence of élan, hard work, and determination even when his short-term objective had not been fully realized.

10

CHECKMATE: SUPPORT TO THE POLITICAL CAMPAIGN

As early as August 1990, when Warden initiated Instant Thunder, he knew that the air campaign plan would have to be accompanied by a "political campaign for the air campaign." He viewed his Checkmate directorate as a link between two portions of the planning activity: the Washington-based political campaign, which sought to convince policy makers of air power capabilities, and the Riyadh-based operational effort, which translated concepts into execution. Thus, in addition to its significant role in developing Instant Thunder and providing the substance of Phases II and III, Checkmate made a third major contribution to the war plan by keeping the senior political and military leadership in Washington apprised of the air campaign and the potential of air power.

Spreading the Word

The success of air power, which became obvious a few days into Operation Desert Storm, had been neither universally expected nor assumed in the previous weeks and months.[1] Skeptics had reminded their audiences that air power had failed to deliver on its promise in the Second World War, in the Korean War, and, most significantly, in the Vietnam War. Many warned that at some point Iraqi troops would have to be forced out of Kuwait at the point of a bayonet, and when that occurred, "American casualties would explode, morale would plummet, and a Vietnam-style antiwar movement would destroy the United Nations coalition."[2] Statistical models based on army doctrine and past wartime experiences forecast fatalities in the thousands and critics asserted that air power's reliance on technology was dubious: "Eventually it would come down to a nineteen-year-old American in the open with an M-16 versus dug-in nineteen-year-old Iraqis with an AK-47, with horrendous resulting casualties."[3] Gen. Edward C. Meyer, a former U.S. Army chief of staff, estimated between ten and thirty thousand American casualties; Joshua Epstein of the Brookings Institution predicted 1,049 to 4,136 deaths and up to 16,059 American casualties.[4]

THE CAMPAIGN AGAINST THE GROUND CAMPAIGN

Against these predictions of a "slugfest" that would result in a disaster at worst and a Pyrrhic victory at best, Warden took it upon himself to explain the capabilities of air power to the capital's decision makers. He made it his personal objective to do everything he could to prevent the ground campaign from taking place.[5] In September he had begun to convey information to senior officials in the White House through various channels, and over the next months he persuaded several prominent politicians and many senior generals to visit Checkmate in his effort to make sure that the president and his closest advisors understood the potentially decisive effects of air power. This, of course, was not a task normally assigned to a colonel in the Air Staff, but Warden respected no such bureaucratic boundaries.

Warden was convinced that "Powell made a concerted effort to control ideas going to the Secretary of Defense, to the Under Secretary of Defense for Policy, to the White House, and to the President . . . going to great lengths to block flows of information."[6] Warden believed that Powell had agreed to accept sanctions without military action for several months while he tried to persuade the president that a second corps would be needed if the United States took the offensive, and suspected that Powell's opinions were influencing members of Congress.

A series of hearings before the Senate Committee on Armed Services in mid-September, which dealt with "sanctions, diplomacy and war," confirmed that Congress was divided. Senator Sam Nunn, among others, strongly opposed U.S. military action to oust Iraqi forces from Kuwait. Warden responded by sending a letter that explained air power advantages:

> The only Service which can move significant fire power in days or weeks is the Air Force. This is not to denigrate the other Services; it is merely to state physical facts. The Navy can arrive in theater quickly, sometimes faster than the Air Force, but normally requires extensive support from land based Air Forces for tankers and electronic warfare aircraft. The Army can provide significant firepower, but must move predominantly by sea. Thus, the Joint Commander has to rely on air power—and predominantly on land based air power—for a lengthy period. The second advantage of air power is its ability to strike enemy centers of power behind the front. These centers may be strategic or operational. With few exceptions, the air power gives the US its greatest advantage over potential enemies. When we use air power against strategic and operational centers, we are fighting on our terms on our ground. Should combat develop in the Persian Gulf, we will depend

on air power to make up the huge imbalance between enemy manpower and Allied manpower.[7]

In early October Warden told General Loh that the USAF needed to "get the [air power] story out," because otherwise it would not be heard. Loh responded that Warden probably knew whom to contact and that he had a "*carte blanche* to talk to anybody."[8] Warden needed no further encouragement.[9] Loh recalls that Powell expressed deep concerns about this "air power undercurrent going around town": the idea that air power could be so decisive that Saddam Hussein would evacuate Kuwait and surrender was finding its way "to the White House" and Powell considered such an argument appalling.[10] Thus, Powell became increasingly irritated with "these air guys running around town telling the President that air power can be totally decisive and that we can leap off on October 15th."[11]

Warden's special relationship with Secretary Rice, and his direct link to senior officers in the Air Staff, enabled him to present his case. Equally important, Warden turned Checkmate into the hub of an internal air force network for information.[12] For example, Checkmate sent analyses and assessments to Lt. Col. John L. Barry, military assistant to the secretary of defense; Lt. Col. Garry R. Trexler, senior military assistant to the deputy secretary of defense; Lt. Col. Lonnie Dail Turner, chief of the Strategy Division in the Joint Staff; Lt. Col. T. K. Kearney in the secretary of the air force's staff group; and Col. Michael V. Hayden on the staff of the National Security Council.[13] All these air force officers knew Warden and appreciated the expertise that his group represented, and often saw to it that the information was forwarded to their respective superiors.

However, Powell's concerns about "freewheeling" made it increasingly difficult for Warden to meet key officials face to face. In early November, when Warden in his characteristic *sub-rosa* fashion contacted Under Secretary of Defense Paul D. Wolfowitz and his deputy, Lewis "Scooter" Libby Jr., to update them on the air campaign planning, the Joint Staff told him not to make the presentation since he did not represent the air force's official viewpoint and was certainly not in the chain of command.[14] Undeterred by such "technicalities" Warden raised the issue with Rice, who talked directly with Cheney, and the secretary of defense favored the idea of his staff's receiving an inside view. When he learned that Warden had briefed Wolfowitz and Libby, Powell complained to McPeak about this unorthodox way of communicating information. As a result McPeak berated Adams for being unable to control his subordinate, and Adams was furious with Warden for "getting out in front." Once more, Adams wanted to fire Warden and shut down Checkmate for good,[15] and once more he thought better of it. Warden's immediate superior, Major General Alexander, recalled many such incidents.[16]

In December Powell again briefed Congress and warned that air power was not a quick, cheap, and certain way to force Iraqi formations out of Kuwait:

> Many experts, amateurs and others in this town believe that this can be accomplished by such things as surgical air strikes or perhaps a sustained air strike. There are a variety of other, nice, tidy, alleged low-cost incremental, may-work options that are floated around with regularity in this town. The fundamental fatal flaw in all such strategies is that it leaves the initiative in Saddam Hussein's hands. He makes the decision as to whether or not he will or will not withdraw. He decides whether he has been punished enough so that it is now necessary for him to reverse direction and take a new political tack. Those strategies may work. But they also may not. The initiative is left in Saddam Hussein's hands.[17]

Powell reiterated the traditional view that air power had some advantages, but that fundamentally it was a "supporting arm" and only ground forces could bring the war to a conclusion.[18] He apparently remained firm in his conviction that air power had never carried the day without action on the surface at sea or on the ground, and he refused to accept that PGMs and stealth technology would ensure victory.

Powell's comments angered Warden. As he saw it, the real situation was the reverse: strategic air power would ensure that Saddam Hussein would be physically incapacitated and therefore all decisions and initiatives would be in the hands of the coalition. After discussing the chairman's position with Glosson and Deptula, Warden sent a memorandum to Secretary Rice suggesting counterarguments.[19] Rice attempted to convince Powell that air power might well eliminate the need for a ground campaign altogether, but, more important, that it could "prevent a bloody ground campaign."[20] When Powell told Loh in a meeting that the United States could not "bomb them into the stone age," Loh responded, "we are talking about a very precise application of air power to control the events and to continue to erode the Iraqi position over time."[21]

Deptula also played an important part in explaining the rationale and potential of the air campaign to Cheney, Wolfowitz, and Libby. Deptula returned to the office of the secretary of the air force twice during the planning period— September 22 to October 12, 1990, and November 5, 1990, to January 2, 1991; on both occasions he worked behind the scenes with Rice to make the air power case to politicians as well as to the Joint Staff.[22]

McPeak Meets with the President

In the meantime Warden had decided to expand his network: he needed to bring his arguments to the president himself. He concluded that the most promising channel was through McPeak, even though the Goldwater-Nichols Act barred the individual service chiefs from meeting directly with the president unless the latter called upon them for advice or the chiefs declared that they had to see the president as a matter of emergency. Since the president had not asked to meet with the chiefs by late November, Warden shared his concerns with Edward Luttwak, holder of the strategy chair at the Center for Strategic and International Studies, who in turn alerted Senator John Warner (Republican, Virginia). Luttwak told the senator that there was a possible divergence of views among the chiefs of staff on how the war should unfold, so that it might be useful for the president to hear their individual opinions. Luttwak recalls that "turning to a member of congress usually includes the risk of a disastrous, publicity-seeking leak, but not in Warner's case; as the former husband of Elizabeth Taylor he needed no publicity and was in fact the soul of discretion."[23] Whether as a direct result or not, within the next few days the president invited all the joint chiefs to Camp David to hear their views about the possible war.

McPeak did not know the reason for the sudden interest, but he was delighted at the chance to present his case. To get ready for the meeting he requested a range of briefings, reports, and data from Warden's Checkmate team.[24] He spent several hours alone with Warden and later admitted that Checkmate "played a big role in preparing me to go to Camp David."[25] On December 1, when the president asked for his opinion, McPeak made a strong case for the decisive impact that air power would have both in central Baghdad and on the battlefield. He predicted that the air campaign would last approximately thirty days and that by then Iraqi ground forces would have less than 50 percent combat effectiveness. McPeak warned that time worked against the United States and that the air force was prepared to act as soon as possible. Drawing on Checkmate's analysis, and using Warden's arguments almost verbatim, he confidently stated that Iraq was less capable than many thought.

President Bush commented later that McPeak was the only chief of staff who was aggressive and forward leaning, and McPeak's confidence in air power apparently impressed him.[26] On January 14, 1991, two days after the U.S. Congress passed a resolution authorizing the use of military force to liberate Kuwait—the narrow Senate vote was fifty-two in favor and forty-seven against—Bush invited McPeak, Cheney, and Scowcroft to a private luncheon in the White House. The UN ultimatum for an Iraqi withdrawal was running out the next day, Powell had recommended that all ground forces be in place prior to the start of an air campaign, and several world leaders insisted that Bush delay a military attack. When Bush asked McPeak's opinion, the general replied that he had just returned from theater and that from an airman's standpoint it would be better to go to war sooner rather than later. The president then asked McPeak if he were as confident about air power as he had been on December 1 and received an affirmative answer.

BRIEFING THE SECRETARY OF DEFENSE

Warden had told his Checkmate team early on to investigate where the president's closest advisors stood on the air power issue. Powell certainly viewed air power merely as a precursor to an inevitable ground campaign, and early reports indicated that Scowcroft held the same opinion. Cheney was Warden's hope, and few really knew where the secretary of defense stood on the matter. Rice had told Cheney in private discussions that the decision to launch an air campaign did not imply that a ground campaign would follow and analyses by Warden's Checkmate group supported the statement.

At Rice's suggestion Cheney agreed to meet with Warden on December 11, immediately prior to a planned trip to Saudi Arabia. Warden began his two-hour briefing with the strategic air campaign and its targeting-for-effects philosophy, showing how 4,600 sorties over a six-day period would paralyze the Iraqi national leadership, eradicate Iraq's strategic offensive and defensive capability, and disrupt Iraq's economy, but would not significantly degrade Iraq's ability to export oil. After setting the stage and focusing on how the combination of stealth and precision had virtually replaced mass, he devoted considerable time to informing the secretary of defense about Checkmate's most recent computer analysis for Phase III. Warden was convinced that the strategic offensive would succeed, but had by then become equally enthusiastic about what air power could accomplish against Iraq's fielded forces. He described how air forces would conduct the operations, the effects expected, the number of sorties, the targets, the predicted rate of attrition of the Iraqi forces, and the time it would take to reduce Iraq's warfighting capability by 50 percent.

Warden insisted that the first part of Phase III would destroy the Republican Guard as a fighting force after rendering the air defense system in Kuwait and southern Iraq helpless. Targeting the elite forces *en masse* would have the spillover effect of weakening the morale of the regular forces and the United States should be prepared for the early surrender of large numbers of troops. In his opinion, eight days of concentrated bombing would destroy half of the artillery in Kuwait, and nine days would destroy half of the armor. Indeed, only fifteen days would be needed to destroy 90 percent of all Iraqi artillery and armor in Kuwait. His predictions assumed good weather, an attack rate of a thousand sorties per day, and a 75 percent target acquisition rate. Thus, Phase III would destroy the Iraqi army in Kuwait and a reoccupation would meet minimal resistance. He suggested that it might be both desirable and possible to use Arab forces to liberate Kuwait and that the U.S. ground forces should be held in reserve as a "Cocked Fist." This, Warden argued, would be "Near Certain Achievement of President's Objectives Without Significant Casualties to Ground Troops."[27] He summarized his argument by stating that the best defense against a tank was not a tank, but an aircraft.

Throughout the briefing Warden emphasized that starting the air campaign did not automatically mean that the coalition would need a ground war, a point Rice had already made several times to Cheney.[28] If need be, air power could simply continue the pressure until the Iraqis gave in, and do so without any significant risk to friendly forces.

In response to Cheney's concerns about losses, Warden offered a worst-case estimate of 40 aircraft in the first phase, 5 in the second, 35 in the third, and 66 in the last: a total of 146 aircraft lost. Warden believed that half of the crewmembers would probably be rescued, a quarter would be killed, and the remaining quarter made prisoners of war and possibly be paraded on television.[29] He predicted between four hundred and two thousand casualties among Iraqi civilians. Cheney asked several detailed questions, but suggested no changes: he seemed receptive, but in his usual fashion he did not reveal his thoughts.[30]

Warden told Glosson and Deptula what he had presented and what the secretary of defense had asked so that they could prepare themselves for the follow-up meeting in Riyadh. Nine days later, on December 20, Horner briefed Cheney and Powell on the air campaign plan in theater, stating that CENTAF's modeling and programming predicted that Phase I would last six days, Phase II one day, and Phase III eleven days. When Cheney asked if he really believed that the air force would reach its 50 percent goal in eleven days, Horner replied that his gut feeling was that it would take twice as long.[31] He also noted that the execution of the phases would not necessarily be discrete or sequential; phases might overlap as resources become available or priorities shifted. Cheney talked at length with Schwarzkopf and told the CINC that he was comfortable with the basic strategy: the air campaign would begin shortly after the UN deadline passed on January 15 and the ground campaign would begin in mid-February, when the strength of the Iraqi ground forces had been reduced by 50 percent.

THE AIR CAMPAIGN BEGINS

On paper the campaign plan consisted of three MAPs that outlined the details of the upcoming air war. The first seventy-two hours were defined minute by minute, aircraft by aircraft, and target by target. Before the first bomb dropped on Baghdad Warden saw the complete picture in his mind's eye: the phones were dead, the lights were out, the regime was under attack but the civilians were not.

On January 16, 1991, Warden sat with the secretary of the air force, the director of plans, and several key planners in Checkmate.[32] When Baghdad went "black" forty-five seconds into the war, Warden recalled: "I'll admit it was a little bit hyperbolic but I rolled back in the chair and threw my arms up and said: 'The war is over; we won. There is nothing now that the Iraqis can do that can prevent us from exercising our military will upon them.' You may argue with that but I would maintain that it was a reasonable statement to make, and after only 45 seconds."[33]

The next few days of air attacks went well and on January 27 Warden felt that the strategic air campaign had been so successful that the coalition should think seriously about how to end the war. In a letter to Secretary Rice he suggested,

> As we move into the next phase of our operations—defeat of the army in Kuwait and liberation of the country, we face several serious questions. The first is whether we should continue the battle with air power and thus avoid US casualties attendant to a land attack. It seems to me that this is a good approach—we have ample sorties and munitions to obliterate enemy forces in Kuwait should we choose to do so. I would hope, however, that imposition of massive casualties on the regular Army of Iraq—an army composed of ordinary citizens—would not be needed. If we are forced to kill or wound additional tens of thousands of Iraqis, I fear the clean victory that seems so possible will be hollow and tarnished both at home and abroad. Several possible courses suggest themselves:
>
> In the next few days, announce that the Coalition is ready to discuss peace with any Iraqi government that declares its adherence to ordinary standards of behavior at home and abroad; that we have no intention or desire to destroy Iraq (although we have the clear potential to do so); that we will give every assistance to rebuilding Iraq as quickly as possible (it can't happen without massive outside help). By taking this approach, we would hope that the right Iraqis—who understand the critical plight of their country even if Saddam Hussein does not—will take the steps necessary to give us the proper assurances of future acceptable behavior. We have now given patriotic or pragmatic Iraqis a clear choice other than the unspoken "unconditional surrender" which many may fear is our aim.
>
> The regular army is taking a terrible beating and has possibly expended its serious offensive potential during the last two weeks—and is unable to defend itself. It and its commanders (perhaps especially the III Corps commander) will soon (if not already) be thinking in terms of retreat or surrender. We should make either option feasible. To carry out either, we may want to establish electronic or personal contact (a la Mark Clark in North Africa) with the III Corps commander and others as appropriate to offer honorable ways of surrender or to assure him that we will not pursue if he begins a withdrawal. Even if the army in Kuwait begins a withdrawal on its own, we probably should not pursue even though doing so is a time-honored precept of

military theory; in this case, our political objectives are better served by avoiding the appearance of excessive bloodshed and by facilitating the return of the right elements to post-war Iraq. Should the Republican Guard oppose a withdrawal, we should be prepared to continue our attack on it as required.

Absent direct contact with the Army in Kuwait, we may want to swing the full fury of our air campaign against the Republican Guards and only return to Kuwait in the event we see preparations for an unlikely offensive. If the Iraqi Army in Kuwait does not begin to move north after we have destroyed the Republican Guard, we can concentrate our air forces against it. If we have made the peace offer previously described, the burden of bloodshed will be on Iraq and not us.[34]

Warden wrote the letter in reaction to a statement Powell had made four days earlier. During a Pentagon news conference intended to summarize the first week of combat, Powell declared that the Iraqi force of more than five hundred thousand in Kuwait is "sitting there dug in, waiting to be attacked and attacked it will be." The United States was contemplating a ground campaign and the strategy was straightforward: "Our strategy to go after this army is very, very simple. First we are going to cut it off, and then we are going to kill it." Cheney, who appeared at Powell's side, said that, because of the damage to Iraq's communication system, the Iraqi president "doesn't know how badly he's been hit." Cheney warned that Iraq might still surprise the allies with air strikes, terrorist actions, and missile attacks, but that Iraq "cannot change the basic course of the war [and] will be defeated."[35]

INFORMING THE WORLD: CHECKMATE'S MEDIA CONNECTION

The night the war began CNN summoned Major General Smith, its expert commentator, at short notice; on his way to the studio he telephoned Warden to gain insight into the air campaign: "That telephone call was probably the most fruitful call I had made in the last ten years," Smith recalled.[36] Smith talked with Warden and the Checkmate team almost every day during the war and as a result he could inform his audience about the capabilities of strategic air power.[37] Televised coverage of the war helped Warden make the air power argument to a worldwide audience. He also conveyed his views through General Dugan, the expert commentator for CBS. Smith and Dugan, with their deep understanding of the characteristics and advantages of air power, educated the public about doctrines, targeting philosophies, and the realities of air combat. Warden suggested to them that they had an opportunity to make sure that the American public and the national leadership recognized air power's potential and how it had changed the conduct of warfare. In their televised comments both general officers stated that the use of air power represented a new paradigm and a doctrinal shift. Warden helped them to succeed as commentators by providing them with an extraordinary source of the facts, analysis, and predictions they needed. Moreover, when some claimed that the coalition was engaged in "relentless bombing" Smith was instrumental in convincing the Pentagon to release photographs from satellites and reconnaissance aircraft that showed how little damage had been done to civilian areas.[38] After the war Smith acknowledged that Warden "became my primary source, the No. 1 source, for information and insight during the period that I worked for CNN."[39]

As the television stations broadcast video accounts of the war over Iraq, accompanied by commentary from such experts as Smith and Dugan, popular attitudes toward air power began to shift. According to Hallion, skepticism and doubts about air power were replaced by praise and hope as pictures of bombs penetrating ventilator ports and elevator shafts demonstrated how air power could deliver lethality and precision without inflicting massive casualties.[40]

ATTEMPTS TO AVERT THE INEVITABLE

The public debate revolved around when the ground offensive should be launched; the hidden subtext concerned whether the effectiveness of air power had reached the point of diminishing returns. Within Checkmate Warden summed up the situation as he saw it:

> We really have to fight two wars simultaneously. . . . The first one and the most direct one is the military war, and that we are fighting against Hussein and we are winning. But the second war in some ways is the more difficult one, it is the political war that we have to fight right here in Washington. And this one, if we lose, could cost us the military war as well and the lives of tens of thousands, perhaps, of ground troops.[41]

At a staff meeting in theater on February 5 Schwarzkopf revealed that Powell had raised the possibility of starting the ground campaign within the next few days.[42] The final date would be set when Powell and Cheney arrived in theater shortly. Warden was worried, and intensified his efforts to convince the secretary of defense that air power would suffice to win the war. Cheney constantly found memoranda and reports from Warden's directorate on his desk, and he seems to have believed that Warden's group was uniquely equipped to give him the insight he needed into what the coalition had so far achieved. Therefore, as he prepared for his trip to Riyadh to make the final decision, he told his staff to set up a meeting, and on February 6 he spent seventy minutes in Checkmate. Warden reviewed every target-set with Cheney. Each slide had three parts: "In the first part of the slide, we stated the objective desired for that particular target category. . . . In the second part of each slide, we talked about what we've accomplished. . . . The third and last part of each slide was what is left—what remains to be done."[43]

During the discussions Cheney expressed misgivings. According to the bomb damage assessments (BDAs) he had received from the national intelligence agencies, the air campaign was not as effective as they had anticipated. Warden responded that although battlefield preparation sorties began on the first night of the war, the total number of sorties was far lower than planned. Checkmate had based its assumptions on fifteen hundred strike sorties per day to accomplish 50 percent attrition, but the actual average was five to six hundred per day, with only around two hundred sorties per day during the first ten days of the war. Approximately half of the attack sorties into Iraq had been diverted to Scud targeting, aircraft shelter attacks, and maritime operations or canceled because of weather-related problems.[44] The impact was cumulative: aircraft were less accurate in bombing; crews were flying too high to determine accurately the damage done by their strikes; and clouds often prevented satellite photography from revealing the true extent of damage.[45] To help illustrate air power's actual effectiveness, Lieutenant Colonel Stanfill narrated an eight-minute video clip of gun camera films, which showed the effect that precision-guided bombs had on aircraft shelters, hardened bunkers of chemical and biological weapons, roadways, and tanks.

As Warden led Cheney and his entourage clockwise around the Checkmate room, filled with maps and information about targets, assessments, and challenges, he elaborated on the rationale of staying committed to the strategic air campaign in Baghdad and explained the cumulative effect of the operational air campaign in detail. Warden believed that the only way to postpone ground operations, and if possible prevent a ground war altogether, was to convince Cheney that air power was in fact accomplishing the U.S. goals, but he had no objective criteria to measure success. He talked at length about the problems that resulted from using tactical measures of merit for a strategic and operational campaign, and once again lauded air power's achievements. As an example, he pointed out that the national intelligence agencies categorized attacks on the AT&T building as failures because the building was still standing, even though its communication systems no longer functioned.

Warden sensed that Cheney might be willing to postpone the start of ground operations by a few days, but he was already certain that the secretary of defense was committed to a ground war. Wolfowitz, for his part, argued that one option was to sustain the air campaign until the end of March, but that eventually boots on the ground would be needed to complete the victory.[46]

Warden dominated the discussions, although Cheney asked a range of questions and both Rice and Adams added comments as they saw fit. When Adams signaled to Warden that he had only five minutes left and needed to "speed this up," Cheney responded "No, no. Let's take all the time that's required here."[47] Toward the end of the briefing Cheney commented, "For the first time I understand why you people are so confident about this whole thing."[48]

Rice talked with Cheney in private after the presentation and reported back to Warden that it seemed as though Cheney would support "staying with air only for a few more weeks."[49] At the time a Checkmate officer noted in his notebook that "everyone was very pleased with Secretary Cheney's visit. Colonel Warden himself was 'on a high' all day. He was very, very happy with what had transpired."[50]

Warden called both Glosson and Deptula and again discussed at length how he believed they should brief Cheney in theater. He also sent them the slides, notes, and some additional arguments that they might want to use. Later that day Lieutenant General Carns, the director of the Joint Staff, received the same briefing in Checkmate and he too seemed "fairly receptive."[51]

The evidence that Glosson presented when Cheney arrived in theater on February 9 convinced the secretary of defense that the air campaign was continuing to inflict impressive damage on the enemy. When Cheney returned to Washington the next day he received additional reports and analyses from Checkmate and advised President Bush that the United States should give the air campaign another two weeks before engaging the Iraqis on the ground. Bush then told reporters that the air campaign was "very, very effective" and that the United States would continue to rely on it "for a while."[52] "Had decision-makers concluded the air campaign had done as much as it could," historian Richard Hallion later stated, "it would have resulted in a premature launching of the ground offensive, with much greater casualties."[53]

On February 11 Russia undertook a separate peace initiative. The Russian envoy, Yevgeni Primakov, met with Saddam Hussein in Baghdad and the Iraqi leader seemingly accepted Primakov's proposal that Iraq withdraw from Kuwait without economic or territorial compensation: "Okay. I'm going to withdraw my troops from Kuwait. I just want to be sure that, as I retreat, they don't shoot me in the back."[54] Unaware that the president and his advisors had already recognized Saddam Hussein's conditions as unacceptable, Warden saw this as a victory: he believed that the offer was genuine and that it eliminated the need for a U.S. ground campaign. He also thought that strategic air power had brought about the Iraqi leader's concessions and argued that the coalition need only continue air strikes while finalizing the diplomatic aspects.[55] Warden also relied on CIA's Charles Allen, who informed Warden on February 10 that the war was "essentially won."[56]

When Warden learned that no F-117s would attack Baghdad because of the al-Firdos incident on February 13,[57] he took his objections to Rice and sent a subordinate to convey his complaints to Cheney's staff. Warden favored using

F-117s to strike internal security facilities,[58] and contended that the strategic air campaign should be intensified in order to avoid a ground war entirely.[59]

With Rice's consent, Warden persuaded Wolfowitz and Libby to visit Checkmate on the morning of February 16. The two stayed for over three hours, but when they left, Rice and Warden had the impression that "the higher-ups in the Department of Defense are bound and determined to have a ground war and that it begins soon."[60] Still, Warden refused to concede and convinced Rice to invite Cheney to Checkmate for the third time. Unbeknownst to Warden, Cheney had already decided to obtain further updates from Checkmate. Without telling his own staff, he took the elevator to the basement level where the division was housed. As it happened, he stepped out of the elevator on a mezzanine, and since he had not brought his security card he was unable to get back in. He called his own office to fetch him, and on the way upstairs he told Lieutenant Colonel Barry to set up a briefing in Checkmate.

Cheney spent thirty minutes with Warden on February 20. Hoping to give the air campaign every possible chance to ensure Iraq's withdrawal without a ground campaign, Warden recommended an "immediate surge effort to maximize air sorties and other firepower assets to concentrate on Iraqi forces in [the] KTO . . . We must conduct maximum effort over the next 2–3 weeks to achieve victory." Warden drew on a Second World War analogy—the "Big Week" air offensive in late February 1944—and used the term "Big Week II" in recommending an intensive three-day operation that would include fourteen hundred sorties a day against the Republican Guard in addition to F-117s and Tomahawk cruise missiles aimed at the internal security organizations in Baghdad.[61] He suggested that it was imperative to capitalize on "cracks in the Iraqi high command"; in his opinion, these attacks would hasten the end of the war by encouraging mass desertions and surrender and might provoke a coup against Saddam Hussein.[62] Combined with the Russian peace initiative, this would lead to unconditional withdrawal. At the very least, Big Week II would prepare the battlefield for a ground campaign, should one be needed.[63]

One attendee noted that Cheney seemed "receptive . . . and he certainly gave Colonel Warden his utmost attention," but Warden's hopes proved unfounded.[64] Warden recalls, "It was clear to me that [Cheney] had made the decision that there was going to be [a ground campaign] . . . he was not as responsive as he had been the first time . . . the die had already been cast, and it was not something that he was either able or willing to try to reopen."[65] Interestingly, at the end of the discussion, Warden told Cheney that if the United States were to launch a ground war, it should at all costs avoid occupying Iraq because of all the grief it would bring, and Cheney agreed wholeheartedly.[66]

Warden found some encouragement in the speech that Powell gave before the Senate Armed Services Committee on February 21—the same day that

Moscow announced that the Iraqi leader had accepted a Soviet peace plan that included "full and unconditional withdrawal" from Kuwait.[67] Powell stated, "Air power is the decisive arm so far, and I expect it will be the decisive arm into the end of the campaign, even if ground forces and amphibious forces are added to the equation . . . if anything, I expect air power to be even more decisive in the days and weeks ahead."[68] In reality, however, he and Schwarzkopf were fine-tuning the start of a ground offensive, and Scowcroft agreed that a ground campaign would be necessary to complete the victory.[69]

Warden was certain that it was Powell who had convinced Cheney to start the ground campaign. A few days earlier, when Schwarzkopf postponed G-Day (the onset of ground operations to liberate Kuwait) for a few days, Powell had responded angrily: "I hate to wait that long. The President wants to get on with this."[70] Warden continued to maintain that the real victory consisted of overthrowing the regime and that the Iraqi army was not the primary enemy. He had even written a memorandum to Secretary Rice in which he suggested that the United States contact the Iraqi Third Corps commander to make a deal: if he led a coup against Saddam Hussein, the United States would give his forces airlift and close air support to get to Baghdad.[71] Rice liked the idea and mentioned it to Cheney, but it was never pursued.

The ground campaign started on February 24 —"the day that everyone in Checkmate hoped to avoid."[72] Air power delivered large numbers of sorties in close air support, following CENTAF's plan for Phase IV. Warden regretted that airmen had been unable to convince the administration that a ground war was not needed; he remained convinced that the United States was missing a huge opportunity to overthrow the Hussein regime via the Iraqi military; and he was concerned about U.S. casualties, although he believed the Iraqis would not be able to muster much resistance.

Leadership Facility Team

Although the relationship between Checkmate and air force intelligence was initially characterized by adversarial relationships, real cooperation between Checkmate and various intelligence branches began in October, when Warden established a special planning group, called the "Leadership Facility Team," tasked with studying the Iraqi regime.

Lieutenant Colonel Harvey, one of the most important players in Checkmate, arranged for meetings in which Checkmate briefed representatives from the DIA, the CIA, and other intelligence agencies on the essence of the strategic air campaign plan. The team would then work with the intelligence officers on obtaining better information and imagery of the inner-ring target-sets, such as leadership, security apparatus, and C³ targets. The team reviewed sites in Tikrit,

Saddam Hussein's movements and sleeping quarters, leadership shelters, government facilities, communication sites, presidential palaces, and headquarters for the special security forces, the Republican Guard, and the Ba'ath Party, concentrating specifically on the Iraqi regime's ability to communicate with its civilian populace, security and intelligence apparatus, and military forces. As part of this initiative, the team spent a significant amount of time with the engineers who had developed the Iraqi telecommunications system, talking with AT&T and with Canada's Northern Telecom. As soon as they obtained relevant information they sent it to the Black Hole, where Deptula used the information to augment the ever-growing target list and to modify the attack plan as appropriate.

The open planning approach demonstrated its value when DIA analyst Charles Kissel came to Checkmate three days before the air campaign began, bringing information about the fiber optic communication network that connected Baghdad with headquarters in Mosul and Basra, as well as with command posts around Iraq.[73] He told Warden's men that the fiber optic cables that transmitted orders for launching Scuds went across two of the major bridges in Baghdad. Destroying these two bridges therefore took on special importance: it would both hinder effective transportation and degrade communications between the Iraqi leadership and its missile commanders.

As soon as the air war began Warden also contacted the Fighter Weapons School at Nellis AFB. After he explained Checkmate's role several officers joined Checkmate and stayed throughout the war, even though TAC headquarters continued to oppose Checkmate's involvement. These officers played key roles in linking targets with weapons and providing that input to the Black Hole.

BOMB DAMAGE ASSESSMENT

During the war the directorate took a particular interest in BDA, one of the most contentious issues of the air campaign. Unhappy with the existing system for assessing air power's achievements, Warden had written a memorandum to Adams on September 24, recommending that his directorate establish a formal relationship with the DIA.[74] His major concern was that the DIA's BDA team did not know how to assess either strategic effects or the operational impact of air power applied directly against Iraqi ground forces. After talking with several mid-level DIA officials in mid-December, Warden tasked Harvey and Howey to assemble a group of officers who would work with the DIA analysts to develop procedures and working methods for dealing with BDA.[75]

Checkmate provided DIA imagery analysts with expertise on weapon systems and their effects and explained the concept of targeting for effects. Key DIA officers with responsibilities for BDA welcomed Checkmate's assistance in training their staff to interpret the capabilities of penetrating weapons.[76] According to the *Gulf War Air Power Survey*:

During the first stage of imagery analysis, the Checkmate cell was involved deeply in the BDA process. An open-line consultation was conducted around-the-clock. During the second stage, Checkmate provided one Air Force analyst to the DIA cell, and Air Force weapon system experts were on call. During stage three, Checkmate also provided an analyst, while weapon system experts and planners were on call for more in-depth consultation.[77]

The cooperation proved highly useful, but it did not overcome the central problem: no proven methodology existed for measuring the effectiveness of strategic attacks against leadership targets, communications facilities, and electricity plants, and neither the military nor the intelligence community had an agreed criterion for assessing damage on the battlefield. As a general rule, the intelligence community tended toward conservative estimates, while the air campaign planners were more inclined to believe the damage estimates from the firsthand evidence of pilot after-action reports and videotapes, even though they were generally regarded as too optimistic. Confronted with the new concept of targeting for effects, the intelligence officers found themselves in unknown territory. Moreover, many of the analysts were reluctant to "abandon Vietnam-era BDA norms that focused on the physical destruction of targets."[78]

As an example, a few days into the air campaign Warden received a report from the DIA that characterized the bombing of the Iraqi power system as a failure. The intelligence officer insisted that his assessment resulted from a straightforward mathematical analysis: destroying twenty out of two hundred electrical facilities amounted to a hit rate of 10 percent, which he considered a bad result. Warden countered that such tactical measurements missed the overall strategic outcome: the lights in Baghdad and the rest of Iraq were out. The same applied to the AT&T building and the bombing of Salman Park: although bombing destroyed three out of four refrigerated storage bunkers for biological warfare, the DIA refused to acknowledge the target as neutralized until the fourth was eliminated.[79] Warden maintained that practical results should constitute the measurement criteria, and that in those terms the campaign had achieved its objectives, but the DIA officer adhered adamantly to the strictly mathematical approach prescribed by his education and by official procedures.

To complicate the situation further, information about the F-117's laser-guided bombs (GBU-27) was classified, which had kept targeteers and intelligence analysts ignorant of the munition. It was thus difficult suddenly to pass judgment on the weapon's effectiveness. The notion of assessing functional and synergistic effects at the strategic and operational levels of war rather than physical and structural damage at the tactical level created an additional challenge.

Much to the disgust of the national intelligence apparatus, Checkmate became CENTAF's primary source in Washington for current information, and this role continued throughout Operation Desert Storm. Warden's BDA team basically took the conservative DIA reports and compared them to the reports from CENTCOM and CENTAF. On February 3 Major Howey concluded, "We have to interpolate and give our own interpretations of what these figures mean and come up with some kind of coherent package that shows that the war is having an effect . . . that it is too early to resort to a destructive ground campaign."[80]

The discrepancies between the estimates had no practical consequences for the timing of the ground attack, because the CENTAF planners relied on the "back channel" information: bomb-camera video data supplied by aircrews and supported by Checkmate's "sanity checks." Even so, the conservative reports prompted division commanders who did not share Schwarzkopf's positive assessment of air power to nominate targets directly in front of their positions. This, in turn, reduced the theater-wide impact of the carefully structured air campaign that established targeting priorities according to the commander in chief's overall theater needs.[81]

In fact, Warden never succeeded in bringing the DIA as an institution to understand the new warfighting concept: the analysts remained incapable of interpreting results across complete target-sets. However, the contacts that developed between Warden's men and individual intelligence officers improved the overall quality of analysis.[82] As the debate raged over the number of tanks destroyed Warden asserted that the exact figure was irrelevant. From an operational perspective, Iraq no longer posed a coherent threat: Iraqi troops refused to fight and massive numbers of soldiers deserted. Over time the DIA team did learn to assess functional rather than physical or structural damage and came to appreciate synergetic effects. After the war key intelligence officers at the DIA expressed deep appreciation of Checkmate's general assistance in meeting the assessment challenge. Col. F. L. Talbot, CENTAF's chief targeteer, later stated that he had no problem with intelligence being provided from Washington, "where there is an abundance of analysts and databases galore and first-rate communication," but he was unhappy "with the manner in which it was provided to CENTAF."[83]

Warden's "intervention" resulted in heated controversy, occasional friction, and even real bitterness between the intelligence community and the air planners, but Deptula came to rely on Checkmate's steady supply of analytical reports. In fact, Warden's group played a central role in BDA reporting for a logical reason: it was the only organization in Washington that understood the philosophy behind the air campaign plan.

Warden also involved individuals from the national intelligence agencies. As the war progressed, Checkmate produced a daily "Strategic Assessment Point Paper"—an evaluation of the war's progress based on all-source analysis of each major strategic target category. Warden made certain that the papers found their way to the decision makers and Checkmate briefed the secretary of the air force and the chief of staff almost every day of the war.[84]

THE WAR ENDS

Despite the stunning results of the ground campaign, Warden continued to deplore the decision by the National Command Authority, which he believed had risked U.S. lives unnecessarily. But when coalition forces completed the defeat of Iraqi forces in less than a hundred hours he was of course "very pleased." He was relieved that the war had ended without any significant occupation of Iraqi territory and without huge numbers of casualties, but still worried that the United States was failing to obtain an "agreement on a post-war policy." Nevertheless, his team had made a real contribution to the success of the war and he believed the event merited special recognition. On February 28, at 1400, Checkmate held a "victory celebration—complete with champagne, caviar, and all the trimmings."[85] Wolfowitz, Rice, and Alexander attended, but, rather pointedly, McPeak did not.

Postwar Assessments

Over the next few days Warden and his Checkmate team began to return to normal. Those not permanently assigned to XOXW went back to their regular workplaces and Warden shifted his focus to after-action reports. Still, several "senior statesmen" found their way to the Air Staff; for example, on March 12 Warden briefed the former air force chief of staff, Gen. David C. Jones, and the former commander of TAC, Gen. William Momyer, on the air campaign and Checkmate's role in the war.[86]

On March 13, when Warden managed to obtain a copy of the briefing that McPeak planned to present live on CNN the next day, he thought it so bad that he had a team prepare an alternative. McPeak rejected Checkmate's alternative and both Horner and Warden recall that his "Mother of All Briefings" went poorly.[87] The general feeling in Checkmate was that it was "too dull, overloaded with dry statistics of bomb tonnage, etc., no good overview of strategy, not photogenic enough for general TV audiences."[88]

Warden had voiced the need for a postwar analysis as early as January 11, 1991, six days before the air campaign began. At that time he wrote a memorandum to General Loh, suggesting that if the air campaign were carried out as planned a "bombing survey would be extremely valuable," especially one conducted by an "independent commission."[89] To ensure credibility, such a report could not be an "in-house product." Little happened until after the war ended, but once again it was Warden who raised the issue. What triggered his initiative was an article by Paul Nitze that strongly criticized what air power had achieved in 1991. Nitze, a highly respected thinker, had participated in the U.S. Strategic

Bombing Survey (USSBS) that examined air power in the Second World War, and Warden considered it harmful to have such an authority "walking around town saying such things."[90] He arranged to give a presentation to Nitze, who, after hearing Warden's evidence, admitted that he had grossly underestimated the results that air power had produced. Shortly after the meeting Nitze told Warden that the Gulf War of 1991 had proved that PGMs could replace nuclear weapons, because they could achieve the objectives without radiation and collateral damage: thus, a new age of effectiveness had arrived.[91]

Warden devoted considerable time to developing after-action reports, and in a letter March 5, 1991, he noted:

> We have learned a couple of campaign lessons from the Gulf War and will incorporate them in a variety of places. (1) We need to have a category labeled "strategic attack." Somewhere in the vicinity of 30% of our effort was directed against strategic targets that were directly related to attaining broad strategic goals (incapacitation of Iraqi national leadership, destruction of nuclear, biological, and chemical research and production, shutdown of national electric and refining operations, etc). (2) We probably also need a category called "direct attack" for air attacks on ground forces where such attack is seen as the primary means of destroying an enemy ground force (as opposed to softening it for subsequent friendly ground attack.)[92]

In a letter to General McPeak on March 10, 1991, Warden called for reevaluating the AirLand Battle doctrine, noting that the doctrine rested on the assumption that the enemy's second-echelon ground forces would move "hundreds of miles to attack a particular US corps and that US ground forces would bear the brunt of responsibility for stopping the attack." With the success of "strategic attack" and "direct attack," Warden raised questions: "Is there a place where a US president would commit significant ground forces to battle before conducting an extended air operation? Would a corps be likely to operate independently?"[93]

GULF WAR AIR POWER SURVEY

Believing that an independent survey modeled after the USSBS would make a good case for the decisiveness of American air power, Warden turned to his colleague Deptula, who had returned to the office of the secretary of the air force. On July 24, 1991, when Rice learned that the Air Staff suggested three separate evaluations under their own institutional control—from the Office of Air Force History, TAC, and RAND—he echoed Warden's warning to Loh, noting that "if there [was] even a hint that we cooked the books, the value of the product would be destroyed."[94] He confirmed that any review should be both civilian-led and independent. At Deptula's suggestion, Rice invited Eliot A. Cohen, professor of strategic studies at the Paul H. Nitze School of Advanced International Studies at Johns Hopkins University, to serve as the editor-in-chief of what became known as the *Gulf War Air Power Survey (GWAPS)*. Rice told Cohen that the survey should "form conclusions on the implications for future air force organization, training and force structure," and stressed that for the survey to be credible Cohen's team needed to "conduct its study according to the highest standards of professional and intellectual integrity and objectivity."[95]

The study became a civilian-led undertaking that involved more than a hundred civilian and military analysts, including a review committee of prominent statesmen, retired officers, and scholars who provided external advice and criticism. Moreover, the study was chaired by Nitze. From August 1991 to early 1993 the survey team conducted extensive research that culminated in a five-volume report. The review committee had cautioned that the most complex issue would be to address the effectiveness of "the strategic air campaign," as there was no access to Baghdad.[96] Indeed, the volume that dealt with the strategic campaign in detail, *Effects and Effectiveness*, written by Thomas A. Keaney and Barry D. Watts, pointed out the most critical "hole" in the evidence: without access to Iraqi leaders and their prewar plans they had only limited insight into Iraqi "intentions before and during the Gulf War."[97]

To Warden's disappointment, the authors rejected the premise that the use of air power had represented a revolution in military affairs, and concluded that the Gulf War demonstrated the "limits of strategic attack encountered at least as far back as World War II."[98] Warden, who was not involved in the survey, naturally believed the strategic air campaign had not received proper credit. In his view, this had happened because the authors had used the standard tactical and attrition-oriented measures of merit, rather than seeking a comprehensive understanding of the overall systemic effects.

Warden maintained that conditions in Iraq immediately after the war confirmed his theories: the enemy system had been destabilized. Two of the country's three major ethnic groups, the Kurds in the north and the Shias in the south, were in open revolt; Iraqi citizens openly criticized the regime to the world's media on the streets of Baghdad; the infrastructure of daily life, such as communications, electricity, and water supply, was broken but not demolished; and the activities into which Iraq had poured its national treasure and hopes, such as its nuclear and chemical programs, were either dismantled or inoperative. While he could not identify the results obtained in any single targeting category as being responsible for the increasing dislocation of the Iraqi system, he saw the cumulative impact of disorder and national paralysis generated by the strategic air campaign as the central factor in weakening the Iraqi regime.

DESERT STORM IN RETROSPECT

Despite the impressive success of Operation Desert Storm, the effectiveness of the strategic air campaign remains a topic of debate. According to Gen. Larry Welch, Dugan's predecessor as USAF chief of staff, Horner and Glosson had masterfully concealed the danger posed by Instant Thunder, which Schwarzkopf ill-advisedly approved, within the context of a much larger air campaign that dealt with the "real" threat: the Iraqi ground forces in Kuwait. Welch and others believed that the real war winner had been the "preparation of the battlefield": to them, the bombing of Iraqi troops, tanks, and artillery in Kuwait accomplished far more than strategic attacks on Baghdad.[99]

Warden presented his own assessment in a paper titled "Employing Air Power in the Twenty-First Century," which used the results of the recent war to support predictions regarding the future role of air power.[100] The paper first described the strategic context: a world that had witnessed great changes with the end of the cold war and the Soviet Union's deteriorating influence as a global military actor.[101] Warden asserted that the United States could no longer rely on containment as a unifying concept and presented arguments for formulating a new national policy. He linked these concepts to speculations as to the kind of war the United States would most likely experience over the next two decades, and how air power would fit into that conceptual framework. Not surprisingly, he identified air power as the American form of war. The essay then discussed how the objectives of war should be linked to the concept of centers of gravity.

Interestingly, Warden had written the text prior to Operation Desert Storm: the first portion derived from a presentation he had given in July 1990, titled "The Future of Air Power: Strategies for a Changing World," and the second repeated "Centers of Gravity: the Key to Success in War," which he had written even earlier. He chose not to modify the substance of these earlier materials; as far as he was concerned, he had developed a theory of warfare well before the invasion of Kuwait and the subsequent air campaign had validated large portions of that theory.

Warden then offered his own assessment of the air campaign, analyzing the overall effect one ring at a time.

> In the winter of 1991 air power overwhelmed Iraq, paralyzing it strategically and operationally. Air power incapacitated the country's leadership, made communication nearly impossible, took away its electricity and gasoline production, inhibited significant movement, and wreaked destruction on every part of its machine. The cost in American blood for complete domination of a country of 16 million people and its million-man war machine was astoundingly low. This significant victory satisfied the legitimate demands of the American people that their

wars use technology to keep human losses—on both sides—to an absolute minimum. This victory provides the strategic model for American operations well into the twenty-first century.[102]

He stressed the importance of targeting the inner ring, but noted that attacks on the other rings were essential to create the strategic paralysis required for victory. He also contended that "The air campaign had imposed not only strategic paralysis on the whole state of Iraq but had imposed operational paralysis on the army in Kuwait."[103] To provide historical perspective he pointed out that the coalition had achieved success with just over ten thousand sorties and twenty thousand tons of bombs, as opposed to over eight million tons dropped on Vietnam in seven years.

The essay concluded by analyzing the implications of the 1991 Gulf War. Warden's main thesis was that precision weapons, used in conjunction with stealth, made it possible to achieve maneuver, mass, and concentration on an entirely unprecedented scale. Indeed, stealth and precision had redefined the old concept of mass and maneuver: stealth reintroduced surprise into air warfare, precision lowered the number of sorties required by orders of magnitude, and the lethality of the weapons made most targets vulnerable. Warden saw the Gulf War as the first "Hyperwar": "one that capitalizes on high technology, unprecedented accuracy, operational and strategic surprise through stealth, and the ability to bring all of an enemy's key operational and strategic nodes under near-simultaneous attack."[104]

Warden made a persuasive case for his theory. His paper was one of the first analyses of what happened in 1991 and was widely quoted as representing the view of the strategic bombardment advocates. As in most of his writings, he left out the details in an attempt to present the big picture. He also did not mention his own role in the war, or that of the Air Staff. Nor did he mention Instant Thunder or the planning process: the paper centered on strategy and ideas, not on the people who turned them into reality. For all the glory he ascribed to air power, he also warned that its reign would come to an end:

> The world has just witnessed a new kind of warfare—hyperwar. It has seen air power become dominant. It has seen unequivocally how defenseless a state becomes when it loses control of the air over its territories and forces. It has seen the awesome power of the air offensive—and the near impossibility of defending against it. It has seen a demonstration of the validity of strategic attack theory. It has seen a war primarily against things but one that produced remarkably few casualties, especially considering the outcome. For the next two decades—and perhaps for much longer—an American commander, whether

the president in Washington or general in the field, will turn first to air power, just as did President George Bush and Gen. Norman Schwarzkopf. We have moved from the age of the horse and the sail through the age of the battleship and the tank to the age of the airplane. Like its illustrious ancestors, the airplane will have its day in the sun, and then it too shall be replaced. Sic transit Gloria mundi.[105]

CHECKMATE AND WARDEN: DIVIDED OPINIONS

In retrospect, Warden's directorate made a remarkable contribution for an organization that had no official role in the war. A staggering number of people at all levels in government and the armed services drew on Checkmate during the planning and execution of Operation Desert Storm. Without Warden's team the air planners in theater would have had far less support and data on which to base their attack plans. The secretary of defense used Checkmate to verify the information that he received from the Joint Staff; he had no equivalent resource for the ground and naval aspects.[106] According to Eliot Cohen, Checkmate served as an interesting model of a centralized targeting staff: "Although most of the work gets done in the theater, I think that it established a precedent for informal ties between Washington and the field that continues to make a difference."[107]

As for the relationship between intelligence and planning, the *Gulf War Air Power Survey* concluded that "intelligence enabled the plan—it did not formulate the plan":

> There is no evidence to suggest that Air Staff Checkmate operational planners who developed the Instant Thunder plan used intelligence information to sculpt their concept of operations. Rather, they used intelligence to locate and define targets within the series of large, objective-oriented target categories upon which their plan, and eventually the Desert Storm air campaign, was built.
>
> The Air Staff, through Air Force Checkmate, provided a variety of services to Black Hole planners in a fraction of the time it would have taken the formal intelligence system. Checkmate officers developed relationships at the staff officer level with individuals and officers in all the major intelligence organizations: DIA, CIA, the National Security Agency, and the Joint Chiefs of Staff. Air Staff action officers were assigned to the intelligence agencies to help gather information needed by the planners in Checkmate and in the theater. As a result of these informal relationships, intelligence information was passed from the intelligence agency to the user quickly and with no intervening processing by the organized intelligence system in theater.[108]

The survey concluded that Checkmate "provided both critical information and a strategic thought process," including suggestions on "targets to attack next."[109] According to air force historian Richard Davis, the Checkmate structure exemplified Warden's "unusual proclivity for setting up working arrangements between organizations and individuals with specific expertise to facilitate his planning."[110] Major Rogers, who worked both in Checkmate and in the Black Hole, noted that "the execution and success of the strategic air campaign were in large part due to the many action officers of Checkmate and Warden's foresight to maintain an airpower support group from August through the end of the war."[111] Even Adams conceded that Warden made a very useful contribution to the war: "I will tell you that I do not think TAC headquarters had a planning staff to do this kind of a job. I spent maybe 15 years in TAC in most of the senior positions in TAC except the commander, but it is not designed to do that."[112]

General McPeak never became fully comfortable with the situation, noting that both Rice and Warden "were helping more than they really needed to help."[113] At times McPeak even questioned why Warden was involved in the war planning, only to ask for a comprehensive presentation the next day. He called upon Warden's team time and again, spending hours with them:

> Sometimes I saw them quite often; like three times a week or something like that . . . I went down there several times and looked at their approach to targeting and what they had up on the walls and how they prioritized the business and so forth, so I paid a lot of attention to it . . . I would consider the work legitimate, period. I mean, we can do whatever we want in the building and mail it to them, and they can ignore it or pay attention to it as they see fit. My view of it was that we had access in this town to some information and to people that they did not have access to, at least on a regular basis, so we were in a position to provide some knowledgeable help in planning that I would have thought they would be grateful to have. That was the sort of thing that I really paid more attention to; "How can we help these guys in ways that they cannot do themselves from the Black Hole?" . . . There is a difference between trying to help and issuing them a plan. I thought we were trying to help, not really issuing them a plan; and if they didn't want the help we provided, they were free to throw it away.[114]

General Loh, who opened the door for Warden's entrance into the planning, has noted that Warden sometimes went to extremes in trying to market the air option, but that he could not have done without him. He asserted that "Checkmate had an honest and justifiable entry into the plan because they were assessing targets that were given to them by the CIA and other unnamed sources, and they were checking those targets out and then sending them over to Deptula to put into the plan."[115] As Loh saw it, Checkmate served as a cell that fed concepts, analysis, and ideas into the joint planning process in theater, while at the same time keeping the decision makers in Washington informed, and therefore deserved considerable praise. Still, he had to admit that Warden occasionally presented him with a predicament: Checkmate received various requests for Warden to brief "very high individuals," but at the same time it was not Warden's plan to brief—it was CENTCOM's plan and "there was a lot of resistance in the JCS to just brief that willy-nilly."[116]

Even Major General Alexander, Warden's immediate superior, saw the colonel as a double-edged sword. From the inception of Instant Thunder through the actual conflict, Alexander repeatedly found himself caught between the proverbial rock and hard place as he tried to keep Warden's ideas flowing without completely alienating General Adams:

> Warden would work it through an informal network. He would get an invitation transmitted to Cheney in an informal way. He claimed to me that Cheney's exec called up and wanted to come down and see the War Room. Well, that just does not happen. You know that, and I know that. Either he worked through the Secretary of the Air Force and the Secretary then told Cheney or through Lopez, who was Cheney's military assistant. Adams made sure he did not show up because there is a problem if he is there briefing SecDef without Schwarzkopf or Powell . . . I never had Warden under control. I just kept trying; you could not control him . . . we would have shouting matches. I would call him in and scream at him. Warden is very resilient . . .
>
> Warden truly marched to the drum beat of a bigger mission and objective . . . I have never really met a fanatic until I met him. . . . Warden was a problem for me the whole time. Warden would have self-destructed with that little plan of his if he was not managed carefully . . . Warden is an absolute fanatic in his faith in what airpower can do and he has unswerving confidence . . . Warden did not have a doubt in his mind about his figures. Warden really did not have the rationale to have as much confidence as he did. There was not the evidence to give him that much confidence. He just had a feel . . . His confidence in airpower is more of a passion. He almost loses reason when extolling the qualities and capabilities of airpower . . . Looking back on it, I can't believe how prophetic he was. He is brilliant, you know.[117]

Alexander reflected that although Warden was "one of the most gifted strategists in the USAF" he constantly had to "assess his liabilities versus his contributions," and at times that balance was only "marginally in his favor."[118]

Finally, Secretary Rice insisted a larger lesson should be learned:

> I think when you look at what was involved in planning the strategic air campaign, it is wholly unrealistic to expect that it could have been done out in Riyadh, the resources that the Checkmate operation was able to pull together in many cases involved accessing things that probably could only have been accessed in Washington. You just could not have done that out in the field. That is not to say they could not have planned some level of strategic air campaign plan out there, but a lot of the details about how the telephone system worked that we got from AT&T and other contractors; a lot of details that we got on the actual construction and layout of the buried bunkers, command and control centers, special facilities in the key Iraqi buildings and palaces; the way the Yugoslav shelters were constructed, and various other things; the Checkmate operation, through intelligence sources and working through diplomatic sources to access foreign companies, as well as our own, [so] we got a tremendous amount of information, sometimes down to the detailed architectural plans for some of the structures that ended up being targets in the attack. I do not see how that level of stuff ever could have been done out in Riyadh . . . Nothing was dictated to General Horner. There was nothing passed out there that he did not have a full opportunity to adopt or reject or modify or do whatever he wanted to do with it. I think that is the right way in which it should operate, and my own personal view is, we will have to do the same kind of thing again the next time the situation arises; and to assume that everything that needs to be done can be done out there without any help from outsiders is just naïve. The technical and analytical and informational base and expertise that has to go into the design of a well structured air campaign is just flat not going to be available out in some desert someplace.[119]

Falling Action

After Operation Desert Storm ended, some leaders in the Air Staff attempted to eradicate the position that Warden and his team had established for themselves by moving Warden's Checkmate division away from the Directorate of Plans into the Directorate of Operations. Such a change made sense from an organizational perspective, but, according to a three-star general who had an inside view, it also carried a deliberate message: "the institutional Air Force was not happy with the influence of John Warden and his organization during Desert Storm."[120] Col.

James Gough, who replaced Warden shortly after the war, recalls that he inherited a "wonderful team," but that the role of Checkmate was a "very, very sensitive issue."[121]

Warden never received explicit recognition for his contribution to the air campaign, but occasional acknowledgments gave him personal satisfaction. After the war President Bush awarded the prestigious Presidential Citizens Medal to Richard N. Haass, the senior director for Near East and South Asian affairs on the staff of the National Security Council, in recognition of his contributions to the development and articulation of U.S. policy during Operations Desert Shield and Desert Storm. Haass, who had visited Checkmate twice during the war, had been greatly impressed by its activities and stated that it had made a significant contribution to the war, "first by designing the strategic portion of the air campaign and then by providing politicians in Washington with information, analysis, suggestions and predictions."[122] Haass favored using air power against the leadership and the command and control apparatus, and believed that Warden had expressed the concept behind the attacks coherently and convincingly. He concluded that Warden's "confidence, enthusiasm and knowledge were both refreshing and insightful."[123] Haass personally invited Warden to the award ceremony and when they met he told the colonel, "You are the one who really should have had this medal."[124]

11

TRANSFORMING THE AIR COMMAND AND STAFF COLLEGE

In July 1991, at the recommendation of the secretary of the air force, Donald B. Rice, and the air force vice chief of staff, Gen. Michael P. C. Carns, Warden became the special assistant for policy studies and national security affairs to Vice President Dan Quayle. After a brief interlude on the White House staff, Warden took on the challenge of revitalizing the Air Command and Staff College. In his three years as commandant, Warden initiated many changes, some of which were the most radical since the college was founded. Warden restructured the academic year to resemble a campaign plan, seeking to match ingredients such as objectives and targeting strategies with resources, constraints, and restraints. Moreover, he set high standards for his faculty members, made major commitments to the use of advanced technology, and encouraged the students to gain deeper understanding of their profession by reading about history and theories underlying the formation of the air force.

Special Assistant to the Vice President

Rice and Carns instigated the move from the Pentagon to the White House partly to ensure that Warden would receive a favorable efficiency report that would support his promotion to brigadier general.[1] General Adams, who left the Air Staff in February 1991 to become the commander in chief of Pacific Air Forces, and his successor, Lt. Gen. Michael A. Nelson, had made it clear that they did not see Warden as flag-rank material.[2] Nelson was apparently uncomfortable with Warden's giving speeches about how "the traditional containment policy of the U.S. has lost its credibility," how the American forces needed "a more global capacity," and how the USAF could play the central role in the U.S. military.[3]

Warden was excited about the new assignment. It was, first and foremost, an opportunity to work with actual decision and policy makers."[4] After all, he noted, "part of the fascination of this whole business is that military plans have little to do with [the] military . . . only five per cent of it is getting military people convinced and selling them on that. The other ninety-five per cent is getting the civilians to sign on to it."[5]

When Warden took up the appointment in June 1991 Quayle was heading the Competitiveness Council and Warden spent the first few months in his new position focusing on how the United States could become more productive and economically competitive. He represented the vice president's office on numerous interagency policy coordination committees conducted at the assistant secretary level. He suggested that the United States focus on developing and supporting a comprehensive program that would "capture the high ground of ideas" by linking education and technology with productivity and a positive and healthy business attitude. He summarized the challenges and solutions in a report titled "New Policies for a New Epoch" that he submitted to the vice president in mid-November 1991. In it Warden stated:

> To change our direction, to realize our extraordinary potential, we need an overarching goal that will help us build an integrated, long term program that will be as encompassing as the Containment Strategy of the Cold War and which will allow us to measure our progress. The goal must be one which is easily understandable, one which is politically acceptable to the majority of Americans, one which gives us a compass for the long haul, and one which will help us evaluate a myriad of existing and yet to be proposed sub-programs.[6]

To meet the goal of doubling the American standard of living within a generation he proposed a program based on five pillars—economic prosperity, education, justice, environmental concerns, and national security—and identified measurable objectives for each. In his typical deductive fashion he presented a range of hypotheses and supported them with examples from successful enterprises around the world. Warden emphasized that the paper represented a leadership plan and that the vice president could play an important role in giving the United States "a compass to replace the one that pointed to Cold War north."[7]

Warden's strongest arguments related to national security matters. At the core he insisted that the United States had to recognize the domestic consequences of being the world's only superpower.[8] Future-oriented and optimistic as always, Warden referred to combining research for civilian and military purposes, using the example of developing a bomber that could operate at an altitude of 200,000 feet and at a speed of Mach 10. For both commercial and military reasons, he concluded that the United States had to "stay well in the forefront of world aviation technology" and that Americans could learn from the Japanese how to do business: "Send military academy and ROTC technical graduates through Japanese school, then on to Japan for a year or two. When they return, let them stay in their service, or go to work for an American enterprise. *They will be serving their country equally in either case.*"[9]

The assignment convinced Warden that many of the ideas and principles he had developed, reintroduced, or explored in planning the air campaign also applied in the political environment of the White House. He capitalized on the similarities between business affairs and military operations at the grand strategic level. He felt comfortable in the policy-making environment, which placed a premium on rapid results, and he appreciated the absence of a rigid military structure and hierarchy. In the political setting Warden's persuasive presentation techniques, combined with his big-picture thinking, were appreciated: he was seen as effective, articulate, and vigorous, and his desire to change things was welcomed.

While many people would have used the opportunity of working in the White House to promote themselves, Warden did not. He made useful contacts, but he focused on his job and did not take part in the social gatherings and informal discussions that advance personal career paths. He certainly wanted to become a general officer, but he believed that his work would speak for itself. While some saw this as proof of his integrity, others interpreted it to mean that he simply did not "understand the game."

Warden enjoyed acting as aide-de-camp to the vice president, but after a year in the White House he was offered what seemed an ideal opportunity: Carns suggested placing this leading air power theorist in charge of educating future air force leaders by making him the commandant of ACSC. Rice fully endorsed the nomination, and McPeak reluctantly agreed. Lieutenant General Boyd, who had been Warden's superior at the Air Staff and was now the commanding officer of Air University, did not have to be asked twice. Rice, Carns, and Boyd believed that Warden's ideas about air power merited further exploration, that his vision of strategic bombardment had restored the USAF's sense of purpose, and that he had the necessary leadership qualities to translate the theoretical foundation into a sustainable education program. All three general officers recognized Warden's academic inclinations, his dedication to air power, his ability to look beyond immediate needs, and his willingness to bypass the bureaucracy when necessary. These qualities, combined with his wartime planning achievements, made him the logical choice. Warden was very pleased with the new challenge: he saw it as an excellent opportunity in which he could make a long-term contribution to air power and the air force.[10] The position also had an added advantage: every commandant in the previous three decades had been promoted to brigadier general during his tour at the ACSC.

Ironically, those who held Warden in contempt supported the assignment:

ACSC was an academic institution far away from Washington, and the job did not involve operational command. After all, as one four-star general commented: "How much damage could Warden possibly cause from the backwater of Montgomery?"[11]

Although Quayle had not worked closely with Warden, the vice president seems to have been impressed by his performance. He credited Warden with having finalized the Manufacturing Technology Initiative: a bilateral agreement that enabled American enterprises to become increasingly familiar with Japanese production technology. Quayle also explicitly acknowledged Warden for having introduced senior U.S. government officials to the "Six Sigma" concept of improving quality control, and for pursuing regulatory reforms that in various ways helped defense companies adapt to the post–cold war economic environment.[12] Thus, when Warden left the White House he received a strong endorsement from the vice president that amounted to a recommendation that he be promoted to brigadier general:

> His unique experience in the areas of national security planning, defense industrial base capabilities, exploitation of emerging technologies, and macro-economic planning focused senior members of the Administration on post-Cold War opportunities to strengthen national security by enhancing industrial competitiveness. In this effort, John started with a blank piece of paper, no turnover and no support staff. He engaged his intellect and exceptional vision to conceptualize and articulate a long range national security and economic plan. His analysis outlined specific action in five different areas: conversion of new technology from military to civilian applications, improving quality control at each level of the production process, expanding overseas demand for American exports, removing governmental impediments that detract from industrial competitiveness, and channeling foreign assistance into areas that will stimulate demand for American goods and services.
>
> I cannot overemphasize the contribution of Colonel Warden. He demonstrates the exceptional vision, superior intellectual capacity, tireless work ethic, broad experienced judgment and moral fabric I expect to find only in general officers. Moreover, John understands the complexity associated with policy development at the highest levels of the government, making him an outstanding choice for senior leadership positions in the Air Force.[13]

Commandant at the Air Command and Staff College

Career air force officers typically move through general education at the undergraduate level and then attend three types of programs at the Air University. The company-grade courses at Squadron Officer's School focus largely on the tactical level of war and the duties of an officer. ACSC, attended primarily by majors and major-selects, represents the intermediate level, while studies at the senior service school, the Air War College, focus on grand strategy; here the students are primarily lieutenant colonels.[14]

ACSC had grown out of the Field Officers' Course established in 1921 by the Army Air Service to "prepare senior officers for higher Air Service Command." Its successor, the Air Service Tactical School, renamed the Air Corps Tactical School (ACTS) in 1931, focused on air power theory, strategy, and doctrine, and quickly established itself as the intellectual center within the Air Corps. However, after ACTS became Air University in 1946, its status began to decline. In 1974 the Department of Defense's Committee on Excellence in Education found that ACSC left a great deal to be desired. Lt. Gen. Raymond B. Furlong, the Air University commander from August 1975 to June 1979, and his successor, Lt. Gen. Stanley M. Umstead, who held the position from July 1979 to July 1981, took these conclusions seriously and sought to remedy the problems, but progress was slow.

The lack of any real improvement became evident when the Skelton Committee documented the institution's unimpressive record in 1989, and RAND analyst Carl Builder confirmed Congress's low opinion two years later. Builder had visited ACSC in the spring of 1991 to remind the students of the fundamentals of their profession, only to realize that the midcareer officers had little interest in either education or their service. The only topics that stimulated discussion dealt with career tracks and promotions. He observed that the USAF suffered from intellectual and professional hollowness rooted in a lack of institutional vision and suspected that many of the problems could be "laid at the doorstep of its neglect of air power theory as the basis for its mission or purpose."[15]

In his book *The Icarus Syndrome* Builder concluded that abandoning air power theory to concentrate on means (aircraft, missiles, and bombs) and ends (deterrence theory) had cast the service adrift from the commitments that had pushed it to its apogee in the 1950s.[16] The challenge would be to motivate the air force and its officers to think about the objectives of warfare rather than focus only on the instruments of warfare. Although Builder's book contains many generalizations built on assertions rather than proof and seeks to convince its audience with its catchy metaphors and readable style, his basic premise is valid: the USAF had grown to greatness with an air power theory built on strategic bombardment, but during the cold war had lost the theoretical foundation that had given the profession its meaning.

When Warden arrived at ACSC in the summer of 1992 he inherited a college that could aptly be described as a "sleepy hollow" with very few academic pretensions. Officers chosen to attend ACSC generally considered the year as an interval away from operational command and therefore unproductive beyond having the opportunity to spend more time with their families and to establish contacts for the future.[17] Moreover, many of the faculty members had little or no real interest in academic matters. ACSC's lack of educational relevance was also obvious from the comments of senior leaders who returned as guest speakers: "That seat has my name on it because I slept there" and "The best thing that happened to me is my golf game improved."[18]

Even though the USAF senior leadership was divided about his credentials, and some thought that the assignment relegated him to professional oblivion, Warden resolved to mold the college according to his own criteria. To do so he decided to emphasize the college's raison d'être—to prepare officers for command and staff positions—and its ability to fulfill that mission, and to implement improvements that would turn ACSC into a "world-class educational institution for mid-career officers."[19] He wanted to reinstate the knowledge about and passion for air power that had bonded the staff and students at the ACTS: to reawaken the institution by orienting its curriculum toward military history, air power theory, and air campaign planning at the strategic and operational levels of war. He also wanted to do it fast.

Warden knew full well that this would not be an easy task: his experience over the past twenty-seven years had demonstrated that air force officers were far more at ease with science than with the ambiguities of the humanities. Pilots were trained to put bombs on target, and thought only in terms of the accuracy and destructive power of weapons and of the speed, range, instrumentation, and maneuverability of aircraft. They had little appreciation of history and strategic thought as the foundation for doctrine, planning, and leadership, and in fact little interest in education beyond improving their technical skills.[20] Airmen tended to be action-oriented futurists, obsessed with technology and numbers at the expense of in-depth reflection and subjective analysis.[21] The apparent lack of initiative and vision among many of the faculty members and staff, the anti-intellectual attitude of the students, and the remoteness of Maxwell AFB from the centers of intellectual and political activity presented major impediments. Nevertheless, Warden was determined to raise the professional level of the college and thus help rescue the USAF from its Icarus Syndrome.[22]

SHAPING THE CURRICULUM

Warden's resolve to do things differently from his predecessors became obvious as soon as he arrived. In his obligatory welcome speech to the students' spouses, rather than provide soothing descriptions of Montgomery as a family-friendly environment, he gave his bewildered audience a lecture on planning an air campaign: he thought they would find it useful to know what would be expected of their husbands or wives during the coming year. His pursuit of change also became evident to the faculty during Warden's "welcome briefing": instead of engaging in the usual pleasantries, he arranged a lengthy meeting in which he reviewed each of the existing courses, explained in detail why he believed the school was teaching the wrong subjects, and outlined his vision for the future. He urged the faculty to think in revolutionary terms: the old system had to be broken rather than adjusted. Warden asserted that ACSC could fulfill a necessary role as an institution that organized comprehensive, creative, and future-oriented studies on air power.[23] He revealed that his goal was "to take the school intellectually to the level of ACTS" and that he appreciated its old motto: "We Progress Unhindered by Tradition."[24] He had decided to establish a new regime under which air power theory would serve as the unifying theme and the instructors would participate in developing, presenting, and improving the curriculum.

Most of the faculty members were impressed by his preparedness and his dedication to his new position, but many doubted his ability to effect transformation. Unaware of the high-level support and unofficial mandate that Warden enjoyed, they feared that he would soon be promoted and would depart, leaving only chaos behind. It was not the first time a commandant had expressed grandiose sentiments, and none of the last four had stayed more than a year.

The Air Campaign Course

Although Warden's plans met with considerable skepticism, they were warmly welcomed by a small but determined group of scholars. Within the first few weeks Lt. Col. Larry Weaver, a recent graduate of ACSC who had become a faculty member, took the initiative to turn Warden's vision into reality: he established a "revolutionary committee" and became the "conspirators" Robespierre. Three others joined him: Richard R. Muller, who was referred to as Carnot; Earl Tilford, who was compared to St. Just; and Lt. Col. Albert Mitchum, who retained his old nickname of "Bull."[25] Weaver believed that "The heart of the revolution was the instructor force" and its understanding of "critical thinking."[26] This core of four, also referred to as "the cabal," recruited eight other instructors who were committed to making changes.[27] The group met regularly during the fall of 1992 to develop a new curriculum that would stimulate students and fellow faculty members to think about air power and air campaign planning at the operational level of war within the context of grand strategy.[28]

Warden and his revolutionaries quickly identified the "seminar packages" on which ACSC relied as a key reason why the curriculum was inadequate for higher learning. These packages consisted of a seemingly random set of seminars that had accumulated over the years. Instructors provided students with reading material and direction as best they could on an ad hoc basis, and students would then study the topic independently. In many cases the instructor knew no more about the subject than the students did, and in an entire seminar students might never hear from a genuine expert.[29] Instructors spent more time on administration than on teaching: indeed, the college seemed to take the view that the main task of a faculty member was to participate in social activities.[30] The result was a series of disorganized courses without a unifying theme, but since they had little in the way of expectations or encouragement neither students nor faculty members had complained.

Under Weaver's direction, the dedicated conspirators constructed a new outline, with an unprecedented Air Campaign Course as the center of a new syllabus. The course was designed to include all aspects of air and space power so that students would learn to view military operations from the national, strategic level all the way down to the minutiae of "bombs on target":

> This course is designed to give the officers a better appreciation of the air campaign planning process. It is an interdisciplinary approach that combines academic discipline and operational art. We will provide an organized structure for asking the questions that accompany the creation of successful air campaign plans. The course is divided into four major parts: the air campaign planning process, contextual elements of air campaign planning, operational art, and practical exercises.
>
> The first block on the campaign planning process will examine the theory and application of campaign planning. Block two will discuss the importance of knowing the strengths and weaknesses of yourself and your enemy. The third block will provide an examination of the operational elements of campaign planning. The final block will prepare you for campaign planning and execute a campaign plan.
>
> This course will encourage each officer to think in strategic and operational terms in order to see beyond the tactical issues of combat. . . . This course will meet the following objectives: comprehend the modern day "revolution in warfare"; comprehend the operational art in the aerospace domain; comprehend the synergetic contributions of airpower to theater campaign plans; apply operational art in the aerospace domain; and analyze examples of operational art in all domains.[31]

The accompanying reading list would include classic and contemporary military history, and the college would establish an environment that encouraged challenges to the old axioms of military thought. Students would be expected to read, study, and discuss essential air power thought and doctrine, and would be urged to think of campaign planning in terms of the political and technological dimensions.

While substance was crucial, Warden was equally adamant about approaches to the subject. To build the requisite academic foundation the students would need a broad understanding of air power concepts, a creative and open mind, and an ability to examine problems in depth.[32] Warden noted that there were two ways to think about a problem: the inductive—aggregating many individually insignificant facts and reasoning about what they might mean—and the deductive—first identifying general principles and then finding the necessary details to support them: "In the Air Force, most of our early training involves us with inductive processes. To become good operational artists and strategists, however, we must learn to think deductively."[33] By combining this methodology with the unifying theme of air power theory, Warden planned to present the college with a radically new educational platform.

> We must not start our thinking on war with the tools of war—with the airplanes, tanks, ships and those who crew them. These tools are important and have their place, but they cannot be our starting point, nor can we allow ourselves to see them as the essentials of war. Fighting is not the essence of war, nor even a desirable part of it. The real essence is doing what is necessary to make the enemy accept our objectives as his objectives.[34]

The "revolutionary committee" worked intensively during the fall of 1992 to create the Air Campaign Course, planning to introduce it in the next academic year. Warden, however, found that the group had made such excellent progress by mid-November that he announced to the students before they left for Thanksgiving vacation that they would be offered the optional Air Campaign Course in the second semester. Both faculty and students were dumbfounded at the short timeline. Even Weaver, the strongest supporter, was dubious. Although the new curriculum was taking shape the college lacked qualified teachers; Weaver recalled, "We had a Ferrari curriculum with Model-T drivers."[35] Moreover, the amount of time and effort required seemed unrealistic, because Warden demanded that instructors deliver the old curriculum as well as the new course and had high expectations for the quality of teaching.[36]

LORD OF THE RINGS

Despite warnings of a heavy workload, 103 of the 580 students chose to enroll in the new program.[37] As part of the Air Campaign Course Warden delivered a series of lectures in which he examined the strategic and operational levels of war in generic terms and in the context of the 1991 Gulf War.[38] The emphasis on these two levels represented a departure from earlier practice, or perhaps more accurately a return to a conceptual approach that had been lost after the Second World War. In a matter of weeks, the ACSC sparked a genuine debate about how to apply air power at the operational level of war and how to define military objectives that would meet political objectives through the lens of effects-based operations.

At the heart of the Air Campaign Course Warden offered the Five Rings Model as an analytical tool: it stimulated big-picture thinking and a systematic approach to linking political objectives with concrete target-sets. He did not present it as a solution; he simply suggested that its utility lay in capturing important features in a simplified form. Many believed that at the very least the model permitted a fresh approach to warfighting, and even those who did not find it universally applicable generally agreed that it was a useful way to categorize and prioritize targets and to allocate resources. In many ways the model combined the art and science of planning: operational art meant identifying the appropriate target-sets in light of the strategic objectives, while tactical science revolved around perfecting ways to destroy those targets.

Still, some faculty members complained that as a targeting theory the Five Rings Model rested on questionable logic and took an overly mechanical approach, and that it was difficult to apply against unconventional, ideologically motivated, adaptive, and asymmetric forces. War could not possibly be so predictable and formulaic.[39] Moreover, Warden's theory did not take into account the enemy's plans, intentions, strategies, psychology, and culture—it simply reduced the enemy to a "passive collection of targets." Warden countered that it was essential to start with the overall generic model and then take complexities into account, making the model more sophisticated as one went into details:

> To make the concept of an enemy system useful and understandable, we must make a simplified model. We all use models daily and we all understand that they do not mirror reality. They do, however, give us a comprehensible picture of a complex phenomenon so that we can do something with it. The best models at the strategic level are those that give us the simplest possible big picture. As we need more detail, we expand portions of our model so that we can see finer and finer detail.[40]

In any event, the model was intended to help warfighters understand the enemy, rather than to predict the enemy's actions. For all its possible limitations, the Five Rings Model provided both students and faculty with a framework for analyzing warfare and a view of air power that differed fundamentally from those used at the time by TAC and SAC. Warden did not require students to accept his particular approach; his point was that airmen needed to understand the strategic, operational, and tactical levels of war, and, importantly, that strategy was not merely an extrapolation of tactics, but required an entirely different mindset.

The faculty received highly encouraging feedback on the new curriculum after the first year, although the Air Campaign Course created a schism between the "have" and "have-not" students. Even some of the dedicated students in the first group found it difficult to redirect their studies in the middle of their academic program. The new curriculum also left much room for improvement in organization and implementation, but most students agreed that the content and the methodology represented the right approach to training future air force leaders.[41]

Warden became so influential that the ACSC was referred to not only as the "Air Campaign College," but also as the "John Warden school of air power."[42] His concept was lightheartedly termed "the Five Rings of Death," and, predictably, he became the "Lord of the Rings."[43] The Five Rings constituted the major focus of ACSC's 1993 yearbook, whose title and recurring theme were "Doing time with the Warden." In keeping with this theme, the figure on the cover represented an ACSC student, dressed in the colors of the American flag, bursting out of the constraints of the academic world (a prison camp) and into the operational (free) world. Grasped in his left hand were three lightning bolts representing the land, sea, and air components of the operational campaign; in his right hand was the shield of defense, with the Five Rings engraved on it. The forehead was stamped "ACTS," a tribute to the tradition of air power advocates and the enthusiasm that had characterized Maxwell since the 1920s. No previous yearbook had devoted so much space to the commandant, whom the students had also selected as the man of the year; and never before had air power theory and air campaign planning been the major topics. Since the commandant and the faculty had no input into the design or content of the yearbook, the strong focus on Warden indicates his popularity. Warden probably found the recognition gratifying, but he might also have reflected, somewhat ruefully, that he would have preferred receiving such accolades for the very different type of command involved in running a wing.

Warden and the faculty continuously revised and updated the course plan, and as the class of 1994 arrived Warden was pleased with what the team had achieved. In a letter sent to the incoming students several months earlier he had recommended books that they should read as preparation and suggested that they would benefit from "familiarizing" themselves with using personal computers. He also declared that his goal was to help the first "post Cold War class" become "the world's best winners, commanders, and staff officers":

> You and your class will be the first to have the benefit of a significantly changed program—a program specifically designed to prepare you to cope with a world experiencing accelerating change in every field of endeavor. . . . We have tried to keep the new curriculum from being a series of isolated subjects, so we have integrated it horizontally across

the year. Every phase is related to all the prior phases. . . . You will start
by honing the skills you will use during the year and in your service
thereafter. You will learn how to convert political objectives into executable military objectives. You will become familiar with broad sweeps
of military history. You will learn how to recognize and exploit strategic and operational centers of gravity. You will study a wide range of
joint force employment options. You will learn how to build an air
campaign that uses the air and space power of all the services in the full
spectrum of operations. You will think about ways to end wars—that
is, to win the peace. You will learn how to conceive, develop, and acquire air forces for future campaigns. Through the whole curriculum
you will find many case studies and war games. From this top down
perspective, you will learn the "why" behind the "what" and "how" our
nation uses its military forces.[44]

The class of 1994 was greeted by a complete course that covered the
conceptual and practical issues involved in mastering the art and science of air
warfare. It centered on ten areas: professional skills; war, conflict, and military
missions; military theory; strategic structures; operational structures; campaign
concepts; air campaign; campaign termination; campaign 2000+; and terminal
exercise. Some of these topics were new, while others had merely been revised by
Warden and his acolytes.

Like an inverted pyramid, this new curriculum will begin with large
conceptual issues of politico-military operations and end in practical
case studies. In these case studies, students will apply their knowledge
and practice application of air power to carefully selected case studies
at the operational level . . . Central to this new curriculum is the understanding that campaigning in general, and air campaigning in particular, is not the sole province of the flyer. A successful campaign requires
full participation from virtually every field in the USAF, from public
affairs to the logistician . . . The past division of the curriculum into
discrete segments of study with arbitrary boundaries will be removed
in favor of a yearlong continuum . . . With a single focal point, all
instructors can work through issues of academic preparation and execution. The corporate nature of this new relationship will replace the
former compartmentalization of tasks within divisions and improve
faculty communication.[45]

Warden not only took an active interest in developing and overseeing the
curriculum, but also spent more time lecturing than his predecessors had. When

he took the stage he emphasized interconnections: air power theory provided the unifying theme at the core of an air force officer's profession; the Five Rings Model served as an explanatory tool for categorizing targets and therefore helped the students to think in terms of effects-based operations; and the top-down methodology that started with the end-state and political objectives and ended with bombs on target offered the key to a comprehensive and holistic understanding of air power.[46]

In revising the curriculum Warden also significantly reduced the number of courses that dealt with administrative and managerial matters and eliminated elective classes that did not relate to the central mission of the school. Courses such as "Executive Fitness," "Cleaning out Your In-Box," "Next Assignment: Pentagon," and "Personal Finance"—somewhat embarrassing examples of the caliber of the curriculum prior to 1992—were not offered during Warden's tenure.[47] Moreover, Warden viewed the existing leadership classes as a hodgepodge more relevant to junior officers than to field-grade officers. He believed that students spent too much time learning facts that they could easily look up, that the courses offered no coherent message, and that the curriculum did not distinguish between management and leadership. He therefore changed the "Professional Skill Course" to "Leadership and Command" and instituted a course built around biographies of great military leaders.[48] After all, Warden argued, what better way to learn about the leadership of Gen. George C. Kenney than to examine his use of air power in the Pacific campaign?

Structural Reforms

Although the Air Campaign Course became the quintessential symbol of Warden's new approach, several related efforts to improve the institution had lasting impact. Warden agreed with the thesis that Samuel P. Huntington had formulated two decades earlier in *The Soldier and the State*:[49] professional military education should have two dimensions—wide, liberal education similar to that required for other occupations, and highly specialized training in the expertise of the students' particular profession. Both parts required substantial study of history and the nature of warfare.[50]

BOOK-BASED CURRICULUM

Before Warden's arrival the reading assignments for ACSC students had been unsystematic, consisting largely of excerpts from papers that the leaders of the various seminar packages considered adequate treatments of a topic. The required reading list for the Military History and Doctrine phase of the curriculum had included only three books.[51] Warden believed that airmen needed in-depth indoctrination in their own field of expertise—air power—but needed the broader orientation as well. He therefore introduced a book-based curriculum that required each student to develop a professional reading list: students were exposed to a range of books and encouraged to study in depth those topics that they found particularly appealing or relevant. He insisted that the ACSC purchase books so that students could build their own libraries. Somewhat optimistically, he suggested that each student should have read a hundred books by the time he or she graduated.[52]

Warden took an active role in reviewing the list of books that ACSC would purchase and did not hesitate to express his opinion, but he did not base the list merely on books whose conclusions he supported.[53] For example, he believed that there was no need to teach Clausewitz: all of the worthwhile elements in *On War* had been incorporated into later thought. Still, when Muller, who was in charge of the history program, protested and justified his reasons Warden conceded and the book became part of the reading list.[54] The books Warden recommended ranged from military classics such as Sun Tzu's *The Art of War* to *General Kenney Reports* and science fiction novels such as *Starship Troopers*. He included the latter to encourage imaginative thinking about the next generation of warfare, and because such titles helped to lighten the required reading. He also made it possible for all students in the classes of 1994 and 1995 to keep their own copies of every book on the reading list. Not surprisingly, he was accused of misusing public money, but he responded that the entire book budget was far less than the cost of one hour of training in the F-15.

To supplement lectures by the faculty, ACSC invited guest speakers with world-class reputations in relevant areas to inform and challenge the students, but Warden reduced the total number of speakers because he believed they distracted the students from their studies. In fact, because of the large amount of reading required Warden and his team decided that students should spend far less time in the classroom. This met with opposition from many long-time faculty members, who believed that "seat time" was the best way to measure the quality of education and that students could not be trusted to use unstructured time wisely. Warden and his team brushed aside the latter objection, pointing out that the students at ACSC represented the top 20 percent of majors in the USAF and that the faculty's job was to provide them with the opportunity to learn, not to ride herd on them.

TECHNOLOGY

The high-technology focus for which the ACSC became known in the latter half of the 1990s originated during Warden's tenure. Most who served with Warden recall that his fascination with technology distinguished him from his predecessors. He was convinced that technology was central to effective instruction and that one could "let machines do the dirty work,"[55] thus freeing the faculty from some mundane tasks. Warden gave Maj. Pat Nutz, the instructor who served as chief of educational technology and war-gaming, an unprecedented task: "put together a proposal for five million dollars to infuse technology into the Air University."[56] For a college accustomed to a budget of half a million dollars per year this seemed like sheer lunacy, but it prompted a creative thought process without self-imposed restrictions.

Laptop computers and local area network connections were obvious necessities, and within two weeks Nutz organized working groups to investigate war-games, hyperlinking, hardware and software purchases, and network integration. One team concentrated on hyperlinking the Five Rings Model into a computer system that could tie strategic goals to detailed sorties against a limited set of targets. The model was also integrated into war-gaming programs.

The concept that Nutz and his team developed, "The Air Campaign Planner," carried the recommended price tag, and Lt. Gen. Jay W. Kelley, who had replaced Boyd as the Air University commandant shortly after Warden arrived, greeted the concept with enthusiasm. He told Warden to present it to the vice chief of staff in the hope of obtaining the funding, and thanks to Warden's advocacy Air University received four-and-a-half million dollars to buy the necessary hardware and software, in addition to books for all the students. Shortly thereafter, each student had a personal laptop and personal computers were available throughout the college.

RESEARCH PROGRAMS

After discussions with faculty members Warden had concluded that very few students had adequate research skills, so he devoted considerable time to building a research program. Since the majority of the students would serve in staff positions, where most reports resulted from team efforts and collaboration, he considered it a waste of effort to have hundreds of USAF officers spend a year writing essentially trivial individual papers that were judged primarily on style, format, and number of footnotes. Content should become the central factor, and with this in mind he introduced comprehensive research programs, with Fridays devoted entirely to collaborative and individual research. He resolved to have the students study topics of value to the USAF and other parts of the Department of Defense, thereby linking the school environment with policy and decision makers. To identify appropriate research areas he drew on the network he had established in the intelligence and political communities during the run-up to Desert Storm. Some research groups also worked on classified projects for the air force chief of staff.[57]

Warden stated that research was "deemed an important part of the ACSC curriculum," and thus credit gained for research could "boost an overall grade point average by 10 percent."[58] Some immediately criticized these changes, noting that several projects would doubtless fail, but Warden insisted that it was "better to fail doing something great than to succeed doing something meaning-less."[59] As it happened, during the second year of Warden's tenure the research program raised grade point averages so much that the proportion of Distin-guished Graduates (DGs) increased from the normal 10 percent to almost 40 percent. Since this seemed excessive, the grading was adjusted the next year, returning the proportion of DGs to 10 percent of the student body.[60]

Advocacy

Warden transformed what had been an isolated academic institution into one that drew the notice of the Pentagon, the Department of Defense, and various research communities. He was not only tenacious in promoting his views but was also a superb communicator.[61] The strength of his convictions, his skillful presentations, and his reputation as a critical planner in Desert Storm stimu-lated unusual enthusiasm for air power theory, strategy, and doctrine. Warden also spent considerable time hosting visitors, "ranging from mundane to the Chairman of the Joint Chiefs,"[62] and he made several trips to the Pentagon and to Congress, where he presented the new curriculum to senior officers and con-gressional staffers. He commanded considerable attention among policy mak-ers, and the ACSC seems to have enjoyed an unparalleled level of recognition in these circles.

Warden's ability to make so many changes resulted in no small part from the strong support he received from his superiors at the Air University: first Boyd and then Kelley. In fact, when Kelley arrived at Maxwell he felt that Warden was "bigger than the Air University," because he received so much attention from senior officers. Kelley had been Secretary Rice's director of public affairs and was fully aware of Warden's controversial reputation. Indeed, he had talked at length with General McPeak and Lieutenant General Glosson, who was now the deputy director of plans and operations in the Air Staff, about how to put Warden's talents to the best use. All had agreed that Warden had a tremendous intellect and needed freedom of action to maintain his enthusiasm for air power and continue to generate new ideas, and Kelley was more than content to give him that freedom.

Controversy

Not surprisingly, Warden proved controversial even in his educational role. A detailed examination of his three-year tour reveals that the majority of the in-structors, students, and staff members appreciated his dedication and shared his objectives, but at the same time he aroused considerable resentment with his insistence on sweeping changes. Since he was not a professional educator by trade, but in many ways a "self-made historian," his ideas on curriculum development, group research, and the primacy of technology attracted both supporters and critics.[63] Some valued this dedicated and demanding commandant who wanted to implement radical changes to an institution that "had fallen into sedentary ways,"[64] while the less-motivated instructors simply wanted to finish the year without exerting too much effort. Still, the relationship between Warden and the faculty was complex: no simple dividing line separated his admirers from his detractors, and most found that they supported him on one issue and opposed him on another.

The more cautious faculty members also raised a legitimate concern: they feared that in his haste to initiate reforms Warden might well replace an admittedly imperfect curriculum with an even worse alternative. To avoid such an outcome they recommended studying an identified problem, developing solutions, testing the ideas, analyzing the results, and only then initiating the change,[65] but Warden was unwilling to devote significant time to reviewing and exploring all possible aspects of any given problem.

Warden's strong convictions, combined with his controversial ideas, led to polarized opinions even within the "intellectual community."[66] He had certainly built enthusiasm for air power as a subject and was well versed in strategy and history, but some of the faculty found themselves engaged in heated debates over the validity of his theories, especially with their counterparts at another component of Air University, the School of Advanced Airpower Studies (SAAS). SAAS was universally considered the "jewel in the crown": the students in the one-year program were normally those who had distinguished themselves at the ACSC the previous year, and the faculty consisted entirely of academics, most of whom held doctorates. While serving as commandant Warden published his most famous paper, "The Enemy as a System," which again presented his air power theory and gave examples of how it had been validated in the 1991 air campaign.[67] Many of the SAAS faculty members voiced detailed criticisms of the paper. They argued that Warden lacked academic credentials and could not substantiate his view of what air power could achieve independently from ground and naval forces.[68] In addition, Warden was not popular with all historians: he was not, and had never been, interested in history for its own sake, but in deriving trends and generalizations that would be useful in developing ideas about the present and future. Some of the SAAS faculty also feared that his faith in the ability of strategic bombing to paralyze the enemy leadership would convince the air force to reduce support for other important air power operations, and believed that he sought to make the application of air power into something that it could never be: an exact science.

Warden, in turn, castigated the SAAS faculty for never having formulated an air power theory of their own, or even an air power template that would provide students with a baseline from which they could construct their own interpretations. Until his opponents could propose a better alternative he would not be swayed from his position.[69] The SAAS faculty insisted that all students develop their own ideas, and that this process would be just as important as the product.[70] Still, the SAAS, like Warden, at least encouraged the students to think systematically and creatively.

Some of Warden's personality traits also contributed to an aura of eccentricity. For example, again remembering that at Bitburg he had been criticized for keeping decision making to himself, he now arranged for his weekly staff meetings to be broadcast live throughout the main building so that all could hear the discussions. This radical step triggered protests and did not survive his tenure. It also caused comment that Warden found his office too small for meetings with staff, faculty, and students, and almost immediately turned a nearby briefing room into his workplace. Some thought this an excellent idea, while others considered it odd.[71]

Perhaps most spectacular was an ACSC graduation ceremony held in the civic auditorium in central Montgomery, which suggested that Warden sometimes succumbed to hubris. The ceremony began with a video clip that showed a picture of Alexander the Great, which morphed first into Napoleon, then into Gen. Ulysses S. Grant, and finally into Warden. In fact, Warden had not been informed about the exact form of the presentation, but the audience simply assumed that as commandant he had encouraged it. Many believed that the linkage was reasonable, but others thought it preposterous. Thus, while most people saw Warden as a humble and dedicated public servant, concerned only for the good of the country, the USAF, and ACSC, such incidents aroused suspicion that he had a monumental ego and immense ambitions. Unfortunately, opponents often used these incidents as examples to support their low opinion of Warden. Beyond this, even Warden's supporters thought that he concentrated too much on his own priorities and paid insufficient attention to personnel issues, interpersonal relations, and group dynamics, and as a result failed to forge connections with the full spectrum of senior and junior faculty members.[72]

LEGACY

Warden's successor, Col. John W. Brooks, later recalled that he appreciated much of what Warden had done for ACSC, stating that Warden had served both the Air University and the USAF well simply because he had challenged the institution and the service to think.[73] However, like Colonel Wiseman, who replaced Warden at Decimomannu, and Colonel Cliver, who replaced Warden in Bitburg, Brooks discovered that Warden had left him with many unfinished tasks. For example, the programs to maintain and upgrade the computers, and much of the infrastructure needed to develop the local area network, had not been organized adequately. The ad hoc system that Warden had put into place functioned, but did not follow established procedures and USAF policy.

Brooks acknowledged that the group research projects incorporated elements that would be useful for future general officers, but not all students belonged to that elite group. He concluded that Warden's ambitious focus should give way to smaller individual papers, with more modest aspirations, so that all students could benefit.[74] In addition, although Warden had commendably shifted the focus of the research program from meaningless topic papers toward significant research, Brooks worried that ACSC was becoming "too much like the RAND Corporation."[75] According to Brooks, Warden's method allowed "loafers" to ride the coattails of the harder-working students. In fact, Warden had been well aware of this potential for free riding, but he considered it a problem for the students to solve themselves.[76] Warden often made the point that students were not intellectually lazy or incapable per se, they were simply not challenged.[77]

As for the Air Campaign Course, Brooks believed it had displaced too many leadership courses. The students certainly studied the operational leadership of Hannibal, MacArthur, Manstein, and Kenney far more than they had in previous years, but Brooks reintroduced the central and separate role of leadership courses and reduced the number of hours that Warden had devoted to the Air Campaign Course.

Despite these adjustments much of the Warden transformation survived. Reflecting on his two years as Warden's superior at Air University, General Kelley provided the following assessment:

> Warden is perhaps the single most influential individual in the development of concepts regarding the employment of air power in modern times. He has stimulated thought on the subject and he has led the way in advocating air power as we have seen it employed throughout the 1990s. He is an extraordinarily talented man, but there is also a challenge here. He is a rebel and a renegade, and sometimes he is so convinced that he is right that he has a hard time adjusting to other considerations. The intensity of his thinking and action provides for extraordinary command and leadership challenges for whom ever he has to report. However, he did marvelously at the Air Command and Staff College and he was a very successful commandant.[78]

Kelley thought it admirable that Warden time and again pursued ideas out of conviction, even when he knew he would not benefit personally.[79] Such integrity, Kelley admitted, was rare in the USAF. He gave Warden a very favorable efficiency report, although he had to defend his assessment against those who felt less positively about the colonel.

Warden does not deserve sole credit for the high scholastic standards at the ACSC, but his vision provided a foundation on which concrete progress was built. During Warden's tenure the ACSC, by its own admission, "undertook the most significant change to its educational program since the school's inception. The school transitioned from a lecture-based to a seminar-centered, active environment with an integrated curriculum geared to problem solving across the continuum from peace to war."[80] Warden saw the school receive several official honors, such as the General Muir S. Fairchild Educational Achievement Award, which was given to ACSC in both 1994 and 1995. He had established a framework that enabled ACSC to respond to the academic needs of the students, and set the standard for the years to come.

When Warden left ACSC Lieutenant General Furlong wrote a personal note to him, stating: "You have been the college's first Commandant who was also its intellectual leader . . . You brought vision, personal competence and brilliance to your duties. At this point you turned to your other long suit, military leadership, and transformed this College in a very few years."[81] The changes that Warden and the "revolutionary committee" made in the 1992–1995 timeframe culminated, in many ways, in ACSC's being granted permission to award master's degrees in Military Operational Art and Science a decade later. Many of the changes that Warden initiated in the curriculum remain solidly in place to this day.[82]

Thus, by any credible system of measurement Warden was a successful commandant: he had the vision to recognize the need for change, the ability to make the necessary improvements, and the courage to expose himself to inevitable negative reactions.[83] Weaver recalls that "Warden arrived like a hurricane cleaning out the ramshackle structures of the mind that had been constructed over the previous 40 years. He brought vision. He brought incredible energy. And he brought clear senior level support."[84] Col. T. K. Kearney, who first worked for Warden in the Air Staff and then as the dean of technology and distance learning at ACSC from 1995 to 1998, uses a biblical analogy to describe the post-Warden fate of the college: the story of Joseph tells us that despite his many achievements, eventually there arose a new Pharaoh "who knew not Joseph."[85]

Historian David R. Mets, professor emeritus at Air University's School of Advanced Air and Space Studies, sums up the Warden legacy in the following terms:

> His real-world combat-flying experience, along with his professional studies and purposefulness, made him stand apart from the other commandants in my experience. Most of them were impressive officers, but none took such an active role in lecturing and reforming the curriculum. None of them did as much to attempt to get his charges started on a serious, personal, and lifelong program of the study of war. None of the commanders in my experience did nearly as much to move the

college out of its existing ways and into new studies and procedures—
with both good and bad effects, I suppose.[86]

The best criterion by which to evaluate Warden's impact is not the extent
to which his changes have survived in the ACSC curriculum, but his influence on
the more than eighteen hundred majors who graduated during his tenure, some
of whom have already reached general rank and others of whom will do so in the
future. One thing is certain: unlike their predecessors of the late 1980s, air force
captains or majors today can explain fairly eloquently what air power brings to
warfighting and how air assets can be employed. This improvement reflects well
on the USAF. According to Professor Muller, a member of the ACSC faculty
before, during, and after the Warden era, Warden's contribution to the education
of USAF officers is all-important:

> Most people will remember John Warden for his contribution to air
> power theory, and those are substantial. But to me, his most lasting
> impact was on air force education, with its potential to shape the think-
> ing of generations of officers. For the first time in a long time, curricu-
> lum content, the quality of the faculty, and intellectual rigor were the
> top priorities. Perhaps most importantly, he made certain that ACSC
> focused on the business at hand—educating people about air power at
> the operational level of war. It was not perfect. In the years after War-
> den, the curriculum continued to develop, and the overall quality of
> the program improved tremendously. Yet, it was Warden who started
> the school down that path. Those were exciting times and it was a
> privilege to be part of it.[87]

12

A FAREWELL TO ARMS

Given Warden's contributions to the air campaign plan for Desert Storm and to the development of modern air power thought, why did he never become a general officer? His experience illustrates that advancement in the military world depends on many factors other than insight and originality of thought.

Promotion Boards

Once a year the secretary of the air force appoints a board of general officers representing different positions and branches within the service to review the records of eligible colonels and select those who will be promoted. The members meet behind closed doors for a week to study the candidates' records, and then give each colonel a score from one to ten. The rule in the military services is "up or out"; the criteria for promotion are clearly defined and the board's deliberations are not made public.

Having proved himself during the planning for Desert Storm, Warden had his best chance when the Brigadier General Promotion Board of 1992 met at Andrews AFB on November 4–10. The board was chaired by Gen. Ronald W. Yates, commander of Air Force Mobility Command (AFMC). The other fifteen members were Lt. Gen. Charles G. Boyd, designated deputy commander of European Command; Lt. Gen. Alexander M. Sloan, surgeon general of the air force; Lt. Gen. Gary H. Mears, director of logistics on the Joint Staff; Lt. Gen. Buster C. Glosson, deputy chief of staff for plans and operations, Headquarters, USAF; Lt. Gen. John E. Jackson, commander, Fifteenth Air Force, AFMC; Lt. Gen. Arlen D. Jameson, commander, Twentieth Air Force, Air Combat Command; Lt. Gen. Howell M. Estes III, deputy commander in chief, United Nations Command Korea; Lt. Gen. Jay W. Kelley, commander of Air University; Maj. Gen. David C. Morehouse, air force judge advocate general; Maj. Gen. Eugene E.

Habiger, vice commander, Air Training Command; Maj. Gen. Donald J. Harlin, air force chief of chaplains; Maj. Gen. Robert E. Linhard, director of plans and policy, U.S. Strategic Command; Maj. Gen. Carl E. Franklin, deputy chief of staff, plans and programs, USAFE; Brig. Gen. Ray F. Garman, military assistant to command surgeon, AFMC; and Brig. Gen. Marcelite J. Harris, vice commander, Oklahoma City Air Logistics Center.[1] Boyd, Estes, Glosson, and Kelley knew Warden well; the others knew him only from reports and rumors.

Before the board met it was already evident that Warden had several strong backers. Secretary Rice had made it clear that Warden should be promoted: in his letter of guidance to the board he stated that there should be room for intellectual leaders among general officers, and although Warden's name was not mentioned explicitly many board members knew that Rice thought very highly of Warden. Rice had also sent the board a signal by naming Warden as ACSC commandant: the assignment was considered a brigadier general slot because no ACSC commandant had retired in the rank of colonel since 1959. In addition, Warden had received personal endorsements from Vice President Quayle and from the air force vice chief of staff, General Carns. The assistant vice chief of staff, Lieutenant General McInerney, also spoke highly of Warden.[2]

However, several factors worked against him. Many defined Warden by his unsuccessful tenure at Bitburg, and although such a perception did not automatically preclude promotion it substantially reduced his chances. Moreover, the efficiency reports that General Adams and Lieutenant General Nelson wrote about his last assignment in the Pentagon did not endorse promotion. Beyond this, the "zone" for promotion normally falls between an officer's twenty-second and twenty-fifth year of service, and Warden was in his twenty-seventh. Finally, it was common knowledge among the fighter pilots that Generals Horner and Russ did not believe that Warden deserved promotion. All of these negative points could have been overcome if the chief of staff had endorsed Warden as his top candidate. Dugan might have done so; McPeak did not.[3]

During the actual voting Warden received an unusual combination of very high and very low scores, but when the votes were tallied he was not among the small and distinguished group recommended for promotion. As the rules allowed, one member of the board requested that they reconsider Warden's case. He expounded on Warden's contributions to the 1991 air campaign and to the development of a coherent and unified air power theory. He maintained that Warden had managed to introduce a new way of using air power that had possibly saved thousands of lives, and had done so even though some senior leaders in the air force had opposed his involvement altogether. Besides, the officer argued, he was about to prove himself as a transformational leader at ACSC. The air force needed such vision and courage, and the general believed Warden had the right qualities to help in shaping the USAF to deal with the challenges of a new world order.[4]

Another officer responded that there was "no way a failed wing commander should make it on the basis of being a good theorist." He emphasized that the Bitburg experience could not be swept under the carpet, that Warden was not a team player, and that he tended to bypass the chain of command whenever he chose. Yet another critic warned that the USAF could "pick up his broken glass as a colonel, but not as a general officer": if he created so many ripples in the USAF as a colonel, they had to think twice about the waves he could cause as a general. Besides, it was suggested, the services had been directed to "think joint" and promoting a man known for his statements about what air power could achieve on its own would hinder close cooperation with the army. The debate grew heated and personal, as pros and cons on Warden were exchanged.

After an hour of discussion General Yates called for a rescore. Again, several gave Warden extremely high marks while others gave him very low marks, and again the composite ranking did not suffice for promotion. The consensus among the "neutral" members seems to have been straightforward: there were plenty of qualified officers, so why place your bets on one who was so controversial? Most members of the board later agreed that the amount of personal attention given to Warden's case was unique, that the range of scores was extraordinary, and that Warden aroused admiration and loathing in roughly equal measures of intensity. One board member recalled that there was a "determined effort to prevent Warden from getting promoted."

When Warden was informed of the outcome he was surprised and obviously disappointed, but he thought he still had a reasonable chance the following year.[5] However, the controversy did not lessen over time. At the next promotion board in September 1993 he was once again the topic of intense debate, but the end result was the same.[6] The details of the selection processes will never be publicly known, but three general officers who did not serve on either board provide some insight as to why Warden was denied promotion.

> I should not pick on John [Warden] because I really do not know, but it is just the way that I received briefings . . . I just know of him from the fighter pilots . . . They had a feeling that he was from academia. They had a feeling that he sat in an ivory tower and thought about all these grand and glorious things, but when it got down to fighting and dropping bombs and shooting people, that he just did not understand. That is the impression that you get from the fighter pilots; so when everybody says he is a "great strategist," they say "Oh, yeah, BS." . . . He probably had something to contribute, but according to the rank

and file, he was a long way from a war fighter! See, Warden is considered—and I do not like to run people down—by the tactical community as a failure, not as a hero . . . It is because he—and failure may be too strong of a term—is not considered to have passed all the tests. He had two or three problems and could not hack it operationally and now he is trying to tell us how to do this . . . that is the kind of feeling that is prevalent in the tactical community . . . The difference between the conceptual individual and the warrior aviator is that you sometimes take what the conceptual guy says and fight the war that way. I am not saying that the conceptual individual is always wrong. He is very valuable. He comes up with a lot of good ideas. It is just that all his ideas are not good or practical. The operator in the theater is a more pragmatic individual . . . It is just that all some people do is sit and theorize.[7]

—Gen. (ret.) Robert D. Russ, December 9, 1991

I gave him some initial tasking, but he was intent on building what I believed at the time to be a bigger campaign than I was willing to go with. As it grew and as the circumstances changed then I became more of a supporter of what he had done. So you could say that he was a visionary or he was just hard headed, but he believed this was the golden opportunity to show what air power can really do and if you read his book you clearly understand. So, I felt my job was to fly top cover for him but to keep him corralled so that he did not get way out in front of the process because what we really had was an Air Force staff office doing operators business for a joint organization and I expressed great nervousness about that from the very beginning and I did not want them out on the street beating their chest about how great air power is and how we could bring the guys to their knees if they could just leave us alone and we did not need those other services. It was not the time for us to make that speech.[8]

—Gen. Jimmie V. Adams, February 3, 1992

John has a fatal professional flaw, and his fatal flaw is that he does what he thinks needs to be done, regardless of what other people that he works for think; so he is, in the vernacular, a wild mustang most of the time, with absolute good intentions. I mean, John Warden is convinced when he does something that is the right thing to do, and I think he is convinced in his own mind that he doesn't need, in making this decision, to bring the boss into the loop . . . There were numerous confrontations between Adams and Warden because of this modus operandi.

What typically would happen was that Adams would find out that something had happened and that Warden had caused it to happen, and he wasn't in the loop at all. That is always upsetting to the boss when that happens. I talked to John I know at least 20 times, and my approach to him was, "Why in the hell do you keep doing this? If you have got a good idea, you can sell the idea to Adams. He is a warfighting guy. He understands how to employ airpower in combat. Why in the hell don't you?" "Well, I didn't think he needed to know it at this point." I said, "John, you are destroying your credibility with Adams, and you don't need to do that. You can have your cake and eat it, too"; but I never could convince him that he needed to sit down with General Adams and say, "Hey, Boss, this is what I think we ought to do," and sell Adams. He was much more comfortable with doing whatever he thought was right and bearing the punishment, verbal albeit, that he received every time when he got the cart before the horse. . . .

[Warden] has spent many hours thinking through, to a much greater extent than most of the people for whom he works, these problems. In my mind he was convinced that he had the answer. He knew what needed to be done, and he was impatient with the process of getting the people for whom he worked to that same conclusion. Time was of the essence . . . People would not have confidence that John would stay on their wing. You are going to look out and think your wing man is protecting you, and John has gone to do something else, which he is absolutely convinced is truth, and he is following through. He is not going to be deterred by the incidentals of rank or position or the need for a consensus building or what have you.[9]

—Lt. Gen. (ret.) Charles A. May Jr., August 21, 1992

One officer who served on the 1992 board stated that Warden's retiring as a colonel after making such a substantial contribution to Desert Storm "suggests the marginal status of air power theorists in the contemporary Air Force," while another recalled that "the Air Force has low tolerance for outside-the-box thinkers—too many oxen gored and egos bruised." In the eyes of the tactical community Warden was not a warfighter and a leader of men, but an air power devotee, and they saw this as counterproductive in creating a close relationship with the other services. Perhaps worst of all, he was considered an arrogant loner who circumvented the chain of command if he believed it was in the service's best interest, and this called the hierarchy itself into question. One three-star general noted that the air force as an institution "did not want to acknowledge that John Warden had as big an influence as he did on the Desert Storm air campaign specifically and air power in general—promotion to brigadier general would have been acknowledgement of his contribution."

Retirement: May the Force Be with You

When Warden's pending retirement became known he received numerous private letters congratulating him on his achievements and wishing him well for the future. The most important, in his view, came from Schwarzkopf:

> I have just learned of your retirement from the United States Air Force on June 30th. I could not let this occasion pass without thanking you for your strategic vision and the superb contribution you have made to the defense of our nation. I will always remember our first meeting in Tampa in early August, where together we mapped out the strategic concept that ultimately led to our country's great victory in Desert Storm.[10]

Warden also received warm praise from Charles Allen, the CIA's national intelligence officer for warning, with whom he had worked closely during the planning and execution of Desert Storm.

> I keenly remember those difficult days in early August 1990, when Maj. Gen. Alexander and you arrived to brief senior CIA officials on "INSTANT THUNDER." I remember how galvanized I was by your "centers-of-gravity" concept for "taking down" Saddam Hussein's regime. In the following months, I came to know you and your extraordinarily able colleagues at CHECKMATE and was privileged to be able to provide targeting and other intelligence support to you and your staff throughout DESERT SHIELD/DESERT STORM. At the time, I remember that many intelligence analysts were skeptical about the efficacy of air power in shutting down not only the Baghdad regime but also in immobilizing the forces deployed in the Kuwaiti Theater of Operations. I never had any doubts! By 10 February, my Staff and I had decided the war was essentially over, that Saddam's command-and-control system had been neutralized, and that his forces in the KTO had been immobilized. We even put that in writing. Asserting that air power, in essence, had won the war by that date was a view not well received within the Intelligence Community.[11]

As Warden's retirement date approached his vice commandant, Col. Ronald A. Winter, who had previously worked for Warden in the Strategy Division in the Air Staff, decided to organize a memorable ending to what he believed had been "an outstanding career."[12] The ceremony, held at the Wright Flyer monument at Maxwell AFB, was more elaborate than that for most generals. Winter, in conjunction with Lieutenant General Kelley and the ACSC protocol officer, Brenda King, arranged for the visits of several distinguished guests, from high-level military officers to the local mayor. A large tent offered shade and refreshments; a string quartet provided background music during the opening proceedings; and a USAF band played the blues before and after the speeches.[13]

In a notable sign of support, Gen. Ronald R. Fogleman, who had succeeded McPeak as chief of staff in October 1994, "went out of his way to travel to Maxwell" to attend the ceremony.[14] It was rare for the chief to preside in person at a colonel's retirement, especially so far away from the capital, but Fogleman believed that "the USAF had made a mistake by not promoting Warden, and he hoped that by attending he would send a signal to the younger officers that the USAF encouraged officers to think outside the box."[15] Fogleman had a strong interest in history and doctrine, and he stated at the ceremony that Warden had contributed substantially not only to the 1991 air campaign, but also to the quest to improve the USAF as a military service. In his opinion, Warden had introduced air power to a new era and the air force owed him "a very great debt."[16] Maj. Gen. (ret.) Perry Smith drove to Montgomery from Augusta, Georgia, for the specific purpose of honoring Warden, whom he considered the "most important airman of his generation."[17]

Characteristically, Warden's speech at the retirement ceremony broke with tradition. It was natural for Warden to devote his final statement as an active duty air force officer to the subject that had consumed most of his life, and about which he felt so passionately: thus, instead of simply thanking all those present, he speculated on the future of air power, tracing its development from ACTS to the unprecedented capability of the current USAF. As a perspective on the war on which his own ideas had left their mark he also delivered a recitation from memory of Byron's 1815 poem, "The Destruction of Sennacherib":[18]

> *The Assyrian came down like the wolf on the fold,*
> *And his cohorts were gleaming in purple and gold;*
> *And the sheen of their spears was like stars on the sea,*
> *When the blue wave rolls nightly on deep Galilee.*
>
> *Like the leaves of the forest when Summer is green,*
> *That host with their banners at sunset were seen;*
> *Like the leaves of the forest when Autumn hath blown,*
> *That host on the morrow lay withered and strown.*

For the Angel of Death spread his wings on the blast,
And breathed in the face of the foe as he passed;
And the eyes of the sleepers waxed deadly and chill,
And their hearts but once heaved, and for ever grew still!

And there lay the steed with his nostril all wide,
But through it there rolled not the breath of his pride;
And the foam of his gasping lay white on the turf,
And cold as the spray of the rock-beating surf.

And there lay the rider distorted and pale,
With the dew on his brow, and the rust on his mail:
And the tents were all silent, the banners alone,
The lances unlifted, the trumpet unblown.

And the widows of Ashur are loud in their wail,
And the idols are broke in the temple of Baal;
And the might of the Gentile, unsmote by the sword,
Hath melted like snow in the glance of the Lord![19]

Warden noted that Byron's vision captured many aspects of the recent Gulf War, but that after Desert Storm "the widows of Baghdad were not loud in their wail" because precision bombing had made it possible to destroy the power of the host without killing its people. Nor were "the sacred icons all broken in the mosques of Balad," because the United States had not gone to war against the religion of the Iraqi people.[20] Moving from Byron to the future Warden ended his speech with the famous Star Wars quotation: "May the Force Be with You."[21] With that he left the stage.

Perspectives:
THE INTELLECTUAL WARRIOR

As the preceding chapters have shown, those who served with Warden hold opinions that cover the full spectrum from uncritical praise to blanket condemnation. Whatever his strengths, weaknesses, and idiosyncrasies, the common denominator is that Warden broke step: he broke step intellectually with existing doctrine and practice regarding the use of air power and he broke rank in his various attempts to implement his ideas. He had a rare ability to identify shortcomings—whether in doctrine, practice, or educational processes—and the equally rare courage to make every effort to remedy them, even at cost to himself. In the process he served as a catalyst for change and played a significant role in reviving the lost art of applying air power strategically with conventional means.

At a time when the air force seemed content to grant the army preeminence in warfighting he advanced a coherent theory for the employment of air forces in support of national objectives—one that accorded the air force equality with the other services. When the traditional approaches of the Joint Staff, the CENTCOM staff, and TAC offered only defensive responses to Iraq's invasion of Kuwait, he circumvented the entrenched bureaucracy to provide Coalition forces with a strategic and offensive plan to overcome the enemy. When the labyrinthine national intelligence process failed to deliver timely information to the planners and combatants in the field, he turned his Air Staff directorate into the key source of timely targeting data for the deployed forces. And when the U.S. Congress criticized the professional education received by air force officers, he instituted a curriculum at the ACSC that challenged the students to explore the intellectual foundations of their service and regain their sense of mission.

The Anatomy of a Maverick
Only a man with particular personality traits could have developed Warden's theories about air power and the conduct of war. While categorizing individuals

is both difficult and often overly simplistic, the Myers-Briggs Type Indicator (MBTI) matrix shows Warden to be Introvert, Intuitive, Thinking, and Judging (INTJ),[1] and indeed his character and actions conform to this profile. According to the generic description:

> People with INTJ preferences have a clear vision of future possibilities and the organization and drive to implement their ideas. They love complex challenges and readily synthesize complicated theoretical and abstract matters. They create a general structure and devise strategies to achieve their goals. INTJs value knowledge highly and expect competence of themselves and others. They especially abhor confusion, mess and inefficiency. INTJs see things from a global perspective and quickly relate new information to overall patterns. They further trust the validity of their insights regardless of established authority or popular opinion. Dull routine smothers their creativity. INTJs use their intuition primarily internally, where they develop complex structures and pictures of the future.[2]

Those who are "introverted and intuitive" are the most intellectually independent of the MBTI's sixteen types; "they have a theory to explain everything," they prefer innovative solutions to conventional wisdom, they are dispassionate judges, and they project an aura of "definiteness" and "self-confidence." In pursuing their objectives INTJs may show "disregard for authority," as they quickly lose respect for anyone—including superiors—whom they consider inefficient or slow to grasp new ideas. Moreover, they do not disguise their opinions: they are often "critical of those who do not see their vision quickly; [becoming] single-minded and unyielding in pursuing it." Furthermore, they take it upon themselves to implement critical decisions without consultation. They also have a gift for seizing opportunities that others might not even notice, but they often overlook details or facts that do not apply to their intuitive patterns, and may fail to offer sufficient encouragement to others. Consequently their strengths (intellectual contributions and forceful planning) are undermined by their weaknesses (perceived arrogance and apparent lack of patience). Indeed, personal relationships are often regarded as their weak spot because they do not readily grasp social rituals.[3]

The air force in which Warden served could scarcely have been a less nurturing environment for a man with these characteristics. Carl Jung once stated that "the world in general, particularly America, is extroverted as hell, the introvert has no place, because he does not know that he beholds the world from within."[4] The fighter pilot community represents an extreme: an extrovert group within an extrovert profession in an extrovert country. It was not Warden's ideas per se that stirred up opposition, but the way he put them into practice. He demanded, and often triggered, change, and change disorients individuals and organizations. Military organizations, even more than most bureaucracies, resist reform, in part because the cohesive officer corps often consists of conservative, like-minded individuals, and in part simply because the military recognizes the reality that until change is fully assimilated it causes inefficiency.

A House Divided

Warden's strengths were his Achilles' heel: the qualities that made him successful as a theorist and strategist were the same ones that made him a difficult leader, colleague, and subordinate. As a personality Warden was fascinating, admirable, but in many ways exasperating, and it is understandable that people have strong and radically different reactions to him. Warden's active duty in the USAF ended on June 30, 1995, but the controversy that had surrounded him throughout much of his career remains. More than a decade after Warden's retirement the very mention of his name still elicits both warm affection and cold contempt inside and outside the USAF.

Several books about the Gulf War in general and the air campaign in particular have praised his involvement. Foremost among these was *Heart of the Storm*, a behind-the-scenes account written by Air Force Col. Richard T. Reynolds and published in 1995 by the Air University Press. This book, based on more than four thousand pages of interviews with key players, revealed that Warden had developed his innovative and daring plan for the air campaign despite serious opposition from the tactical community. It also depicted several air force general officers as hostile to Warden and obstructionist in their efforts to oppose him.

Lieutenant General Kelley, the commandant of Air University and therefore responsible for Air University Press, faced a dilemma: should he publish what was essentially a critique of the air force's ability to plan and an outright condemnation of many leaders at TAC? He sent the manuscript to all the players mentioned in Reynolds's book; the response was divided. General Russ commented, "You can imagine how disappointed I was when I read the manuscript, and I read it three times. . . . I sincerely believe that this effort will add little, if any, honest understanding of what occurred in the development of the campaign plan."[5] Lieutenant General Glosson concluded that "this document has no place in the annals of Air Force history."[6] General Adams and Major General Henry thought TAC was unfairly treated and General Horner agreed.[7] However, most reviewers praised the book and Kelley decided in favor of publication, although he acknowledged his reservations:

When I first read Heart of the Storm, I was—and remain—deeply concerned about the way people are characterized by the author. I worry that there was a preconceived notion about who really planned and built the air campaign. So, I wrote many of the principal people in Heart of the Storm, sent them a copy of the manuscript, and asked their opinions. That correspondence is filed with the documentation in the Air Force Historical Research Agency. I must tell you that most of them said there were inaccuracies, words and events taken out of context, a definite bias in favor of Col John Warden and his team, and undocumented flourishing / spicing up in the style of Tom Clancy. While I respect these concerns, I did read the interviews, and I did cross-check the work.[8]

General Fogleman made certain that both Warden's *The Air Campaign* and Reynolds's *Heart of the Storm* were included on the chief of staff's professional reading list for officers. The latter became an immediate best-seller for a book published by a military press, and provoked fierce debate about Warden's role in Desert Storm. It also became the primary record to which researchers turned for insight into the genesis of the strategic air campaign plan, and the principal source used by award-winning author David Halberstam when he dealt with the subject in his book *War in a Time of Peace*, published in 2001:

> If one of the newsmagazines had wanted to run on its cover the photograph of the man who had played the most critical role in achieving victory, it might well have chosen Warden instead of Powell or Schwarzkopf . . . He was considered by some military experts to be an important figure, emblematic not just in the air force but across the board among a younger generation of officers eager to adjust military thinking, planning, and structure to the uses of the new weaponry. The principal opponents of Warden's radical ideas turned out to be not, as one might expect, army men or civilian leaders, but senior officers in his own branch of service, especially the three- and four-star officers who dominated much of air force strategy and technology and came from the Tactical Air Command (TAC). They had a much more conventional view of the order of battle and believed airpower was there to support the army on the ground and interdict enemy forces. They despised Warden and his ideas, a hostility that never lessened.[9]

While he praised Warden for his pivotal contribution to the air campaign, Halberstam also portrayed TAC as an incompetent institution, captive of the U.S. Army and unable to think holistically about air power strategy.[10]

GENERAL CREECH STRIKES BACK

Such viewpoints, especially when presented to a large public by a well-known author, only increased TAC's hostility. Many air force officers saw Warden and his ideas as criticism of everything they stood for. The aircraft and weapon systems developed and used by TAC had performed superbly in Desert Storm, and TAC's leaders believed that the postwar analyses should have portrayed the conflict as TAC's finest hour. Instead, they felt, Warden and his conceptual thinking had usurped their place in the sun, and they resented him accordingly.

Gen. Wilbur L. Creech, the commander of TAC from 1978 to 1984 and widely acknowledged as one of the most influential airmen in the recent history of the USAF, took issue with what he characterized as "myths which emerged from the Gulf War success."[11] Creech, who had mentored an entire generation of air force leaders and stayed in contact with serving general officers long after his own retirement, vehemently denied that Warden had played a major role in the success of the air campaign: he claimed that all Warden did was answer Schwarzkopf's call "to do some targeting in the aftermath of the Iraqi invasion."[12] Creech also challenged the implication that TAC did not know how to apply strategic air power.[13] Eighteen years after his own retirement, Creech wrote to senior leaders in all the military services, encouraging a "counter-battery fire" to "set the record straight."[14]

If Warden's ideas on strategic air power represented a "revolution," Creech sought revisionism through a "counter-revolution." In the process, several high-ranking USAF officers attempted to demean Warden's contribution by stifling debate and restricting the distribution of books, papers, presentations, and other information concerning Warden's theories and actions. Warden, who had been asked to speak at the Air University every year since he retired, was suddenly no longer invited. Gen. John P. Jumper, the chief of staff from October 2001 to November 2005, made sure that Creech's own book, *The Five Pillars of TQM*, was placed on the chief's reading list, while *Heart of the Storm* and *The Air Campaign* were removed.[15] On several occasions both Creech and Jumper asserted that Warden's role in developing the 1991 air campaign had been exaggerated and that he had received far more attention and credit than he deserved.

Warden's Legacy: Breaking Step

It is difficult to assess one man's influence on strategic thought, but there is more than circumstantial evidence that Warden strongly influenced the air force. The *Gulf War Air Power Survey*, which remains the most thorough research on the Desert Storm air campaign, documents how Warden managed to define the debate on the military strategy for 1991 through his presentations to Generals Powell and Schwarzkopf. The U.S. Air Force History Office, after extensive research, concludes that Warden introduced a new approach for the conduct of war: an air- and leadership-centric paradigm diametrically opposed to the AirLand Battle doctrine that relegated air power to a supporting role.[16]

Although best known for his advocacy of strategic air power, Warden—through intellect, tenacity, connections, and persistence—set up a multidisciplinary, multiservice intra- and intergovernmental organization that provided key answers and options to the in-theater cell charged with the planning and execution of the air campaign. Warden established an umbilical cord between the Black Hole and Checkmate, and this reach-back agency made three crucial contributions to helping the deployed planners complete the air campaign plan and put it into effect. First, from late August to mid-October, when the Black Hole was under great pressure to produce an executable ATO but lacked the necessary resources to do so, Warden's team provided data and ideas for fine-tuning and improving Phase I, the strategic air campaign plan. The plan that Powell and Schwarzkopf declared ready for execution on September 13, and that the National Command Authority approved on October 11, was Instant Thunder revised. Second, from mid-October 1990 to mid-January 1991, Checkmate took the lead in developing the conceptual underpinnings for Phases II and III. Warden's team provided a range of analyses that included destruction rates, ammunition consumption, and possible aircraft losses. The air planners in theater turned the data from Checkmate into a functional plan and presented it to Schwarzkopf, who in November 1990 stated that he was immensely impressed with the overall coherence of the air effort and decided to delay the ground offensive until air power had ensured 50 percent attrition of the Iraqi tanks, artillery, and armored personnel carriers. Third, Checkmate kept the senior political and military leadership in Washington abreast of the air campaign and the potential offered by air power. Warden briefed Secretary of Defense Richard Cheney in person three times and Checkmate provided Cheney with reports throughout the war. The expertise accumulated by Warden and his planning cell led senior political and military leaders to view Checkmate as the natural source of the information they needed about the war effort.[17]

None of this means that Warden single-handedly won the war—a claim that neither he nor his supporters ever made or even suggested. Neither does it mean that the war was planned in Washington, DC. All operational and tactical decisions were made in theater, under the guidance of Schwarzkopf and Horner. Although the meeting between Horner and Warden on August 20 represented a clash of views, their radically differing perspectives, when brought together, created synergy that produced a better air campaign plan than either man alone would have formulated. Glosson and Deptula then turned many of Warden's ideas into reality. Warden significantly influenced the planning process, but once the air campaign actually began his input became less important because of the influx of information from other organizations and agencies, including CENTCOM itself.

Yet Warden's contribution to air power thinking extends far beyond any specific conflict. His statements about air superiority and his subsequent development of the Five Rings Model to illustrate an air campaign represented critical steps in the evolution of understanding and thinking about the purpose and potential of air power. When Warden joined the air force, all military thinking other than the Single Integrated Operational Plan focused almost exclusively on Western Europe and large-scale conventional war with Warsaw Pact forces. The overwhelming numbers and close proximity of the enemy eliminated the luxury of planning to conduct defense in depth, and thus air power seemed limited to forward commitment in support of the ground forces. While the dominant AirLand battle doctrine, largely accepted by air force and army alike, reflected and codified this view of air power, that commitment, like the Fulda Gap scenario itself, was unique in time and place. Warden offered a much broader perspective on how air power could serve the nation's interests. By linking specific categories of targets to stresses in the enemy system as a whole, and by daring to suggest that air power be used for offense rather than merely defense, he created the framework on which others could build. Most important, he had the moral courage to insist that his ideas be heard and considered.

Fundamentally, in the context of air power Warden broke the momentum of the Fulda Gap mentality. He created the space and the intellectual sanctuary in which the potential of air power could be creatively considered, and this, in turn, contributed to its effective use. The most immediate result may have been fewer casualties in Operation Desert Storm. The longer-term result seems to have been the subsequent emergence and acceptance of Warden's main ideas, specifically his belief in what is now known as effects-based operations—a central tenet of today's joint doctrine.

Through Warden, the USAF regained its own unifying theory for strategic operations, a regeneration that began in the mid 1980s and manifested itself in Desert Storm and the decade that followed. According to Edward Luttwak:

> It would be a foolish exaggeration to say that John Warden found the U.S. Air Force tactical and left it strategic. An entire strategic culture was in place long before he arrived, and there was immense strategic capability—but it was all nuclear, so much so that the non-nuclear was automatically "tactical," even though the wings of Tactical Air Command still had a large inventory of nuclear weapons. What no one can deny is that Warden revived the lost art of strategically intelligent targeting, that had matured through painful trial and error during the Second World War only to be suddenly abandoned in 1945 when the

advent of nuclear weapons made it seem entirely unnecessary. The introduction of precision weapons decades later in increasingly post-nuclear conditions was only the necessary condition of the revival. The sufficient condition was Warden's systematic thought on how to use them—not to destroy bridges, etc., but to win wars.[18]

WARDEN'S AIR POWER THEORY: SYSTEMIC PARALYSIS

In his theoretical writings Warden identified ten key findings for the use of air power: the importance of strategic attack and the fragility of states at the strategic level of war; the fatal consequences of losing strategic air superiority; the overwhelming effects of parallel warfare; the value of precision weapons; the fragility of surface forces at the operational level of war; the fatal consequences of losing operational air superiority; the redefinition of mass and surprise by stealth and precision; the viability of air occupation; the dominance of air power; and the importance of information at the strategic and operational levels of war. Under the umbrella of those findings, the term "systemic paralysis" probably best summarizes the goals espoused by Warden's air power theory. His work quintessentially deals with ends, ways, and means: air strategists must appreciate the political objectives sought by military action, rather than view that action as an end in itself (ends); they should use the Five Rings system to determine the best military strategy to induce or force the enemy to acquiesce in those political objectives (ways); and they should identify which target-sets to subject to parallel attacks with precision-guided munitions (means).

The theory rests on three primary tenets. First, the strategic approach to a challenge differs distinctly from the tactical approach. A true strategist must appreciate the general nature and specific content of national political objectives, since these identify the behavioral changes expected of the enemy leadership and suggest the level of paralysis needed to produce the changes. Thus, a strategist should examine war-termination criteria and the desired end state before thinking about aircraft, tanks, ships, and weapon systems. To Warden, strategic thinking entails finding leverage points—centers of gravity—to manipulate the leadership or nation directly rather than through forces in the field.

Second, with the strategic picture in mind, the strategist must determine how to achieve the desired effects. Strategic paralysis implies temporarily freezing the enemy at the strategic level of war; that is, making the enemy's actions and decisions irrelevant to the outcome of the conflict. In strong contrast to previous military thinking, which saw victory as resulting from either annihilation or attrition of fielded forces, strategic paralysis calls for attacks on the national-level targets directly connected to the enemy's ability to follow its chosen course of action; the theory is only secondarily concerned with the enemy's warfighting efforts or capability. This approach, characterized by producing effects as opposed to destruction, by economical use of assets, and even by using nonlethal means, holds promise for changing or blocking the enemy's behavior at a relatively low cost to both sides. Given the objective of strategic paralysis, it is paramount to view the enemy as a system, and Warden believed that his Five Rings Model applies at the strategic, operational, and tactical levels of war. Leaving aside the specifics of where different targets fit into the model, the theory maintains that planners need to define centers of gravity within the enemy system, and that only rigorous categorization can produce understanding of the interrelationships among different components and thus of the systemic strengths and weaknesses on both sides of a conflict.

Finally, to create systemic paralysis the attacker must operate quickly and decisively over a range of target-sets nearly simultaneously: success depends on hitting the targets at a rate that precludes competent enemy reaction because of the ensuing paralysis. An enemy regime attacked with high intensity from the opening moments of war will find itself shocked, disoriented, and unable to act. In Warden's view, precision represents a crucial capability to enhance the effectiveness of such parallel attacks, and the ability to hit the designated targets with near certainty distinguishes current operations from the pre-Vietnam era.

In retrospect, Operation Desert Storm was unique in the sense that the fighting unfolded without much of the fog, friction, and uncertainty that had marked all previous major wars. The strategic air campaign prevented the Iraqi regime from acting in a timely and meaningful way—dumb, blind, and mute as it was after only forty-eight hours of bombardment—and over thirty-eight days air power destroyed Iraqi tanks, artillery, and troops at will without engagement on the ground. Thus, the outcome of Desert Storm depended on air power to an extent entirely unprecedented in the annals of warfare. In this war Warden's theory of systemic paralysis, which is both leadership-centric and effects-based, represented an advance of the first order. His insistence that air power should not merely seek attrition or destruction, but could create decisive effects by delivering non-nuclear precision weapons rapidly and intensively against targets categorized in terms of systems, has proved noteworthy.

Regional wars in the ensuing years have generally followed the Desert Storm pattern. Air power proved itself in Operation Deliberate Force (1995) and the air commander, Gen. Michael E. Ryan, stated that Warden's template was "very useful."[19] Lt. Gen. Michael C. Short has never given Warden much credit, but as the air commander of Operation Allied Force (1999) he suggested that he would have preferred to target downtown Belgrade on the opening night, conducting strategic attacks against the leadership apparatus, communication centers, and infrastructure, rather than focus on Serbian ground forces.[20] In Operation Enduring Freedom (2001) overwhelming air power, coupled with special operations and indigenous ground forces such as the Northern Alliance, played a crucial role in defeating a much larger land-oriented adversary. Finally, in Operation Iraqi Freedom (2003), where "regime change" was a stated objective, the USAF once again led the way. Although for various reasons the air commanders were not always allowed to execute air campaigns as they wished, all presented Warden-like arguments: focus on leadership rather than tanks and artillery, effects rather than destruction, and centers of gravity rather than a list of targets.

Thus, many of Warden's ideas have entered the mainstream. Some commanders, from all services, have used air power better than others, but none has resurrected the AirLand Battle option. Today's military leaders accept that air power can be either the supporting or supported force in war, or can act independently. Army officers seldom consider air power merely as an auxiliary of land power, and potential enemies know that they cannot confront the United States force-on-force and inflict huge losses, because air power will diminish their fighting capability. The USAF as an institution now maintains that air power can be used with precision against the enemy leadership from the opening moments of a war, and routinely talks about centers of gravity and effects rather than destruction.

FINAL THOUGHTS

Invariably, great ideas arise as a synthesis of a range of experiences and people, and few events in human history have single causes. Nevertheless, ultimately someone must combine these experiences and ideas, and then formalize, advance, and popularize them. Carl von Clausewitz does not deserve sole credit for the notion of a "center of gravity," or Basil Liddell Hart for the "indirect approach," but their articulation of these concepts brought them into the mainstream and made important contributions to modern military theory. Warden succeeded in crystallizing and popularizing a new—or more accurately, forgotten—theoretical construct for applying air power and helped make it possible for large parts of his concept to prove their value in Desert Storm.[21] The individual concepts that underlie the theory of "systemic paralysis" were not unprecedented when viewed through the lens of history, but Warden correlated them, added new insight, formulated them, and knew how to apply them in time of war. His true achievement is that he took a series of unconnected ideas and gathered them into a coherent theory; matched the theory to the new technology that could implement it; and had the strength of character and the opportunity to push the theory through a huge bureaucracy, despite serious opposition, at a critical point in time. Warden served as a catalyst, an intellectual leader who returned air power theory to its rightful place on the air force agenda. As such, Warden has become the main symbol of the renaissance in aerospace thinking that has characterized the 1990s and continues to this day.

EPILOGUE

W arden established his own company, Venturist, Inc., in Montgomery shortly after he retired from the air force. He had toyed with the idea of becoming an entrepreneur for some time and was convinced that his approach to planning air campaigns applied equally to the world of commerce. He also found the notion of not having to report to a superior appealing. As a consultant focusing on education and training programs he has since 1995 offered private businesses, academia, and governmental institutions insight into the meaning of strategy and the importance of thinking and acting strategically.

Warden did not find it difficult to make the transition from air power strategy to business strategy. Ever since he entered the Air Force Academy he had been interested in strategy—far more than in air operations. Even in his later military career he saw air power simply as the most practical and attractive means of achieving strategic objectives at the national level, and his air power theory was not designed to justify long-range fighter-bombers. Indeed, he never saw aircraft as an end in themselves, although he appreciated their capabilities and very much enjoyed flying them. He had always used business analogies: in "Planning to Win" (1983) he had warned that "the company with a strategy aimed at protecting its market share rather than increasing it quickly falls prey to competitors with a positive strategy,"[1] and in promulgating the ninety-three initiatives at Bitburg (1987) he had stated "the commercial graveyards of the world are filled with companies that stopped growing because they thought they had found perfection . . . The company, country, or military unit that does not grow, that does not search everyday for a better way to get the job done, is doomed."[2] His year in the White House had further strengthened this awareness of competitiveness. By focusing explicitly on business strategy Warden came full circle.

Shortly after establishing Venturist Warden decided to capture his universal methodology in a book, but he did not act upon the impulse until he met

Leland A. Russell at a workshop for Texas Instruments. Russell, the founder of GEO Group and an innovator in leadership development and knowledge management, was immediately impressed by Warden's conceptual understanding and grasp of strategy. He recalled that he thought Warden's ideas were "well articulated, logically structured and easy to comprehend,"[3] and he considered Warden a "genius." The two joined forces in 1999 and developed a concept they called the Prometheus Process: it combined Warden's strategic outlook, military experience, and interest in history with Russell's knowledge of how businesses succeeded and failed. Recalling ancient Greek mythology, they saw Prometheus as an ideal symbol for their philosophy, since the rebel Titan represented both forethought and passion (fire) for accomplishing a goal. According to Warden and Russell, the Prometheus Process is "a mindset and a method for rapid, decisive strategic action" and the recipe for success is to "think strategically, focus sharply and move quickly":

> The Prometheus Process is a systematic and proven method for designing winning strategies that is simple enough for everyone to grasp, yet sophisticated enough to plan, execute and complete projects of any scope and complexity. It guides you to focus on the future and to decide what the real measurements of success need to be; it teaches you how to find the right "targets" for action that will give you the most return on your energy; it shows you how to think about different organizational concepts; and it leads you to plan as carefully for the end of product and business cycles as for the beginnings. Prometheus includes a common strategic vocabulary that is shared across the organization . . . It is also fractal, which means that the same process pattern can be repeated over and over at an ever-smaller scale.[4]

The Warden-Russell partnership resulted in the book *Winning in Fast Time*, published in August 2001. The title reflected the book's primary message: the need to compress the greatest number of actions into the smallest period of time to achieve the highest probability of success. The first half of the book, the Prometheus Touchstones, provides the philosophical and methodological basis for principles and laws governing strategic planning, while the second part presents the four imperatives that constitute the Prometheus Process: Design the Future, Target for Success, Campaign to Win, and Finish with Finesse.

To a large extent the book repackages Instant Thunder, the Five Rings Model, and the ideas that Warden developed while serving in the Pentagon, albeit augmented by new insights, adaptations, perspectives, and a range of military and commercial illustrations. Not surprisingly, the book is persuasive: it offers both simplicity and a holistic approach that has been successfully tested.

It also partly lifts the mantle of mystery that tends to be associated with strategic thinking.

Winning in FastTime resembles Warden's previous writings in that its message is not unprecedented, but it suggests a range of factors that businesses must evaluate and does so in a coherent way. Like *The Air Campaign*, it is prescriptive, containing four "imperatives," eight Instant Thunder "principles," nine Promethic "laws," twelve cardinal "rules," and twelve "key descriptors." The Prometheus Process applies the principles that guide what Warden termed the "orchestration of war" in *The Air Campaign* to planning a business campaign, stresses the fundamental importance of seizing and maintaining the offensive, and translates the concept of "reserves" from troops and weapons to financial budgets and other organizational resources. Like all motivational books it is intentionally optimistic; it omits nuances and claims to present revolutionary ideas. Moreover, the book encourages the reader to think strategically rather than tactically, provides guidelines for dealing with an underlying problem rather than its symptoms, emphasizes the importance of thinking positively instead of complaining about restrictions, and proposes a set of principles that at the very least merit consideration. The Prometheus Process is more encompassing than many other well-respected business strategies and is still evolving.

Venturist has expanded in the decade since its inception. The collaboration between Warden and Russell ended in 2002, but Warden continues to develop new courses and training materials to make the Prometheus Process available to private companies, government agencies, and individuals. Although most of the company's activities take place in the United States, including a series of courses at the Prometheus Academy in Montgomery, Warden also holds seminars and gives talks worldwide, traveling to China, South America, and Europe. Venturist's program has earned praise from companies such as Texas Instruments, Pfizer, Prudential Bank, North Shore Medical Center, EPS Solutions, Jay Cashman Construction, McDonald's Corporation, and Bama Foods Ltd. George Consolver at Texas Instruments states that Warden's strategic insight has helped the company considerably, and when the Bama Companies, Inc., received the Malcolm Baldrige National Quality Award in 2004 its CEO, Paula Marshall-Chapman, gave much of the credit to Warden.[5]

Still driven by his intellectual curiosity and his impatience with established boundaries, Warden continues to explore and extend the meaning and significance of strategy in all spheres of human endeavor.

Appendix 1:

"INSTANT THUNDER"

In response to the Iraqi invasion of Kuwait on August 2, 1990, Col. John A. Warden's small group of air power advocates in the Pentagon, the so-called Checkmate team, proposed a strategic air campaign designed to drive the Iraqi army from Kuwait by a sustained effort against the major sources of Iraqi national power. Warden termed the proposal "Instant Thunder." Although changes were made, the concept remained at the heart of what became the strategic air campaign in Operation Desert Storm. Instant Thunder has become the very symbol of the U.S. Air Force reintroducing strategic attacks by conventional means to the forefront of air campaign planning.

The first draft of Instant Thunder was presented to Gen. H. Norman Schwarzkopf on August 10, 1990, while the second was presented seven days later. The following slides were those presented to General Schwarzkopf in Tampa, Florida, on August 17, and to Lt. Gen. Charles A. Horner in Riyadh, Saudi Arabia, on August 20. The original presentations contained more than thirty slides; these twenty-two have been declassified.

IRAQI AIR CAMPAIGN INSTANT THUNDER

1

IRAQ AIR CAMPAIGN
INSTANT THUNDER

WHAT IT IS: A **FOCUSED, INTENSE** AIR CAMPAIGN DESIGNED TO INCAPACITATE IRAQI LEADERSHIP AND DESTROY KEY IRAQI MILITARY CAPABILITY, IN A **SHORT** PERIOD OF TIME.

AND IT IS

DESIGNED TO LEAVE BASIC IRAQI INFRASTRUCTURE INTACT

WHAT IT IS NOT: A GRADUATED, LONG-TERM CAMPAIGN PLAN DESIGNED TO PROVIDE ESCALATION OPTIONS TO COUNTER IRAQI MOVES.

2

WHY ?

- SEIZE THE INITIATIVE – ATTACK HEART OF THE PROBLEM
- EXECUTABLE IN THE NEAR TERM
- AVOID PROLONGED GROUND COMBAT/LOSSES
- PROVIDE FRIENDLY ARAB STATES ABILITY TO CONDUCT FOLLOW-ON OPERATIONS/ RECONSTITUTION

 TIME IS ON HIS SIDE

3

STRATEGY ELEMENTS

- ISOLATE HUSSEIN
- ELIMINATE IRAQI OFFENSIVE AND DEFENSIVE CAPABILITY
- INCAPACITATE NATIONAL LEADERSHIP
- REDUCE THREAT TO FRIENDLY NATIONS
- MINIMIZE DAMAGE TO ENHANCE REBUILDING

4

STRATEGIC AIR CAMPAIGN
INSTANT THUNDER

CONCEPT OF OPERATIONS: Conduct powerful and focused attacks on strategic centers of gravity in Iraq over a short period of time (days not weeks)

- Target Hussein regime, not Iraqi people
- Minimize civilian casualties and collateral damage
- Minimize American and allied losses
- Pit U.S. strengths against Iraqi weaknesses

5

HOW WE EFFECT THE
STRATEGY

- EMPLOY PSYOPS & DECEPTION
- GAIN AIR SUPERIORITY
  - DESTROY HIS DEFENSES
  - ATTACK HIS AIRFIELDS
  - ATTRIT HIS FORCES WITH DEFENSIVE COUNTER-AIR AND OFFENSIVE COUNTER-AIR SWEEP
- ATTACK A **SELECT** STRATEGIC TARGET SET
  - LEADERSHIP
  - C^2
  - KEY INTERNAL PRODUCTION & DISTRIBUTION
  - NUCLEAR, BIOLOGICAL, CHEMICAL
  - OFFENSIVE AIR & MISSILE CAPABILITY
- EMPHASIZE PRECISION MUNITIONS

6

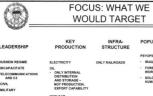

FOCUS: WHAT WE WOULD TARGET

LEADERSHIP	KEY PRODUCTION	INFRA-STRUCTURE	POPULATION	FIELDED FORCE
HUSSEIN REGIME	ELECTRICITY	ONLY RAILROADS	PSYOPS	DESTROY STRAT AIR DEFENSE
-INCAPACITATE	OIL		• IRAQIS	
TELECOMMUNICATIONS AND C3	• ONLY INTERNAL DISTRIBUTION AND STORAGE – NOT PRODUCTION, EXPORT CAPABILITY		• FOREIGN WORKERS	DESTROY STRAT OFFENSE – BOMBERS
-CIVIL			• SOLDIERS IN KUWAIT	- MISSILES
-MILITARY				
	NUCLEAR, BIOLOGICAL, CHEMICAL RESEARCH FACILITY			
	MILITARY RESEARCH, PRODUCTION AND STORAGE			

7

TARGET CATEGORIES

STRATEGIC AIR DEFENSE – 10	OIL (INTERNAL CONSUMPTION) – 6
STRATEGIC CHEMICAL – 8	RAILROADS – 3
NATIONAL LEADERSHIP – 5	AIRFIELDS – 7
TELECOMMUNICATIONS – 19	PORTS – 1
ELECTRICITY - 10	MILITARY/SUPPORT PRODUCTION & STORAGE DEPOTS - 15

TOTAL TARGETS: 84

8

ESSENTIAL TARGET SETS

- Strategic Air Defense
  - Render Iraq defenseless and minimize threat to friendly forces
- Strategic Offense Capability
  - Reduce threat to adjacent states . . . now and in the future
- Hussein Regime
  - The most important center of gravity
- Telecommunications and C3
  - Rupture Hussein's link to people and military

9

ESSENTIAL TARGET SETS   (Cont'd)

- Electricity
  - Cripple production and create confusion
- Oil (refined products)
  - Paralyze domestic and military internal movement
- Railroads
  - Complicate movement of goods and services
- Nuclear/Biological/Chemical Research Facility
  - Reduce long-term international threat
- Military Research, Production and Storage
  - Limit offensive capability – short and long-term

10

EXPECTED STRIKE RESULTS

- Strategic Air Defense - Destroyed
- Strategic Chemical - Long Term Setback
- National Leadership - Incapacitated
- Telecommunications - Disrupted/Degraded
- Electricity - 60 Percent Baghdad, 35 Percent Country
- Oil (Internal Consumption) - 70 Percent
- Railroads - Disrupted/Degraded
- Airfields - Disrupted/Degraded
- Ports - Disrupted
- Key military Production/Storage - Disrupted/Degraded

11

INTENSITY: WHAT WE WOULD USE

- US AIR FORCE, NAVY, MARINE
  - LONG RANGE CONVENTIONAL BOMBERS
    - 2 B-52 SQUADRONS
    - 1 F-111 SQUADRON
    - 1 F-15 SQUADRON
  - 32 FIGHTER/ATTACK SQUADRONS
  - SPECIALIZED AIRCRAFT
    - 1 F-117 SQUADRON
    - 3+ DEFENSIVE SUPPRESSION SQUADRONS
    - COMPASS CALL
    - AWACS
  - TLAM
  - PSYCHOLOGICAL OPERATIONS
    - VOLANT SOLO
  - MULTI-NATIONAL AIR-FORCES INTEGRATED WHERE POSSIBLE

12

INTENSITY:
HOW WE WOULD USE

- ROUND THE CLOCK OPERATIONS

  - INITIATED BY MULTI-AXIS, MULTI-TARGET NIGHT STRIKE

  - FOLLOW-ON MULTI TARGET ATTACK SAME NIGHT

  - THEREAFTER, 1 STRIKE PER PERIOD (AM/PM/NIGHT)

  - APPROX 6 DAYS DURATION
    - 1200 STORTIES DAY 1
    - 900 SORTIES/DAY, DAYS 2-6

13

TARGETING PRIORITIES

- DAY 1 & 2: Coverage of Strategic Target List
- DAY 3 & 4: Reattack of Strategic Target List
  Based on BDA With Emphasis on OCA Targets
- DAY 5 & 6: Maximum Effort Against Chemical Production
  and Military Support Infrastructure

14

EXECUTION PLAN

- Initiate with Night Attack (2 Waves)
- Wave 1 – One hour post-sunset (163 sorties)
  - SEAD Packages
  - Air Defense, C2, Airfields
  - Chemical, OCA/Leadership
  - LRBs impact as aircraft egress (timing GPS dependent)
- Wave 2 – One hour pre-sunrise (131 sorties)
  - SEAD Packages
  - Airfields/south
  - Chemical/Leadership
- Follow-on: One strike per period (AM/PM/Night)
- Deconfliction
  - USAF – Western Baghdad & Central Iraq
  - USN – Eastern Baghdad (Red Sea CVBG)
    Southeast area (Independence)
  - USMC – Southern and Central target set

15

EXPECTED RESULTS

- NATIONAL LEADERSHIP, C2 DESTROYED

- IRAQ'S STRATEGIC OFFENSE & DEFENSE
  (MISSILES AND LONG – RANGE AIRCRAFT)
  ELIMINATED FOR EXTENDED PERIOD

- INTERNAL ECONOMY DISRUPTED

- IRAQ'S CAPABILITY TO EXPORT OIL NOT SIGNIFICANTLY
  DEGRADED

- PENINSULA NATIONS WOULD HAVE COMBAT
  CAPABILITY TO DEAL EFFECTIVELY WITH RESIDUAL IRAQI
  FORCES

16

WHAT IF: IRAQ ATTACKS SAUDI ARABIA
IN RESPONSE TO INSTANT THUNDER

- Available for immediate engagement
  - 4 A-10 Squadrons (96)
  - 2 AV-8B Squadrons (40)
  - 3 F/A-18 Squadrons (36)
  - 2 AH-1W Squadrons (30)
  - 4 AH-64 Squadrons (75)
- Instant Thunder addresses many common targets
  - Air Superiority
  - Command and Control
  - Interdiction
- Combined Instant Thunder and battlefield air
  operations can stop ground advance
- Minimal impact on Instant Thunder

17

PSYCHOLOGICAL AND
DECEPTION OPERATIONS

- PSYOPS CRITICAL ELEMENTS OF CAMPAIGN

  - DESTROY IRAQ TV & BROADCAST STATIONS

    - SUBSTITUTE US BROADCASTS

    - SEPARATE HUSSEIN REGIME FROM SUPPORT
      OF PEOPLE AND MILITARY
- DECEPTION

  - REDUCE CASUALTIES

  - FACILITATE MILITARY OPERATIONS

    - **NOT** CRITICAL FOR SUCCESS

18

ISSUES AND LIMFACS

- Night PGM Capability
  - F-111D's have no laser designation capability
  - More night designators for leadership and air defense targets
- USE OF MULTINATIONAL ASSETS
  - Significant aid to Instant Thunder air superiority and offensive counter-air plan
  - Integration poses a challenge
- AIRSPACE CONTROL PLAN
  - Simple airspace control plan required
  - Must not inhibit air superiority weapons employment
- MUNITIONS DISTRIBUTION
  - Must get to proper bases

19

ISSUES AND LIMFACS   (Cont'd)

- TANKER NUMBERS (Boomers and Fuel Upload)

TOTAL AIRCRAFT	MIN REQUIRED	OPTIMAL
~75 NOW	94	114

- Targeting
  - Must refine constantly to meet strategic situation and new intelligence information
    - For example, need to target National Palace Guard and Muhabarat headquarters, dispersal fields, etc
  - Long-Range Missiles
    - Chemical-capable long-range SCUDs present real problem
  - Political
    - Status of Turkey, Iran

20

ISSUES AND LIMFACS   (Cont'd)

- Psychological War
  - Can Hussein use Kuwait TV and radio
  - VOLANT SOLO not in the flow – modified for ME TV
- RESCUE
  - Joint Rescue Coordination Center (JRCC), Scott AFB, IL, not tasked; needs to be co-located with TACC

21

EFFORTS TO DATE

- JOINT STAFF/SERVICE PARTICIPATION
- ANALYSIS OF TARGET BASE, SYSTEM CAPABILITIES, SUPPORT REQUIREMENTS, AND LOGISTICS
  - CJCS/SERVICE CHIEFS BRIEFED
- REFINEMENTS CONTINUING
- PLAN READY FOR REVIEW BY CINCCENT

22

Appendix 2:

"CENTCOM AIR CAMPAIGN PLAN"

The U.S. Air Force's Tactical Air Command at Langley Air Force Base, Virginia, did not like Colonel Warden's Instant Thunder, and thus proposed an alternative plan for General Schwarzkopf, which it faxed to the Air Staff on August 10. The alternative focused on gradual escalation and demonstrative strikes, rather than massing air power aggressively against Iraq's leadership from the outset. It was meant to give Schwarzkopf options, but it never reached him because Warden's group had already made its case to Schwarzkopf, receiving approval of Instant Thunder's basic concept in the process.

Senior officers in the Air Staff, and Warden's group in particular, referred to the "CENTCOM Air Campaign Plan" as a possible repetition of the failed strategy in Vietnam. The following slides were those faxed to the Air Staff on August 10. They outline an approach that represents the antithesis to the Instant Thunder philosophy of air power as a war-winning concept.

CENTCOM AIR CAMPAIGN PLAN

1

PRESIDENT'S OBJECTIVES

- Immediate, Complete, and Unconditional Iraqi Withdrawal From Kuwait
- Restore Kuwait's Legitimate Government
- Security and Stability of Persian Gulf
- Protect Lives of US Citizens Abroad

2

USCINCCENT OBJECTIVES

- Deter Further Iraqi Aggression While Supporting Political/Diplomatic/Economic Endeavors to Resolve Crisis.
- Conduct Defensive and Offensive Operations To Protect Saudi Arabian/Gulf States Sovereignty.
- Be Prepared To Conduct Offensive Operations To Force Iraqi Forces To Withdraw From Kuwait.
- Be Prepared to Conduct Operations To Force Cessation of Hostilities On Terms Favorable To The US and Allied Governments

3

PLANNING FACTORS

- Target is Iraqi War Machine Vice Iraqi Nation
  - "Focused Destruction" (Focus on Iraqi Capability to Project Power)
  - Attack His Vulnerabilities
  - Minimize Civilian Casualties/Collateral Damage
- Joint & Multinational Forces Involved in Air Campaign
- Appoint a JFACC
  - Closely delineates "Who's In Charge"
  - Directs a focused air campaign using all air assets
  - OPCON not required (need only tasking authority)
- Avoid War of Attrition
  - Rapid, Intensive Air Campaign
  - Minimize Force-On-Force

4

EXPECTED OUTCOME

- Overthrow/Termination of Hussein
- Restoration of Kuwait Sovereignty
- Establish Regional Military Balance of Iraq Vis-A-Vis Neighbors
- Assure World Access to Oil Resources

5

MILITARY OPTIONS

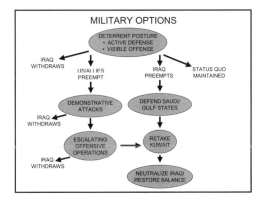

6

CONDITION: IF IRAQ HAS ATTACKED
SAUDI ARABIA

CONDUCT OFFENSIVE OPERATIONS
TO
DEFEND SAUDI ARABIA
AND
RESTORE REGIONAL STABILITY

7

AIR STRATEGY
(IRAQ ATTACKS SAUDI ARABIA)

DEFEND and PRESERVE SOVEREIGN
INDEPENDENCE of SAUDI ARABIA

- Establish Air Superiority Through a
  Comprehensive Counter-Air Campaign
- Attack and Destroy All Means to Conduct
  Chemical Operations
- Support Ground Scheme of Maneuver of
  Ground Force Commander
- Interdict Critical Items of Resupply to
  Iraqi Field Forces

8

CONDITION: IF IRAQ HAS NOT ATTACKED
SAUDI ARABIA NOR
WITHDRAWN FROM KUWAIT

CONDUCT OFFENSIVE OPERATIONS
TO
PRECLUDE STALEMATE
AND
LIBERATE KUWAIT

9

AIR STRATEGY

- DEMONSTRATE OUR ABILITY TO CONDUCT
  OFFENSIVE OPERATIONS AGAINST
  IRAQI TARGETS OF OUR CHOOSING
  - Begin with Demonstrative Attacks
    Against High-Value Targets
  - Select Type/Location to Emphasize
    Ability to Attack Whenever and
    Wherever We Wish
  - Concentrate on Those Systems that
    Hold Our Forces at Risk
    - Surface-to-Surface Missiles
    - Long-Range Aircraft
  - Destroy Systems that are Offensive to the
    World and Pose a Long Term Threat to Everyone
    - Chemical Capability
    - Nuclear Capability
  - Primary Night Attacks
    - „We Own the Night"
    - Our Strength vs Their Weakness

10

AIR STRATEGY
(CONTINUED)

- ESCALATE AS REQUIRED UNTIL ALL
  SIGNIFICANT TARGETS ARE DESTROYED
  - Still Primarily Night Ops
  - Include More Strategic Targets
  - Concentrate on Targets that
    Reduce His Ability to Project Power
    - Field Armies
    - Infrastructure to Support
      Offensive Operations
- KEEP UP THE PRESSURE UNTIL IRAQI POWER
  HAS DIMINISHED TO THE POINT THAT
  REGIONAL STABILITY HAS BEEN RESTORED
- THIS STRATEGY ALLOWS TIME AND OPPORTUNITY
  FOR HUSSEIN TO REEVALUATE HIS SITUATION AND
  BACK OUT WHILE THERE IS SOMETHING TO SAVE

11

TARGET PRIORITIES

- Long-Range Delivery Assets
  - Aircraft
  - Missiles

  > Systems that have the
  > ability to bring
  > Friendly forces under
  > attack

- Chemical Capability
  - Stockpiles
  - Production

  > Systems that have
  > international implications
  > & pose long term threat

- Military Forces (First Echelon)
  - Armor
  - Artillery
- Reinforcement & Resupply
  - Lines of Communication
  - Transportation Assets
  - POL
  - Water

12

TARGET PRIORITIES
(CONTINUED)

- Command and Control
  - Ground Forces – Division & Above
  - Air Force Integrated Air Defense System
  - National Communications to
    Field Commanders
- Strategic Targets

13

NUCLEAR REACTOR TARGETING

PRO:
- Very Visible – Sends Strong Signal to World
- Easily Locatable
- National Pride (Symbolic Target)
- Hussein Thinks Invulnerable
  - Numerous SAM Systems
  - AAA on berm around facility

CON:
- Reactor Breach Could Result in Nuclear
  Type Incident and Adverse World Opinion
- Heavily Defended

14

KEY INSTALLATIONS
(Max Effort/One Lauch/One Night)

- Three Transhipment Points (Rail to Truck)
- One Sector Operations Center (SOC)
- Two CW Production Plants
- Two AMMO Storage Sites
- Fixed SSM Sites (SCUD)

15

SUMMARY

AIR CAMPAIGN PROVIDES:

- Options to Achieve President's and CINC's
  Objectives

- Current and Reasonable Assumptions
  and Results

- Variety of Options with Targeting Priorities

16

NOTES

Introduction: The Power of Ideas

1. Gen. H. Norman Schwarzkopf, *It Doesn't Take a Hero*, with Peter Petre (New York: Bantam Books, 1992), 369–371.
2. Colin L. Powell, *My American Journey*, with Joseph E. Persico (New York: Ballantine Books, 1995), 460.
3. David Halberstam, *War in a Time of Peace: Bush, Clinton and the Generals* (London: Bloomsbury, 2002), 47–49.
4. See for example, Rick Atkinson, *Crusade: The Untold Story of the Gulf War* (London: Harper Collins Publishers, 1994); Eliot A. Cohen, study director, *Gulf War Air Power Survey*, vol. 1, *Part I: Planning* (Washington, DC: Government Printing Office, 1993); United States Department of Defense, *Conduct of the Persian Gulf War: Final Report to Congress* (Washington, DC: Government Printing Office, 1992); Michael R. Gordon and Gen. Bernard E. Trainor, *The Generals' War: The Inside Story of the Conflict in the Gulf* (New York: Little, Brown and Company, 1995); Col. Edward C. Mann, *Thunder and Lightning: Desert Storm and the Airpower Debates* (Maxwell AFB, AL: Air University Press, 1995); Col. Richard T. Reynolds, *Heart of the Storm: The Genesis of the Air Campaign Against Iraq* (Maxwell AFB, AL: Air University Press, 1995); U.S. News and World Report, *Triumph without Victory: The Unreported History of the Persian Gulf War* (New York: Random House, 1992).

   Warden's contribution is also acknowledged by the official USAF historians: Diane T. Putney, *Airpower Advantage: Planning the Gulf War Air Campaign 1989–1991* (Washington, DC: Air Force History and Museums Program, 2005); Richard G. Davis, *On Target: Organizing and Executing the Strategic Air Campaign Against Iraq* (Washington, DC: Air Force History and Museums Program, 2002); Richard P. Hallion, *Storm over Iraq: Air Power and the Gulf War* (Washington, DC: Smithsonian Institute Press, 1992); Perry D. Jamison, *Lucrative Targets: The U.S. Air Force in the Kuwaiti Theater of Operations* (Washington, DC: Air Force History and Museums Program, 2001).
5. Robert Frost (1874–1963), "The Road Not Taken," in *The Norton Anthology of American Literature*, 3rd ed., vol. 2 (New York: W.W. Norton and Company, 1989), 1099.

Chapter 1: Origins: The Early Years

1. R. Manning Ancell, *The Biographical Dictionary of World War II Generals and Flag*

Rank Officers: The U.S. Armed Forces, with Christine M. Miller (Westport, CT: Greenwood Press, 1996), 336. The author is grateful to Joanne Knight at the Combined Arms Research Library for having provided him with this citation, and to Luther Hanson at the Quartermaster Museum for having provided general background on Warden.

2. Brig. Gen. John Ashley Warden was married to Jane Robinson Abernathy. They had two sons and one daughter: John A. Warden, Jr., (April 28, 1913–July 9, 1983); Henry "Pete" Warden (1915–); and Nancy Jane Warden (later married Love, 1918–).

3. Fort D. E. Russell was renamed Fort F. E. Warren in 1930.

4. Lori S. Tagg, *Development of the B-52: The Wright Field Story* (Wright-Patterson AFB, OH: Aeronautical Systems Center, 2004), 8–10.

5. Walter J. Boyne, correspondence with author, May 19, 2004.

6. Tagg, *Development of the B-52*, 92; Lori Tagg, correspondence with author, July 21, 2004.

7. In the end his military record earned him the Asiatic-Pacific Theater Ribbon with three Bronze Stars and one Bronze Arrowhead, in addition to the Philippine Liberation Ribbon with two Bronze Stars.

8. The author is grateful to Steve Showers at the Otis Historical Archives for having provided him with these citations.

Chapter 2: Learning to Fly: From the Air Force Academy to Spain

1. David R. Mets, "Airpower History and Professional Education in the U.S. Air Force" (paper presented at the Society for Military History in Bethesda, MD, May 22, 2004).

2. Col. John A. Warden, in *Desert Story Collection*, May 30, 1991, 2. The *Desert Story Collection*, held in the archives of the Air Force Historical Research Agency at Maxwell Air Force Base, Alabama, consists of audiotapes and transcripts of interviews conducted from 1991 to 1993 by Air Force lieutenant colonels (later colonels) Suzanne B. Gehri, Edward C. Mann, and Richard T. Reynolds.

3. J. F. C. Fuller, *The Generalship of Alexander the Great* (London: Wordsworth Editions, 1998), 7.

4. Quoted in Azar Gat, *Fascists and Liberal Vision of War; Fuller, Liddell Hart, Douhet, and other Modernists* (Oxford: Clarendon Press, 1998), 25.

5. J. F. C. Fuller, *The Foundations of the Science of War*, reprint (Fort Leavenworth, KS: U.S. Army Command and General Staff College Press, 1993), 18.

6. Gen. Howell M. Estes III (ret.), interview with author, May 25, 2004; Gen. Michael E. Ryan (ret.), interview with author, May 7, 2004; Lt. Gen. Michael C. Short (ret.), interview with author, February 6–8, 2001.

7. Margie Warden, interview with author, August 11, 2004.

8. The author is grateful to Christopher Stewart at the USAF Academy for having made the extract available.

9. C. R. Anderegg, *Sierra Hotel: Flying Air Force Fighters in the Decade after Vietnam* (Washington, DC: Air Force History and Museums Program, 2001), 5. CEP is the radius of a circle within which half of all the weapons targeted for the center of that circle can be expected to land.

10. Warden, interview with the author, December 4, 2004.

11. Lt. Col. Mark Clodfelter (ret.), "Air Power Versus Asymmetric Enemies: A Framework for Evaluating Effectiveness," in John Andreas Olsen (ed.), *Asymmetric Warfare* (Trondheim: Royal Norwegian Air Force Academy, 2002), 35.

12. Ibid., 37.

13. Warden, in *Desert Story Collection*, May 30, 1991, 6.
14. Lt. Col. Gary B. Mcintire (ret.), interview with author, August 12, 2004.
15. Halberstam, *War in a Time of Peace*, 48–49; Warden, interview with author, December 4, 2004.
16. Mcintire, interview, August 12, 2004.
17. Warden, in *Desert Story Collection*, May 30, 1991, 6.
18. Brig. Gen. Kenneth F. Keller (ret.), interview with author, July 7, 2005.
19. Capt. John A. Warden, "Employment of Tactical Air in Europe," memorandum, August 1, 1972; Warden, in *Desert Story Collection*, May 30, 1991, 9.
20. Warden, "Employment of Tactical Air in Europe," 7.
21. Warden, in *Desert Story Collection*, May 30, 1991, 8.
22. Ibid.
23. Warden, interview, December 4, 2004.
24. Mcintire, interview, August 12, 2004.

Chapter 3: The Making of a Strategic Thinker

1. Warden, interview, December 4, 2004.
2. Capt. John A. Warden, "The Grand Alliance: Strategy and Decision," M.A. thesis (Texas Tech University, 1975), 3, in author's private collection.
3. Ibid., 1–3.
4. Ibid., 17, 142.
5. Fuller, *Generalship of Alexander the Great*, 312.
6. Warden, "The Grand Alliance," 140.
7. Ibid., 35.
8. Ibid., 143.
9. Ibid., 146–148.
10. Ibid., 150–151.
11. H. P. Willmott, *When Men Lost Faith in Reason: Reflections on War and Society in the Twentieth Century* (Westport, CT: Praeger, 2002), 5, 114.
12. Ibid., 79.
13. Warden, "The Grand Alliance," 1.
14. Ibid., 32.
15. Warden, in *Desert Story Collection*, May 30, 1991, 13.
16. B. H. Liddell Hart, *Strategy* (London: Meridian Books, 1957), 212.
17. Keller, interview, July 7, 2005.
18. Warden, in *Desert Story Collection*, October 22, 1991, 24.
19. Warden, in *Desert Story Collection*, May 30, 1991, 34.
20. Gen. Richard L. Lawson (ret.), interview with author, May 24, 2004.
21. Ibid.
22. Ibid.
23. Keller, interview, July 7, 2005.
24. Warden, in *Desert Story Collection*, October 22, 1991, 10–11; May 30, 1991, 39–40.
25. Warden, in *Desert Story Collection*, October 22, 1991, 4; May 30, 1991, 35–36.
26. Maj. Gen. Richard B. Goetze Jr. (ret.), interview with author, June 28–29, 2004.
27. Brig. Gen. William M. Constantine (ret.), interview with author, August 18, 2005.
28. Ibid.
29. Gen. Lew Allen Jr. (ret.), interview with author, March 2, 2004.
30. Ibid.
31. Ibid.

32. Gen. Joseph W. Ashy (ret.), interview with author, June 28, 2004.
33. Ibid.
34. Constantine, interview, August 18, 2005.
35. Ashy, interview, June 28, 2004.

Chapter 4: Operational Assignments
1. Anderegg, *Sierra Hotel*, 149.
2. Warden, interview, May 21 2004.
3. Gen. Gregory S. Martin, interview with author, May 21, 2004.
4. Maj. Gen. Stanton R. Musser (ret.), interview with author, July 1, 2004.
5. Warden's recorded title for the period became "Self-Inspection Manager." Cheryl A. Nolan, historian at the Thirty-third Fighter Wing, correspondence with author, September 7, 2004.
6. John Q. Smith, Air Combat Command historian, correspondence with author, July 2, 2004.
7. Gen. John L. Piotrowski (ret.), interview with author, June 18, 2004.
8. Modern-day double-digit mobile surface-to-air missiles may have changed the equation.
9. Lt. Col. John A. Warden III, "Planning to Win," *Air University Review* 34 (Mar–Apr 1983), 94–97.
10. Musser, interview, July 1, 2004.
11. Col. Jack Petry, interview with author, August 12, 2004.
12. Col. Eugene L. Vosika (ret.), interview with author, August 12, 2004.
13. Ibid.
14. Ibid.
15. Col. Douglas B. Cairns (ret.), interview with author, March 15, 2004.
16. Col. John Golden (ret.), interview with author, July 18, 2005.
17. Piotrowski, interview, June 18, 2004.
18. John Smith, correspondence with author, July 2, 2004.
19. Gen. Billy G. McCoy (ret.), interview with author, June 18, 2004; Col. Joe Prater (ret.), interview with author, September 12, 2004; Lester R. Moore, interview with author, July 19, 2005; Gen. Michael J. Dugan (ret.), interview with author, March 15, 2003.
20. Maj. Gen. Harald G. Hermes (ret.), interview with author, June 2, 2004; Golden, interview, July 18, 2005; Maj. Gen. William A. Peck Jr. (ret.), interview with author, July 20, 2005; Prater, interview, September 12, 2004; McCoy, interview, June 18, 2004.
21. Prater, interview, June 16, 2004.
22. Col. Robert A. Ator (ret.), interview with author, June 16, 2004; Peck, interview, July 20, 2005.
23. Lt. Gen. John R. Baker, interview with author, January 21, 2005.
24. Prater, interview, September 12, 2004, and interview, June 16, 2004; McCoy, interview, June 18, 2004; Peck, interview, July 20, 2005; Moore, interview, July 19, 2005; Ator, interview, June 16, 2004.
25. Dugan, interview, March 15, 2003.
26. Piotrowski, interview, June 18, 2004; McCoy, interview, June 18, 2004; Hermes, interview, June 2, 2004.
27. McCoy, interview, June 18, 2004.
28. Piotrowski, interview, June 18, 2004; McCoy, interview, June 18, 2004.
29. Hermes, interview, June 2, 2004.

30. Ator, interview, June 16, 2004; Moore, interview, July 19, 2005; Peck, interview, July 20, 2005; Prater, interview, June 16, 2004.

31. Anderegg, *Sierra Hotel,* 50–51.

32. Lt. Gen. Buster C. Glosson (ret.), interview with author, June 1, 2004; Ator, interview, June 16, 2004.

33. Moore, interview, July 19, 2005.

34. Incidentally, some of the British Tornados were painted "desert pink" when they flew in the Gulf War of 1991.

35. Ator, interview, June 16, 2004; Moore, interview, July 19, 2005.

36. Golden, interview, March 23, 2004; Ator, interview, June 16, 2004; Cairns, interview, March 15, 2004; Prater, interview, June 16, 2004; Richard L. Boyd, interview, June 22, 2004.

37. Ashy, interview, June 28, 2004; Glosson, interview, June 1, 2004; Ator, interview, June 16, 2004.

38. Elizabeth (Warden) Dierlam, interview with author, September 25, 2005.

39. Col. John A. Warden, "End-of-Tour Report," July 1985, in author's private collection.

40. Ibid.

41. Maj. Richard Dan Taylor (ret.), interview with author, March 27, 2004.

42. Warden, "End-of-Tour Report."

43. Richard Boyd, interview, June 22, 2004.

44. Ibid.; Taylor, interview, March 27, 2004.

45. Taylor, interview, March 27, 2004.

46. Brig. Gen. Frederic A. Zehrer III (ret.), interview with author, July 30, 2005.

47. Warden, "End-of-Tour Report."

48. Zehrer, interview, July 30, 2005.

49. Warden, "End-of-Tour Report."

50. Col. Omar R. Wiseman (ret.), interview with author, August 12, 2004.

51. Ibid.

52. Ibid.

53. Ibid., September 29, 2004.

Chapter 5: The Art of Air Warfare: *The Air Campaign*

1. This concept of operational art originated in Russia in the aftermath of the 1904–1905 war against Japan. After witnessing devastating civil wars and a recent world war, Soviet scholars and military officers realized that war had become so large and complex that commanders needed to identify a dimension between the strategic and tactical levels: one that dealt with campaigns rather than battles. The American awakening followed the war in Vietnam and began to influence the armed forces in the late 1970s and early 1980s.

2. For a discussion of the AirLand Battle concept, see John L. Romjue, *From Active Defense to AirLand Battle: The Development of Army Doctrine, 1973–1982* (Fort Monroe, VA: U.S. Army Training and Doctrine Command, 1984); Richard G. Davis, *The 31 Initiatives: A Study in Air Force–Army Cooperation* (Washington, DC: Office of USAF History, 1987).

3. Mann, *Thunder and Lightning,* 29.

4. Col. John A. Warden III, *The Air Campaign: Planning for Combat* (Washington, DC: Brassey's, 1988), 3.

5. Ibid., 7.

6. Ibid.

7. Ibid., 141.

8. Ibid., 10.

9. Ibid.

10. Ibid., 13.

11. Ibid., 15.

12. Ibid., 20.

13. Ibid., 68, 70.

14. Ibid., 22.

15. Ibid., 23.

16. Ibid., 32.

17. Ibid., 30.

18. Ibid., 33.

19. Ibid., 34.

20. Ibid., 40.

21. Ibid., 44.

22. Ibid., 47.

23. Ibid., 54.

24. Ibid., 60.

25. Ibid.

26. Ibid., 66.

27. Ibid., 72.

28. Ibid., 80–81.

29. Warden, interview, July 1, 2003.

30. Warden, *The Air Campaign*, 80, 125.

31. Ibid., 125, 147–148. When Warden developed an air power theory several months later he insisted that both these limitations had been largely overcome.

32. Ibid., 84–85.

33. Ibid., 87.

34. Ibid., 89–90.

35. Ibid.

36. Ibid., 101.

37. Ibid., 111–112.

38. Ibid., 115–116.

39. Ibid., 123–124.

40. Ibid., 125.

41. Giulio Douhet, *The Command of the Air*, translated by Dino Ferrari (New York: Coward-McCann, 1984); Brig. Gen. William Mitchell, *Winged Defense* (New York: G. P. Putnam's Sons, 1925) and *Skyways* (Philadelphia: J. B. Lippincott, 1930); Maj. Alexander de Seversky, *Victory through Air Power* (New York: Simon and Schuster, 1942).

42. David R. Mets, *The Air Campaign: John Warden and the Classical Airpower Theorists* (Maxwell AFB, AL: Air University Press, 1998), 65.

43. Col. John A. Warden, interview with Williamson Murray, Barry D. Watts, and Thomas A. Keaney, February 21, 1992, cited in Eliot A. Cohen, *Gulf War Air Power Survey*, vol. 2, *Part I: Operations*, 21.

44. Col. Peter Faber, "The Evolution of Airpower Theory in the United States: From World War I to Colonel John Warden's *The Air Campaign*," in Olsen, *Asymmetric Warfare*, 45–115.

45. John Shy, "Jomini," in Peter Paret, ed., *Makers of Modern Strategy: From Machiavelli to the Nuclear Age* (Oxford: Clarendon Press, 1986), 144.

46. Lt. Col. Barry D. Watts (ret.), interview with author, April 20, 2005. See also Barry D. Watts, "Clausewitzian Friction and Future War," *Institute for National Strategic Studies*, McNair Papers no. 68, 2004.

47. See Col. Dennis Drew (ret.), "Air Theory, Air Force, and Low Intensity Conflict: A Short Journey to Confusion," in Phillip S. Meilinger, ed., *The Paths of Heaven: The Evolution of Airpower Theory* (Maxwell AFB, AL: Air University Press, 1997), 343–344.

48. Niklas Zetterling, "John Warden, *The Air Campaign*—En Kritisk Gransking," *Kungl Krigsveteskaps-akademiens Hanlinger och Tidsskrift*, no. 1 (1998): 107–130. For a positive review, see Timothy G. Murphy, "A Critique of the Air Campaign," *Airpower Journal* 8, no. 1 (Spring 1994): 63–74.

49. Warden, interview, January 26, 2006; *The Air Campaign*, 13.

50. Zetterling, John Warden, *The Air Campaign*; Col. Al L. Gropman (ret.), interview with author, November 14, 2004. Gropman is very critical of Warden's use of history.

51. Philip A. Crowl, "Alfred Thayer Mahan: The Naval Historian," in Paret, *Makers of Modern Strategy*, 455.

52. I. B. Holley Jr., "Reflections on the Search for Airpower Theory," in Meilinger, *Paths of Heaven*, 593.

53. Hallion, *Storm over Iraq*, 116–118.

54. Mets, *The Air Campaign*, 55–56.

55. Maj. Gen. Perry M. Smith (ret.), interview with author, January 14, 2006.

56. Maj. Gen. Perry M. Smith (ret.), in *Desert Story Collection*, June 18, 1992, 4.

57. Lt. Gen. Bradley C. Hosmer, "Foreword" in Warden, *The Air Campaign*, xiii.

58. Smith, in *Desert Story Collection*, June 18, 1992, 5.

59. Gen. Charles L. Donnelly Jr., "A Theater-Level View of Air Power," *Air Power Journal* 1, no. 1 (Summer 1997): 3–8. The article had been extracted from the text of a speech that Gen. Donnelly presented on May 19, 1986, to the NWC.

60. Ibid. 3–8.

61. Donnelly, cited in Warden, *The Air Campaign*, xvii.

62. Martin, interview, May 24, 2005.

Chapter 6: Wing Commander: Ninety-Three Initiatives

1. SrA Michael J. Ramsey, "Col. Warden Becomes Vice Wing Commander," *Bitburg Skyblazer*, Bitburg AB, Germany, vol. 37, no. 6 (July 3, 1986): 1.

2. Maj. Gen. Peter D. Robinson (ret.), interview with author, October 21, 2004.

3. Daniel F. Harrington, historian, USAFE, correspondence with author, December 10–13, 2004.

4. Robinson, interview, June 22, 2004.

5. Lt. Gen. George K. Muellner (ret.), interview with author, November 8, 2004.

6. Col. Emery M. Kiraly (ret.), interview with author, October 20, 2004; Robinson, interview, October 21, 2004.

7. Robinson, interview, June 22, 2004.

8. Muellner, interview, November 8, 2004.

9. Anderegg, *Sierra Hotel*, 45.

10. The two-star general, with whom the author talked at length, prefers to not be named.

11. The air force officer, with whom Warden served, prefers not to be named.

12. Col. John A. Warden, "Wing Commander Efficiency Report," March 22, 1988, in author's private collection.

13. Col. John A. Warden, "36th Tactical Fighter Wing Goals Fiscal Year 1988," Department of the Air Force, Headquarters Thirty-sixth Tactical Fighter Wing USAF, September 26, 1987.

14. Lt. Gen. William R. Looney III, interview with author, September 8, 2004; Maj. Gen. Jeffrey G. Cliver (ret.), interview with author, July 6, 2004; Maj. Gen. Jay D. Blume Jr. (ret.), vice commander and commander at Fifty-second TFW, Spangdahlem Air Base, June 1985–June 1988, interview with author, June 30, 2004.

15. Warden, in *Desert Story Collection*, October 22, 1991, 13.

16. Warden, *The Air Campaign*, 63, 165.

17. Ibid., 61.

18. Brig. Gen. Frank Gorenc, interview with author, July 20, 2005.

19. Cliver, interview, July 6, 2004.

20. Ibid.

21. Ibid.

22. Ibid.

23. Ibid.

24. Buster C. Glosson, *War with Iraq: Critical Lessons* (Charlotte, NC: Glosson Family Foundation, 2003), 84.

25. Gen. Charles A. Horner (ret.), interview with author, March 21, 2004.

26. Ibid.

27. Ibid.

28. Lt. Gen. Thomas G. McInerney (ret.), interview with author, February 26, 2004.

29. Gen. William L. Kirk (ret.), interview with author, March 9, 2004.

30. Warden, interview, March 16, 2003.

31. Kirk, interview, March 9, 2004.

32. Kirk, interview, January 7, 2003.

33. Gen. Robert L. Rutherford (ret.), interview with author, June 5, 2004; Glosson, interview, June 1, 2004; Blume, interview, June 30, 2004.

34. Glosson, interview, June 1, 2004.

35. Ibid.

36. The self-help shop system has since expanded and is now taken for granted at every base.

37. Kirk, interview, January 7, 2003.

38. Lt. Gen. Richard M. Pascoe (ret.), interview with author, August 12, 2004.

39. Warden, interview, December 4, 2004.

40. Looney, interview, September 8, 2004; Gorenc, interview, July 20, 2005.

41. Gorenc, interview, July 20, 2005.

42. Looney, interview, September 8, 2004. However, Lt. Gen. McInerney introduced the concept of using F-15s in big formations when he was the one-star commander of the 313th Air Division at Kadena Air Base, Japan, between February 1981 and June 1983. Lt. Gen. David A. Deptula, interview with author, March 7, 2006.

43. Gorenc, interview, July 20, 2005.

44. There was no MEI, ORI/TACEVAL during Warden's tenure, but there was one HQ USAFE Unit Effectiveness Inspection (November 16–23, 1987) with the overall rating of Satisfactory. Details are as follows within the wing-areas: Outstanding (2): Judge Advocate and Wing Intelligence; Excellent (8): Quality Assurance Evaluation; Safety; Deputy Commander for Ops Staff; Squadron Operations; Transportation;

Civil Engineering; Personnel; and Services; Satisfactory (15): Public Affairs; Wing Staff Support Functions; Resource Control; Comptroller; Supply; Deputy Commander for Maintenance Staff; Aircraft Generation Squadron; Component Repair Squadron; Equipment Maintenance Squadron; Security Police; Disaster Preparedness; MWR (Morale, Welfare and Recreation); Base Administration; Communications; and Other Support (Contracting, Exchange and Commissary); Marginal (1): Social Actions. The number of non-judicial punishments (Article 15) was 114 over the first seven months of 1987 and 62 for the period in which he was the wing commander: August (9); September (19); October (11); November (9); and December (14). The author is grateful to Daniel Harrington, historian, USAFE, for providing the data.

45. Lt. Gen. Harley A. Hughes (ret.), interview with author, March 8, 2004.
46. Piotrowski, interview, June 18, 2004.
47. Harrington, interview, December 10, 2004.
48. McInerney, interview, October 21, 2004.
49. Maj. Gen. Richard M. Pascoe, "Colonel Warden's 'Wing Commander Efficiency Report,'" February 9, 1988, in author's private collection.
50. McInerney, "Colonel Warden's 'Wing Commander Efficiency Report,'" March 22, 1988, in author's private collection.
51. Kirk, "Colonel Warden's 'Wing Commander Efficiency Report,'" March 22, 1988, in author's private collection.
52. Kirk, interview, March 9, 2004.
53. Halberstam, *War in a Time of Peace*, 49.
54. Col. Richard T. Reynolds (ret.), interview with author, April 17, 2002.
55. Col. Steve G. Wilson, in *Desert Story Collection*, December 11, 1991, 4.
56. Reynolds, interview, October 23, 2001.
57. Horner, interview, March 8–9, 2006; Kirk, interview, March 9, 2004; Ashy, interview, June 28, 2004; Estes, interview, May 25, 2004; Lt. Gen. James F. Record (ret.), interview with author, June 26, 2004; Lt. Gen. Joseph J. Redden (ret.), interview with author, June 30, 2004; Maj. Gen. Everett H. Pratt Jr. (ret.), interview with author, August 18, 2005.
58. Smith, in *Desert Story Collection*, June 18, 1992, 5–7, 12–13; March 15, 2006.
59. Harrington, interview, December 10, 2004.
60. The general officer asked not to be quoted, but the sentiment was reflected in several interviews for this book.

Chapter 7: Air Power Theory: Creation, Loss, and Recovery

1. Hughes, interview, March 8, 2004.
2. Col. Dennis Drew (ret.), "Educating Air Force Officers: Observations after 20 Years at Air University," *Airpower Journal* 11, no. 2 (Summer 1997): 37–44.
3. Lt. Col. James C. Slife, *Creech Blue: General Bill Creech and the Reformation of the Tactical Air Forces, 1978–1984* (Maxwell AFB, AL: Air University Press, 2004), 9; Lt. Col. James C. Slife, interview with author, October 1, 2004.
4. Creech, cited in Slife, *Creech Blue*, 38–39.
5. Ibid., 107.
6. Gen. Robert D. Russ, "The Air Force, the Army, and the Battlefield of the 1990s," *Defense* 88 (July–August 1988): 13.
7. Col. Phillip S. Meilinger (ret.), "The Problem with Our Air Power Doctrine," *Airpower Journal* 6, no. 1 (Spring 1992): 24–31; Lt. Col. David A. Deptula, "Global Reach—

Global Power: Changing the Face of the Air Force," 1, in author's private collection.

8. Dugan, interview, February 24, 2004.

9. Col. John A. Warden, "Project Air Power," May 1988, in author's private collection.

10. Lt. Col. Barry D. Watts (ret.), "Doctrine, Technology and Air Warfare," in Richard Hallion, ed., *Air Power Confronts an Unstable World* (London: Brassey's, 1997), 20; Gen. Charles G. Boyd (ret.), interview with author, May 24, 2004.

11. Davis, *On Target*, 60.

12. Maj. Gen. Charles G. Boyd decided that Warden should be in charge of what used to be called the Deputy Directorate for Planning Integration (XOXI). With the reorganization taking place Warden suggested that it should be the Deputy Directorate for Strategy and Operational Matters (XOXS). In the end it became the Deputy Directorate for Warfighting Concepts (XOXW).

13. Davis, *On Target*, 60–61; Boyd, interview, May 24, 2004.

14. Warden, interview, February 6, 1992, cited in Davis, *On Target*, 61.

15. Warden, interview, December 4, 2004.

16. Col. John A. Warden, "XOXW Goals," memo, August 3, 1988, in author's private collection.

17. Warden, in *Desert Story Collection*, October 22, 1991, 21.

18. Ibid., 28; Boyd, interview, May 24, 2004; Col. Stephen Cullen (ret.), Strategy Division, interview with author, January 4, 2005.

19. Richard G. Davis, *Decisive Force: Strategic Bombing in the Gulf War* (Washington, DC: Air Force History and Museums Program, 1996), 9; Col. T. K. Kearney (ret.), interview with author, February 3, 2005; Col. Ronnie A. Stanfill (ret.), interview with author, May 19, 2004; Col. John W. Roe (ret.), interview with author, December 8, 2004; Boyd, interview, May 24, 2004; Kiraly, interview, October 20, 2004.

20. Lt. Gen. Michael J. Dugan, "The Air Campaign," memorandum to "All Officers DCS Plan & Operations," November 15, 1988, cited in Watts, "Doctrine, Technology and Air Warfare," 41.

21. Maj. Gen. David A. Deptula, interview with author, June 3, 2005.

22. Lt. Gen. Charles G. Boyd to Maj. Gen. James H. Ahmann, memorandum, drafted by Col. John A. Warden, June 5, 1988, in author's private collection.

23. Lt. Gen. Michael M. Dunn, interview with author, March 11, 2004; Col. Jeff Watson (ret.), interview with author, January 18, 2005; Roe, interview, January 13, 2005; Baker, interview, January 21, 2005; Cullen, interview, January 4, 2005.

24. Col. John A. Warden, "Global Strategy Outline," May 1988, in author's private collection.

25. For combining the Five Rings Model with Maslow's theory, see Lt. Col. Peter W. W. Wijninga and Col. Richard Szafranski (ret.), "Beyond Utility Targeting: Toward Axiological Air Operations," *Aerospace Power Journal* 14, no. 4 (Winter 2000), 45–59.

26. Davis, *Decisive Force*, 12.

27. Warden, "Global Strategy Outline."

28. Ibid.

29. Ibid.

30. Putney, *Airpower Advantage*, 393.

31. Col. John A. Warden III, "Centers of Gravity: The Key to Success in War," in author's private collection. In March 1990, at a symposium on "Operational Art and Analysis" sponsored by the Military Operations Research Society (MORS) at the National Defense University, Warden delivered his "centers of gravity" paper.

32. Warden, "Centers of Gravity."
33. Lt. Col. David S. Fadok, "John Boyd and John Warden," in Meilinger, *Paths of Heaven*, 361.
34. Warden, in *Desert Story Collection*, October 22, 1991, 18; Boyd, interview, May 24, 2004.
35. Terrence Colvin, interview with author, July 18, 2005.
36. Lt. Col. David A. Tretler, cited in Davis, *On Target*, 66.
37. Warden, in Tom Clancy, *Fighter Wing: A Guided Tour of an Air Force Combat Wing* (New York: Berkley Books, 1995), 41. See also Putney, *Airpower Advantage*, 394.
38. Col. Phillip S. Meilinger (ret.), interview with author, October 4, 2005.
39. Davis, *On Target*, 66.
40. Warden, in *Desert Story Collection*, October 22, 1991, 22.
41. Williamson Murray, interview with author, April 26, 2005.
42. Williamson Murray, "Grading the War Colleges," *National Interest*, Winter 1986/1987; Lt. Col. David A. Tretler, "Point Paper on Report of Skelton Panel on Military Education," May 22, 1989, in author's private collection.
43. Tretler, "Report of Skelton Panel."
44. Murray, interview, April 26, 2005.
45. Gen. Jack T. Chain, interview with author, June 14, 2004; Donald B. Rice, interview with author, July 17, 1999.
46. Donald B. Rice, in *Desert Story Collection*, December 11, 1991, 31–32.
47. Gen. Robert D. Russ (ret.), in *Desert Story Collection*, December 9, 1991, 76.
48. Mann, *Thunder and Lightning*, 194.
49. Kearney, interview, February 3, 2005.
50. Mann, *Thunder and Lightning*, 164–165.
51. Lt. Col. Daniel T. Kuehl (ret.), Doctrine Division, interview with author, March 22, 2005.
52. United States Air Force, "AFM 1-1 Air Force Doctrine: Employing Aerospace Power," draft, May 25, 1990, 13, in author's private collection.
53. "Parallel operations" were defined as "efforts that are separate from but working in conjunction with concurrent surface operations to achieve broad common objectives," as opposed to what the term came to mean during and after Desert Storm: air attacks conducted simultaneously against several target-sets. United States Air Force, "AFM 1-1 Air Force Doctrine," 22.
54. Ibid., 58–59.
55. Col. Lonnie Dail Turner (ret.), interview with author, April 17, 2003.
56. Warden, in *Desert Story Collection*, May 30, 1991, 110.
57. Lt. Col. David A. Deptula used this expression with Lt. Gen. Charles A. Horner during Operation Desert Storm, and he subsequently posted the statement in the Black Hole to emphasize his view. Deptula, interview, March 7, 2006.
58. Col. Dennis Drew (ret.), "Inventing a Doctrine Process," *Airpower Journal* 9, no. 4 (Summer 1995): 42–52. In March 1992 the air force presented its new doctrine as a concise twenty-page document with references to a second volume that contained essays with historical examples and more detail on the core set of ideas.
59. Cohen, *Gulf War Air Power Survey: Planning*, 191.
60. Turner, interview, April 17, 2003; Warden, interview, December 4, 2004.
61. Warden, "Global Strategy Outline."
62. Brig. Gen. Henry Viccellio, "Composite Air Strike Force," *Air University Quarterly Review* 9, no. 1 (Winter 1956–1957): 27–38.

63. Col. John B. Piazza, "The Air Legion: A Close Encounter with Bureaucratic Politics," short paper, National War College, December 1990, 2.

64. RAND is an independent, non-profit, public service institution that conducts research and analysis of problems of national security and domestic affairs.

65. Col. John B. Piazza (ret.), interview with author, April 1, 2003; Warden, interview, December 4, 2004; Turner, interview, April 17, 2003.

66. Rice, interview, July 17, 1999; Mann, *Thunder and Lightning*, 164.

67. Lt. Col. David A. Deptula, memorandum for Secretary Rice, "Feedback on 'Air Battle Force' concept and briefing," December 7, 1989, in author's private collection.

68. Warden, Deptula, and Piazza, "Air Battle Force: Victorious Tonitus Violentus," undated slides from presentations developed by XOXW and the Office of the Secretary of the Air Force, in author's private collection.

69. Ibid.

70. Martin, interview, May 24, 2005.

71. Russ, in *Desert Story Collection*, December 9, 1991, 3.

72. Warden, in *Desert Story Collection*, May 30, 1991, 109.

73. Ashy, interview, June 28, 2004.

74. Deptula, "Airpower in the 21st Century: The Air Battle Force," Fall 1990, 6, in author's private collection.

75. Ibid., 8.

76. Welch, cited in Piazza, "The Air Legion," 1.

77. Ibid.

78. Gen. Merrill A. McPeak, interview with author, June 22, 2004. See also Merrill A. McPeak, "For the Composite Wing," *Airpower Journal* 4, no. 3 (Fall 1990): 4–12.

79. United States Air Force Report to the 102nd Congress of the United States of America, Fiscal Year 1992/93 (Washington, DC: Government Printing Office, 1991), 2.

80. Welch, interview, April 30, 2004.

81. Deptula, "Airpower in the 21st Century," 8.

82. Col. John A. Warden, "The Future of Air Power: Strategies for a Changing World," July 22, 1990, in author's private collection.

83. Rice, interview, July 17, 1999.

84. Maj. Gen. Ronald J. Bath, interview with author, January 18, 2005.

85. Ibid.

86. Col. Warden with comments from Maj. Meilinger, "Global Airpower and Power Projection," unpublished draft, April 6, 1990, 6, in author's private collection.

87. Hallion, *Storm over Iraq*, 253.

88. Lt. Gen. Michael V. Hayden, interview with author, November 29, 2004; Jeffrey Barnett, interview with author, November 29, 2004; Watson, interview, January 18, 2005.

89. The twenty-eight-page document, "A View of the Air Force Today," in author's private collection.

90. Hayden, interview, November 29, 2004; Barnett, interview, 29 November 2004; Watson, interview, 18 January 2005.

91. Meilinger, "Dog Days for the Air Force: What Is Wrong and How Can It Be Fixed," October 9, 2005, in author's private collection; Hayden, interview, November 29, 2004.

92. Secretary of the Air Force, *The Air Force and the U.S. National Security: "Global Reach—Global Power: Reshaping for the Future"* (Washington, DC: Department of the Air Force, June 1990), 6.

93. Ibid., 8. See also Gen. John M. Loh, "Advocating Mission Needs in Tomorrow's World," *Airpower Journal* 6, no. 1 (Spring 1992): 4–13.

94. Carl H. Builder, *The Icarus Syndrome: The Role of Air Power Theory in the Evolution and Fate of the U.S. Air Force*, 4th printing (New Brunswick: Transaction Publishers, 1998), 269–270, 274–275; Stephen Budiansky, *Air Power: The Men, Machines, and Ideas That Revolutionized War; From Kitty Hawk to Gulf War II* (New York: Viking, 2004), 414.

95. Christopher Bowie, civilian analyst assigned to the office of the secretary of the air force, interview with author, January 21, 2005.

96. Col. John W. Brooks was the chief of Rice's staff group.

97. Hallion, *Storm over Iraq*, 120.

98. Ibid.

99. Rice, interview, July 17, 1999; Dugan, interview, March 15, 2003.

100. Ellen Piazza, interview with author, June 3, 2005.

101. Gen. Jimmie V. Adams (ret.), interview with author, June 19, 2004; Gen. Richard E. Hawley (ret.), director of operations (XOO), interview with author, March 11, 2004; Baker, interview, January 21, 2005.

102. Halberstam, *War in a Time of Peace*, 49.

103. Warden, cited in Fadok, "John Boyd and John A. Warden," 23; Fadok, interview with author, January 31, 2005.

104. Roe, interview, December 8, 2004.

105. Ibid.

106. Brig. Gen. David A. Deptula, interview with author, March 11, 1998; Barnett, interview, November 29, 2004.

107. Davis, *On Target*, 60; Hawley, interview, March 11, 2004; Baker, interview, January 21, 2005; Hayden, interview, November 29, 2004.

108. Reynolds, interview, October 28, 2001; Baker, interview, January 21, 2005; Hayden, interview, November 29, 2004.

109. Wayne Thompson, interview with author, March 1, 1999; Richard G. Davis, interview with author, March 9, 1998; Deptula, interview, March 11, 1998; Hawley, interview, March 11, 2004; Baker, interview, January 21, 2005.

110. Maj. Mark B. Rogers, in *Desert Story Collection*, June 4, 1991, 95.

111. *The Mint*, an account of Lawrence's experiences in the Royal Air Force, was published in 1955. Hugh Trenchard (1873–1956) established the British Independent Air Force in 1918 and served as chief of the air staff from 1919 to 1929.

112. Piazza, interview, 3 June 2005; Halberstam, *War in a Time of Peace*, 47.

Chapter 8: Instant Thunder: Victory through Air Power

1. Cohen, *Gulf War Air Power Survey: Planning*, 17–54, 223.

2. Horner, interview, March 8–9, 2006.

3. Horner, in *Desert Story Collection*, December 2, 1991, 3.

4. Mann, *Thunder and Lightning*, 28.

5. Putney, *Airpower Advantage*, 15; Horner, interview, March 8, 2006.

6. Cohen, *Gulf War Air Power Survey: Planning*, 225.

7. Ibid., 25–54; Putney, *Airpower Advantage*, 17, 348–349.

8. For the Internal Look 90 Mission List, see Cohen, *Gulf War Air Power Survey: Planning*, 53.

9. Ibid.

10. Cohen, *Gulf War Air Power Survey: Planning*, 48–49, 193.

11. Ibid., 46.

12. Note: On August 2, 0100 local time, Iraq invaded Kuwait (that is 0200 Baghdad time and August 1, 1800 in Washington, DC).

13. Putney, *Airpower Advantage*, 22.

14. Ibid., 24.

15. Maj. Gen. Burton R. Moore (ret.), in *Desert Story Collection*, September 21, 1992, 26.

16. Jamison, *Lucrative Targets*, 18.

17. Horner, in *Desert Story Collection*, December 2, 1991, 13.

18. Horner, interview, March 8, 2006.

19. Putney, *Airpower Advantage*, 27.

20. Ibid.

21. Department of Defense, *Conduct of the Persian Gulf War*, 65.

22. Horner, in *Desert Story Collection*, December 2, 1991, 30.

23. Schwarzkopf, *It Doesn't Take a Hero*, 371.

24. Margie Warden, interview, August 11, 2004.

25. Warden, in *Desert Story Collection*, October 22, 1991, 35–36.

26. Warden's view proved largely to be correct and has been confirmed. See for example Moore, in *Desert Story Collection*, September 21, 1992, 5–6.

27. Cohen, *Gulf War Air Power Survey: Planning*, 223. See also Thomas A. Keaney and Eliot A. Cohen, *Revolution in Warfare? Air Power in the Persian Gulf* (Annapolis: Naval Institute Press, 1995), 25: "Exercise-ending attacks against the enemy homeland reflected the decades of planning for East-West conflict in Europe in which such strikes were closely associated with the escalation of nuclear conflict. Furthermore, CENTCOM classified the Internal Look 90 simulated attacks as 'long-range interdiction,' a term considerably different in its connotations from the 'strategic attacks' of Desert Storm. And finally, the concluding strikes of Internal Look 90 in no way matched the weight and intensity of the air campaign that began on 17 January 1991."

28. Moore, in *Desert Story Collection*, September 21, 1992, 5–6.

29. A hard look at those CENTCOM plans tends to support his view. See Mann, *Thunder and Lightning*, 27.

30. Warden, interview, December 4–5, 2004; Dunn, interview, March 11, 2004.

31. Lt. Gen. Robert M. Alexander, in *Desert Story Collection*, May 30, 1991, 1.

32. Ibid.; Cohen, *Gulf War Air Power Survey: Operations*, 36–37.

33. Adams, in *Desert Story Collection*, February 3, 1992, 2; Brig. Gen. Paul R. Dordal (ret.), staff officer in the Joint Operations Division, J-3, Joint Staff, from June 1990 to July 1992, interview with author, June 1, 2005.

34. Gordon and Trainor, *The Generals' War*, 75–76; Schwarzkopf, *It Doesn't Take a Hero*, 313.

35. Davis, *On Target*, 58; Putney, *Airpower Advantage*, 33; Adm. William A. Owens, (ret.), senior military assistant to the secretary of defense, interview with author, January 13, 2006.

36. Gen. H. Norman Schwarzkopf (ret.), interview with author, May 25, 2004.

37. Lt. Gen. Charles A. May Jr. (ret.), in *Desert Story Collection*, August 21, 1992, 85; Moore, in *Desert Story Collection*, September 21, 1992, 13.

38. Reynolds, *Heart of the Storm*, 24.

39. Loh, in *Desert Story Collection,* September 26, 1991, 3.

40. Dugan, interview, February 24, 2004.

41. Ibid.
42. Horner, in *Desert Story Collection*, December 2, 1991, 33.
43. Davis, *On Target*, 59.
44. Ibid.
45. Tom Peters, *Thriving on Chaos: Handbook for a Management Revolution* (New York: Alfred A. Knopf, 1987).
46. Reynolds, *Heart of the Storm*, 28.
47. Kearney, interview, February 3, 2005.
48. Putney, *Airpower Advantage*, 44–45; Cohen, *Gulf War Air Power Survey: Planning*, 109.
49. Cohen, *Gulf War Air Power Survey: Planning*, 111.
50. Mann, *Thunder and Lightning*, 146–147.
51. Ibid., 100–101 and 125; Warden, in *Desert Story Collection*, May 30, 1991, 57–58.
52. "'Instant Thunder,' Proposed Strategic Air Campaign," August 13, 1990, cited in Cohen, *Gulf War Air Power Survey: Operations*, 23.
53. Warden, in *Desert Story Collection*, May 30, 1991, 114.
54. Reynolds, *Heart of the Storm*, 34.
55. Putney, *Airpower Advantage*, 32.
56. Col. James R. Blackburn, in *Desert Story Collection*, April 21, 1993, 16.
57. Reynolds, *Heart of the Storm*, 52.
58. Ibid.
59. Alexander, in *Desert Story Collection*, May 30, 1991, 13.
60. Ryan objected to Instant Thunder on two counts: Horner should have been involved and it was too aggressive. Ryan, interview, May 7, 2004.
61. Putney, *Airpower Advantage*, 54.
62. Rice, in *Desert Story Collection*, December 11, 1991, 8, 18.
63. Rice, interview, July 17, 1999; February 16, 2006.
64. Reynolds, *Heart of the Storm*, 52; Alexander, in *Desert Story Collection*, May 30, 1991, 26.
65. Putney, *Airpower Advantage*, 51.
66. Warden, in *Desert Story Collection*, December 11, 1991, 11; October 22, 1991, 58.
67. On precision bombing, see for example Lt. Gen. Buster C. Glosson, "Impact of Precision Weapons on Air Combat Operations," *Airpower Journal* 7, no. 2 (Summer 1993): 4–10; Lt. Col. Edward C. Mann, "One Target, One Bomb: Is the Principle of Mass Dead?" *Airpower Journal* 7, no. 1 (Spring 1995): 35–43.
68. Reynolds, *Heart of the Storm*, 105.
69. Lt. Col. Bernard E. Harvey, memorandum for record, August 10, 1990, 1830, Subject: "Instant Thunder" briefing to U.S. CINCCENT, 10 August/1320-1400/HQ CENTCOM/J3 Office/MacDill AFB, FL. Attendees: CINCCENT General Schwarzkopf, deputy commander CINCCENT, Lieutenant General Rogers, J-3 Major General Moore, AF/XOX Major General Alexander, AF/XOXW Colonel Warden and AF/XOXWS Lieutenant Colonel Harvey. See also Alexander, in *Desert Story Collection*, May 30, 1991, 29–30; Cohen, *Gulf War Air Power Survey: Planning*, 112. See also Schwarzkopf, *It Doesn't Take a Hero*, 318.
70. Reynolds, *Heart of the Storm*, 57; Alexander, in *Desert Story Collection*, June 3, 1992, 26.
71. Reynolds, *Heart of the Storm*, 58.
72. Schwarzkopf, interview, May 25, 2004.
73. Moore, in *Desert Story Collection*, September 21, 1992, 37.

74. John T. Corell, "The Strategy of Desert Storm," *Air Force Magazine* 89, no. 1 (January 2006).

75. Loh, in *Desert Story Collection,* September 26, 1991, 17.

76. Russ, in *Desert Story Collection,* December 9, 1991, 2.

77. Adams, in *Desert Story Collection,* February 3, 1992, 6–8, 22; Russ, in *Desert Story Collection,* December 9, 1991, 19–20, 49; Warden, in *Desert Story Collection,* May 30, 1991, 110.

78. Russ, in *Desert Story Collection,* December 9, 1991, 20.

79. Ibid., 67.

80. Gen. Jack T. Chain Jr., in *Desert Story Collection,* August 12, 1991, 15–16.

81. Russ, in *Desert Story Collection,* December 9, 1991, 23.

82. Ibid., 9–10.

83. Ibid., 10, 31.

84. Adams, in *Desert Story Collection,* February 3, 1992, 12, 15; Loh, in *Desert Story Collection,* September 26, 1991, 16–17; Warden, in *Desert Story Collection,* May 30, 1991, 110.

85. Col. Richard D. Bristow, in *Desert Story Collection,* November 9, 1992, 10–11.

86. Ibid.; Reynolds, *Heart of the Storm,* 102.

87. Putney, *Airpower Advantage,* 60.

88. Russ, in *Desert Story Collection,* December 9, 1991, 49.

89. Putney, *Airpower Advantage,* 60.

90. Russ, in *Desert Story Collection,* December 9, 1991, 11.

91. Ibid.

92. Ibid., 12–13.

93. Maj. Gen. Thomas R. Griffith to Maj. Gen. Robert M. Alexander, "CENTCOM Air Campaign Plan," briefing, August 11, 1990, cited in Cohen, *Gulf War Air Power Survey: Operations,* 25.

94. Ibid.; Adams, in *Desert Story Collection,* February 3, 1992, 8.

95. Griffith, "CENTCOM Air Campaign Plan," cited in Cohen, *Gulf War Air Power Survey: Operations,* 25.

96. Cohen, *Gulf War Air Power Survey: Operations,* 25.

97. Warden, interview, December 4, 2004.

98. Putney, *Airpower Advantage,* 58–59.

99. Ibid., 59.

100. Ibid., 61; Reynolds, *Heart of the Storm,* 71.

101. Atkinson, *Crusade,* 60; Alexander, in *Desert Story Collection,* May 30, 1991, 36.

102. Cohen, *Gulf War Air Power Survey: Operations,* 32.

103. Reynolds, *Heart of the Storm,* 72.

104. Lt. Col. Ben Harvey, memo, August 11, 1990, cited in Cohen, *Gulf War Air Power Survey: Effects and Effectiveness,* 74.

105. Reynolds, *Heart of the Storm,* 72.

106. Loh, in *Desert Story Collection,* September 26, 1991, 20.

107. Ibid., 22; Loh, interview with author, June 29, 2004.

108. Alexander, in *Desert Story Collection,* May 30, 1991, 38.

109. Reynolds, *Heart of the Storm,* 71.

110. Putney, *Airpower Advantage,* 62.

111. Ibid.

112. Adams, in *Desert Story Collection,* February 3, 1992, 36, 40; Alexander, in *Desert Story Collection,* May 30, 1991, 38.

113. Warden, in *Desert Story Collection*, October 22, 1991, 71.
114. Wayne Thompson, interview, March 1, 1999.
115. Alexander, in *Desert Story Collection*, June 3, 1992, 15.
116. Putney, *Airpower Advantage*, 63.
117. Powell, *My American Journey*, 459–460.
118. James Coyne, *Airpower in the Gulf* (Arlington, VA: Air Force Association Book, 1992), 45; Kiraly, interview, October 20, 2004.
119. Bristow, in *Desert Story Collection*, November 9, 1992, 22.
120. Ibid., 26–27.
121. Ibid., 72.
122. Adams, in *Desert Story Collection*, February 3, 1992, 7.
123. Adams, interview, June 19, 2004.
124. Adams, in *Desert Story Collection*, February 3, 1992, 40; Adams, interview, June 19, 2004.
125. Adams, interview, June 19, 2004.
126. Adams, in *Desert Story Collection*, February 3, 1992, 3.
127. Ibid., 23.
128. Putney, *Airpower Advantage*, 68.
129. Adams, in *Desert Story Collection*, February 3, 1992, 23.
130. Alexander, in *Desert Story Collection*, June 3, 1992, 15.
131. Putney, *Airpower Advantage*, 68.
132. Ibid.
133. Ibid., 69.
134. Cohen, *Gulf War Air Campaign Survey: Planning*, 113.
135. Davis, *On Target*, 73.
136. Ibid., 71; Reynolds, *Heart of the Storm*, 74.
137. Davis, *On Target*, 74.
138. Rice, interview, July 17, 1999.
139. Dugan, in *Desert Story Collection*, August 15, 1991, 14.
140. Deptula, in *Desert Story Collection*, November 1, 1990, 3; Warden, in *Desert Story Collection*, October 22, 1991, 88–89.
141. Ibid.
142. Davis, *On Target*, 74.
143. Reynolds, *Heart of the Storm*, 101.
144. Deptula, in *Desert Story Collection*, May 22, 1991, 20; Col. Ben Harvey, memorandum for Col. Richard Reynolds, "Comments on March 1994 Draft, *Heart of the Storm*," June 2, 1994, in author's private collection.
145. Cullen, interview, January 4, 2005.
146. Cohen, *Gulf War Air Power Survey: Planning*, 126; Putney, *Airpower Advantage*, 77.
147. Harvey, "Comments on *Heart of the Storm*."
148. Davis, *On Target*, 76.
149. Reynolds, *Heart of the Storm*, 108.
150. Deptula, in *Desert Story Collection*, May 22, 1991, 25.
151. Ibid., 26.
152. Putney, *Airpower Advantage*, 81.
153. Ibid.
154. Deptula, in *Desert Story Collection*, May 22, 1991, 28.
155. Ibid.; Reynolds, *Heart of the Storm*, 107–109.
156. Jamison, *Lucrative Targets*, 25, 169.

157. Reynolds, *Heart of the Storm*, 110.
158. As he noted on a piece of paper during Warden's presentation: "1. Instant Thunder; 2. Suppression of air defenses over Kuwait; 3. Attrition of enemy forces by fifty percent; and 4. Ground attack (?)" See Schwarzkopf, *It Doesn't Take a Hero*, 320.
159. Schwarzkopf, interview, May 25, 2004.
160. Reynolds, *Heart of the Storm*, 43; Davis, *On Target*, 32.
161. Davis, *On Target*, 82.
162. Adams, in *Desert Story Collection*, February 3, 1992, 17.
163. Ibid., 13.
164. Wilson, in *Desert Story Collection*, December 11, 1991, 11; Adams, in *Desert Story Collection*, February 3, 1992, 14.
165. Col. Samuel J. Baptiste (ret.), interview with author, August 30, 2005; Wilson, in *Desert Story Collection*, December 11, 1991.
166. Adams, in *Desert Story Collection*, February 3, 1992, 17.
167. Ibid., 27.
168. Deptula, in *Desert Story Collection*, May 22, 1991, 9; Putney, *Airpower Advantage*, 16.
169. Putney, *Airpower Advantage*, 121.
170. Maj. Gen. Larry L. Henry (ret.), interview with author, June 29, 2004.
171. Lt. Gen. Patrick P. Caruana (ret.), interview with author, August 30, 2005; Baptiste, interview with author, August 31, 2005.
172. Putney, *Airpower Advantage*, 94.
173. Jamison, *Lucrative Targets*, 27.
174. Henry, interview, June 29, 2004. Critics have often argued that the early iterations of Instant Thunder were incomplete, but it should be noted that Warden and company were able, in the span of forty-eight hours, to produce and present a strategic outline with enough detail to win the approval and support of both the chairman of the joint chiefs and the CENTCOM commander in chief; seven days later, with an expansion of his initial team, Warden provided Schwarzkopf with a document of more than a hundred pages and detailed annexes for an undertaking at the operational level.
175. Horner, interview, March 8, 2006.
176. Deptula, in *Desert Story Collection*, May 23, 1991, 20–24; Harvey, "Comments on *Heart of the Storm*."
177. Warden, in *Desert Story Collection*, October 22, 1991, 108.
178. Horner, interview, March 8, 2006.
179. Deptula, in *Desert Story Collection*, May 22, 1991, 26.
180. Reynolds, *Heart of the Storm*, 124.
181. Ibid., 118; Putney, *Airpower Advantage*, 127.
182. Deptula, in *Desert Story Collection*, May 22, 1991, 38.
183. Maj. Gen. Larry L. Henry, interview with Williamson Murray and Barry D. Watts, August 1992, in author's private collection; Lt. Col. Ben Harvey, notes, August 20, 1990, cited in Cohen, *Gulf War Air Power Survey: Operations*, 27. Horner, interview, July 20, 1999.
184. Deptula, in *Desert Story Collection*, May 23, 1991, 26–38.
185. Harvey, cited in Reynolds, *Heart of the Storm*, 126.
186. Gordon and Trainor, *The Generals' War*, 75; Deptula, in *Desert Story Collection*, May 23, 1991, 55.
187. Putney, *Airpower Advantage*, 127.
188. Warden, in *Desert Story Collection*, October 22, 1991, 109; Deptula, in *Desert Story Collection*, May 23, 1991, 40–46.

189. Putney, *Airpower Advantage*, 130.
190. Deptula, in *Desert Story Collection*, May 23, 1991, 43–46.
191. Horner, interview, March 8, 2006.
192. Horner, interview with Jamison, Davis, and Barlow, March 4, 1992, 31.
193. Tom Clancy, *Every Man a Tiger*, with Gen. Chuck Horner (ret.) (New York: G. P. Putnam's Sons, 199), 260–265.
194. Horner, interview, March 8, 2006.
195. Putney, *Airpower Advantage*, 131.
196. Warden, in *Desert Story Collection*, October 22, 1991, 71.
197. Ibid., 110.
198. Davis, *On Target*, 84.

Chapter 9: Checkmate: Support to the Military Campaign

1. Alexander, in *Desert Story Collection*, May 30, 1991, 45.
2. Harvey, notes, in Deptula, in *Desert Story Collection*, May 23, 1991, 56.
3. Putney, *Airpower Advantage*, 135–136, 155.
4. Ibid., 135, 150.
5. Ibid., 136.
6. Horner, interview, March 9, 2006.
7. Horner, interview, August 20, 1999; in *Desert Story Collection*, March 1992, 15; Glosson, in *Desert Story Collection*, June 4, 1992, 31.
8. Putney, *Airpower Advantage*, 132–133; Henry, interview, June 29, 2004.
9. Putney, *Airpower Advantage*, 138; Henry, interview, June 29, 2004.
10. Glosson, *War with Iraq*, 14; Glosson, in *Desert Story Collection*, June 4, 1991, 46.
11. Horner, interview, March 8, 2006.
12. Glosson, *War with Iraq: Critical Lessons*, 17.
13. Glosson, cited in Cohen, *Gulf War Air Power Survey: Operations*, 28.
14. Glosson, *War with Iraq*, 17; Glosson, in *Desert Story Collection*, May 29, 1991, 30.
15. Glosson, *War with Iraq*, 18.
16. Ibid., 16.
17. Glosson, in *Desert Story Collection*, June 4, 1992, 5, 9, 28.
18. Putney, *Airpower Advantage*, 144.
19. Glosson, *War with Iraq*, 24; Deptula, in *Desert Story Collection*, May 23, 1991, 148.
20. Glosson, *War with Iraq*, 29; Glosson, in *Desert Story Collection*, May 29, 1991, 51.
21. Putney, *Airpower Advantage*, 146; Henry, interview, June 29, 2004.
22. Horner, in *Desert Story Collection*, December 2, 1991, 40; Putney, *Airpower Advantage*, 146.
23. Putney, *Airpower Advantage*, 148.
24. Cohen, *Gulf War Air Power Survey: Command and Control*, 164–167; Cohen, *Gulf War Air Power Survey: Planning*, xiii.
25. Deptula, cited in Putney, *Airpower Advantage*, 146.
26. Cohen, *Gulf War Air Power Survey: Planning*, 92–95.
27. Glosson, *War with Iraq*, 33.
28. Putney, *Airpower Advantage*, 136, 179.
29. Ibid., 359.
30. Allan W. Howey, "Checkmate Journal: The Gulf War Air Campaign from Inside the Pentagon," CAFH Working Papers (Washington, DC: Center for Air Force History Air Staff Division, 1994), 19.
31. Horner, interview, March 9, 2006.

32. Deptula, interview, March 7, 2006.

33. Putney, *Airpower Advantage*, 164.

34. Davis, *On Target*, 92. Note that Deptula introduced the phrase "Master Attack Plan" (MAP): after Desert Storm, for joint reasons, the term was modified to "Master Air Attack Plan" (MAAP). Cohen, *Gulf War Air Power Survey: Operations*, 42.

35. Deptula, in *Desert Story Collection*, December 10, 1991, 25–26.

36. Putney, *Airpower Advantage*, 168.

37. Deptula, in *Desert Story Collection*, May 22, 1991, 39.

38. Ibid.; Adams, in *Desert Story Collection*, February 3, 1992, 53.

39. Capt. John R. Glock, interview, January 30, 1992, cited in Cohen, *Gulf War Air Power Study: Command and Control*, 176.

40. Davis, *On Target*, 178.

41. Baptiste, in *Desert Story Collection*, September 24, 1992, 25.

42. Putney, *Airpower Advantage*, 180.

43. Ibid.,180–181.

44. Ibid., 188.

45. Ibid., 186.

46. Ibid., 88.

47. Ibid.,184.

48. Schwarzkopf, *It Doesn't Take a Hero*, 353–354.

49. Putney, *Airpower Advantage*, 189.

50. Ibid., 190.

51. Glosson, *War with Iraq*, 26.

52. Putney, *Airpower Advantage*, 190.

53. Adams, in *Desert Story Collection*, February 3, 1992, 22, 40.

54. Ibid., 40.

55. Alexander, in *Desert Story Collection*, June 3, 1992, 56.

56. Putney, *Airpower Advantage*, 192.

57. Ibid., 146; Horner, in *Desert Story Collection*, December 2, 1991, 61.

58. Horner, interview, June 30, 2005.

59. Putney, *Airpower Advantage*, 191.

60. Charles E. Allen, interview with author, July 12, 2004.

61. See Davis, *On Target*, 225.

62. Rogers, interview, September 9, 2003. Warden had already tasked Rogers with the AT&T project on September 6, 1990. See also Putney, *Airpower Advantage*, 195.

63. Putney, *Airpower Advantage*, 212–213.

64. Horner, interview, March 8, 2006.

65. Horner, in *Desert Story Collection*, March 4, 1992, 31.

66. Gen. Michael J. Dugan, quoted in Rick Atkinson, "U.S. to Rely on Air Strikes if War Erupts," *The Washington Post*, September 16, 1990, A1.

67. "U.S. War Plan: Air Strikes to Topple Hussein Regime," *Aviation Week and Space Technology*, September 24, 1990, 16–18.

68. Dugan, in *Desert Story Collection*, August 15, 1991, 25.

69. Glosson, *War with Iraq*, 45.

70. Ibid.

71. Lt. Gen. Robert M. Alexander (ret.), interview with author, June 28–29, 2004.

72. Dugan, in *Desert Story Collection*, August 15, 1991, 31.

73. Bob Woodward, *The Commanders* (New York: Simon and Schuster, 1992), 292–293.

74. Hallion, *Storm over Iraq*, 146; Loh, in *Desert Story Collection*, October 16, 1991, 53.

75. Howey, "Checkmate Journal," 2.

76. Putney, *Airpower Advantage*, 207.

77. Adams, interview, June 19, 2004.

78. Rogers, interview, September 9, 2003.

79. Henry, interview, June 29, 2004.

80. Putney, *Airpower Advantage*, 205.

81. Warden, "Point Paper on BQM-74," September 14, 1990, in author's private collection.

82. May, in *Desert Story Collection*, August 21, 1992, 33, 121.

83. Adams, interview, June 19, 2004; Alexander, interview, June 28–29, 2004.

84. Warden, in *Desert Story Collection*, October 22, 1991, 117.

85. Rogers, interview, September 9, 2003.

86. Putney, *Airpower Advantage*, 206.

87. Ibid., 205.

88. Jamison, *Lucrative Targets*, 28.

89. Putney, *Airpower Advantage*, 204.

90. Instant Thunder Brief, "Campaign Flow," August 16, 1990, cited in Cohen, *Gulf War Air Power Survey: Operations*, 117–118.

91. Putney, *Airpower Advantage*, 220.

92. Glosson, *War with Iraq*, 57.

93. Ibid., 58.

94. Gordon and Trainor, *The Generals' War*, 135–141.

95. Davis, *On Target*, 105.

96. Putney, *Airpower Advantage*, 222.

97. Davis, *On Target*, 105.

98. Putney, *Airpower Advantage*, 222.

99. Cohen, *Gulf War Air Power Survey: Operations*, 29.

100. Davis, *On Target*, 132.

101. Cohen, *Gulf War Air Power Survey: Operations*, 29; Glosson, *War with Iraq*, 63.

102. Diane T. Putney, "From Instant Thunder to Desert Storm: Developing the Gulf War Air Campaign's Phases," *Air Power History* 41, no. 3 (Fall 1994): 48; Loh, in *Desert Story Collection*, October 16, 1991, 75–76.

103. George Bush and Brent Scowcroft, *A World Transformed* (New York: Alfred A. Knopf, 1998), 384.

104. Glosson, *War with Iraq*, 48; Putney, *Airpower Advantage*, 225.

105. Putney, *Airpower Advantage*, 232.

106. Ibid., 233.

107. Project AIR FORCE, "Gulf Crisis Analysis," October 6, 1990 (34 slides), in author's private collection.

108. Putney, *Airpower Advantage*, 232.

109. Ibid.

110. Ibid., 234.

111. Ibid., 235.

112. Warden, cited in Putney, *Airpower Advantage*, 235.

113. Warden, cited in Cohen, *Gulf War Air Power Survey: Planning*, 172.

114. Cohen, *Gulf War Air Power Survey: Planning*, 172.

115. Maj. Roy "Mac" Sikes, "Kuwait Offensive Air Campaign: Phases II & III," presented to General Loh, October 26, 1990, 7, in author's private collection.

116. Ibid., 21.

117. Thompson, interview, March 1, 1999; Cohen, *Gulf War Air Power Survey: Planning*, 172.

118. Putney, *Airpower Advantage*, 237.

119. Warden, "Modeling methodology," October 14, 1990, in author's private collection.

120. Col. T. N. Dupuy (ret.), "Casualty Forecasts, Attrition Anderson's War Toll Estimate Widely Inaccurate," *Washington Post*, November 7, 1990.

121. It is difficult to assess who came up with the 50 percent analogy first, but it was Warden and his Checkmate team that first provided substance on how to achieve 50 percent attrition (Glosson, *War with Iraq*, 69). The attrition rate suggested by Checkmate proved too optimistic for a number of reasons. First, the weather was worse than planned for; second, the coalition had to fly higher than planned (resulting in less accurate bombing); and, third, Checkmate planners assumed that the F-16 would use Mavericks against enemy equipment, but the F-16 community had not prepared itself in peacetime to employ that antitank missile. See Cohen, *Gulf War Air Power Survey: Operations*, 254–258.

122. Glosson, cited in Putney, *Airpower Advantage*, 238.

123. Rogers, interview, September 9, 2003.

124. Putney, *Airpower Advantage*, 239.

125. Meilinger, "Dog Days."

126. Gen. Merrill A. McPeak, in *Desert Story Collection*, November 5, 1992, 2; McPeak, interview, June 22, 2004; Warden, interview, June 9, 2006.

127. Warden had suggested this proposition in early October. Warden, "Campaign Plan," October 9, 1990, in author's private collection.

128. Putney, *Airpower Advantage*, 242.

129. Alexander, interview, June 28, 2004.

130. Putney, *Airpower Advantage*, 238.

131. Capt. Mike "Carlos" Johnson (ret.), interview with author, February 27, 2003.

132. Ibid., 242–243.

133. Cohen, *Gulf War Air Power Survey: Planning*, 172.

134. Putney, *Airpower Advantage*, 242.

135. Glosson, *War with Iraq*, 70; Putney, *Airpower Advantage*, 245.

136. Putney, *Airpower Advantage*, 246. See also Cohen, *Gulf War Air Power Survey: Planning*, 175.

137. Putney, *Airpower Advantage*, 248.

138. Col. Daniel W. Jacobowitz, interview with author, February 9, 2005.

139. Davis, *On Target*, 57.

140. Putney, *Airpower Advantage*, 298–299.

141. Ibid., 298.

142. Warden, memorandum for General Loh, November 1, 1990, in author's private collection.

143. Horner, in *Desert Story Collection*, December 2, 1991, 42; March 4, 1992, 7.

144. Gordon and Trainor, *The Generals' War*, 492–493

145. Deptula, in *Desert Story Collection*, May 22, 1991, 33, 40.

146. Adams, in *Desert Story Collection*, February 3, 1992, 12; Alexander, in *Desert Story Collection*, June 3, 1992, 67; Maj. Gen. John A. Corder, in *Desert Story Collection*, February 4, 1992, 51; Smith, in *Desert Story Collection*, June 18, 1992, 51.

147. Glosson, in *Desert Story Collection*, June 4, 1992, 5, 9, 28.

148. Ibid.; 115; May 29, 1991, 122–123.

149. Putney, *Airpower Advantage*, 192.

150. Jamison, *Lucrative Targets*, 29.

151. The author is grateful to Maj. William E. "Dollar" Young for having suggested this analogy. For the origins and significance of effects-based operations, see for example Maj. Gen. David A. Deptula, "Effects-Based Operations: Change in the Nature of War," in John Andreas Olsen, ed., *A Second Aerospace Century* (Trondheim, Norway: Royal Norwegian Air Force Academy, 2001), 135–174.

152. Horner, interview, March 9, 2006; Adams, interview, June 19, 2004.

Chapter 10: Checkmate: Support to the Political Campaign

1. Hallion, *Storm over Iraq*, 1–2.

2. Ibid., 2.

3. Ibid., 4.

4. Joel Achenbach, "The Experts in Retreat," *Washington Post*, February 28, 1991; John J. Fialka and Andy Pasztor, "Grim Calculus: If Mideast War Erupts, Air Power Will Hold Key to U.S. Casualties," *New York Times*, November 15, 1990. Cited in Hallion, *Storm over Iraq*, 2–3.

5. Warden, in *Desert Story Collection*, December 11, 1991, 48–49.

6. Warden, in *Desert Story Collection*, May 30, 1991, 88.

7. Warden, "Answer to Nunn Questions," September 26, 1990, in author's private collection.

8. Loh, in *Desert Story Collection*, September 26, 1991, 49.

9. Glosson was also very frustrated with Powell's apparent attitude to air power. See Glosson, *War with Iraq*, 58.

10. Loh, in *Desert Story Collection*, October 16, 1991, 49.

11. Ibid., 30.

12. Rice, interview, July 17, 1999.

13. Howey, "Checkmate Journal," 23. Lt. Col. Garry R. Trexler was the military assistant to the secretary of defense (July 1989–June 1990) and then the senior military assistant to the deputy secretary of defense (June 1990–July 1991). Lt. Col. John L. Barry was the military assistant to the secretary of defense (July 1990–August 1992).

14. Warden, in *Desert Story Collection*, May 30, 1991, 91.

15. Alexander, in *Desert Story Collection*, June 3, 1992, 60; Howey, "Checkmate Journal," 63.

16. Alexander, interview, June 28–29, 2004. September 14, 1990, Rice invited Wolfowitz, Libby, and Lt. Gen. Dale Vesser (ret.) to see the Instant Thunder presentation in his office; October 2 Libby requested some additional information on the strategic air campaign and went to Checkmate for a presentation; November 8 Libby requested information on Phase III and again went to Checkmate for a presentation; November 16 Libby requested a brief for Wolfowitz and Henry Rowan, but the Joint Staff told Major General May that Warden should not give such a briefing. Warden, "Memo for General May," October 13, 1990, in author's private collection.

17. Gen. Colin Powell speaking on the Crisis in the Persian Gulf Region: United States Policy Options and Implications to the Committee on Armed Services, S. Hrg. 101-1071, 101st Cong., 2nd sess., *Congressional Record* 663 (December 3, 1990).

18. Putney, *Airpower Advantage*, 264.

19. Deptula, in *Desert Story Collection*, December 10, 1991, 39.

20. Rice, in *Desert Story Collection*, December 11, 1991, 19.

21. Loh, in *Desert Story Collection*, October 16, 1991, 49.

22. Deptula, interview, March 25, 2006.
23. Edward N. Luttwak, interview with author, February 27, 2006.
24. McPeak, interview with author, June 22, 2004.
25. McPeak, interview, November 5, 1992, 14.
26. Bush and Scowcroft, *A World Transformed*, 432, 448.
27. Warden to Secretary of Defense Richard Cheney, briefing, December 11, 1990, in author's private collection; Gordon and Trainor, *The Generals' War*, 178.
28. Jamison, *Lucrative Targets*, 115.
29. The USAF lost fourteen aircraft in the war.
30. Horner, in *Desert Story Collection*, December 2, 1991, 45; Rice, interview, July 17, 1999.
31. Putney, *Airpower Advantage*, 360–361; Horner, interview, March 8, 2006. As it happened, on February 23, the CINCCENT BDA indicated after thirty-nine days air power had destroyed 1,688 tanks (39 percent); 1,452 artillery pieces (47 percent); and 929 armored personnel carriers (32 percent).
32. The air campaign's strike forces available January 15 totaled 1,316 aircraft: 73 F-5s; 98 F-14s; 133 F-15Cs; 48 F-15Es; 210 F-16s; 162 F/A-18s; 64 F-111s; 36 F-117s; 105 A-6Es; 22 A-7s; 60 AV-8Bs; 144 A-10s; 42 B-52s; 53 Tornados; 28 Jaguars; 12 Mirage 2000s; 8 Mirage F1s; and 18 CF-18s. Horner went to war with the following ten target categories and 238 targets: Strategic Air Defense (28); Strategic Chemical and Scuds (25); Leadership (32); Republican Guard and Military Support (44); Telecommunications (26); Electricity (16); Oil (7); Railroads (28); Airfields (28); and Ports (4). As it happened, from January 17 to February 28, the coalition made 11,610 strikes against twelve targets sets, excluding the Republican Guard: Leadership (260); Electric Power (280); Naval targets (370); Oil (540); Telecommunication and C3 (580); IADS and KARI (630); Military industry (970); NBC (990); LOCs (1,170); SAMs (1,370); Scuds (1,460); and Airfields (2,990).
33. Warden, "Planning to Win," in Shaun Clarke, ed., *Testing the Limits* (Fairbairn, Australia: Air Power Studies Centre, 1998), 78.
34. Warden, letter to the Secretary of the Air Force, January 27, 1991, in author's private collection.
35. Dan Balz and Rick Atkinson, "Powell Vows to Isolate Iraqi Army and 'Kill it,'" *Washington Post*, January 24, 1991, A01.
36. Smith, in *Desert Story Collection*, June 18, 1992, 4. See also Perry M. Smith, *How CNN Fought the War: A View from the Inside* (New York: Birch Lane Press, 1991). Smith resigned from CNN on June 13, 1998, over the CNN special "The Valley of Death," which accused the U.S. military of using lethal nerve gas (sarin) to kill American defectors in Laos during the Vietnam War.
37. Smith, interview, January 14, 2006.
38. Smith, in *Desert Story Collection*, June 18, 1992, 124.
39. Ibid., 5.
40. See Hallion, *Storm over Iraq*, 197–200.
41. Howey, "Checkmate Journal," 29.
42. Glosson, *War with Iraq*, 201, 208.
43. Howey, "Checkmate Journal," 30.
44. Cohen, *Gulf War Air Power Survey: Effects and Effectiveness*, 202–203.
45. Ibid., 100.
46. Warden, interview, December 4, 2004; Glosson, *War with Iraq*, 209.
47. Howey, "Checkmate Journal," 33.

48. Halberstam, *War in a Time of Peace*, 52; Warden, "Airpower in the Gulf," *Daedalus Flyer* 36, no. 1 (Spring 1996): 15; Trexler, in *Desert Story Collection*, May 11, 1992, 19.
49. Glosson, *War with Iraq*, 209.
50. Howey, "Checkmate Journal," 34.
51. Ibid.
52. Hallion, *Storm over Iraq*, 226.
53. Ibid.
54. Yevgeni Primakov, interview, *BBC Frontline*, part one, 3; Ken Fireman, "Hussein's Peace Feeler: Says He'll Cooperate with Soviets," *New York Newsday*, February 13, 1991.
55. Warden, in *Desert Story Collection*, December 11, 1991, 114.
56. Charles Allen, interview with author, July 12, 2004.
57. On February 13, 1991, coalition bombs struck the al-Firdos bunker, killing several hundred Iraqi civilians who had sought shelter there. On the basis of the data available to them the planners believed that the facility had been converted to a C^3 military command post and was being used by the Iraqi secret police. Thereafter the NCA considered such bombardments too risky. Michael Lewis, "The Law of Aerial Bombardment in the 1991 Gulf War," *American Journal of International Law* 97 (2003), 481–509.
58. Cohen, *Gulf War Air Power Survey: Operations*, 243.
59. Ibid., 291.
60. Howey, "Checkmate Journal," 48.
61. Ibid., 54.
62. Warden's idea of a coup was based on intuition, albeit inspired by Edward Luttwak's *Coup d'État* (Cambridge, MA: Harvard University Press, 1968). Warden, interview, December 4, 2004.
63. Jamison, *Lucrative Targets*, 115.
64. Howey, "Checkmate Journal," 54.
65. Warden, in *Desert Story Collection*, December 11, 1991, 45, 115.
66. Warden, interview, February 13, 2006.
67. "Soviets Say Iraq Accepts Kuwaiti Pullout," *New York Times*, February 22, 1991, 1.
68. Powell, cited in Hallion, *Storm over Iraq*, 201.
69. Lt. Gen. Brent Scowcroft (ret.), interview with author, January 24, 2006.
70. Glosson, *War with Iraq*, 216.
71. Warden, in *Desert Story Collection*, December 11, 1991, 119.
72. Howey, "Checkmate Journal," 55.
73. Putney, *Airpower Advantage*, 299; Warden, interview, February 22, 2006.
74. Warden, "Memorandum for General Adams," September 24, 1990, in author's private collection.
75. Howey, "Checkmate Journal," 3.
76. Putney, *Airpower Advantage*, 281. At the DIA Center, Maj. Jeff Lord became the Checkmate representative to the Phase II BDA cell, while Lt. Col. Steve Stern became the Checkmate representative to the Phase III BDA cell.
77. Cohen, *Gulf War Air Power Survey: Command and Control*, 288.
78. Cohen, *Gulf War Air Power Survey: Effects and Effectiveness*, 34.
79. Howey, "Checkmate Journal," 9.
80. Ibid., 29. For insight into the cooperation between DIA and Checkmate on BDA, see Putney, *Airpower Advantage*, 278, 281.
81. Hallion, *Storm over Iraq*, 206–207.

82. Cohen, *Gulf War Air Power Survey: Operations*, 76.

83. Putney, *Airpower Advantage*, 285.

84. Howey, *Checkmate Journal*, 14.

85. Ibid., 62–64.

86. Ibid., 72.

87. Horner, interview, March 8, 2006; Warden, December 4, 2004.

88. Ibid., 71–73.

89. Gian Gentile, *How Effective Is Strategic Bombing? Lessons Learned from World War II to Kosovo* (New York: New York University Press, 2001), 170.

90. Warden, interview, December 4, 2004.

91. Ibid.

92. Warden, letter to Col. Mike Chesney, U.S. Army (ret.), March 5, 1991, in author's private collection.

93. Warden, "Your Initiative to Improve Air Forces/Army Combat Operations," memorandum for Gen. McPeak, March 10, 1991, in author's private collection.

94. Gentile, *How Effective Is Strategic Bombing*, 174.

95. Ibid., 172.

96. Ibid., 183.

97. Ibid., 184.

98. Ibid., 188.

99. Welch, in *Desert Story Collection*, May 1991, cited in Mann, *Thunder and Lightning*, 170. The difficulty of measuring the effectiveness of the strategic air campaign led other analysts, perhaps most notably Robert A. Pape, to conclude that the strategic portion had made little difference. Robert A. Pape, *Bombing to Win: Air Power and Coercion in War* (Ithaca, NY: Cornell University Press, 1996).

100. Warden, "Air Theory for the Twenty-first Century," in Karl Magyar, ed., *Challenge and Response: Anticipating US Military Security Concerns* (Maxwell AFB, AL: Air University Press, 1994), 326–329.

101. Warden, "Employing Air Power in the Twenty-first Century," in Richard H. Schultz Jr. and Robert L. Pfaltzgraff, *The Future of Air Power: In the Aftermath of the Gulf War* (Maxwell AFB, AL: Air University Press, 1992), 57–83.

102. Ibid., 57.

103. Ibid., 78.

104. Ibid., 79.

105. Ibid., 81–82.

106. Maj. Gen. John L. Barry (ret.), interview with author, January 6–8, 2006.

107. Eliot A. Cohen, interview with author, January 15, 2006.

108. Cohen, *Gulf War Air Power Survey: Command and Control*, 185, 214.

109. Ibid., 260.

110. Davis, *On Target*, 68; Hallion, *Storm over Iraq*, 245.

111. Rogers, interview, September 9, 2003.

112. Adams, in *Desert Story Collection*, February 3, 1992, 29.

113. McPeak, interview, November 5, 1992, 5.

114. Ibid., 3–5; Deptula, in *Desert Story Collection*, December 12, 1991, 97.

115. Loh, in *Desert Story Collection*, October 16, 1991, 63–64.

116. Ibid., 65.

117. Alexander, in *Desert Story Collection*, May 30, 1991, 36–58; June 3, 1992, 59, 75–77.

118. Ibid., 61–62.

119. Rice, in *Desert Story Collection*, December 11, 1991, 9, 37; Trexler, in *Desert Story*

Collection, May 11, 1992, 30–35.

120. The officer preferred not to be named.

121. Col. James Gough (ret.), interview with author, November 19, 2004.

122. Richard Haass, interview with author, December 21, 2004; Hayden, interview, November 29, 2004.

123. Haass, interview, December 21, 2004.

124. Ibid.

Chapter 11: Transforming the Air Command and Staff College

1. Rice, interview, February 16, 2006.

2. Adams, interview, June 19, 2004; Lt. Gen. Michael Nelson (ret.), interview with author, July 20, 2005; Warden, interview, February 20, 2006.

3. Adams, interview, June 19, 2004; Nelson, interview with author, July 20, 2005; Warden, interview, February 20, 2006; "Colonel Urges Increased Role for Air Force in U.S. Military," *Daily Free Press*, February 16, 1990. Warden gave the presentation at the Institute for the Study of Conflict, Ideology and Policy at Boston University, February 15, 1991.

4. Warden, interview, March 25, 2006.

5. Warden, in *Desert Story Collection*, May 30, 1991, 94.

6. Warden, "New Policies for a New Epoch," November 1991, in author's private collection.

7. Ibid.

8. Ibid.

9. Ibid.

10. Warden, interview, March 25, 2006.

11. The officer preferred not to be named.

12. Vice President Dan Quayle, letter to Gen. Michael P. C. Carns, September 1, 1992, in author's private collection.

13. Ibid.

14. Mets, "Airpower History and Professional Education." See also Col. Dennis M. Drew, "Educating Air Force Officers."

15. Builder, *The Icarus Syndrome*, xviii.

16. Ibid., xiii. Icarus, according to Greek mythology, was the son of Daedalus, with whom he escaped from Crete, flying with wings made of wax and feathers. Heedless of his father's warning, he flew too close to the sun, which caused the wax to melt, and he fell into the Aegean Sea and drowned.

17. Grant T. Hammond, interview with author, June 7, 2004; Lewis B. Ware, interview with author, March 12, 2004.

18. Col. Larry Weaver (ret.), interview with author, October 22, 2004.

19. Stephen L. Butler, "Toward the Twenty-First Century Air Command and Staff College: The Curriculum from Theory to Practice," *EDL* 631 (Spring 1995).

20. Earl H. Tilford, interview with author, March 1, 2004.

21. Mets, "Airpower History and Professional Education."

22. Ibid., 2. Warden declared the mission for the "new" ACSC: "educate midcareer officers to develop, advance, and apply air and space power in peace and war."

23. Weaver, interview, October 22, 2004.

24. See Maj. Mason Carpenter and Maj. George T. McClain, "Air Command and Staff College Air Campaign Course: The Air Corps Tactical School Reborn?" *Airpower Journal* 7, no. 3 (Fall 1993): 72–83.

25. The author is particularly grateful to Richard R. Muller, David R. Mets, Larry Weaver, and Pat Nutz for their insight into Warden's three years as commandant.

26. Butler, "Twenty-First Century Air Command," 5.

27. Carpenter and McClain, "Air Command and Staff College"; *Oakleaf 1993*, the ACSC yearbook (Maxwell AFB, AL: Air Command and Staff College, 1993), 15: Lt. Col. Tom Falconer and majors: Gary Burg, Sy Caudill, Rick Cosby, Dave Goebel, Larry Key, Gaylord Liby, and John Pardo.

28. Mets, *The Air Campaign*, 58.

29. Larry Weaver, "Interview with Lt Col Larry Weaver," May 26, 1995, at ACSC, Maxwell AFB, AL, in author's private collection.

30. Weaver, "Interview with Lt Col Larry Weaver."

31. "Air Campaign Course Syllabus, Spring 1993," as of November 10, 1992, in author's private collection.

32. Carpenter and McClain, "Air Command and Staff College," 72–83.

33. Warden, "The Enemy as a System," *Airpower Journal* 9, no. 1 (Spring 1995): 40–55.

34. Ibid.

35. Weaver, interview, April 12, 2002.

36. Carpenter and McClain, "Air Command and Staff College," 83.

37. Ibid., 72–83.

38. Warden, "Notional Strawman Elective Course on Airpower and the Air Campaign," draft paper, 1992, in author's private collection.

39. Meilinger, "Dog Days."

40. Warden, "Enemy as a System."

41. "Air Command and Staff College Academic Year 1992–1993: End of Course Critique," prepared by Office of Evaluation, July 1993, in author's private collection.

42. Grant T. Hammond, interview with author, May 15, 2002.

43. Ibid.

44. Warden, letter to all students of the Class of 1994, presented in June 1993, which contains a direct reflection of the new curriculum that was developed in the autumn of 1992, in author's private collection.

45. Carpenter and McClain, "Air Command and Staff College," 72–83.

46. Weaver, interview, April 12, 2002.

47. Richard R. Muller, interview with author, September 15, 2005.

48. Weaver, "Interview with Lt Col Larry Weaver."

49. Samuel Huntington, *The Soldier and the State: The Theory and Politics of Civil-Military Relations* (Cambridge, MA: Harvard, 1957).

50. Ibid., 8.

51. According to Weaver and Muller the following three books were compulsory reading for the Military History and Doctrine phase of the curriculum: Russell F. Weighley, *The American Way of Warfare: A History of United States Military Strategy and Policy* (London: Macmillan Publishers, 1973); Dennis M. Drew and Donald M. Snow, *Making Strategy: An Introduction to National Security Processes and Problems* (Maxwell AFB, AL: Air University Press, 1998); Larry H. Addington, *The Patterns of War since the Eighteenth Century* (Bloomington: Indiana University Press, 1984).

52. As the popular saying goes: "it is only a lot of reading if you do it."

53. The reading list for the pilot project of the air campaign course included a total of thirty-five books.

54. Muller, interview, February 25, 2002.

55. Butler, "Twenty-First Century Air Command," 5.

56. Col. Pat Nutz (ret.), interview with author, November 5, 2004.

57. Weaver, interview, April 12, 2002.

58. ACSC, "Seminar Guidebook, Academic Year 1994," 8.

59. Weaver, interview, April 12, 2002.

60. Muller, interview, January 4, 2006.

61. Col. Dennis M. Drew (ret.), interview with author, May 7, 2003.

62. Warden, interview, February 12, 2006.

63. Meilinger, "Dog Days."

64. Mets, *The Air Campaign*, 66–67.

65. Weaver, "Interview with Lt Col Larry Weaver."

66. Interestingly, Robert A. Pape, a young scholar at SAAS, would later become Warden's strongest intellectual opponent. His book *Bombing to Win* concluded that strategic bombing had never worked, did not work in Operation Desert Storm, and would not have any value in the future. Indeed, in the late 1990s the air power debate was presented as one between Warden and Pape. For insight into the Warden-Pape debate, see Robert A. Pape, "The Limits of Precision-Guided Air Power," *Security Studies* 7, no. 2 (Winter 1997/98): 93–114; Barry D. Watts, "Ignoring Reality: Problems of Theory and Evidence in Security Studies," *Security Studies* 7, no. 2 (Winter 1997/98): 115–171; Warden, "Success in Modern War: A Response to Robert Pape's *Bombing to Win*," *Security Studies* 7 (Winter 1997/98)," 172–190; Karl Mueller, "Strategic Coercion: Denial, Punishment, and the Future of Air Power," *Security Studies* 7, no. 3 (Spring 1998): 182–238; Benjamin S. Lambeth, "Bounding the Air Power Debate," *Strategic Review* 25, no. 4 (Winter 1997): 42–55.

67. Warden, "Enemy as a System." For critiques, see for example Col. Richard Szafranski, "The Problem with Bees and Bombs," *Airpower Journal* 9, no. 4 (Winter 1995), 94–98; "Parallel War and Hyperwar: Is Every Want a Weakness?" in Barry R. Schneider and Lawrence E. Grinter, eds., *Battlefield of the Future: 21st Century Warfare Issues* (Maxwell AFB, AL.: Air University Press, 1995); Lewis Ware, "Ware on Warden: Some Observations on the Enemy as a System," *Airpower Journal* 9, no. 4 (Winter 1995), 87–93; Jason B. Barlow, *Strategic Paralysis: An Airpower Theory for the Present* (Maxwell AFB, AL: Air University Press, 1994).

68. Drew, interview, May 7, 2003.

69. Tilford, interview, March 1, 2004.

70. Meilinger, interview, May 12, 2003.

71. Col. Ronald A. Winter (ret.), interview with author, November 18, 2004.

72. Ware, interview, March 12, 2004; Tilford, interview, March 1, 2004.

73. Maj. Gen. John R. Brooks (ret.), interview with author, February 20, 2003.

74. Karl Mueller, interview with author, April 8, 2002.

75. Brooks, interview, February 20, 2003.

76. Meilinger, interview, May 12, 2003.

77. Weaver, "Interview with Lt Col Larry Weaver."

78. Lt. Gen. Jay W. Kelley (ret.), interview with author, January 9, 2006.

79. Ibid.

80. Cited from the official ACSC web site, http://wwwacsc.au.af.mil/aboutACSC.asp (accessed January 7, 2007); Albert Mitchum, interview with author, December 6, 2004; Kearney, interview, February 3, 2005; Hammond, interview, June 7, 2004.

81. Lt. Gen. Raymond B. Furlong, letter to Col. John A. Warden III, June 26, 1995, in author's private collection.

82. Lt. Gen. John W. Rosa, ACSC commandant from August 1998–March 2000, inter-

view with author, November 18, 2004; Brig. Gen. Ronald R. Ladnier (ret.), ACSC commandant from June 2002–October 2004, interview with author, November 8, 2004; Col. Richard Szafranski (ret.), interview with author, February 8, 2002.

83. Muller, interview, September 15, 2005; October 7, 2005.
84. Weaver, interview, April 12, 2002.
85. Kearney, interview, February 3, 2005.
86. Mets, *The Air Campaign*, 69.
87. Muller, interview, September 15, 2005; October 7, 2005.

Chapter 12: A Farewell to Arms

1. The author is grateful to Rick Bennett at the Air Force Senior Management Office for providing this list.
2. McInerney, interview, October 21, 2004.
3. McPeak, interview, June 22, 2004; Dugan, interview, March 15, 2003; Gen. Ronald R. Fogleman (ret.), interview with author, February 2006.
4. The board members spoke with the author under the agreement that he would not reveal information beyond what is stated in the text.
5. Warden, interview, March 25, 2006.
6. The generals with whom the author spoke prefer not to be named.
7. Russ, in *Desert Story Collection,* December 9, 1991, 24–26, 51–52, 70–71.
8. Adams, in *Desert Story Collection*, February 3, 1992, 19–20.
9. May, in *Desert Story Collection*, August 21, 1992, 34. May did not express negativity towards Warden: the quotation presents his explanation of why Warden was considered contentious.
10. Schwarzkopf, letter to Warden, June 30, 1995, in author's private collection.
11. Charles Allen, letter to Warden, June 1995, in author's private collection. Zilliso, who worked in the National Security Council, was equally full of praise for Warden and his contribution to the air campaign: Philip D. Zilliso, letter to Col. John A. Warden, June 27, 1995, in author's private collection.
12. Winter, interview, November 18, 2004.
13. Ibid.
14. Smith, interview, March 17, 2006; Fogleman, interview, February 20, 2006; Winter, interview, November 18, 2004.
15. Fogleman, interview, March 10, 2004; February 20, 2006.
16. Ibid.; Nutz, interview, December 5, 2004.
17. Smith, interview, March 16, 2006.
18. Mets, interview, 18 December 2005; Brooks, interview, 20 February 2003; Warden, interview, 1 March 2003; Col. John A. Warden, "Final Speech – 30 June 95," in author's private collection.
19. Lord Byron, "The Destruction of Sennacherib," cited in Warden, "Final Speech."
20. Warden, "Final Speech."
21. Reynolds, interview, April 14, 2002.

Perspectives: The Intellectual Warrior

1. Isabel Briggs Myers, "Introduction to Type," 5th edition, European English Version, *Oxford Psychologists Press*, 1998, 12. The MBTI categorizes personalities according to four scales: where do you prefer to focus your attention? (Extroversion-Introversion scale); how do you take in information and find out about things? (Sensing-Intuition scale); how do you make decisions? (Thinking-Feeling scale); and how do you orient

toward the outer world? (Judging-Perceiving scale). This leads to a matrix of sixteen types. Warden filled out the form for the author in July 2002.

2. Myers, "Introduction to Type," 4–5.

3. Ibid.

4. William McGuire and R. F. C. Hull, eds., *Jung Speaking* (Princeton, NJ: Princeton University Press, 1977), 303.

5. Gen. Robert D. Russ (ret.), letter to Lt. Gen. Jay W. Kelley, July 5, 1994, in author's private collection.

6. Glosson, "Memorandum for AU/CC (Lt Gen Kelley)," June 20, 1994, in author's private collection.

7. Henry, interview, June 29, 2004.

8. Kelley, "Note from the Commander of Air University," in Reynolds, *Heart of the Storm*, iii.

9. Halberstam, *War in a Time of Peace*, 47–49.

10. Ibid.

11. Gen. Wilbur Creech (ret.), letter, August 2, 2002, in author's private collection. For a wider perspective, see Slife, *Creech Blue*. Creech's opposition to Warden has been confirmed in a range of interviews.

12. Creech, letter, August 2, 2002.

13. See Gen. John P. Jumper, foreword to Slife, *Creech Blue*, vi.

14. Creech, letter, August 2, 2002; Adams, interview, June 19, 2004.

15. Gen. Bill Creech (ret.), *The Five Pillars of TQM: How to Make Total Quality Management Work for You* (New York: Truman Talley Books, 1994).

16. Scholars such as Alan Stephens, Richard P. Hallion, Phillip S. Meilinger, Robert A. Pape, and Edward N. Luttwak all agree that Warden is one of the most influential strategists since the Second World War.

17. Alexander, in *Desert Story Collection*, May 30, 1991, 45.

18. Edward N. Luttwak, interview with author, September 4, 2005.

19. Ryan, interview, May 7, 2004.

20. See for example Lt. Gen. Michael C. Short (ret.), "An Airman's Lessons from Kosovo," in John Andreas Olsen, ed., *From Manoeuvre Warfare to Kosovo?* (Trondheim, Norway: Royal Norwegian Air Force Academy, 2001), 257–288; John A. Tirpak, "Short's View of the Air Campaign," *Air Force Magazine* 82, no. 9 (September 1999).

21. The author is grateful to Alan Stephens for this argument.

Epilogue

1. Warden, "Planning to Win," 94–97.

2. Warden, "36th Tactical Fighter Wing."

3. Leland A. Russell, interview with author, July 30, 2004.

4. John A. Warden and Leland A. Russell, *Winning in Fast Time: Harness the Competitive Advantage of Prometheus in Business and Life* (Montgomery, AL: Venturist Publishing, 2001), 5.

5. George Consolver, interview with author, September 13, 2004; Paula Marshall, interview with author, November 25, 2004.

SELECTED BIBLIOGRAPHY

Addington, Larry H. *The Patterns of War Since the Eighteenth Century.* Bloomington: Indiana University Press, 1984.

Ancell, R. Manning. *The Biographical Dictionary of World War II Generals and Flag Rank Officers: The U.S. Armed Forces.* With Christine M. Miller. Westport, CT: Greenwood Press, 1996.

Anderegg, C. R. *Sierra Hotel: Flying Air Force Fighters in the Decade after Vietnam.* Washington, DC: Air Force History and Museums Program, 2001.

Arkin, William M. "Baghdad: The Urban Sanctuary in Desert Storm." *Airpower Journal* 11, no. 1 (Spring 1997): 4–20.

Atkinson, Rick. *Crusade: The Untold Story of the Gulf War.* London: Harper Collins, 1994.

Barlow, Jason B. *Strategic Paralysis: An Airpower Theory for the Present.* Maxwell Air Force Base, AL: Air University Press, 1994.

Belote, Howard D. "Paralyze or Pulverize? Liddell Hart, Clausewitz, and Their Influence on Air Power Theory." *Strategic Review* 27, no. 4 (Winter 1999): 40–46.

Blackwell, James. *Thunder in the Desert: The Strategy and Tactics of the Persian Gulf War.* New York: Bantam Books, 1991.

Budiansky, Stephen. *Air Power: The Men, Machines, and Ideas That Revolutionized War; From Kitty Hawk to Gulf War II.* New York: Viking, 2004.

Builder, Carl H. *The Icarus Syndrome: The Role of Air Power Theory in the Evolution and Fate of the U.S. Air Force.* 4th printing. New Brunswick: Transaction, 1998.

———. *The Masks of War: American Military Styles in Strategy and Analysis.* Baltimore, MD: Johns Hopkins University Press, 1989.

Bush, George, and Brent Scowcroft. *A World Transformed.* New York: Alfred A. Knopf, 1998.

Butler, Stephen L. "Toward the Twenty-First Century Air Command and Staff College: The Curriculum from Theory to Practice." *EDL 631,* Air University (Spring 1995).

Carpenter, Mason, and George T. McClain. "Air Command and Staff College Air Campaign Course: The Air Corps Tactical School Reborn?" *Airpower Journal* 7, no. 3 (Fall 1993): 72–83.

Clancy, Tom. *Every Man a Tiger.* With Gen. Chuck Horner (ret.). New York: G. P. Putnam's Sons, 1999.

———. *Fighter Wing: A Guided Tour of an Air Force Combat Wing.* New York: Berkley Books, 1995.

Clausewitz, Carl von. *On War*. Edited and translated by Michael Howard and Peter Paret. London: Everyman's Library, 1993.

Cody, James R. *AWPD-42 to Instant Thunder: Consistent, Evolutionary Thought or Revolutionary Change?* Maxwell Air Force Base, AL: Air University Press, 1996.

Cohen, Eliot A., et al. *Gulf War Air Power Survey*. Vol. 1, *Part I: Planning*. Washington, DC: Government Printing Office, 1993.

———. *Gulf War Air Power Survey*. Vol. 1, *Part II: Commando and Control*. Washington, DC: Government Printing Office, 1993.

———. *Gulf War Air Power Survey*. Vol. 2, *Part I: Operations*. Washington, DC: Government Printing Office, 1993.

———. *Gulf War Air Power Survey*. Vol. 2, *Part II: Effects and Effectiveness*. Washington, DC: Government Printing Office, 1993.

———. *Gulf War Air Power Survey*. Vol. 5, *Part A: A Statistical Compendium*. Washington, DC: Government Printing Office, 1993.

Corell, John T. "The Strategy of Desert Storm." *Air Force Magazine* 89, no. 1 (January 2006). http://www.afa.org/magazine/jan2006/0106d_storm.asp.

Coyne, James P. *Airpower in the Gulf*. Arlington, VA: Air Force Association Book, 1992.

Davis, Richard G. *Decisive Force: Strategic Bombing in the Gulf War*. Washington, DC: Air Force History and Museums Program, 1996.

———. *On Target: Organizing and Executing the Strategic Air Campaign Against Iraq*. Washington, DC: Air Force History and Museums Program, 2002.

———. *The 31 Initiatives: A Study in Air Force–Army Cooperation*. Washington, DC: Office of USAF History, 1987.

Department of the Army. *Field Manual (FM) 100-5: Operations*. Washington, DC: Government Printing Office, 1982.

Deptula, David A. *Firing for Effect: Change in the Nature of Warfare*. Defense and Airpower Series. Arlington, VA: Aerospace Education Foundation, 1995.

De-Seversky, Alexander P. *Victory through Air Power*. New York: Simon and Schuster, 1942.

Donnelly, Charles L., Jr. "A Theater-Level View of Air Power." *Air Power Journal* 1, no. 1 (Summer 1997): 3–8.

Douhet, Giulio. *The Command of The Air*. Translated by Dino Ferrari. New York: Coward-McCann, 1984.

Drew, Dennis M. "Educating Air Force Officers: Observations after 20 Years at Air University." *Airpower Journal* 11, no. 2 (Summer 1997): 37–44.

———. "Inventing a Doctrine Process." *Airpower Journal* 9, no. 4 (Winter 1995): 42–52.

Drew, Dennis M., and Donald M. Snow. *Making Strategy: An Introduction to National Security Processes and Problems*. Maxwell Air Force Base, AL: Air University Press, 1998.

Felker, Edward J. "Airpower, Chaos, and Infrastructure: Lords of the Rings." Maxwell Paper 14. Maxwell Air Force Base, AL: Air War College, 1998.

Fuller, J. F. C., *The Foundations of the Science of War*. Reprint. Fort Leavenworth, KS: U.S. Army Command and General Staff College Press, 1993.

———. *The Generalship of Alexander the Great*. London: Wordsworth Editions, 1998.

Gat, Azar. *Fascists and Liberal Vision of War: Fuller, Liddell Hart, Douhet, and Other Modernists*. Oxford: Clarendon Press, 1998.

Gentile, Gian P. *How Effective Is Strategic Bombing? Lessons Learned from World War II to Kosovo*. New York: New York University Press, 2001.

Glosson, Buster C. "Impact of Precision Weapons on Air Combat Operations." *Airpower Journal* 7, no. 2 (Summer 1993): 4–10.

————. *War with Iraq: Critical Lessons*. Charlotte, NC: Glosson Family Foundation, 2003.

Gordon, Michael R., and Gen. Bernard E. Trainor. *The Generals' War: The Inside Story of the Conflict in the Gulf*. Boston: Little, Brown and Company, 1995.

Halberstam, David. *War in a Time of Peace: Bush, Clinton and the Generals*. London: Bloomsbury, 2002.

Hallion, Richard P. *Storm over Iraq: Air Power and the Gulf War*. Washington, DC: Smithsonian Institution Press, 1992.

————, ed. *Air Power Confronts an Unstable World*. London: Brassey's, 1997.

Hammond, Grant T. *The Mind of War: John Boyd and American Security*. Washington, DC: Smithsonian Institution Press, 2001.

Hansell Jr., Haywood S., *The Air Plan That Defeated Hitler*. New York: Arno Press, 1980. First published 1972.

Hosmer, Stephen T. *Psychological Effects of U.S. Air Operations in Four Wars 194—1991: Lessons for U.S. Commanders*. Santa Monica, CA: RAND, 1996.

Howey, Allan W., "Checkmate Journal: The Gulf War Air Campaign from Inside the Pentagon," CAFH Working Papers. Washington, DC: Center for Air Force History Air Staff Division, 1994.

Huntington, Samuel. *The Soldier and the State: The Theory and Politics of Civil-Military Relations*. Cambridge, MA: Harvard, 1957.

Jamison, Perry D. *Lucrative Targets: The U.S. Air Force in the Kuwaiti Theater of Operations*. Washington, DC: Air Force History and Museums Program, 2001.

Keaney, Thomas A., and Eliot A. Cohen. *Gulf War Air Power Survey: Summary Report*. Washington, DC: Government Printing Office, 1993.

————. *Revolution in Warfare? Air Power in the Persian Gulf*. Annapolis, MD: Naval Institute Press, 1995.

Kenney, George C. *General Kenney Reports*. USAF Warrior Studies. Washington, DC: Office of Air Force History, 1987.

Lambeth, Benjamin S. "Bounding the Air Power Debate." *Strategic Review* 25, no. 4 (Winter 1997): 42–55.

Liddell Hart, Basil H. *Strategy* (London: Meridian Books, 1957).

Luttwak, Edward N. *Coup d'État*. Cambridge, MA: Harvard University Press, 1968.

————. *Strategy: The Logic of War and Peace*. Rev. and enlarged ed. Cambridge, MA: Belknap Press of Harvard University Press, 2001.

Magyar, Karl P. *Global Security Concerns: Anticipating the Twenty-First Century*. Maxwell Air Force Base, AL: Air University Press, 1996.

————, ed. *Challenge and Response: Anticipating US Military Security Concerns*. Maxwell Air Force Base, AL: Air University Press, 1994.

Mann, Edward C. "One Target, One Bomb: Is the Principle of Mass Dead." *Airpower Journal* 7, no. 1 (Spring 1995): 35–43.

————. *Thunder and Lightning: Desert Storm and the Airpower Debates*. Maxwell Air Force Base, AL: Air University Press, 1995.

McGuire, William, and R. F. C. Hull, eds. *Jung Speaking*. Princeton, NJ: Princeton University Press, 1977.

McPeak, Merrill A. *Selected Works 1990–1994*. Maxwell Air Force Base, AL: Air University Press, 1995.

Meilinger, Phillip S. "Dog Days for the Air Force: What Is Wrong and How Can It Be Fixed." October 2005. In author's private collection.

————. "The Problem with Our Air Power Doctrine." *Airpower Journal* 6, no. 1 (Spring 1992): 24–31.

———, ed. *The Paths of Heaven: The Evolution of Airpower Theory.* Maxwell Air Force Base, AL: Air University Press, 1997.

Mets, David R. *The Air Campaign: John Warden and the Classical Airpower Theorists.* Maxwell Air Force Base, AL: Air University Press, 1998.

———. "Airpower History and Professional Education in the U.S. Air Force." Paper presented at the Society for Military History, Bethesda, MD, May 22, 2004.

Mitchell, William. *Skyways: A Book on Modern Aeronautics.* Philadelphia: J. B. Lippincott, 1930.

———. *Winged Defense: The Development and Possibilities of Modern Air Power Economic and Military.* New York: G. P. Putnam's Sons, 1925).

Mueller, Karl P. "Strategies of Coercion: Denial, Punishment, and the Future of Air Power." *Security Studies* 7, no. 3 (Spring 1998): 182–228.

Murphy, Timothy G. "A Critique of the Air Campaign." *Airpower Journal* 8, no. 1 (Spring 1994): 63–74.

Murray, Williamson. *Air War in the Persian Gulf.* With Wayne W. Thompson. 2nd printing. Baltimore, MD: Nautical and Aviation Publishing Company of America, 1995.

———. "Grading the War Colleges." *National Interest,* no. 6 (Winter 1986/1987): 12–19.

Olsen, John Andreas. *Strategic Air Power in Desert Storm.* London: Frank Cass, 2003.

———, ed. *Asymmetric Warfare.* Trondheim, Norway: Royal Norwegian Air Force Academy, 2002.

———, ed. *A Second Aerospace Century.* Trondheim, Norway: Royal Norwegian Air Force Academy, 2001.

———, ed. *From Manoeuvre Warfare to Kosovo?* Trondheim, Norway: Royal Norwegian Air Force Academy, 2001.

Pape, Robert A. "The Air Force Strikes Back: A Reply to Barry Watts and John Warden." *Security Studies* 7, no. 2 (Winter 1997/1998): 191–214.

———. *Bombing to Win: Air Power and Coercion in War.* Ithaca, NY: Cornell University Press, 1996.

———. "The Limits of Precision-Guided Air Power." *Security Studies* 7, no. 2 (Winter 1997/1998): 93–114.

Paret, Peter, ed. *Makers of Modern Strategy: From Machiavelli to the Nuclear Age.* Reprint. Oxford: Clarendon Press, 1994.

Peters, Tom. *Thriving on Chaos: Handbook for a Management Revolution.* New York: Alfred A. Knopf, 1987.

Powell, Colin. *My American Journey.* With Joseph E. Persico. New York: Ballantine Books, 1996.

Putney, Diane T. *Airpower Advantage: Planning the Gulf War Air Campaign 1989–1991.* Washington, DC: Air Force History and Museums Program, 2005.

———. "From Instant Thunder to Desert Storm: Developing the Gulf War Air Campaign's Phases." *Air Power History* 41, no. 3 (Fall 1994): 38–50.

Reynolds, Richard T. *Heart of the Storm: The Genesis of the Air Campaign Against Iraq.* Maxwell Air Force Base, AL: Air University Press, 1995.

Romjue, John L. *From Active Defense to AirLand Battle: The Development of Army 1973–1982.* Fort Monroe, VA: U.S. Army Training and Doctrine Command, 1984.

Scales, Robert H. *Certain Victory: The U.S. Army in the Gulf War.* London: Brassey's, 1997.

Schelling, Thomas C. *Arms and Influence.* New Haven, CT: Yale University Press, 1966.

———. *The Strategy of Conflict.* 16th printing. Cambridge, MA: Harvard University Press, 1997.

Schneider, Barry R., and Lawrence E. Grinter, eds. *Battlefield of the Future: 21st Century Warfare Issues*. Maxwell Air Force Base, AL: Air University Press, 1995.

Schwarzkopf, H. Norman. *It Doesn't Take a Hero*. With Peter Petre. London: Bantam Books, 1993.

Shultz Jr., Richard H., and Robert L. Pfaltzgraff Jr. *The Future of Air Power in the Aftermath of the Gulf War*. Maxwell Air Force Base, AL: Air University Press, 1992.

Slife, James C. *Creech Blue: Gen. Bill Creech and the Reformation of the Tactical Air Forces, 1978–1984*, Maxwell Air Force Base, AL: Air University Press, 2004.

Smith, Perry M. *The Air Force Plans for Peace*. Baltimore, MD: John Hopkins Press, 1970.

———. *How CNN Fought the War: A View from the Inside*. New York: Birch Lane Press, 1991.

Summers Jr., Harry G. *On Strategy II: A Critical Analysis of the Gulf War*. New York: Dell Publishing, 1992.

Sun Tzu. *The Art of War*. London: Hodder and Stoughton, 1995.

Szafranski, Richard. "The Problem with Bees and Bombs." *Airpower Journal 9*, no. 4 (Winter 1995): 94–98.

Tagg, Lori S. *Development of the B-52: The Wright Field Story*. Wright-Patterson Air Force Base, OH: Aeronautical Systems Center, 2004.

Toffler, Alvin, and Heidi Toffler. *War and Anti-War: Making Sense of Today's Global Chaos*. London: Warner Books, 1995.

United States Air Force. *The Air Force and the U.S. National Security: "Global Reach–Global Power: Reshaping for the Future."* Washington, DC: Department of the USAF, June 1990.

———. *Air Force Manual 1-1: Basic Aerospace Doctrine of the United States Air Force*. Washington, DC: Government Printing Office, 1984.

———. *Air Force Manual 1-1: Basic Aerospace Doctrine of the United States Air Force*. Vol. 2. Washington, DC: Government Printing Office, 1992.

———. "Global Reach Global Power: Reshaping for the Future." *USAF White Paper*. Washington, DC: Department of the USAF, 1991.

United States Department of Defense. *Conduct of the Persian Gulf War: An Interim Report to Congress*. Washington, DC: Government Printing Office, 1991.

———. *Conduct of the Persian Gulf War: Final Report to Congress*. Washington, DC: Government Printing Office, 1992.

U.S. News and World Report. *Triumph without Victory: The Unreported History of the Persian Gulf War*. New York: Times Books, 1992.

Viccellio, Henry. "Composite Air Strike Force." *Air University Quarterly Review* 9, no. 1 (Winter 1956/1957): 27–38.

Warden, John A., III. *The Air Campaign*. Washington, DC: Brassey's, 1988.

———. "Airpower in the Gulf." *Daedalus Flyer* 36, no. 1 (Spring 1996).

———. "Centers of Gravity; The Key to Success in War." March 1990. In author's private collection.

———. "Employment of Tactical Air in Europe." Memorandum, August 1, 1972. In author's private collection.

———. "The Enemy as a System." *Airpower Journal* 9, no. 1 (Spring 1995): 40–45.

———. "Global Strategy Outline." May 1988. In author's private collection.

———. "The Grand Alliance: Strategy and Decision." M.A. thesis, Texas Tech University, 1975.

———. "The New American Security Force." Vortices. *Airpower Journal* 8, no. 3 (Fall 1999): 75–91.

————. "Planning to Win." *Air University Review* 34 (March–April 1983): 94–97.

————. "Success in Modern War: A Response too Robert Pape's *Bombing to Win*." *Security Studies* 7, no. 2 (Winter 1997/1998): 172–190.

————. "36th Tactical Fighter Wing Goals Fiscal Year 1988." Department of the Air Force, Headquarters Thirty-sixth Tactical Fighter Wing USAF, September 26, 1987. In author's private collection.

Warden, John A., and Leland A. Russell. *Winning in FastTime: Harness the Competitive Advantage of Prometheus in Business and Life*. Montgomery, AL: Venturist Publishing, 2001.

Ware, Lewis. "Ware on Warden: Some Observations on the Enemy as a System." *Airpower Journal* 9, no. 4 (Winter 1995): 87–93.

Watts, Barry D. "Clausewitzian Friction and Future War." Institute for National Strategic Studies, McNair Papers no. 68, 2004.

————. *The Foundations of U.S. Air Doctrine: The Problems of Friction in War*. Maxwell Air Force Base, AL: Air University Press, 1984.

————. "Ignoring Reality: Problems of Theory and Evidence in Security Studies." *Security Studies* 7, no. 2 (Winter 1997/1998): 115-171.

Weighley, Russell F. *The American Way of Warfare: A History of United States Military Strategy and Policy*. London: Macmillan Publishers, 1973.

Wijninga, Peter W.W., and Richard Szafranski. "Beyond Utility Targeting: Toward Axiological Air Operations." *Aerospace Power Journal* 14, no. 4 (Winter 2000): 45–59.

Willmott, H. P. *When Men Lost Faith in Reason: Reflections on War and Society in the Twentieth Century*. Westport, CT: Praeger, 2002.

Woodward, Bob. *The Commanders*. New York: Simon and Schuster, 1992.

Zetterling, Niklas. "John Warden, *The Air Campaign*—En Kritisk Granskning." *Kungl Krigsveteskapsakademies Handlinger och Tidsskrift*, no. 1 (1998): 107–130.

INDEX

ABOUT THE AUTHOR

A lieutenant colonel in the Royal Norwegian Air Force, John Andreas Olsen is head of the division for strategic studies at the Norwegian Defence Command and Staff College in Oslo. He graduated from the German Armed Forces Command and Staff College as the best international student in 2005, served as an expert commentator for Norwegian media during Operation Iraqi Freedom in 2003, and received a doctorate in history and international relations from De Montfort University in 2000. He has lectured widely in Europe and the United States. His previous publications include *Strategic Air Power in Desert Storm* (London: Frank Cass, 2003).